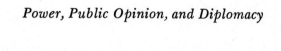

Power, Public Opinion, and Diplomacy

POWER, PUBLIC OPINION, AND DIPLOMACY

Essays in Honor of Eber Malcolm Carroll
By His Former Students

Edited by Lillian Parker Wallace *and* William C. Askew

The Contributors: Lillian Parker Wallace, *Professor of History, Meredith College;* Lucien E. Roberts, *President, Middle Georgia College;* Frederic B. M. Hollyday, *Instructor in History, Duke University;* Mary Elizabeth Thomas, *Associate Professor of History, Florida State University;* John A. Murray, *Assistant Professor of History, St. John Fisher College;* William C. Askew, *Professor of History, Colgate University;* Rodney O. Davis, *Assistant Professor of History, Gustavus Adolphus College;* C. Waldron Bolen, *Professor of History and Government, Clemson College;* J. Bowyer Bell, *Trinity School, New York City;* William R. Rock, *Instructor in History, Bowling Green State University;* John Clinton Adams, *Professor, Department of Russian Civilization, Dartmouth College*

DUKE UNIVERSITY PRESS   DURHAM, NORTH CAROLINA   1959

© 1959, Duke University Press

Cambridge University Press, London, N.W. 1, England

Library of Congress Catalogue Card number 59-12042

Printed in the United States of America
by the Seeman Printery, Inc., Durham, N. C.

Ernest W. Nelson

E. Malcolm Carroll

Acknowledgments

In this volume we honor a distinguished American scholar, an inspiring teacher, and an exacting taskmaster, who made European diplomatic history live for each of us, gave us our start in the study of this complex subject, and carried each of us through to the completion of the doctorate. He has our unending gratitude, esteem, and best wishes as he retires from teaching. We also seek, by drawing upon our current research interests, to illuminate certain aspects of the history of the nineteenth and twentieth centuries.

Our essays all deal with one or more of the factors of power, public opinion, and diplomacy. The title was selected long ago. No other could have expressed adequately the nature of the volume contemplated. Other writers have subsequently published works of somewhat similar title. We saw no reason to change our original decision.

We are grateful to many people who have been helpful in the preparation of this volume. We thank especially Professor William T. Laprade for the introduction, and for reading all of the manuscript. Dr. Frederic B. M. Hollyday not only prepared the list of Professor Carroll's writings, a considerable task, but helped in countless ways in the checking of details. Professor Ernest W. Nelson supplied the photograph used as frontispiece. Professor Robert H. Woody was most helpful in the initial planning stages. Professors A. William Salomone, Kent Roberts Greenfield, Mario Toscano, and Augusto Torre read the chapter on "The Austro-Italian Antagonism, 1896-

1914." Professor Carl H. Pegg read the entire manuscript. We owe much to the wise advice and good judgment of Mr. Ashbel Brice of the Duke Press.

We deeply regret that one of our number, Dr. John A. Murray, did not live to see the finished work.* Professor Arthur J. May read Dr. Murray's essay.

Any shortcomings in our contributions must be traced to our human frailties, as we have tried to emulate the master whom we seek to honor.

LILLIAN PARKER WALLACE

WILLIAM C. ASKEW

---

* Dr. Murray died on January 12, 1959.

Contents

Foreword

I am glad to commend this volume of substantial essays contributed in honor of Professor E. Malcolm Carroll by former students, who thus acknowledge their obligations for his instruction and guidance. The essays illustrate the diverse facets of Professor Carroll's interest in the recent history of Western European countries and in the relations of these countries with each other and with the rest of the world. A reader is impressed by the complexity of affairs in the generations with which Professor Carroll and his students have concerned themselves.

As a colleague closely associated with Professor Carroll during most of his active career as a teacher and scholar, I venture here a few comments in a personal vein. I have often thought that writers of history might be stimulated to a better understanding of the difficult tasks to which they apply themselves if, after reaching maturity, each would try the experiment of using in a study of his own career the cultivated faculties essential for the pursuit of his profession. Records and relics, however ample, never convey to a biographer information as intimate as an observant historian ought to have concerning his own experience. Such a study of his personal adventures might make the historian less certain of his conclusions, less dogmatic in his pronouncements concerning the connections between other events that are related sequentially in time.

Professor Carroll was born at Coldwater, Michigan, March 13, 1893. He had proceeded to the degrees of bachelor of arts, master of arts, and doctor of philosophy in the University of

his native State, had served in the Ambulance Corps of the
United States Army from 1917 to 1919, accompanying the
expeditionary force in France and Germany, and from 1919 had
been Instructor in History in the University of Michigan before
he came to Trinity College in the autumn of 1923 to accept
an appointment that ended with his retirement as Emeritus
Professor of History in Duke University in 1959. He thus did
his work and made his career in the most eventful period the
world has hitherto known.

Trinity College was a comparatively small institution in
1923 devoted chiefly to giving instruction in the liberal arts.
The number of students had increased following the first World
War, and the three members of the Department of History then
on the staff felt the need of an additional colleague ready and
willing to apply himself to the study of the changing events of
that generation. For obvious reasons, such men were scarce
at that juncture, and among the few available it was not easy to
find one disposed to accept an offer from a small college south
of the Potomac River. When Professor Carroll's old teacher,
U. B. Phillips, suggested him for the post at Trinity College,
the three members of the history staff already there closed with
the proposal despite the fact that the major field of the candidate's graduate study had been the political history of the
United States prior to the Civil War. After all, however, he
knew the two major languages used in Western Europe, French
and German, and he had perforce traveled in the area while
with the army.

In this manner a young scholar of promise migrated to a
section of the country previously unfamiliar to him to embark
upon a new adventure. He had to return in 1924 to teach in
the summer session of the University of Nebraska, where he had
taught in the summer of 1923. Not until the summer of 1925
could he go to Paris to begin a long devotion to his new subject. Like others in the time, he began with 1870, which
seemed to emerging scholars in the field to be a sort of water-

shed, separating the old from the new or different. The work in that first summer turned up material for an article published in the *American Historical Review* in July, 1926: "French Public Opinion on the War with Prussia in 1870." This initial success intensified the apprentice's interest in his new subject.

He had need to be busy about it. Mr. James B. Duke announced, December 11, 1924, an offer to begin at once the process of building a university around Trinity College as a nucleus. Members of the faculty of the College were thus challenged to demonstrate their capacities to grow up to the opportunities offered to them. The John Simon Guggenheim Memorial Foundation provided a fellowship to support a residence in France during the academic year 1927-1928. The study in that year prepared the way for the publication in 1931 of *French Public Opinion and Foreign Affairs, 1870-1914.*

The publication in 1925 of *Origins of the Whig Party* was the author's farewell to his first field of interest. His efforts to find out how the Whig party got started and went on to win a presidential election was a useful introduction to the study of the political contents of the French press in the generation before 1914. The Whig party did not achieve its first national success by a united support of any principles upon which its members agreed. Instead, in the wake of an economic depression, crowds rallied about miniature log cabins, partook of hard cider, if nothing stronger, and went to vote for an aging general, a scion of the Harrisons of Virginia who had moved west, who did not survive to the end of the first year of his administration.

Professor Carroll thus launched himself at a propitious time in the field of study destined to occupy his attention through the remainder of his active life. Professor Sidney Fay published in 1928 his two volumes: *Origins of the World War.* His preliminary articles in the *American Historical Review* had demonstrated that historians in the United States had reached a stage enabling them to canvass with some objectivity the issues in a conflict which came to involve their own country as an active participant and to publish the findings in the national organ of their profession. Professor Bernadotte Schmitt's *The Coming of the War* appeared in 1930. Other writers were already joining in, and the controversy was at times heated.

Few scholars viewing these discussions in perspective would now say that they opened a clear road to truth. Much of what was written was analogous to examining with a microscope the available diplomatic correspondence and the memoirs which had begun to appear. Professor Carroll's book, published in 1931, at least tried to add for one country an atmosphere that would contribute to enrich narrations based largely on the diplomatic interchange. In any case, the pioneers in that whole enterprise had to learn their trade empirically while trying at the same time to teach it to others.

Professor Carroll's third book: *Germany and the Great Powers, 1866-1914: A Study in Public Opinion and Foreign Policy,* published in 1938, suggests that the author, and doubtless most of his colleagues in the field, had made progress in educating themselves as historians. The complexity of the subject began to be more apparent, and a simple adequate narrative by a single author began to seem to be practically impossible. Nor did it prove to be easy to allocate to many writers of monographs the tasks of investigating subjects that needed to be explored and then to mold their findings into a coherent single story. Professor Carroll's third book revealed that he had found it necessary to investigate the history of foreign relations for himself if he was to relate his readings in the press to pertinent events of the time.

By 1938, moreover, it was beginning to be clear that too much emphasis had been placed on the study of the diplomatic correspondence before 1914, that the Western European nations would never in the twentieth century return to the stable patterns that seemed to prevail in the last decades of the nineteenth. Instead of a league to enforce peace, of which some talked, or the less ambitious League of Nations, which Woodrow Wilson tried to organize, the peoples of the world took Wilson at his word and started on a binge of "self-determination." The peace which the leaders in the War tried to make at Versailles did not last.

Russians were induced to rally around Lenin and Stalin in the name of Communism; Italians around Mussolini in the name of Fascism; Germans around Hitler in the name of National Socialism. Under these dictators declining nations were revived and attempts made to project new empires at a time when those of Great Britain and France began to be static if not to decline. Professor Carroll's *Germany and the Great Powers* was thus not excessively complex, as a reviewer hinted was the case. He and other writers before that time had omitted factors necessary to be treated if one is ever to understand how the present we now endure emerged from the antecedent past.

Sensing this fact, Professor Carroll began to gather materials to recount the events between 1919 and 1939. Before he had gone far it was impossible to ignore the fact that the history of the modern Western world had acquired another major dimension. Centuries of penetration of the Orient by the West had equipped the Japanese to invade the mainland of Asia and then, with Europe in a desperate turmoil precipitated by the current dictators, to attack the United States at Pearl Harbor and in the Philippines.

Professor Carroll's long study of the history of international relations had qualified him for national service in this crisis, when the United States found itself again involved in a major war. He went first to Washington in the summer of 1942 and thence to Europe after the invading army of the allies had established itself on the Continent, serving in several responsible capacities as occasion offered. His previous studies and his association with the invading army made Professor Carroll an appropriate scholar to help represent the United States among those examining captured German documents to select such as were suitable to be microfilmed or published. These national duties interrupted for five years the routine of teaching and the systematic study of history.

As a recognition of these services to his institution and his country, it was fitting that Professor Carroll should be included among the select group of James B. Duke Professors as a public mark of distinction. Before he retired he served for several years as Chairman of the Department of History.

Perhaps this bare narrative of the career of a single man helps little one who speculates concerning the vicissitudes of fate to decide why of two men in a field one is taken and the other left. Many men who made careers in the period extending from the last decade of the nineteenth century through the first six of the twentieth took responsible parts in rapidly changing events in a troubled time. But the forces that brought Eber Malcolm Carroll from Coldwater, Michigan, to Durham, North Carolina, and impelled him to serve notably his profession and his country do not become simpler when the stages of his career are examined and placed in order, nor is any design in the general pattern of events made clear.

W. T. Laprade

Power, Public Opinion, and Diplomacy

PIUS IX AND
LORD PALMERSTON, 1846-1849*

Lillian Parker Wallace

The year 1846 brought into the limelight in Europe two persons who were destined to play significant roles in the unfolding drama on the European stage, and within a fortnight of each other.[1] In Rome, Mastai Ferretti was elected by the Conclave on June 14 and assumed the name Pius, becoming Pius IX; in London, on June 26, the formation of a new Whig Government brought to the office of Foreign Secretary Henry John Temple, 3rd Viscount Palmerston. The one was absolute ruler of the oldest institution in Europe, the other the representative in international affairs of Europe's oldest national government. These two historic events had at the moment no connection with each other; no Cardinal had carried in his pocket any nomination to the Holy See; no word from Rome brought about the failure of the Tory cabinet. England was Protestant,

---

* This title was suggested by a letter from Louis Charles Farini to the Director of the *Rivista Contemporanea* in 1856 (Farini, *Lettres sur les affaires d'Italie* [Paris, 1860], p. 145), who wished him to review a French article on the Pontifical Government; Farini replied that if he wrote such an article to the Parisians they would not believe it—they would make a couple of visits to Italy, studying their history and taking their documents from the leading Cardinals; then to set their consciences at ease "they would write an oration which would have for title: 'Pius IX and Lord Palmerston, or, a Commentary on Pontifical Government.'"

[1] The publication of the news of the election of the new Pope preceded in London by only five days the announcement of the fall of the Peel cabinet. See *Times* (London), June 22, 1846.

and had for three centuries been separated from direct spiritual
or diplomatic relations with the See of Rome.   Nevertheless,
the two drew near each other for a space of time, and in so
doing influenced the course of events.   Their drama was not
played out on an isolated stage but in the midst of the tensions
and countertensions, the alarms, seditions, and wars of much
of Europe.

The change of parties was not a world-shaking affair; to the
aristocratic Tories succeeded the equally aristocratic Whigs.[2]
The Tories, composed of the lesser nobility, devoted almost
equally to the Queen, the Church of England, and their prejudices, quarreled within their own ranks over the Corn Laws,
whose abolition Sir Robert Peel, their leader, espoused, and
opened the door for the return of the Whigs.   In fact, the
Whigs might have taken over the reins of government six
months earlier except for the fact that Lord John Russell's
Whig cabinet would of necessity have brought back to the
Foreign Office Lord Palmerston,[3] a circumstance from which
they wished devoutly to be delivered if possible.   The great
change was a change of personalities.   Commotion would be
the result of the eruption, for such it must be called, of this

[2] *Univers* (July 17, 1847), the Catholic daily in Paris, commenting on the
English parties remarked, "Are Whigs still Whigs, and Tories Tories?   There
has been between the two during the past three years such an exchange of
view that one can no longer clearly distinguish one from the other."

[3] *Times* (London), June 29, 1846.   See editorial referring to Russell's attempt
in December, 1845, to form a cabinet, and the bitter attack made on Lord
Palmerston at the time.   *Revue des Deux Mondes* (I, Dec. 15, 1846) was sure
that Palmerston was regarded as a liability by the Whigs, but Russell saw no
ministry possible without him.   When the fall of the Peel ministry seemed imminent Palmerston visited France to improve his relations with the French, who
were fearful of losing their *entente cordiale* with England, an entente sedulously
cultivated by his predecessor, Lord Aberdeen.   See Donald Greer, *L'Angleterre, la
France et la Révolution de 1848: Le Troisième ministère de Lord Palmerston
au Foreign Office 1846-1851* (Paris, 1925), p. 9.   French apprehension had, indeed, been very considerable.   See *Revue des Deux Mondes*, I (1846), Jan. 14,
p. 168.   See also Princess Lieven (residing in Paris) to Lord Aberdeen, July 1,
1846.   *Correspondence of Lord Aberdeen and Princess Lieven 1832-1854* (2 vols.;
Royal Historical Society, Camden, 3rd ser., Vol. LX, London, 1931), I, 259.   She
remarked that "there is not a diplomat here who is not frightened"; the policy
would again be "uneasy, mischief-making and arrogant."

fiery, audacious, intractable, and very able non-Whig, whose peerage, being Irish, did not prevent him from occupying a seat in the House of Commons, where his ability to turn a phrase with telling effect,[4] made him a colorful and unforgettable figure.

Pius IX's election was much more world-shaking—almost a nuclear explosion. He was destined to reign over the Catholic Church for thirty-two years; the most important events, religious, social, and political, were to be unfolded during his pontificate. He was not a mere spectator of these events.[5]

The Conclave[6] astonished the world and the Church no less by its brevity than by its choice of Ferretti to wear the Triple Crown.[7] Rumor, in fact, was that the anti-Austrian members hastened to elect in order to have finished before the arrival of the Cardinal from Milan with Austria's *non placet* in his

[4] This ability appeared also in his voluminous correspondence. One of his witty remarks in a letter to Granville in 1832 illustrates the point: "Metternich has made April Fools of us . . . . It (the agreement regarding Belgium) is only a piece of parchment which might as well be on the back of its own sheep. . . ." Quoted in C. K. Webster, *Palmerston, Metternich and the European System 1830-1841* (London, 1934), p. 18.

[5] The most recent biographer of Pius IX, E. E. Y. Hales, entitles his book *Pio Nono: Creator of the Modern Papacy* (New York, 1954), and not without justification.

[6] There were seventy-two Cardinals at the time of Gregory XVI's death. Not all arrived before the election. Naturally those who lived in Italy or near by, of whom there were many, reached Rome first. Each of the Catholic monarchs had the right to be represented by an envoy. One of these was Pellegrino Rossi, envoy of the King of France, whose career and death were to be so intimately connected with Pius IX and the Revolution of 1848. At the death of the Pope all power, temporal and spiritual, passes into the hands of the Conclave as a body, and remains until the new pontiff is elected. Petitions for reform, redress, or decision, may be presented to the body as though it were St. Peter himself. Such was the case in 1846, when feeling ran high between reactionaries and liberals in the Papal States.

[7] The *Times* (London, June 19, 1846) referred to the election as "sudden" and "unexpected"; its "precipitancy," thought the *Times*, was probably due to the need for changes in Italy. "The reported liberal views of the new Pope," it went on, "suggest to some of the journals before us the idea that concessions would be made to the demands of the discontented; but the Sacred College, which opposed itself to all species of temporal reform during the life of Gregory XVI, will probably overrule in like manner the wise dispositions and moves of his successor."

pocket to be used against any liberal chosen.[8] As Bishop of
Imola the newly elected Pope had been esteemed for his chari-
table works, his saintliness of character, and the purity of his
private life. Recognized as a liberal (he was known to have
read Gioberti, whose works were the very Bible of Italian liberals) he was succeeding the reactionary Gregory XVI. Here
was change indeed. The pontificate of Pius IX began more
auspiciously than the entrance of Lord Palmerston into the
Foreign Office in England.

Although there were domestic questions which pressed upon
and complicated British foreign relations, Palmerston's policy
was to be in the main a return to that which he had maintained during his earlier years in the Foreign Office, when the
Whigs had been in power. Lord Aberdeen, the Tory Foreign
Secretary, had in general retained the same lines of procedure,
but in a calm, dignified, and less explosive way. He left, however, to Lord Palmerston a foreign problem whose outcome
was to start a spiraling series of events. This was the question
of the Spanish marriages. Both the Queen of Spain and her
sister the Infanta were of an age to contract marriage alliances,
and the matter was of interest not only in Spain but in Europe.
Outside Spain the greatest concern was in France and England;
in France, that the choice should be limited to a member of
the House of Bourbon,[9] that is, a descendent of Philip V of

[8] See G. F. H. and J. Berkeley, *Italy in the Making* (3 vols.; Cambridge,
1940), II, 34, for examination and rejection of this claim. See also Raffaele
Ballerini, *Premières pages du pontificat de Pie IX* (Rome, 1909), p. 6. Ballerini gives two reason sometimes assigned for the short duration of the Conclave: (1) that it was a formality, the Pope being already chosen; (2) that it
was precipitated to check the rising split between two powerful factions, one led
by the liberal Mastai, the other by the Papal Secretary of State, Lambruschini.
Ballerini maintains that the first claim is disproved by the fact that the choice
did not come on an early ballot, and for the second, that unanimity grew.
Special interest attaches to Ballerini's study because his work, although not published until 1909, was written during the lifetime of Pius, who read the manuscript and made a few notations in the margin. Further volumes were contemplated but for some reason did not materialize, and this first volume did not
appear in print until after Ballerini's death.

[9] Guizot, *History of France* (8 vols.; New York, 1885), VIII, 368. Guizot

Spain; in England, that France should not seek to promote the interests of an Orleanist, thus uniting the policies of France and Spain. The name of Prince Leopold of Saxe-Coburg had been introduced into the Spanish court and met with the favor of the Spanish Queen and Christina, the Queen Mother.[10]

Guizot, insisting that Leopold was a British candidate because of the family relationship between the Queen of Britain and the Saxe-Coburg House, had informed Aberdeen that any attempt to promote the candidacy of Leopold would absolve France from the promise not to support an Orleanist. Lord Aberdeen had not been disturbed, as he favored Don Enrique, an eligible Bourbon prince. This was the situation to which Palmerston fell heir when he took over the Foreign Office.

When the name of Prince Leopold began to be discussed favorably in Madrid, consternation reigned in the French capital.[11] Guizot wanted assurance that England would act jointly with France in recommending Don Enrique. This Palmerston refused to do. He would co-operate, but not act jointly, because France was attempting to dictate in Spain; England was not.[12] While exchanges of letters were taking place and the

said, as early as 1842, in a letter to his ambassador in Vienna, "It is for us a French interest of the first order; and in my opinion . . . it is also a European interest." In the same year Lord Aberdeen, after conferring with the French ambassador in London, informed his representatives in Spain, Austria, and France that Louis Philippe would renounce all pretensions of a son of his own. Aberdeen said it was a question for Spain to decide. *British and Foreign State Papers* (hereinafter cited as *B.S.P.*), XXXV, 717.

[10] So Palmerston reported to Queen Victoria. *Letters of Queen Victoria* (3 vols.; New York, 1907), II, 106.

[11] Lord Cowley to Lord Palmerston, Paris, July 13, 1846, *B.S.P.*, XXXV, 724. Palmerston precipitated the crisis by mentioning Prince Leopold's name in a letter (July 18) to his representative in Madrid and showed the letter to the French ambassador in London. *Letters of Queen Victoria*, II, 107.

[12] Palmerston to Queen Victoria, Aug. 19, 1846, *Letters of Queen Victoria*, II, 115. At the Queen's insistence Palmerston enjoined Bulwer not to take sides in Spanish politics; England's interest was to maintain the independence of Spain; France's to establish predominant influence. Victoria wanted no interference internally in Spain and no "steering" of the Government "for the avowed purpose of counteracting the influence of France." Such a policy might lead to a quarrel between England and France the consequences of which, she said,

news from Madrid was that the French ambassador was authorized to respect the wishes of the Spanish Queen,[13] came the
sudden word that Isabella had decided to marry the Bourbon
Don Francisco, and that immediately after, a marriage had
been arranged between the Infanta and the Duc de Montpensier, son of Louis Philippe.[14]

Palmerston expostulated both in Paris and in Madrid[15] but
it was too late; the diplomacy of Guizot had defeated the
British Foreign Secretary. Palmerston was furious, and his
wrath was not easily allayed. The most serious aspect of the
affair was that Guizot had deliberately, in the interest of Louis
Philippe's dynasty, brought a rupture in the relations of England and France, at a critical time in the history of Rome, as
of all Europe.[16] In serving Louis Philippe's personal ambitions
he had not served France.[17] In reaching for an additional

"we can hardly foresee." Queen Victoria to Lord John Russell, Aug. 17, 1846,
Ibid. II, 113. See also Palmerston to Bulwer, July 19, 1846, in Sir Henry
Lytton Bulwer (Lord Dalling), *The Life of Henry John Temple Viscount
Palmerston with Selections from his Correspondence* (3 vols.; London, 1870-
1874), III, 262.

[13] *Times* (London), Sept. 3, 1846.

[14] Bulwer to Palmerston, Madrid, Aug. 29, 1846, *B.S.P.*, XXXV, 735. Bulwer
asserted that Christina took a hand; she told Isabella to marry Don Francisco
or not marry for several years; Isabella consented; it was twelve o'clock at night;
Count Bresson (the French ambassador) immediately asked the hand of the
Infanta for the Duc de Montpensier, saying he was fully authorized; so the
whole affair was concluded on the spot.

[15] Palmerston to Normanby, Sept. 22, and to Bulwer, Sept. 18, 1846, *B.S.P.*,
XXXV, 741-743, 744. *B.S.P.* (p. 758) includes an extract from the Spanish
Constitution of 1845: "Neither the King nor the immediate successor can contract
marriage with any person excluded by law from the succession to the crown."
It had been expressly stipulated, by treaty, when the Bourbon Philip V had
ascended the Spanish throne that the two crowns of Spain and France should
never rest on the same head.

[16] Ballerini declared (*Premières pages,* p. 85) that the failure of England and
France to agree about Rome was at least in part due to the Spanish marriages.

[17] Guizot's behavior throughout was equivocal, and was generally so regarded,
in spite of his attempts to justify his actions. Both Tories and Whigs united
in support of Lord Palmerston. When Queen Victoria learned of the outcome
of the affair she wrote to her uncle, the King of the Belgians, that it was unfortunate—"our *entente wantonly* thrown away." Guizot's conduct, she said
further, "is beyond all belief shameful and so shabbily dishonest." *Letters of
Queen Victoria,* II, 128. Palmerston not only disliked Guizot, he had also a

crown for the Orleanist House, he contrived to make the crown of France totter on the head of the Bourgeois Monarch. Palmerston was presently richly revenged. In the meantime, however, the rift in the *entente cordiale* was viewed with pleasure by Russia, Prussia, and Austria—the Northern Courts. The weakening of the solidarity of the western liberal states would be of assistance to the reactionary policies of these three great powers.

While events were thus shaping up unsatisfactorily during the first months of Palmerston's occupation of the Foreign Office, His Holiness, Pius IX, was making excellent progress with changes in the Papal States. The misgovernment and corruption in public affairs under Gregory XVI was widely recognized at the time, in Italy and far beyond. It did not require the hand of Mazzini,[18] skilled in writing, to make the facts known. Some of the criticisms were very severe. One article in a Paris journal declared that Rome had become the "systematic ally of thrones against nationalities."[19] The long-

---

poor opinion of Louis Philippe, as a man "on whom one could not sincerely count," but if he had been "an honest man, scrupulous and of high character, he would not now be King of France." *Cambridge History of Foreign Policy*, II, 291. Palmerston was also annoyed at Metternich's failure to intervene in the affair, thus giving tacit support to the French position. See Prince Metternich's *Mémoires, documents, et écrits divers* (Paris, 1881), VII, 162. See also Antonin Debidour, *Histoire diplomatique de l'Europe* (2 vols.; Paris, 1891), I, 437.

[18] Giuseppe Mazzini, *Scritti editi e inediti* (Imola, 1921), XXXI (*Politics*, Vol. X), 85-190. This particular work, "Gli Stati Pontifici," gives a detailed description of the operation of government, its mismanagement, confusion, and venality. According to Ballerini (*Premières pages*, p. 10), not only Pius but the Sacred College as well recognized the necessity for change. See also Montanelli to Mazzini, Pisa, April 1, 1847, in Giuseppe Montanelli, *Memorie sull 'Italia e specialmente sulla Toscana dal 1814 al 1850* (2 vols., 2d ed.; Turin, 1855), I, 258.

[19] *Siècle* quoted in *Univers* (Paris), June 6, 1846. It stated that Rome (the Holy See), "in times past the support of oppressed classes, the refuge of liberty, of science and letters, declares itself the ally . . . of ignorance and darkness against light and progress." The article also attacked the "Holy Alliance" whose object was to promote "Christian fraternity and peace," as really tending to "immobilize institutions and peoples." Alphonse Balleydier (*Histoire de la révolution de Rome; tableaux religieuses, politiques, et militaires des années 1846-1850 en Italie* [Geneva, 1851], I, 11) speaks of one work published in 1846 which advocated not only the assassination of the Pope but of the Cardinals,

standing ills of Italy were regarded by many as stemming from two principal causes: the domination of the clergy (who occupied all public positions great and small in the Papal States), and the preponderance of Austria, which, having a legal claim to portions of northern Italy, "extended its influence over the whole peninsula."[20] While the Conclave was in session petitions were drawn up in many places to present to it, setting forth the widespread desire for reforms. All of the documents asked for amnesty for political prisoners and exiles; they asked also for provincial councils to present the wishes of the people to the Government. The Conclave was so brief that most of these did not arrive in time, but those that did exhibited a revolutionary character.[21] Revolutionary refugees from Poland had already been brought in and distributed widely in Italy even before the death of Gregory XVI and the meeting of the Conclave.[22]

Addressing himself first to the most widely demanded reform, Pius IX took up the question of amnesty. The problem was whether to pardon or to expunge. Conservatives favored the former, radicals the latter. Pius chose the latter.[23] From

---

priests, and members of religious orders, and laid out a program of insurrection to be carried on by secret societies.

[20] Farini, *Lettres*, p. ii. Austria, in fact, upon the death of Gregory XVI, increased its armaments at Ancona in Italy, according to the report of the English consul to Lord Aberdeen (June 27, while Aberdeen was still Foreign Secretary); eleven days later another consul reported that because of ferment in the Marches, Ancona, and Umbria, the Austrians had increased their forces at Ferrara and were watching the coast. *B.S.P.*, XXXVI, 1180-1181.

[21] Ballerini, *Premières pages*, pp. 4-5. See also Montanelli, *Memorie*, I, 172.

[22] Metternich to Buol (at Turin), Vienna, May 29, 1846, in Metternich, *Mémoires*, VII, 341. He thought Charles Albert of Sardinia should be prepared to take steps against radicals; in this he would be seconded by Austria. In a confidential letter of the same date (p. 233) he remarked that Charles Albert "followed the flag of liberalism in 1820; that flag was worn out; it is the flag of radicalism that has replaced it." In Metternich's view there was no middle ground: to depart from conservatism was to go over to "Carbonarism." Yet Metternich realized that excessive harshness produced no salutary effects.

[23] Metternich commented on this point. He disapproved, and especially of expunging the wrong doing from the record—the "forgetting the whole thing." See his *Mémoires* (Aug. 6, 1846), VII, 178. Paschini says that military persons and priests were excluded from the amnesty. See Pio Paschini, *Lezioni di storia*

this moment on there was serious difference of opinion between Pius and Metternich.[24] The proclamation of amnesty was posted in Rome on July 17, 1846.[25] On the same day Pius fulfilled the custom of Roman pontiffs and held a consistory to thank the Sacred College for electing him. After making the confession of faith he took oath to the apostolic constitutions. Two, the one promulgated in 1564 by Pius V, and the other in 1660 by Alexander VII, are especially significant: they forbid the "alienation in any manner whatsoever of the territories of the Roman Church."[26]

Lord Palmerston, viewing with approval the initial activities of the Pope, sought to know the French attitude toward reform; he would see with pleasure both the granting of amnesty by Pius and further reforms, suggested in the memorandum which had been presented to the papacy in 1831 by the Five Powers.[27] Guizot's reply, expressed through Lord

ecclesiastica (3 vols.; Turin, 1955), III, 503. Spellanzon asserts that the documents show that "the Roman amnesty of July, 1846, was known and approved in advance by Metternich (*"preventivamente conosciuta e approvata"*). See Cesare Spellanzon, *Storia del Risorgimento é del unità d'Italia* (5 vols.; Milan, 1933-1950), III, iii. Nevertheless, Metternich did not approve the expunging.

[24] Cowley (English ambassador in Paris) to Palmerston, July 17, 1846. *B.S.P.*, XXXVI, 1195-1196. Lord Cowley said that reports to Paris from Vienna and Rome indicated that Metternich was afraid of the too-liberal policy of Pius.

[25] See *ibid.* (pp. 1197-1198) for a copy of the proclamation. A facsimile appears in Spellanzon, *Risorgimento*, III, 9.

[26] Ballerini, *Premières pages*, pp. 63-65. Pius later referred to this oath when he wrote to Emperor Francis Joseph from Gaëta on December 4, 1848. See the Latin version in Spellanzon, *Risorgimento*, V, 1035.

[27] Palmerston to Cowley, July 21, 1846. *B.S.P.*, XXXVI, 1196. A copy of the memorandum was sent to Lord Russell by Palmerston with a letter dated July 30. See this letter in Evelyn Ashley, *The Life and Correspondence of Henry John Temple Viscount Palmerston* (2 vols.; London, 1879), II, 12-14. Palmerston points out in the letter the intolerably bad government in the Papal States and goes on that "nothing can make men submit to misrule, but physical force and despair of outside assistance"; if affairs in Italy were not remedied the peace of Europe was likely to be upset; why should not the Whigs "take advantage of the liberal inclinations of the new Pope to encourage and induce him to make reforms"; he would try to get the other four powers to support Pius in this reforming policy. Rosselli insists that Palmerston's program was to encourage the liberation of Italy from Austrian domination without throwing it into the arms of France, and to encourage the liberalizing of political institutions. Nello Rosselli, *Inghilterra e regno di Sardegna dal 1815 al 1847* (Turin, 1954), p. 852.

Cowley, was that Pius was going ahead on his own steam and did not need any advice.[28] Pius, in fact, appointed the liberal Gizzi as Cardinal Secretary of State and went serenely on with his contemplated changes.[29] Some of his reforms were in the realm of economics and improved living conditions among his subjects, such as proposals for railway construction, a project to light the streets with gas, an Agricultural Institute, customs reforms, improvement in proceedings in criminal courts, financial reforms, and betterment of administration.[30]

This reforming zeal in the papal dominions not only brought approbation from liberals everywhere[31] but received enthusiastic response from all Italians who were not ultraconservative.[32] The granting of the amnesty, freely, persuaded the people that here at last was a really liberal Pope. For the time being the radical organizations lost ground; Young Italy lost many members. Protestants and schismatics alike joined in the general chorus of praise to Pius. The hatred for the papacy which had built up under Gregory XVI abated; love and veneration filled the hearts of the Pope's subjects. Unfortunately the organized radicals, a small minority, taking advantage of the return of affiliates from exile and of the exuberance of joy

[28] *B.S.P.*, XXXVI, 1199.

[29] See Abercrombie's (Turin) review of the events of 1846 in a report to Palmerston on January 12, 1847, *ibid.*, XXXVI, 1201. Gizzi was appointed on August 6, 1846. See Ballerini, *Premières pages*, p. 66.

[30] Hales, *Pio Nono*, pp. 58-59. See also Balleydier, *Révolution de Rome*, I, 36; Farini, *Lettres*, p. 176.

[31] *Times* (London), Sept. 2, 1846. An editorial referred to the *Journal des Débats* (Paris) eulogizing the policy of Pius IX. The *Times* editorial goes on in approval of the appointment of a liberal as Secretary of State and says that Pius "will strengthen that religion of which he is the light and guide"; that Catholic religion has never brought real opposition except when people believed, "erroneously, no doubt," that the heads of the Church wanted to curtail human progress.

[32] *Constitutionnel* (as quoted in *Times* [London], Sept. 2, 1846) stated that Charles Albert of Sardinia had written to Pius in flattering vein "complimenting him on his reforms." The Paris journal regarded this as very important; it would be the "death blow to the retrograde party and to Austrian influence"; it expressed encouragement to Cardinal Gizzi to proceed with the reform program; the King of Naples, on the other hand, indicated hostile intentions "toward the Pontifical Court."

legitimately felt by the citizens of the Papal States, used every
occasion for exaggerating the shouting and confusion; crowds
were turned into mobs, which might be more easily dominated.
This was one of the reasons for the later series of tragic events
in the city of the Caesars. The radicals did not fear violence;
they were ready to resort to it. On the other hand, it must be
remembered that reactionary authorities did not refrain from
violence when opportunity offered. The path of genuine liberalism was then, as later, a difficult one to follow. Moreover,
the rejoicing was beginning to take on a nationalist tinge.

The first warning not to misunderstand the nature of the
new Pope's liberalism came in a circular[33] which emphasized
the undesirability of innovations which might interfere with
the tranquillity which every government needs for the welfare
of its subjects. This declaration went almost unheeded; the
liberals tried to prevent its being read. Actually, the greatest
dangers to the tranquillity in Rome were the dangers of radicalism, on the one hand, and of blind conservatism of some
classes on the other.[34] An event outside the boundaries of
Italy which occurred during November formed a prelude to
the violence which was to beset Europe in the next few years.
This was the annexation of the Free City of Cracow and its
territory to the dominions of His Imperial Majesty, the Emperor of Austria.[35] This breaking of the Settlement of 1815
was brought about by the emboldening of the Northern Courts
because of the rupture of the *entente cordiale*. Palmerston,
after the rebuff involved in the Spanish marriages question,

[33] The circular was dated August 24, 1846. See Ballerini, *Premières pages*,
p. 66. This displeased those who wanted extensive reforms. Some said it was
written by a subordinate in the secretariat desirous of sowing discord between
the sovereign and his people.

[34] This was the opinion, fully justified by later events, of Comte Auguste de
Liedekerke de Beaufort, ambassador to the Holy See from The Netherlands,
as expressed by A. M. Ghisalberti, who edited Liedekerke's *Rapporti delle cose
di Roma 1848-1849* (Rome, 1849). See Ghisalberti's foreword, p. xii.

[35] Ponsonby to Palmerston, Vienna, Nov. 18, 1846, *B.S.P.*, XXXV, 1086.

could not be expected to support Guizot in the type of vigorous
protest demanded by the French people.[36]

Whatever the coolness in the relations between England
and France, Lord Palmerston and Pius IX were very cordial.
Pius continued his reforms, although at a slower pace, and
England approved. Feeling that some direct contact would
be advantageous in these days of change, a proposal was made
to put the relations of the two courts on a firmer basis. The
British ambassador in Paris reported a conversation with the
Nuncio there. The Pope's representative had told him His
Holiness desired a more active moral support from England;
he was having trouble, not only through "jealous interference
of Austria" but because France was not supporting him strongly,
and, "if her interests were otherwise engaged" would not be
likely to aid him; he thought such English support would be of
the "greatest service to the progress of social improvement in
Italy."[37] Lord Palmerston in his reply asked exactly what he
could do; his Government had "every desire" to do whatever
might "properly be in their power to comply with any wishes
expressed by the Pope."[38] Normanby, in another conference
with the Nuncio, told him that it was "well known that England would have none but disinterested motives in giving support to the independence of the Italian States"; how could
moral support be given? The Nuncio replied that it could
not be given effectively without "direct communication." If
a Minister could not be established in Rome, he went on, it
would be a great support to His Holiness if someone in the
confidence of Her Majesty's Government could have temporarily an opportunity of personally communicating with the
Pope and his Minister.[39]

[36] This is the well-founded view of Debidour, expressed in his *Histoire
diplomatique*, I, 435.

[37] Normanby to Palmerston, Paris, April 19, 1847, *B.S.P.*, XXXVI, 1205.
(Normanby had replaced Cowley). Cf. Spellanzon, *Risorgimento*, III, 284.

[38] Palmerston to Normanby, April 27, 1847, *B.S.P.*, XXXVI, 1206.

[39] Normanby to Palmerston, April 30, 1847, *ibid.*, p. 1207.

Out of this exchange of letters developed two Government-sponsored projects: the extraordinary mission of Lord Minto, and a move to establish diplomatic relations with the Papal Court. The first was undertaken immediately; the second awaited the arrival of the special envoy in Rome to confer with the Pope.

The man selected for the mission was Earl Minto, father-in-law of the Prime Minister, Lord Russell, and Lord Privy Seal in his cabinet. Lord Minto had had a distinguished career in both Houses and in several cabinets; he enjoyed the confidence of both parties. Queen Victoria approved of his selection and also of his mission, "on the understanding that the object of it will be communicated beforehand to the Courts of Vienna and Paris. . . ."[40] Lord Palmerston notified his representatives in the courts to which Lord Minto was accredited, and said he was being sent on "extraordinary Mission."[41] He directed Lord Minto to proceed to Switzerland, Turin, Florence, and Rome.

The situation which the special envoy was to investigate in Switzerland[42] was part of the crescendo of demand for reform not only in Italy, where the papal reforms had been undertaken so auspiciously by Pius IX, but also in central Europe, where the tempo of reform had been even faster. His Holiness, Lord Palmerston, and other statesmen of Europe were all disturbed, for varying reasons, over the Swiss struggle. Switzerland (whose neutrality had been guaranteed in 1815 by the powers) was divided between Catholic Cantons and a Protestant majority in the Federal Diet. Not all of the Cantons were of the same political complexion, as they were not all alike religiously. The liberals by introducing an article on ecclesiastical reform in their program had added to the political quarrel a religious one. In reply the Catholic Cantons formed a union, the Sonderbund, designed to protect their way of life. The Federal Diet in attempting to form a closer federal arrangement among all

[40] Victoria to Russell, Sept. 3, 1847, *Letters of Queen Victoria*, II, 151.
[41] *B.S.P.*, XXXVI, 1268. Cf. Spellanzon, *Risorgimento*, III, 288.
[42] Palmerston to Lord Minto, Sept. 18, 1847, *B.S.P.*, XXXVI, 1268.

of the Cantons and to break up the Catholic cantonal union
undertook to discipline this minority.   It became inevitably a
question of international diplomacy.   Would the Cantons be
permitted to settle the issue among themselves by force?   Would
any of the powers intervene to dictate a settlement?   The Pope
himself, keen as might be his interest, could not interfere in
any other way than by admonition, which in this case would be
a futile gesture.   The two great Catholic powers, however, had
a vital interest in defending the Catholic minority.   When a
radical group gained control of the Federal Diet both of these
powers became alarmed at the gravity of the situation.[43]

Lord Minto carried out his instructions to look at Switzerland and later, at Rome, tried to persuade the papal government to "recall the Jesuits from Switzerland, or at least to take
some decided step with regard to them" which might be "calculated to lay the ground for an avoidance of civil war."[44]   He
conferred with the Cardinal Secretary of State with reference
to the matter.   He found the Pope's Minister "not altogether
averse to the interposition of authority, if by such means a
conflict might be prevented in Switzerland."   This the Pope
was not prepared to do; all he felt he could give was advice,
"and it has, I fear," reported Lord Minto, "been given to those
who are unlikely to listen to anything short of a command."

[43] Metternich, *Mémoires*, VII, 178. See also *Univers* (Paris), Oct. 21, 1847.
The article in the Catholic paper stated that not only were the radical Cantons
trying to deprive the Catholic Cantons of their liberty but were endeavoring as
well to reform the Pact of 1815.   Federal action in Switzerland rested on a
famous article in each of the capitulations: "Every political question which
might be raised and which is not of the power of military command will be
submitted to the decision of the Federal Diet."   Radicals in several Cantons,
by changing their constitutions, had made the issue a "political" one, which was
to be referred to the Diet, which sided with them.   See also the issue of Feb.
6, 1848.   The Basle correspondent pointed out that one of the main questions
was the presence of the Jesuits, whom the radicals wished to exclude.   Cf.
Spellanzon, *Risorgimento*, III, 264.

[44] T. C. Hansard, *Parliamentary Debates of Great Britain* (hereinafter cited
as Hansard), 3rd ser., XCVI, 784.   Palmerston said further that "in the present
case the Pope has it in his power, by an exercise of his unquestionable authority,
to remove at once a cause which threatens to involve a hitherto peaceful and
happy nation in all the miseries and crimes of civil conflict."

He said he would continue to press for papal interposition of authority.[45]

Lord Palmerston, not expecting any miracle to be performed in Switzerland by Pius IX, whatever might be the Pope's disposition to allay friction, took a hand himself in order to circumvent the plans of Metternich and Guizot, the ministers of the two Catholic powers.

Metternich having approached France in the summer with a suggestion of intervention, Guizot replied (July 2), in a message full of circumlocutions about the prospect of civil war, declaring that if the public voice, raised "from the heart of Switzerland" should be addressed to Europe, as the only way of re-establishing peace and order, he thought a direct intervention of the powers might be efficacious.[46] Guizot suggested that Austria send troops into Switzerland, then France would do the same, as a counterbalance. Metternich was suspicious of this move. He proposed sending jointly a threatening note, warning Switzerland that war would result if the Sonderbund were attacked. France wanted the *five* powers to act, including England especially.[47] Lord Palmerston used delaying tactics. A conference of the powers was planned to take place at Basle.[48]

[45] *Ibid.*, 3rd ser., XCVI, 785. This exchange of letters between Palmerston and Lord Minto was referred to by Lord Stanley in the debate on restoring diplomatic relations with the Holy See.

[46] *Univers* (Paris), Feb. 2, 1848. This correspondence was brought out in the debate (February 1) in the French Chamber over this issue (by that time actually ended).

[47] Guizot was being reproached by the French for allowing the *entente cordiale* to fail because of his coup for the dynasty in the matter of the Spanish marriages. See Debidour, *Histoire diplomatique*, I, 446. See also Normanby's dispatch to Palmerston of March 13, 1848, in Ashley, *Palmerston*, II, 67-68. The Ambassador said he had sat through three weeks of debate in which Guizot's foreign as well as his domestic policy had been under attack; Guizot was reproached for the Spanish affair, which was labeled a "selfish and anti-nationalist policy." In the course of the debate the Minister of War admitted that while Guizot was proposing mediation in the Swiss affair "he had smuggled, for the benefit of the Sonderbund, arms and ammunition out of the Royal Arsenal at Besançon." When Normanby's report was written the French Government and Guizot had already fallen.

[48] Guizot to French ambassadors in London, Berlin, Vienna, and Rome (Holy

On November 4[49] the Swiss Diet rendered a decree of execution
against the Sonderbund and prepared for immediate beginning
of hostilities. The British ambassador conferred with the Swiss
Government.[50] Palmerston quibbled, and delayed still further, suggested moving the conference to London; he proposed
different wording for a joint note; he discussed with the French
ambassador the possibility of getting the Pope to induce the
Jesuits to evacuate Switzerland; he insisted that mediation
should be employed rather than any threat of force.[51] The
result of the war was the victory of the Protestant Cantons over
the Sonderbund by force of arms.[52] The radicals in Rome were
pleased at the defeat of the Catholic Cantons and demonstrated
against the Jesuits. Pius was pained.[53]

Intervention in Switzerland was a dead issue. Palmerston,
interpellated in the House of Commons on whether he had any
information which "would prevent or render unnecessary, any
mediation, on the part of this country between the contending
parties in Switzerland" replied that civil war in Switzerland was
"in point of fact at an end. Now, as mediation meant an interposition between two contending parties, it was evident that
when there was an end of contention, there must also be an

See), Nov. 4, 1847. *Univers* (Paris), Feb. 2, 1848 (giving debate of February 1).
Guizot said the powers could not remain indifferent to a crisis which imperiled
the Federal pact.

[49] The very day of Guizot's announcement to his representatives.

[50] *Univers* (Paris), Nov. 9, 1847.

[51] Palmerston to Ponsonby, Nov. 20, 1847, in Ashley, *Palmerston,* II, 8. Again
on December 1, 1847, Palmerston tried through Ponsonby to dissuade Metternich
from intervention on the ground that France would certainly intervene also—
and adversely to Austria. See Palmerston to Ponsonby, Dec. 21, 1847, *ibid.,* II, 10.

[52] The subsequent repression of customary church forms in the Catholic
Cantons drew a pained expression of alarm and astonishment from Pius. See
Univers (Paris), Nov. 8, 1848, for a statement from the Papal Secretary of State.
Pius could not understand the prohibition of the wearing of ecclesiastical cos-
tume. The statement further recalled that when the Holy See in 1820 authorized
the clergy to take the oath of fidelity to the state it was understood that they
would not be obliged to do anything "contrary to the *principles* of the Catholic
faith nor to the ordinances of the Church." [Italics in the original.]

[53] Hales, *Pio Nono,* p. 69.

end of mediation."[54]   Metternich had been unable to move, and
Guizot had played an inglorious part.   The *entente cordiale*
had indeed broken apart, and at a time when its hand to support or to restrain, its voice to approve or counsel caution, were
to be sadly needed.   The Government of France in debating
the issue in the Chamber was inclined to insist on continuing
to use moral force rather than active coercion.   This point of
view was challenged, it is true, and an anti-Government speaker,
without deprecating the value of an English alliance, insisted
that occasions arose when the policy of England was in opposition to that of France; that was the situation in the Swiss
affair; the Constitution of Switzerland ought not to be
changed.[55]   This debate was not only a post-mortem on events
past but a prelude to the overthrow of the French monarchy
before the month was out.

   The visit of Lord Minto to Switzerland had been a side
issue; the real object of his mission was to encourage reform in
Italy, and especially in Rome, and to discuss the question of
putting the relations between the Vatican and London on a
firmer basis.   Lord Palmerston regarded the Pope's reforms as
highly praiseworthy and deserving of encouragement, and instructed his envoy to let it be known that "Her Majesty's Government could not see with indifference any aggression committed upon the Roman territories, with a view to prevent the
Papal Government from carrying into effect those internal improvements which it may think proper to adopt."   He also sent
Lord Minto a copy of the notable memorandum of 1831 which
had been handed to the Cardinal Secretary of State at that time
by each member, separately, of the Conference assembled at
Rome, and urged on the Pope (Gregory XVI) for adoption.[56]
Lord Minto was not officially accredited to the Pope, because of

[54] Hansard, 3rd ser., XCV, 701.   Session of Dec. 6, 1847.
[55] *Univers* (Paris), Feb. 2, 1848.
[56] Palmerston to Earl Minto, Sept. 18, 1847, *B.S.P.*, XXXVI, 1268.

the lack of regular diplomatic intercourse between the two
courts, or to Naples until long after he had left England.[57]

After leaving Switzerland Lord Minto went on, first to
Turin and then to Florence. At Turin he was instructed to
say to Charles Albert that the British Government sympathized
with Sardinia and felt "surprise and regret" at the suggestion
of Austrian interference with Sardinia's internal reforms;
Britain was pleased that Charles Albert had promised friendly
and defensive support of the Pope. In general he was to express there and elsewhere that he regarded it as "undeniable
truth, that if an independent sovereign . . . shall think fit to
make within his dominions such improvements in the laws and
institutions of his country as he may think conducive to the
welfare of his people, no other Government can have any right
to attempt to restrain or to interfere with such an employment
of one of the inherent attributes of independent sovereignty."[58]
Lord Palmerston was always of the opinion that the surest way
to ward off more revolutionary demands was to make needed
reforms in time.

Having made his scheduled stops along the way, Lord Minto
arrived in Rome in November and proceeded to carry out his
instructions. The request for Pius to intervene in the Swiss
affair bore no fruit, as has been earlier observed. He did encourage the Pope in his reforms, and in the reassurance that
Austria was not likely to interfere.[59] The envoy was to tell the

[57] Ashley, *Palmerston*, II, 42-43. Palmerston said Lord Minto was to go to
Rome "not as a Minister accredited to the Pope, but as an authentic organ of
the British Government, enabled to explain its views and to declare its sentiments upon events" then taking place in Italy.

[58] *Ibid.*, II, 43. Charles Albert wrote Pius that Lord Minto had praised the
papal government and recommended the union of Italian princes to assure "wise
and moderate reforms." See Rosselli, *Inghilterra e regno di Sardegna*, p. 889.

[59] Palmerston told Lord Minto in a letter dated October 29, 1847, that Austria
had been "headed" and would not "break for cover towards Italy," for which the
Pope ought to feel thankful. See Ashley, *Palmerston*, II, 45. As for encouragement of papal reforms, Nicomede Bianchi (*Storia documentata della diplomazia
europea in Italia dall' anno 1841 all' anno 1861* [8 vols.; Turin and Naples, 1869],
V, 84) says that Lord Minto saw the Pope caught between two opposing forces, one
to go on to further experiments, the other to hold him back; Lord Minto thought

Pope that an act of Parliament would be necessary to enable England to establish diplomatic relations with him. Although Lord Minto was advised in a dispatch sent to him after he left England that this was not a propitious moment for bringing to the Pope's attention a bill to accomplish this end, he did discuss the matter with His Holiness during his sojourn in Rome. He was further to suggest that the Pope "exert his authority over the Irish priesthood, to induce them to abstain from meddling in politics . . . and to inculcate in their flocks greater respect for the law." In a letter in early December Palmerston advised Lord Minto to go beyond his original memorandum and let people around the Pope know that many of the Irish clergy were inciting their flocks to murder and violence. Pius was shocked at the news of the behavior of the priests and expressed strong disapproval.[60]

While Lord Minto was still sojourning in Rome the question of establishing regular diplomatic intercourse was actually taken up in London. Such relations had not existed between London and Rome for three centuries. Several factors in the nineteenth-century situation seemed conducive to a resumption of such intercourse: the popularity of Pius IX, whose reforming zeal had won many hearts, was at a high peak; the Whigs desired to win the Catholic vote;[61] the difficulties in Ireland,

the second danger the greater; Pius asked him whether he knew that the nature of his government did not admit the development of "liberal institutions" such as other states could undertake; Lord Minto recognized this, in view of the sovereignty of the Church over the state in Rome, but thought this should not prevent the Pope as temporal sovereign from introducing reforms for the public welfare. Metternich's representative, Lützow, on the other hand, advised Pius not to make any more concessions as temporal sovereign. See Lützow to Metternich, Jan. 9, 1848, in Spellanzon, *Risorgimento*, III, 595.

[60] Ashley, *Palmerston*, II, 49.

[61] An evidence of this was the proposal of a Bill entitled "Roman Catholic Relief Bill," introduced to remove most of the provisions in the Catholic Emancipation Bill (1829) specifically put in at that time to protect the Protestant Establishment. See *Times* (London), June 25, 1846. There was extended debate (December 8, 1847) on this Bill, in the course of which the question of mixed marriages, frowned on by the Catholic Church, had been brought up by the opponents of the Bill. See Hansard, 3rd ser., XCV, 852.

where Catholic priests were accused of inciting their parishioners
to violence, suggested to some that a word from a Pope friendly
to Britain might help to allay the strife.[62]   Because of Catholic
Emancipation there were Catholic representatives sitting in
Parliament, ably presenting the cause of Ireland, its economic
ills, its nationalist spirit, its religious burdens.[63]

The President of the Council, Lord Landsdowne, brought in
a "Bill for Legalizing Diplomatic Intercourse with Rome," before the House of Lords on February 7, 1848, depositing it
"with breathless haste."[64]   It was vigorously debated.[65]   Lord
Stanley objected to the unceremonious way in which the matter
was put before them.   He reflected that the Government was
proposing to alter a practice in existence for "180 years, or perhaps it is more correct to say for 300 years," and that such a
proposal should have been brought in with dignity, first in a
message from the Crown—but no—

Instead of that [Stanley expostulated] when your Lordships' attention was about to be called to a subject of a totally different
character—when you were about to discuss the price of sugar and
the complaints of the West Indian planters . . . the noble Marquess
[Lansdowne] rose, and with no more ceremony than if he were
proposing to lay a turnpike trust Bill on the table, announced to

[62] *Univers* (Paris), Sept. 8, 1847. The paper states that one word from Pius
would be worth more than 100,000 soldiers in pacifying Ireland, and that Pius
would give that word—which Gregory XVI had refused.

[63] *Ibid.*, Feb. 10, 1848. The Catholic daily commented on the skilful tactics
of O'Connell and the Irish minority to delay and control votes in the House of
Commons. Two paradoxes of the nineteenth century were rarely perceived
and commented on. One was the interest of England in freeing Italian states
from "foreign interference" while maintaining at home that the Irish question
was a purely domestic issue. The other was the fear expressed by statesmen,
especially in Protestant lands, of the interference of the Catholic Church in their
internal politics, while at the same time, when it suited them, seeking a "word
from Rome" to admonish Catholic subjects not to stir up trouble.

[64] Hansard, 3rd ser., XCVI, 775-790. See also CI, 150-151. Disraeli called
attention to the fact that the usual lapse of time between the first and second
reading was waived at the Government's request "on account of the exigency
of the case." He discussed the Minto Mission in the House of Commons at a
session on August 16.

[65] Hansard, 3rd ser., XCVI, 767, Feb. 17, 1848.

your Lordships, without preface or introduction, a Bill to enable Her Majesty to enter into diplomatic intercourse with Rome.[66]

The debate centered around several points: whether or not the Crown had the right to send ambassadors wherever it pleased anyway—if that were true then the Bill was totally unnecessary; the fact that there had been from time to time direct contacts whenever necessary, by persons (such as Lord Minto) appointed on direct missions, or by members of the Admiralty seeking supplies and stores from the Pontiff when plying in Mediterranean waters—so why not keep on with these existing arrangements; the question of whether the representative would be sent to the Pope as a religious head, or head of a tiny principality; the question of reciprocity—would it be necessary to receive a nuncio if an ambassador were sent; the difficulty of withdrawing an accredited ambassador by way of diplomatic rebuff—a common practice in dealing with lay states; the question of the use of the term "Sovereign Pontiff," because of its connotations. Lord Aberdeen noted the fact that by agreement at Vienna diplomats were divided into ranks; in the top rank, that of ambassador, were included legates and nuncios; in Catholic countries the nuncios took "precedence of all ambassadors and all ministers" instead of this being determined by the length of stay.[67] Lansdowne for the Government examined the question of having a bill in order to legalize such intercourse; he said the necessity rested in the interpretation of the Bill of Rights and the Act of Succession, passed under William and Mary, acts not to be meddled with except after "mature deliberation"; he said his view was that the Acts were designed to prevent a spiritual or ecclesiastical reconciliation and did not debar from establishing diplomatic relations; he recognized, however, that others viewed this as illegal unless an enactive measure were passed; for these reasons the Government decided to bring in a bill. As to the reasons for making

[66] Hansard, 3rd ser., XCVI, 781-783.
[67] Hansard, 3rd ser., XCVI, 880.

any change at all, Lansdowne rehearsed the history of the
use of private persons (as when Walpole sent his brother
Horace), and the requests of the Government (1793) for His
Holiness to supply water for the British fleet. He quoted Burke,
who had said, "Nobody can be so squeamish as to refuse benefits . . . because they come from the Pope . . . . Who should
scruple the receipt of those indulgences called *Munitions de
Guerre and de Bouche*' from a prince-prelate that believes in
Purgatory?"[68]

Attempts to delay the decision were beaten down by the
Government, but an amendment was introduced to safeguard
the supremacy of the Crown in ecclesiastical as in civil matters.
This was accepted by Earl Grey, who also mentioned that Eng-
land could do like Prussia and refuse to admit an ambassador,
without writing it into the law; that power was already in the
Government.[69] The Earl of Eglinton wanted to amend the
Bill so that the representative received in London must not be
"in holy orders in the Church of Rome, nor a Jesuit or member of any other religious order, community, or society of the
Church of Rome, bound by monastic or other religious vows."[70]
Lord Stanley called attention to the fact that all Catholic states
"whether Portugal, Spain, Austria, France, or any other" placed
legal restrictions on the exercise of diplomatic functions with
the Court of Rome—and on the diplomats of no other states.[71]

The bill, as amended, finally passed into law; but the unwillingness of England to receive any ecclesiastic as representative from the Holy See (the Eglinton amendment) met with
so much disapproval in Rome that Pius IX refused to send a

[68] *Ibid.*, 3rd ser., XCVI, 761-769.
[69] *Ibid.*, 3rd ser., XCVI, 794-796.
[70] *Ibid.*, 3rd ser., XCVI, 876. See also Normanby to Palmerston, Paris, March
13, 1848 (Ashley, *Palmerston*, II, 68), in which Normanby reported a conversation mostly about trivialities, with King Louis Philippe on the eve of the
collapse of the July monarchy, in which His Majesty spoke of the proposed
renewal of diplomatic relations with Rome and of "the difficulty of receiving
a priest at St. James's in full canonicals. . . ."
[71] *Ibid.*, 3rd ser., XCVI, 790.

minister and declined to receive one from England under the circumstances.[72] Meanwhile the issue had been pending during the stormy events of the revolutionary period. As for Lord Palmerston's views, he wrote subsequently to Clarendon that he could not have made himself "responsible for receiving an ecclesiastic as Roman envoy." He went on, "As for the idea that we could manage the Irish priests by means of a Roman priest in London, I am convinced that the presence of such a man would only have given the Irish priests an additional means of managing us."[73]

The involvement of the Irish question in the attempted *rapprochement* of London and the Holy See was indeed puzzling to both Lord Palmerston and His Holiness. Because the Young Ireland party was antireligious, as were most extreme radicals everywhere, the statesmen might easily join forces with the Irish priests against it. The problem was complicated by the fact that the clergy of Ireland were not of one mind—two factions were struggling against each other, not only in Ireland itself but also in Rome for the ear of the Pope, and by the fact that a new educational policy introduced by Peel had further set these parties at variance with each other.[74] This proposal was for England to pay for colleges to be attended by both Catholics and Protestants, the government paying the salaries of the Catholic clergy, and providing that all religious instruction to Catholic students was to be given by them. This plan for "mixed colleges" was opposed by one of the factions, approved by the other. This latter group knew that the money if not used in this way would be put into Protestant colleges, which Catholic youths would insist on attending, having no other.

[72] Ashley, *Palmerston*, II, 53-54.
[73] *Ibid.*, II, 54.
[74] See a memorandum (*ibid.*, II, 48) signed by Lord Clarendon. It seems that one group, led by Bishop McHale, sent resolutions to Rome which they said were passed by the clergy in "synod assembled." Archbishop Murray, Primate of Ireland, said no synod was held and the first he saw of the resolutions was in the newspapers.

The cabinet attempted to come to some amicable agreement which would suit all factions.[75]

The outcome of the matter was that Pius issued a rescript against the mixed colleges, saying that they would constitute a "grave danger to the Catholic faith"; his decision was that "institutions of this sort must be judged to be detrimental to religion."[76] Lord Palmerston promised to send Lord Minto a memorandum on this.[77] The effect of the decision was to cool enthusiasm for Pius. Lord Clarendon thought the Pope had committed a "hostile, ill-judged, and unnecessary act."[78] Pius was now regarded by some of the English as a mediocre spirit, an indecisive and weak character."[79]

Meanwhile, in Rome, Lord Minto was invited to visit Naples. He had not been originally scheduled to do so and had to await his credentials. These were issued December 7 and were presented on February 7, 1848.[80] His activities there were soon concluded and he returned to Rome.

[75] This proposal on the part of the British Government was highly commended by *Univers* (Paris, May 5, 1847). Archbishop McHale, according to *Univers* on word from Rome, had gone to Rome for the purpose of combating the British attempt at conciliation.

[76] *Univers* (Paris), Oct. 30, 1847. The paper went on to say that Ireland was afraid of the *rapprochement* that was taking place between London and the Vatican, and that it might have been better to delay any display of a nature to compromise the negotiations to be carried on by Lord Minto, whose visit to Rome was at hand.

[77] Ashley, *Palmerston*, II, 46.

[78] Memorandum quoted in Ashley, *Palmerston*, II, 47. Clarendon said it was hostile, because the clergy were ordered to denounce what Parliament and the Queen had sanctioned; ill-judged, because most Irish Catholics wanted the colleges; it produced resentment among English Protestants and Irish Catholics.

[79] *Univers* (Paris), Nov. 11, 1848.

[80] Palmerston mentioned these dates in defending his policy in the House of Commons, where it had been suggested by the Opposition that the Sicilian revolt was a result of Lord Minto's activities; he thought Lord Minto could scarcely have been the cause of the revolution in view of the fact that it was already under way before he got there. See Hansard, 3rd ser., XCV, 365. Metternich was not willing to exculpate Palmerston from complicity in the affair; "Lord Palmerston," he wrote to Dietrichstein on February 23, 1848, "sets the house on fire, disables the firemen, and then presents himself as moderator of the fire." See A. J. P. Taylor, *The Italian Question in European Diplomacy 1847-1849* (Manchester, 1934), p. 69.

As a sort of roving ambassador Lord Minto was not in an enviable position in the spring of 1848. Events were moving far too rapidly for the means of communication then available to make consultation with the home government possible. The telegraph was not yet in effective use. All diplomatic instructions and reports were sent by mail, or by pouch, and these by slow modes of travel. Newspapers in some places received bare announcements "by telegraph," but detailed accounts would be days later. The grapevine of revolution ran faster. There had been ominous warning notes before the spring of 1848: the Swiss disturbance; the seizure of Cracow; banquets in France; the scattered publication of the protests of radical and liberal writers, socialists, anarchists, and nationalists; but most of all, the flood of petitions and demands for reform in Italy, where the misgovernment in Naples and in the Papal States had created an increasing pressure. The movements toward liberalism and nationalism stirred by Napoleon I in the Italian peninsula had not died out. To the fires boiling the cauldrons of revolution came to be added in the nineteenth century the economic and social demands of the proletarian class, wherever the Industrial Revolution spread. The upheaval was too great to be met by the grant of gas lights and railroad trains. As Pius set in motion one reform after another during 1847 the demands grew. In part they were genuine, for a constitutional government; in part they were deliberately stirred up by republican nationalists, in order to turn the demands into a nationalistic channel.[81]

When the revolution in Paris in February brought the end

[81] Ballerini (*Premières pages,* p. 87) called them "rabble rousers." He thought their interest in securing reforms was to be able to move to new vantage points in the struggle, hoping to set up radical republics under the "mob," where the voice of the people would replace the authority of prince or pope. For a discussion of Mazzini's tactics (to build up the Pope so as to terrify Austria to the point of making insistent demands upon him, thus increasing the hatred of Italians for the Austrian Empire) see Ettore Rota, *Questioni di storia del Risorgimento e dell Unità d'Italia* (Milan, 1951), p. 413. Mazzini's instructions to his associates were written in 1846 and were widely distributed.

of the July monarchy, and with it Guizot, the flame spread with
unbelievable rapidity, setting on fire the Hapsburg realms to rid
themselves of Metternich, planting incendiary sparks in the
Germanies, and causing the Italian peninsula to burn from the
Alps to the toe of the boot with determination and hope. Lord
Minto went to Italy to knock on the doors of rulers; he might
soon have difficulty in locating the doors. It is true that Lord
Palmerston was of the opinion that the mission had been salu-
tory in holding the revolutionary wave in legitimate channels.
He wrote to Lord Minto (on March 28, 1848): "Fortunate has
it been for Italy that you crossed the Alps last autumn."[82] "As
for the poor Pope," he had written earlier, "I live in daily
dread of hearing of some misadventure having befallen him.
Events have gone too fast for such a slow sailor as he is. I only
hope he will not be swamped by the swell in the wake of those
who have outstripped him for this would perhaps bring the
Austrians into the Roman States; and we should have a regular
European row."[83]

Pius IX had indeed proceeded with reforms in the political
sphere in 1847. In June he had formed a Council of Ministers;
in July he had armed the national guard, forestalling a plot
planned for the anniversary of the amnesty; on October 14 he
had announced the formation of a *Consulta*, which admitted
nonclerics, under the presidency of a Cardinal;[84] in November
with his approval the Papal States had signed with Sardinia and

[82] Ashley, *Palmerston*, II, 57.

[83] Palmerston to Lord Minto, February 24, 1848, *ibid.*, II, 55. O'Reilly maintained (Bernard O'Reilly, L.D., *A Life of Pius IX* [New York, 1878], pp. 57-58)
that the Minto Mission was an "intrigue"; he was convinced that the whole
purpose of Palmerston was to "work the destruction of the Holy See." It is
obvious that O'Reilly did not have access to the British documents, and read
back into the events of 1847-1848 the attitudes which developed much later,
because of changing circumstances. Every evidence points to the desire to see
the Holy See peacefully established in the Papal States; the Pope was encouraged
to reform, not that he might be destroyed but that he might be saved.

[84] Cardinal Antonelli, who had not been made Cardinal until June of that
year, was president. See Michele Rosí, *L'Italia Odierna: due secoli di lotta, di
studi e di lavoro per l'independenza e la grandezza della Patria* (2 vols.; Turin,
1918-1926), II (Tomo I), 377.

Tuscany a customs union, planned along the lines of the German *Zollverein*;[85] he had reorganized (in October) the municipal Government of Rome, and altered, by a *motu-proprio* of December 29, the Council of Ministers, converting it into nine departments.[86] The liberal Cardinal Gizzi was out, having resigned in July, because Pius, to his view, was going too far. Cardinal Ferretti, a relative of the Pope, was now occupying the post as Secretary of State.[87]

These reforming activities met with varying responses outside as well as inside Italy. The conservatives in the Pope's domains were alarmed at the changes, thoroughly disapproving of them, and biding their time until they might be annulled or modified;[88] the radicals disapproved, actually, because the improvements would give them fewer talking points in stirring up the mass of people, and they therefore feared that they would not be able to direct the flow of events toward their own goals; the King of Naples disapproved, as these changes would be

[85] Palmerston approved Lord Minto's advice about setting this up. See his dispatch on October 27, 1847, *B.S.P.*, XXXVI, 1304. Cf. Spellanzon, *Risorgimento*, III, 250. This question has produced extended debate among writers on the *Risorgimento*. Was this customs union to be a first step in the development of a league of the sovereign states of Italy, in which the Pope would take the lead, and of which he would become head? Since such a league was in process of negotiation until April of the following spring, but never materialized, this would be a purely academic question which could be set aside, were it not that the riddle of Pius' own intentions with regard to Italian unification was wrapped up in it. The riddle is insoluble from the documents. He had told the French ambassador, David Rossi, at the beginning of his pontificate (August 26, 1846) that it was "utopian to think of an Italian league of which the Pope would be the head." See Spellanzon, *Risorgimento*, III, iii, 254; IV, 215. Doubts, however, remain as to whether he subsequently entertained the idea.

[86] See a report from Petre in Rome (December 31, 1847) for a detailed description of this *motu-proprio*. *B.S.P.*, XXXVII, 815.

[87] Ferretti was "of resolute character and liberal opinions," according to Petre's report of July 21, 1847. *B.S.P.*, XXXVI, 1227.

[88] *Univers* (Paris, July 29, 1847) in its lead article deplored the fact that "among the highest dignitaries of the Church" there were some who were fanatically attached ["*opinionâtrement attachés*"] to "the administrative abuses of the past" and who judged the most necessary reforms as "the beginning of a horrible revolution." The article went on to say that these "fanatics of the past, the radical Carbonari, and Austria, were equally interested in checking the Pope. . . ."

likely to inflame the people of Naples and Sicily; the King of
Sardinia approved and promised to back up and defend His
Holiness against outside interference, although knowing that
the Pope's idea (borrowed originally from Gioberti) of an
Italian confederation, and his own plans for creating a united
Italy, did not really coincide. Abroad, the changes made by
Pius, and by other reforming princes in the peninsula, aroused
keenest misgivings on the part of Metternich, endangering his
control, as they would, in the Austrian provinces of northern
Italy,[89] and threatening to remove Austrian predominance from
the rest of the states. Palmerston and the Whig Government
in England approved of the reforms, the *via media,* and proposed to encourage and protect the Pope against any intrusion
of Austria,[90] even to the point of sending in a flotilla of the
Navy to a point where it might be effective against Austrian-
held ports.[91] France, wavering between the Austrian-oriented
policy of Guizot and the traditional French interest in Italian
reform, pursued a weak-kneed and confused policy, opposing all
thought of any possible territorial changes in the peninsula,
while counseling administrative and purely internal reforms.[92]

[89] Metternich to Dietrichstein, Sept. 27, 1847. Metternich, *Mémoires,* VII,
422. Metternich said Austria's right to maintain order in her own possessions
was recognized; he disclaimed any idea of using this right in order to make
any aggression against the Papal territories. Of course, Metternich was not
talking for Dietrichstein's ears.

[90] Palmerston to Ponsonby, Aug. 12, 1847, *B.S.P.,* XXXVI, 1223. Palmerston
called the reforms "laudable undertakings."

[91] Victoria to Russell, Sept. 3, 1847, *Letters of Queen Victoria,* II, 151. Sir
William Parker was sent to the West Coast of Italy "to give countenance to the
sovereigns engaged in Liberal Reform," and exposed both to Austrian inroads
and republican popular movements.

[92] See Alfredo Signoretti, *Italia e Inghilterra durante il Risorgimento* (Milan,
1940), pp. 34-35, for a modern Italian view of the question; the contemporary
French view was expressed in the lead article in *Univers* for September 8, 1847.
This article contended that France, in exchange for Austria's tacit assistance
in the matter of the Spanish marriages, had promised to leave Austria a free
hand in Italy, "if not to assist her." It commented on the rupture between
England and Austria, and said that the French viewed with pleasure the ruin
of the Ghibelline influence in Italy. The proposal to restore diplomatic intercourse between London and Rome would always be opposed by Austria.

The year 1848 was to demonstrate to Pius IX that reforms could not continue into the field of constitutionalism which might jeopardize his absolute control, in view of the peculiar character of his position as head of a universal church. To nineteenth-century liberals, who by no means universally approved of a wide extension of the suffrage,[93] the essence of liberalism was constitutional restraint upon the absolutism of the ruler, exercised through ministers responsible to parliaments. Obviously the Pope could never do, at the behest of ministers interested in a secular program for a part of Italy,[94] what would be out of harmony with his decisions respecting the world outside. Such a situation would have him approving at home as a temporal ruler what he condemned abroad as Sovereign Pontiff.[95] The people of Italy did not understand or appreciate this fact; having built up a concept of Pius as a "liberal" they read into his actions promises of liberalism and patriotism which it would be impossible for him to fulfil. The events of 1848 were to begin to demonstrate this fact, and to lead to the catastrophes of 1849.

Meanwhile, the Fundamental Statute for the Temporal Government of the States of the Church was issued on March 14, 1848.[96] The intention of Pius was from the beginning to open

[93] Lamartine, leading French liberal, asked about universal suffrage, commented only in the famous epigram: *"Il est une énigme et il contient un mystère"* (a mystery wrapped up in an enigma). Alphonse de Lamartine, *Histoire de la Révolution de 1848* (2 vols.; Brussels, 1849), I, 125.

[94] P. Pietro Pirri, *Pio IX e Vittorio Emanuele dal loro carteggio privato* (2 vols.; Rome, 1944), I, 29. It was the consensus of the ambassadors to the Pope expressed at a conference at Gaëta in the spring of 1849 that "a government of the pontifical state in democratic garb seemed to them like the problem of squaring the circle."

[95] Metternich wrote to Fiquelmont in Milan on December 9, 1847 (*Mémoires,* VII, 443), that a "liberal Pope is not a possibility. A Gregory VII could become the master of the world, a Pius IX cannot become that. He can destroy but he cannot build. What the Pope has already destroyed by his own liberalism is his own temporal power; what he is unable to destroy is his spiritual power; it is that power which will cancel the harm done by his worthless counsellors." He had previously characterized Pius as "warm of heart and weak of intellect." *Ibid.,* p. 341.

[96] *B.S.P.,* XXXVI, 879-888. This Statute provided for two Councils: a Council

to his people a corridor for complaints, not a channel of control.[97]

The year had opened with the Sicilian revolt, viewed with more than complacency by England, for the British fleet patrolled the straits between Naples and Sicily. Lord Minto, invited to visit Naples and instructed by his Government to counsel the way of moderation (as has been noted), found that events were ahead of him. The mainland became involved, in the wake of the Sicilian revolt, as the Neapolitan people demanded constitutional government. The Bourbon king of the Two Sicilies yielded to pressure. The question was, Would Austria intervene to restore to him his absolute power, as it had done in 1820?[98] Austria certainly did not view the matter with indifference; her envoys, together with those of Russia and Prussia, expostulated.[99]

All Italy was soon aflame with the demand for liberalism and with hatred for Austria. Constitutions were granted in other Italian states;[100] armies were recruited to take the field against the hated foreigner. Pius IX had set the pattern; the people were gladly following him. He became not only the

of Deputies and a Council of State; legislative procedure involved passage of proposed laws through both houses, consideration in Secret Consistory (a vote being taken), and decision by the Pope on accepting or rejecting the measure (an irreversible veto).

[97] At the opening of the Council of State Pius said: "He would be greatly deceived who should see in the Council of State which I have just created the realization of his own utopias and the germ of an institution incompatible with pontifical sovereignty . . . . Let him know I retract nothing of the sovereignty of the pontificate." Quoted in Cesare Vimercati, *Histoire de l'Italie en 1848-1849* (2d ed.; Paris, 1954), p. 14.

[98] *Times* (London) quoted in *Univers*, Feb. 11, 1848.

[99] Lord Napier to Palmerston, Naples, Jan. 31, 1848, *B.S.P.*, XXXVII, 853. The collective note, according to Napier, warned the Neapolitan king not to yield to demands that he grant a constitution, as it would be contrary to "some secret convention or agreement contracted between their respective governments and the Sicilian Crown." The King of Naples claimed that his forces were insufficient for him to refuse. The Prussian Government subsequently disclaimed any connection with the *démarche*.

[100] Charles Albert's proclamation of a Fundamental Statute providing for a responsible ministry is given in *B.S.P.*, XXXVII, 856.

symbol of liberal reform but of the nation; he was to be the "liberator of Italy."[101] In a *motu-proprio* of February 10, 1848, the Pope used words which seemed to promise much: "Therefore, O Lord God, bless Italy and preserve for her this most precious gift of all—the faith. . . ."[102]

News of the revolution in Paris (February 24) still further inflamed the minds of Italians. Not only were liberal constitutions granted in various sovereign Italian states but before March was out a revolution occurred in Milan, which declared its independence of Austria and chose to be transferred to Sardinia; Venice in revolt set up an independent republic, throwing off the Austrian yoke. Austria, weakened by a liberal revolt in her own territories, was for the time being unable to cope with the situation in Italy; Sardinia declared war. Troops from the Papal States, as well as other Italian states, to the number of twenty thousand, joined the Sardinian forces. Lord Minto cheered Italian independence from the balcony of the Quirinal.[103]

This was the high moment of Pius' career as an Italian and as a temporal ruler; he was the object of adulation on the part of Italians everywhere; he was praised abroad in liberal countries; but he realized the incompatibility of his desires in this direction with the demands made upon him by his position as Sovereign Pontiff of all Catholics everywhere in the world. The time had come for a forthright statement which could not be misunderstood; he issued, therefore, the famous allocution of April 29.[104] In this allocution, from which he omitted any

[101] These words had been spoken during the obsequies at Rome for O'Connell, spokesman for Ireland in the British Parliament, who had died en route to Rome; the preacher had said that O'Connell had "at the end of a life devoted to the advocacy of freedom, and the emancipation of the peoples by peaceful and unbloody means, to do homage to Pius IX, who would be the liberator of Italy." See O'Reilly, Pius IX, p. 142.

[102] Spellanzon, *Risorgimento*, V, 602. See also Giuseppe Montanelli, *Introduzione ad alcuni appunti storici sulla rivoluzione d'Italia* (Turin, 1854), p. 18.

[103] Balleydier, *Révolution de Rome*, I, 57.

[104] *Univers* (Paris, May 25, 1848) tells the story of the document. The authorities in Rome had not permitted the printing of the statement; Pius had

reference to the Constitution he had granted in March, Pius
declared that his reforms were simply carrying out the memorandum of the powers submitted in 1831; he maintained that
he could not declare war on anyone (although he could not prevent his subjects from volunteering if they chose); and, finally,
he stated that he was opposed to any plan to make Italy a federation of republics under his presidency.[105]

The first phase of the Risorgimento was over. The popularity of Pius waned rapidly in Italy, more slowly abroad, as
the contents of the allocution became known.[106] His ministry

it secretly printed in the Quirinal. The *Gazette of Rome* was the only journal
which gave it official publication; it was publicly burned. The bearers of the
allocution were stopped outside Rome, to prevent its dissemination. See also
Petre's report from Rome on May 2, 1848 (*B.S.P.*, XXXVII, 1070), in which
he states that as soon as the proclamation was posted in Rome the placards were
torn down.

[105] For an analysis of this allocution see Spellanzon, *Risorgimento*, IV, 210-215.
Vimercati (*Italie en 1848-49*, pp. 293-296) gives further details about the circumstances of its issuance. The employment of papal troops, which crossed
over the Po and entered Austrian territory, has given rise to considerable controversy. Hamilton's dispatch to Palmerston (April 27, *B.S.P.*, XXXVII, 1045)
asserted "that the Pope had given positive orders that his troops should not
pass the Po," but apparently General Durando had done so on his own
authority. This dispatch is in sharp contrast to the claim made by Farini
(*Lettres*, p. 176) that the order for the pontifical troops to pass the Po was
not given by his ministers without the Pope's knowledge. Farini states further
that Cardinal Antonelli, who had become Papal Secretary of State in March,
succeeding Cardinal Ferretti, along with other ministers signed a paper recommending prosecution of the War of Independence. An ambiguous statement of
Pius (quoted in Berkeley, *Italy in the Making*, III, Appendix I) fails to resolve
the question; Pius in an interview with the Florentine envoy, Bargagli, frank
in tone, remarked that he had told General Durando, leading the papal troops,
"to do anything for the safety of the state and the tranquillity of the people."
Rosi (*L'Italia Odierna*, II [Tomo I], 466) says that Antonelli insisted on the
Pope taking some kind of decisive stand, or saying that desiring peace he "could
not prevent war from being made"; so followed the allocution.

[106] Lord Palmerston received it on May 11, 1848. *B.S.P.*, XXXVII, 1062. An
interesting observation made by the Dutch ambassador to the Papal Court soon
after the issuance of the allocution throws some light on the question. "His
heart," says Liedekerke (*Rapporti*, p. 51), referring to Pius, "is so good, he is so
fundamentally Italian, he needs to be surrounded by the love and confidence
of his subjects, he puts so high a price on being saluted by their acclamations,
that I would not be surprised to see him one of these days, originate acts de-
structive little by little of the import of the allocution of April 29." Hales
(*Pio Nono*, chap. ii) attempts, not very successfully, to refute this estimate

in Rome resigned; the swing towards radicalism was given new impetus. The papal forces were withdrawn from the war against Austria; the Neapolitan troops were also withdrawn; Sardinia, early so successful in the north, was unable to defeat a revived Austrian force and was vanquished at Custozza in July. The day of moderation was almost over; the day of radicalism, and ultimate failure, was near at hand.

Lord Palmerston's policy was inevitably altered by these events. His hopes for a strong state in the north[107] based on Sardinia, to act as a buffer between Austria and France and to keep Austria out of Italy,[108] were threatened. Such a state as that envisioned by Palmerston would be a support to Pius in resisting outside interference. Although naval demonstrations might give added weight to Palmerston's diplomatic pen,[109] he hoped to secure his ends by diplomacy and moral support to his allies, contemplating war only when he felt some vital interest of England jeopardized; diplomatic mediation, suggested by France, should be sufficient to get Austrian troops out of Italy, leaving Lombardy to Sardinia, and preserving Venice as

---

of Pius. Montanelli (*Memorie,* II, 57) had pointed out to Pius on November 2, 1847, the difference in meaning between the "Viva Pius IX" of the crowd and their "Viva the Pope." Pius admitted that he found pleasure in both.

[107] Victoria to Russell, Aug. 21, 1848, *Letters of Queen Victoria,* II, 227. "Lord Palmerston," wrote the Queen, "*will* have his kingdom of Upper Italy under Charles Albert."

[108] Lord Russell, in a memorandum of May 1, 1848, noted: "It is advisable, therefore, that we should use our efforts in communication, though not in direct concert, with France, to produce a frank abandonment of Lombardy and Venice on the part of Austria." Spencer Walpole, *The Life of Lord John Russell* (2 vols.; London, 1899), II, 41.

[109] Queen Victoria "read in the papers" that it "was confidently stated that a French and *British* squadron" with troops was to "*make a demonstration in the Adriatic.*" She said she "*could not consent* [italics, as usual, those of the Queen] to such a proposal." Victoria to Palmerston, Sept. 2, 1848, *Letters of Queen Victoria,* II, 229. Palmerston had stated a year before to the Sardinian ambassador in London that England "had a fleet in the Mediterranean which could make itself felt at Venice and at Trieste. . . ." See Comte de Revel to Solaro della Margarita, London, Sept. 3, 1847, in Bianchi, *Storia della diplomazia,* V, 406. In spite of these words the second phase of the *Risorgimento,* that under Charles Albert's leadership, was about over.

as independent republic.[110]   On August 16 the whole question
was aired in the House of Commons. Disraeli, speaking against
the Government, mentioned the attempt to establish diplomatic
intercourse with the Papal See; he discussed the Minto Mission,
calling it a "defunct campaign." Lord Minto had gone, according to Disraeli, to prevent Austria from invading Sardinia—
Sardinia invaded Austria; he came to terms with the Pope—
when the Pope ceased to have any diplomacy to look after; he
had been equally unsuccessful in Naples; now England was
proposing mediation—with France—in northern Italy—to what
end? and by what means? Was the principle of that mediation,
he asked, to be a "political principle, founded upon the law of
nations and the stipulation of treaties, or upon this modern,
newfangled, sentimental principle of nationality, which will
lead to inextricable confusion, and difficulty, and danger." He
declared that the French ought not to invade Italy; England had
already interfered there, and had sent the fleet to protect Sicily
against the King of Naples. "I protest," he said finally, "against
the attempt to regulate the world by a contrived concert with
the Jacobin party."[111] Palmerston in reply explained the Minto
Mission[112] and the invitation, while Lord Minto was in Rome,
to visit Naples; he described the effect throughout Italy of the

[110] As for acting in co-operation with France, Queen Victoria expostulated
vigorously against pursuing any common policy with a nation "not even legally
constituted" (since the February revolution) which could neither guarantee
nor carry out any engagement. See her letter to Palmerston on July 24, 1848,
and to Russell on July 25, *Letters of Queen Victoria*, II, 220-221. France was
as much opposed, according to the French Foreign Minister (Lamartine was
replaced by Bastide when the Provisional Government gave way to the Constituent Assembly), to setting up a powerful state under Charles Albert as he
was to restoring Lombardy to Austria. *Ibid.*, II, 221. For the details of this
part of Palmerston's policy consult (*passim*) Taylor, *The Italian Question*,
written from archival sources in the chancelleries.

[111] Hansard, 3rd ser., CI, 149-163. Disraeli remarked with his usual wit that
Lord Minto had gone "to teach politics in the country in which Machiavelli
was born."

[112] Palmerston had written to Lord Minto (March 28, 1848): "If the Italian
sovereigns had not been urged by you to move on, while their impatient subjects were held back, there would by this time have been nothing but Republics
from the Alps to Sicily." Ashley, *Palmerston*, II, 57.

"altered policy" of the newly elected Pius IX; he detailed the request of the French that England should join—in an effort to avoid war—in an "endeavour to settle matters by a mediation"; this joint work was to be one of peace. Palmerston answered the charge of "Jacobinism" by stating that the plea had come from France before the fall of the monarchy, and that the republican government of France was desirous of continuing to be in unison with the policy of Britain.[113]

With the situation in Rome deteriorating after the allocution of April 29, Pius IX, to restore order, accepted the liberal Mamiani, and a new ministry was formed on May 4.[114] The Roman people and the officials installed by Pius begged him not to impede them in their work of liberating Italy. Pius, feeling intimidated by his reactionary Cardinals, and obviously unable to seek help from Austria under the circumstances, turned to France and requested (through General Cavaignac) an armed guard.[115] The reply promised to send some frigates to Civita Vecchia, but troops could not be sent without publicly debating the issue. The Cardinals told Pius he could not appeal to Protestant England; the only way out was to make peace with Austria.[116] This, under pressure from the Sacred College, in which Antonelli was the outstanding figure, Pius now attempted to do. He agreed to write to His Imperial Majesty to withdraw from Italy. The people were delighted; they concluded that the Pope had returned to the liberal path.[117] Unable to support wholeheartedly the liberal ministry, Mamiani resigned.[118] After another unsuccessful ministry Rossi was called to the cabinet.

[113] Hansard, 3rd ser., CI, 164-175.

[114] *Univers* (Paris), May 25, 1848. Report from Rome.

[115] *Contemporanea* (Rome, May 16), quoted in *Univers* (Paris, May 25, 1848), held out to France the glory of a war that would "wash away the stain of Waterloo"; if any nation chose to frighten France with her navy—"say the word 'Ireland!' "

[116] Vimercati, *Italie en 1848-49*, pp. 303-305.

[117] *Univers* (Paris), Nov. 8, 1848. Several Italian papers are quoted.

[118] He could not hold the middle way against the resistance of Pius and the Sacred College to laicization of the state, under the formula: "The Pope reigns, but does not govern." See Rota, *Risorgimento*, p. 418.

Although he had influence with Pius no political party gave
him support. As an economist he was interested in internal
economic reforms, not in liberating Italy.[119] The only bright
spot on the horizon was the cessation of the advance of the
Austrian troops, who, having crossed the Po, had been advancing into the Papal States. This advance was halted by
the signing of an armistice between Austria and Sardinia.[120]

On November 15 Rossi was assassinated.[121] Rome was swept
by the radical flood into setting up what, like the others, proved
to be an ephemeral republic;[122] Pius hastily left Rome for
Gaëta possibly planning to leave Italy;[123] he remained, however,
under the Bourbon King of Naples, most unpopular ruler in
Italy, waiting for the turning point in the tide, or until the
faithful outside Italy might rally to his cause. A conference at
Gaëta of the diplomats accredited to the Holy See could suggest
no way to restore him to his authority in Rome. They were all

[119] Count Pellegrino Rossi after a spectacular career as economist and public
figure in three countries had been sent by France to Rome as ambassador. He
became Minister of the Interior and chief minister of Pius. See Spellanzon,
Risorgimento, V, 906.

[120] Ashley (*Palmerston,* II, 88) credits Palmerston with arranging this
armistice through Abercrombie, in Turin. Taylor (*The Italian Question,* p.
148) insists that while Palmerston, with the co-operation of Bastide (French
Foreign Minister), was offering mediation, the armistice had been agreed to
independently by Sardinia and Austria. He agrees that Europe might well
have become involved in war if England had not joined France in a mediating
effort. This whole question is thoroughly handled by Taylor. It is not central
in the study of Pius IX and Palmerston.

[121] Liedekerke (*Rapporti,* p. 117) reported to his Government (November
24, 1848) that the action was regarded in Rome by the majority of the people
as "heroic"; it was the "fatherland delivered," it meant the "independence of
Italy"; it was "Rome reborn."

[122] Farini thought that the attempt at a republic was not the "fruit of free
choice, but of despair." Farini to Gladstone, Dec. 20, 1852, *Lettres,* p. 129.
Thus was ushered in the third phase of the *Risorgimento,* not resting upon
a personality but upon the people themselves. See Michele Rosi, *Il Risorgimento
italiano e l'azione d'un patriota cospiratore e soldata* (Rome-Turin, 1906), p.
59. See also Pasquini, *Lezioni di storia ecclesiastica,* III, 504.

[123] For the offers of asylum in France, Spain, or even Malta, offered by
England, see Spellanzon, *Risorgimento,* IV, 988. For the problem of the ambassadors as to whether to follow the Pope to Gaëta, on the soil of the King
of Naples, or remain in Rome, which seemed impossible as the Pope did not
recognize the Roman Government, see Rosi, *Risorgimento,* p. 63.

agreed, including Antonelli, the Papal Secretary of State, that the Pope's own forces were insufficient for the purpose. The suggestion that Naples and Piedmont undertake the task met with no approval except from the French representatives. Antonelli said Piedmont could not be included as Turin was in alliance with the faction in Rome most hostile to the Temporal Power. The Austrian plenipotentiary pointed out that war had been resumed between Piedmont and Austria.[124] The international situation did not seem propitious; of the great powers one was schismatic and two were Protestant; those within the Catholic fold were rent by internal revolution.

As for stirring up the faithful, this Pius endeavored to do, and with some success. The various Provincial Councils emphasized the dangers of the times and sought to fortify the churches against encroachments of revolutionary governments and draw themselves into a closer union.[125] The French clergy bestirred themselves in support of the Holy See, and also to regain ground lost in France since 1830.

Under Louis Philippe public education had been undertaken, against the will of the hierarchy. Nevertheless, the Bourgeois Monarch remained a consistent support of the Pope's control over the temporal possessions. It was, therefore, with mixed feelings that sincere Catholics witnessed in February, 1848, the overturn of the monarchy[126] and the setting up of a Provisional Government which was republican in form, possibly the only form which could act as a unifying force.[127] The

---

[124] Pirri, *Pio IX e Vittorio Emanuele II*, I, 24.

[125] See Mansi, *Collectio Conciliorum Recentorium Ecclesiae Universae*, XL, 98; and, especially, *Acta et Decreta Sacrorum Conciliorum Recentorium, Collectio Lacensis*, IV, 2-4; 55-57. A mild foretaste of the later *Syllabus of Errors* appears in the synodal letters.

[126] Lord John Russell attributed the revolution to Louis Philippe, who should have adhered to "moderate and constitutional government at home," and abstained from "ambitious projects for his family abroad"; Queen Victoria thought Guizot more to blame. See exchange of letters in April, 1848. *Letters of Queen Victoria*, II, 201.

[127] Lamartine, *Révolution de 1848*, I, 125. As Foreign Minister Lamartine had a dominant position in the new Provisional Government.

French Government was disposed to make common cause with
the liberal movement in the peninsula and to view the Holy
See as an ally.[128] Lamartine proclaimed that the treaties of
1815 no longer existed in the eyes of the French people, and
that, the hour having struck for oppressed nationalities to re-
constitute themselves, if Italy, for one, were invaded to prevent
their consolidation, France would be justified in "arming herself to protect these legitimate movements. . . ."[129] In trying
to follow a moderate path between the revolutionist Montagnards, of all shades, led by Ledru Rollin, and the reactionaries of the right, Lamartine was supported by both
through mutual fear.[130] The apprehension aroused among
moderates as well as conservatives by the revolutionary activities
of the Montagnards,[131] culminating in the riotous June Days,
resulted in the complete defeat of the left. Discredited, and
many of them in flight, they were unable to counterbalance the
pressure from the right, and the way of moderation was imperiled. Elected to the presidency under the Constitution by
direct vote of the people,[132] Louis Napoleon Bonaparte found
it politically expedient to placate the conservatives and clericals,
in spite of his own early revolutionary career. He assumed the
presidency shortly after Pius IX "quitted" Rome.

The Constituent Assembly (which had replaced the Pro-

[128] *Ibid.*, II, 293. Lamartine was laboring under the delusion that the Pope
was abandoning his temporal control and accepting the idea of a federation
with Rome as a center. *Ibid.*, p. 294.

[129] Debate in the Constituent Assembly, May 23, 1848. See *Univers* (Paris),
May 24, 1848.

[130] Alexis de Tocqueville, *Souvenirs* (6th ed.; Paris, 1942), p. 73. Tocqueville
was a member of the Constitutional Commission, and gives an illuminating
description of the problems, parties, and personalities involved. The whole constitution which they sketched in was set aside by the march of events.

[131] This aroused the British fear of a return of Jacobinism, to which reference
has already been made.

[132] See *Univers* (Paris), especially Nov. 4 and 6, 1848. The election was
to occur on December 10. Catholic *Univers* refused to choose between Lamartine
and Louis Napoleon; neither (it felt) was a candidate for a sincere Catholic
to tie to, but either would be better than the others on the list. Louis Napoleon
won by an overwhelming majority.

visional Government in May, 1848) still had a few months to run, after the presidential election, before relinquishing its position to the Legislative Assembly. During this period the Government continued to work in harmony with Great Britain to get a settlement of the Italian question, the war between Austria and Sardinia having been resumed in the spring of 1849. Then came the crushing defeat of Sardinia at Novara. When the left in the French Chamber proposed to take steps to carry out the long-standing resolution to free Italy,[133] the views of the moderates Thiers and Barrot prevailed. Thiers put the matter succinctly, addressing Ledru-Rollin, the leader of the left. He said the policy of moderation, of seeking means short of war, to deal with the question of upper Italy, had been the policy of the year before; when Austria at that time offered France "the accession of Lombardy to Piedmont and the independence of Venetia," the left refused these advantageous conditions because they would have benefited the monarchy of Charles Albert, and the left opposed monarchy everywhere; now that Italy was beaten it was no time to speak of war against Austria.[134] Barrot promised to continue an armed negotiation, benevolent toward Sardinia, but stated categorically that France would not "wage war with the prospect of having for auxiliaries insurrections already carried out or to be carried out."[135] France refused recognition to the Republic of Rome partly because it had been established by events involving murder, and partly because of the lines of complicity between it and the Jacobins of France. Her refusal had nothing to do, insisted Barrot, with the temporal power of the Pope.[136]

Peace was concluded between Austria and Piedmont by direct negotiation while France and England were trying to

[133] Session of March 30, 1849. *Univers* (Paris), March 31, 1849.
[134] *Ibid.*, April 1, 1849.
[135] Odilon Barrot, *Mémoires Posthumes* (3 vols.; Paris, 1876), III, 140. Barrot was president of the Council.
[136] *Ibid.*, III, 140.

mediate on Sardinia's behalf.   Although Lombardy was restored to Austria, the Sardinians lost nothing they had had
before, and paid a modest war indemnity.   Venice also fell to
Austria in August.   The conditions of 1815 had indeed returned, in spite of Lamartine's fiery boast of a year before that
the treaties of 1815 no longer existed.

France did, however, intervene in Italy—not on the side of
republicanism, but to take over Rome.   A French contingent
under General Oudinot was dispatched by executive action.
Led to believe that he would be welcomed by the Roman citizens and that the republicans would not be able to oppose his
entry into the city, the General was astonished to find his force
repulsed at the barriers and made to retire.   A week later
the Constitutent Assembly in Paris, just before it was to give
over to the newly elected Legislative Assembly, forbade the
Government to attack Rome.   Three days later the order to
attack was transmitted to the French army, in flagrant disobedi-
ence to the Chamber's directions.[137]   When this news reached
Paris there was a great stir.   On June 12 Ledru-Rollin demanded, in the Assembly, the impeachment of the President
and his cabinet.[138]   An insurrection of the left failed and in any
event it would have been impossible to reverse the decision of
fate.   There was a rapid swing now in France against the Montagnards; this enabled the conservatives to take control of the
situation; the day of the moderates was over.

The Austrians, successful against Sardinia, were also attacking papal territories (as has been noted) in the interest of
re-establishing the old order of things, and hopeful of preventing the French from deriving too much benefit from General
Oudinot's invasion.   The French troops, ostensibly sent to
operate against Austria, were actually operating against Italian

[137] Tocqueville, *Souvenirs*, p. 193.   Tocqueville was to be Foreign Minister
in the new Government, headed by Odilon Barrot.

[138] *Ibid.*, p. 194.   In the course of the debate his opponents called Ledru-
Rollin "demagogue"; he replied by labeling them "Cossacks," because the Tsar
had intervened on behalf of Austria and put down the Hungarian republic.

liberalism and nationalism.[139] England had little interest in defending the Roman Republic, or republics in general, in Italy. Such republics would be oriented toward France, birthplace of the French Revolution and Jacobin ideas. These ideas were foreign to the British ruling classes. Their interest in northern Italy had not come into conflict with their monarchical views. With the passing of authority in France away from the revolutionaries and moderates toward the conservative and reactionary groups the chance of any intervention on behalf of the Roman Republic disappeared completely. The Government of Louis Napoleon was turning clerical; the intervention in Italy would be on behalf of Pius IX and to prevent any extension of Austrian control. This was demonstrated in the executive-sponsored attack on Rome without authorization from the Assembly. The success of this attack, for the original repulse had presently been followed by a successful entry, now opened the door for the setting up of a government under papal control, and the wiping out of the Mazzinian republic. Pius expressed his thanks to God who had "guided the Catholic arms to sustain the rights of humanity crushed under foot, the rights of the faith which suffered attack and the rights of the Holy See and of our Sovereignty."[140]

The only question which still remained, as the Government in Rome was taken over by Cardinals under the Pope's orders, was the question of whether the changes effected by His Holiness before his departure from the city were to be retained under the restoration, or whether the pendulum would swing back to the conditions of his predecessor. On this point Lord

[139] *Univers* (Paris), July 24. Dispatch from Rome. Tocqueville (*Souvenirs*, p. 221), in justifying France's intervention alone in Rome, said that there was no power with which they might have joined; they were reduced to the "sterile good will of England." Palmerston had forecast in the fall of 1848, after the election of Louis Napoleon, that France would intervene in Italy without much delay, but mistakenly thought that the intervention would be to gain glory by liberating Italy from the Austrian yoke. See Bianchi, *Storia della diplomazia*, V, 335.

[140] Letter of Pius IX, July 17, 1849. *Univers* (Paris), July 31, 1849.

Palmerston and Louis Napoleon were in basic agreement, at
least for the time being. The British view was that diplomatic
intervention (which the French were now supporting with
arms) should have as its object an understanding between the
Pope and his people whereby the constitutional institutions of
1848 should be retained and should include a real separation
between the spiritual and temporal authorities. Palmerston
thought France and Naples should urge the Pope to confirm the
Constitution he had granted in 1848; but would France do so?
This was debatable. "My own belief," he wrote Normanby in
Paris, "is that the priestly and absolutist party is beginning to
prevail in the French Cabinet about the affairs in Rome, and
that the French Government is preparing to re-establish the
Pope, leaving it to his generosity . . . to grant *de novo* to his
subjects such reforms of the Gregorian abuses as he may on reconsideration think expedient . . . considering all done in 1848
as null and void."[141]

The French President's instinctive reaction was to agree
with this point of view. He was astute enough as a politician,
however, to realize that he could not base his policy on a discredited left, and the moderates were too few; for a sound
foundation he must court the right, composed of monarchists
and clericals. The clericals could be won by reversing the
policy of Louis Philippe as regards education, and by giving
unquestioning support to His Holiness in dealing with his subjects. Louis Napoleon yielded to the exigencies of the situation
and permitted Pius to resume absolute control over the Roman
state; the Constitution of 1848 was left permanently in the
discard.[142]

[141] July 7, 1849. Ashley, *Palmerston,* II, 95-96. The instructions to the
French Ambassadors to the Holy See and to Naples said that while it was necessary to re-establish the Pope it was also necessary "that the populations of
the States of the Church be placed under protection against the return of the
detestable regime which was the original cause of all the calamities of recent
times." Barrot, *Mémoires,* III, 201.

[142] It is the opinion of Hales (*Pio Nono,* p. 152) that the decision, ostensibly
that of the Pope, was actually that of Cardinal Antonelli, who, according to

With his abandonment of the liberal path England's enthusiasm for Pius IX waned still further. When Pius, after his restoration to the Vatican, promulgated an ill-timed brief restoring the Catholic hierarchy in England, with Cardinal-Archbishop Wiseman at its head,[143] the tide of public opinion turned; cries of "No popery!" were heard, and Parliament passed a measure invalidating the "assumption of British territorial designations by Papists." The Prime Minister denounced Pius as "an insolent and invidious enemy of Great Britain."[144]

The tentative steps taken by Lord Palmerston toward bringing England into closer relations with the Holy See had failed, and were not renewed during the nineteenth century. His views in 1849, with regard to Pius IX were summed up in a letter to Normanby: "The Papal supremacy, both spiritual and political, has received an earthquate shock from which it can never recover, and all that can be done is to patch up the rent as well as circumstances permit, so that the fabric may last for a time; but there will be shock after shock, till all crumbles to the ground."[145] How right and how wrong Palmerston was in his crystal-ball gazing—right, in that the attacks of the Italian nationalists would not give over until

---

Hales, "employed his exceptional powers of prevarication to prevent Pio Nono from becoming committed" to the milder policy which Napoleon desired. Montanelli called Antonelli a "cunning little fellow!" (*"che furbacchiolo* Antonelli!") *Memorie*, II, 55. For later relations between Pius and his Secretary of State see my *The Papacy and European Diplomacy, 1869-1878* (Chapel Hill, 1948).

[143] When Cardinal Wiseman's statement that the "Appeal to the Reason and Good Feeling of the English People on the Subject of the Catholic Hierarchy" had been shown to Lord Minto in Rome there was vigorous debate and questioning in the House of Lords. Lord Minto denied that it had been shown him, and said he had no recollection of any such document being mentioned. See Hansard, 3rd ser., CXIV, 181.

[144] A bill was brought in "To Prevent the Assumption of Certain Ecclesiastical Titles in respect of Places in the United Kingdom." See Hansard, 3rd ser., CXV, 1676. It remained a dead letter and was repealed some twenty years later (July 13, 1871) by Gladstone. See Hansard, 3rd ser., CCVII, 1544. Gladstone thought it was not in harmony with the principles of religious liberty. See Philip Magnus, *Gladstone* (New York, 1954), p. 101. See also *Letters of Queen Victoria*, II, 325, 338.

[145] Ashley, *Palmerston*, II, 98.

they had wrested the Temporal Power from the papacy, wrong, because in being divested of the encumbrance of the role of temporal prince the papacy would be able to recover its spiritual ascendancy and carry its religious leadership to heights not hitherto reached.

EGYPT AS A
FACTOR IN EUROPEAN POWER
POLITICS, 1875-1878

Lucien E. Roberts

Benjamin Disraeli's master stroke of purchasing the Suez Canal shares in November, 1875, brought Egypt directly into the stream of European power politics. The purchase of the canal shares had greater significance than that of a merely financial transaction; it was the initiation of a new departure in British policy in regard to the Eastern Mediterranean. It is doubtful whether very many Englishmen saw clearly the full implications of the purchase of the Suez shares. Lord Derby, the British Foreign Secretary, expressed the hope during negotiations that the English would not be driven to purchase the Suez shares, because it would be a bad financial bargain.[1] William E. Gladstone, the veteran leader of the Liberal party, wrote on November 22: "If the thing has been done in concert with other powers, it is an act of folly, fraught with future embarrassment. If without such concert, it is an act of folly fraught also with personal danger."[2] However, the calculated

[1] Lord Newton, *Lord Lyons* (2 vols.; London, 1913), II, 87; Gavard to Decazes, London, Nov. 20, 1875, *Documents diplomatiques français, 1871-1875* (hereinafter cited as *D.D.F.*), 1st ser., II, 97. See also John Marlowe, *A History of Modern Egypt and Anglo-Egyptian Relations, 1800-1953* (New York, 1954), pp. 91-92.

[2] Gladstone to Granville, Nov. 22, 1875, in Sir Arnold Talbot Wilson, *The Suez Canal: Its Past Present and Future* (London, 1933), p. 51.

interests of England in the Suez Canal and the public reception of the purchase of the shares was such as to overcome the caution of those who considered it an overventuresome departure.[3]

It is doubtful whether the French would have allowed the British to make the purchase without registering a much greater outcry on both the domestic and foreign scenes had they not been convinced that the British were much more concerned with the broader political implications than merely with a financial interest in the canal.   In fact, the failure of Decazes, the French Foreign Minister, to push the matter with the *Crédit Foncier* was doubtless due to clear warnings which he received through Gavard, French *chargé d'affaires* in London, on November 19 and 20, concerning England's renewed interest in the East and in European affairs.   He especially emphasized England's economic and political interest in India. Since she was the leading power in the East, Gavard said, she did not wish merely an equilibrium but a preponderance in Asia.   Furthermore, Gavard pointed out, Russia had the same aims in Asia and aspired no less than England to become a great Asiatic power.   Therefore, the conflict was inevitable, sooner or later, as England saw danger in two future possibilities, Russia's advance into central Asia, and a Russian menace to the English communications with the Indian Empire.[4] The French *chargé d'affaires* saw evidence that the English would be willing to take a firm stand in protecting the canal and possibly go as far as to take steps to prevent Russia from occupying Constantinople if it became neecssary to do so.[5]   On the following day Derby informed Gavard that England considered her interest in the canal superior to that of any other power.   Despite French ownership of more than half the shares, he based his

[3] Gavard to Decazes, London, Nov. 20, 1875, *D.D.F.*, 1st ser., II, 87; Granville to Bright, Walmer Castle, Dec. 31, 1875, in Edmond Fitzmaurice, *George Leveson Gower, Earl Granville, 1815-1891* (2 vols., 2nd ed., New York, 1905), II, 158-159.
[4] Gavard to Decazes, London, Nov. 19, 1875, *D.D.F.*, 1st ser., II, 15-19.
[5] Gavard to Decazes, London, Nov. 19, 1875, *ibid.*, 1st ser., II, 15-19.

contention on the fact that England used the canal more than all the other powers combined. Since the Khedive had acted as a check upon de Lesseps in the past, England felt that a mortgage or sale of his shares to French interests would seriously concern her.

When pressed directly upon the question of the English attitude toward allowing the shares to fall into French hands, Derby insisted that such an eventuality under the circumstances would produce a bad effect and probably lead to a renewed rivalry between England and France.[6]   Decazes wrote Laboulaye, the French *chargé d'affaires* at St. Petersburg, on November 27, that the English Consul-General in Cairo would not consent to the Khedive's selling to French capitalists, and as a result the Khedive stopped his negotiations with them.[7]

The purchase of the Khedive's shares under conditions of secrecy and without calling Parliament into session was not due entirely to a fear of French competition. The Disraeli cabinet feared complications at home on the part of the Liberal opposition under Gladstone's leadership. Gladstone, Bright, and Granville were committed to a policy which opposed vigorous imperialism. That such was the case was demonstrated by the Liberal policy from 1871-1874 and by the first reactions of the Liberal leaders at learning of the Suez transaction.[8]

Whatever resentment France may have felt, it did not take the form of a press campaign. Though the possibility that complications might cause England eventually to occupy Egypt disturbed French official and public opinion, there was no concerted French attack against the actual purchase of the shares by England. Ferdinand de Lesseps assured Lyons that he considered the transaction as a step toward greater co-operation between English and French capital in the development of a great international waterway, which would be advantageous in

[6] *Ibid.*, 1st ser., II, 19-20.
[7] Decazes to Laboulaye, Paris, Nov. 27, 1875, *ibid.*, 1st ser., II, 21-22.
[8] Wilson, *The Suez Canal*, pp. 51-52.

the future development of the canal.[9] Decazes did not express any very strong objection to the measure itself, Lyons reported, but he brought up the question of whether the Khedive had the right to sell the shares without the consent of the Sultan. "The shares," Decazes said to Lyons, "might be considered as a safeguard for the influence of the [Ottoman] government over a very important establishment on the territory of the Empire; and if so, the Khedive could hardly be entitled to throw away this safeguard, and transfer to a foreign power the influence afforded by it."[10]

On November 25 Decazes informed St. Petersburg regarding the rumors in the English press relative to an eventual occupation of Egypt by Great Britain and said that he counted upon the Russian Government to block such plans.[11] The next day he communicated with the French diplomatic posts with the view of determining the attitude of the various powers. He was especially anxious to secure the Russian reaction to the possible disintegration of the Ottoman Empire.[12] His nervousness was apparently the result in part of the tone of the English press. The clerical French paper *L'Univers* called attention to a statement in the *Pall Mall Gazette* that if Russia imposed her influence at Constantinople, England would occupy Egypt.[13] A *Times* editorial held on November 26 that it was "impossible to separate in our thoughts the purchase of the Suez Canal from the question of England's future relations with Egypt, or the destiny of Egypt from the shadows that darken the Turkish Empire.[14]

The purchase of the shares was greeted by the *Times* as a decisive step toward a great increase in British influence in everything connected with the security and welfare of Egypt

---

[9] Lyons to Derby, Paris, Nov. 30, 1875. MSS, Public Record Office, London, F.O. (hereinafter cited as F.O.), 27/2116, No. 958.

[10] Lyons to Derby, Paris, Nov. 30, 1876, F.O., 27/2116, No. 959.

[11] Decazes to Laboulaye, Paris, Nov. 25, 1875, *D.D.F.*, 1st ser., II, 21.

[12] *Ibid.*, 1st ser., II, 26-27.   [13] *L'Univers*, Nov. 27, 1875.

[14] Gavard to Decazes, London, Nov. 19, 1875, *D.D.F.*, 1st ser., II, 12.

and as the beginning of a new era in British relations. The *Times* saw more importance in the purchase of the shares for England's prestige in the Mediterranean and Egypt than for the commercial advantages to be derived.[15]

On November 29 the Paris correspondent of the *Times* described the French reaction to the British purchase of the canal shares. "In the middle and even in the lower classes," he wrote, "it has produced a kind of melancholy admiration. In the higher class, that of thinkers free from political passion, people are chiefly struck with the care taken by the English government in acquiring an interest in the canal by the agency of an intermediary."[16] On December 1, the *République Française*, the organ of Leon Gambetta, the fiery Republican leader, saw in the affair only a pretext for overthrowing a ministry. "The Duc Decazes," this newspaper complained, "has not yet resigned. After the check which our diplomacy has received in the Egyptian Question, any other but the present Minister of Foreign Affairs would not have hesitated to resign his portfolio to the President of the Republic." "The minister has, in this circumstance, given proof," the *République Française* of November 27 wrote, "of a blindness unequaled except in the worst days of imperial diplomacy."[17]

The most significant development growing out of the purchase of the Suez Canal shares was the immediate discussion in the newspapers of the possibilities of an eventual English occupation of Egypt. Attention was thereby distracted from the commercial implications of the transaction and concentrated upon the broader political aspects. Lyons' dispatch to the British Foreign Office on November 23 analyzed the probable French reaction to a British occupation of Egypt:

The dispatches in the English newspapers on the necessity of the acquisition of Egypt by England, have not provoked in France

---

[15] *Times* (London), Nov. 27, 1875.   [16] *Times*, Nov. 30, 1875.

[17] *Times*, Dec. 1, 1875; Gabriel Hanotaux, *Histoire de la France Contemporaine, 1871-1900* (4 vols.; Paris, 1903-1908), III, 454.

the storm of indignation which would have burst forth had the
slightest hint of anything of this kind been given six years ago. . . .

It must not, however, be supposed that the old French feeling
about Egypt has so far subsided, that France would not strenuously
resent not only the occupation of Egypt by England, but any increase of English influence there, if she were in a position to do
so . . . . It is a sense of want of power which is the real cause
of the apparent calmness with which the question has recently been
regarded. The disposition of France to acquiesce will certainly
decline in exact proportion to her recovery from the state of prostra-
tion to which she was reduced by the war.[18]

Lyons believed that the purchase of the canal shares had
irritated as well as mortified the French. "They feel, however,"
he wrote, "that France cannot undo what has been done and
that she has no means of effectually resenting it; they think
therefore that it is better to put up with their annoyance than
to place themselves on bad terms with England." He believed
that the thing most dreaded by the thinking public in France
was a disturbance of the peace by the rise of any great European
question before France had fully recovered her strength.[19]

The official reactions to the purchase on the part of the
European powers were such as to discourage Decazes from any
attempt at causing serious embarrassment to England. The
Porte was reported as dissatisfied and seemingly disappointed at
not having been consulted before the transaction was completed.[20] Italy expressed confidence in the conservative policy
of England and claimed that Lord Derby had assured her that
England had none of the sinister intentions of which she had
been accused by the press. Moreover, England had assured
her that she did not intend to seek any territorial aggrandize-
ment.[21]

In regard to Russia, Lord Loftus, the English ambassador in
St. Petersburg, wrote that Prince Gorchakov, the Russian Chan-

[18] Lyons to Derby, Paris, Nov. 23, 1875, F.O., 27/2116, No. 948.
[19] Lyons to Derby, Paris, Nov. 30, 1875, F.O., 27/2116, No. 959.
[20] Decazes to Bourgoing, Paris, Nov. 29, 1875, D.D.F., 1st ser., II, 27.
[21] Noailles to Decazes, Rome, Nov. 28, 1875, ibid., 1st ser., II, 25-26.

cellor, had evaded the subject of the canal. As to the more general reaction in the Russian capital, Loftus spoke of the excitement caused in political and commercial circles by the danger of complications, but he asserted that "one of the most influential statesmen here expressed to me yesterday his satisfaction at the step taken by Her Majesty's government, and of his admiration for the manner in which it was carried out." He added that he was not alone in his appreciation and that there were many who shared his views.[22]

On December 1 the Pan-Slavic Moscow *Gazette* had strongly denounced the act as tending to complicate affairs in the Near East and emphasized the political rather than the commercial significance of the incident. The *Russki Mir,* the organ of the landed gentry, viewed the English purchase with satisfaction and believed that it might lead to an understanding between England and Russia on the Eastern question. Representing the commercial classes, the *Exchange Gazette* expressed satisfaction at the English acquisition of the shares. However, the newspapers which generally reflected the opinion of the Russian Government carefully abstained from comments.[23] In a communication of December 21, Loftus observed that since the purchase of the canal shares Russian attention had been directed to the importance of the Dardanelles and the Bosporus, which the *Russki Mir* designated as an "entrance gate without which the Russians are not masters of their own house." He stated that the *Russki Mir* in a second article had advocated an alliance between Russia and England. The *Golos,* a representative of the radical press, did not consider the measure directed against the peace of Europe or as ground for alarm. Lord Loftus observed that the tone of the Russian press was in general moderate and favorable to England, with the exception of the Moscow *Gazette.*[24]

[22] Loftus to Derby, St. Petersburg, Dec. 8, 1875, F.O., 65/930, No. 370.
[23] Loftus to Derby, St. Petersburg, Dec. 8, 1875, F.O., 65/930, No. 370.
[24] Loftus to Derby, St. Petersburg, Dec. 21, 1875, F.O., 65/930, No. 393.

The French ambassador in St. Petersburg, General Le Flô, reported to Decazes that the Tsar was disturbed by reports he had received from Constantinople and Berlin that the Porte had offered to hand over Egypt to England in return for support in resisting foreign intervention.[25] In spite of this attempt to set the French on edge, the Russian Government made no important move. On April 12, 1876, Prince Gorchakov told Le Flô that Russia could not do anything in the interest of France in Egypt and the Suez Canal. He could not afford to side against England, he said, in a question where Russia did not have direct interests.[26]

Prince Bismarck gave England full support and was willing, in fact, for England to take Egypt. As early as November 12, 1875, Odo Russell wrote: "Anything calculated to break the influence of France in the East, which is thought to be too great, would be popular in Germany . . . . England may have Egypt if she likes. Germany will graciously not object."[27] Russell informed Derby on November 29, 1875, that Prince Bismarck desired to congratulate the British Government on having done the right thing at the right moment. "He gives the measure his full support and has written in that sense to Paris, St. Petersburg and Vienna."[28]

Russell also pointed out that Bismarck had told him on former occasions of his apprehension lest the interests of England and Russia lead to a conflict in the East. Bismarck had impressed upon Gorchakov and Shuvalov how the danger might be diminished if England were guaranteed a free passage to India.[29]

The English public was gradually brought to understand the political significance of the purchase. Disraeli in the course of debate said on February 21: "I have never recommended this

[25] Le Flô to Decazes, St. Petersburg, Jan. 9, 1876, *D.D.F.*, 1st ser., II, 38-39.
[26] Le Flô to Decazes, St. Petersburg, April 12, 1876, *ibid.*, 1st ser., II, 47.
[27] Newton, *Lord Lyons*, II, 89.
[28] Russell to Derby, Berlin, Nov. 29, 1875. F.O., 65/831, No. 487.
[29] Russell to Derby, Berlin, Nov. 29, 1875. F.O., 65/831, No. 487.

purchase as a financial investment . . . . I do not recommend it either as a commercial speculation . . . . I have always and do now recommend it to the country as a political transaction. . . ."[30]

France was undoubtedly unhappy at England's purchase of the shares, but she was probably much more concerned with the effect it would have upon Anglo-Russian relations. "Under the influence of this apprehension," Lyons wrote, "was the chance of its producing a difference between England and Russia which might precipitate events in the Levant. They [the French] felt that in such a case France would be driven to side with one or the other; that she could hardly take the same side as Germany; and that therefore the results would be that she would find either Germany and England or Germany and Russia united in opposition to her."[31]

The reactions of the European powers emphasized the political rather than the economic significance of the affair. The British press was almost unanimous in pointing out the political implications of Disraeli's stroke. In France there was naturally a feeling of disappointment in seeing the British gain a strong position in the management of the canal, but France was primarily concerned with whether this was a first step toward a stronger British policy in Egypt and the Near East. Bismarck attempted to minimize the political significance in his conversations with the French ambassador, but the reactions of the German press and his statements to the British ambassador indicate that he considered the English action as politically significant. In fact, he interpreted it as an indication that England was prepared to take a stronger position in European affairs. The noncommittal attitude of the Russian Government suggests that the Tsar probably emphasized rather than minimized the political meaning of the purchase. The more or less independent Russian press gave varying interpretations, but all

[30] T. C. Hansard, *Parliamentary Debates of Great Britain* (hereinafter cited as Hansard), 3rd ser., CCXXVII, 651-660.

[31] Lyons to Derby, Paris, Nov. 30, 1875, F.O., 27/2116, No. 959.

saw the possibility that England might take a greater part in
the affairs of the Near East and in Central Asia.

The excitement caused by the purchase of the canal shares
had hardly subsided before another phase of the Egyptian question was thrust upon the foreign offices and stock exchanges of
Europe. The financial embarrassment which caused the
Khedive to sell his canal shares had become so critical by the
close of 1875 that he was faced with virtual bankruptcy. His
debts were owed principally to the capitalists of the leading
European powers, especially England and France. His creditors
had allowed him to increase the funded debt of Egypt from
approximately three million pounds in 1863 to nearly seventy
million pounds in 1876.[32]

Faced by a financial crisis during the closing days of 1875,
The Khedive, Ismaïl Pasha, asked the British Government to
investigate his finances; whereupon Stephen Cave, an experienced financier and Member of Parliament, was given this
mission.[33] The appointment was favorably received by the
Times, which saw in it an opportunity to go beyond investigation and suggestion and to bring about a thorough reform of
the Egyptian finances.[34] Before the end of March the cabinet
had received Cave's report, but the Government declined to
make it public on the ground that the Khedive had not given
his consent because of the unsettled state of Egyptian finances.[35]
Disraeli's statement to that effect in the House of Commons in
fact caused a short panic in Egyptian securities.[36] However, on
March 31, the Prime Minister assured the Commons that the
report was ready for presentation.[37]

The Cave Report pointed out that "the expenditure, though

[32] Earl of Cromer, *Modern Egypt* (one vol. ed.; New York, 1916), I, 11.

[33] W. F. Monypenny and G. E. Buckle, *The Life of Benjamin Disraeli* (6
vols.; London, 1920), V, 154; Edward Dicey, *The Story of the Khedivate* (London, 1902), p. 133.

[34] *Times*, Dec. 30, 1875; Theodore Rothstein, *Egypt's Ruin* (London, 1910),
pp. 12-14.

[35] Hansard, 3rd ser., CCXXVIII, 480.

[36] *Annual Register*, 1876, CXVIII, 8-9.

[37] Hansard, 3rd ser., CCXXVIII, 1038.

heavy, would not of itself produce the present crisis, which could be attributed almost entirely to the ruinous conditions of the loans raised for pressing requirements, due in some cases over which the Khedive had little control." Cave left the impression that the Egyptian debt was only seventy-five million pounds and that the prospects were reasonably good for the Khedive to pay 7 per cent interest on that amount.[38] The general effect of the report tended to restore confidence in Egypt on the part of the financial interests.

In the meantime, on February 14, Decazes had suggested to Lyons that France and England should reach a better understanding on the Egyptian question. "Politically as well as financially," he said, "the only remedy for the evils of the present condition of Egyptian finances would be found in a close understanding between the English and French governments."[39] He pointed out the political advantages of an understanding in Egypt instead of rivalry. He went so far as to indicate that he would not object to bringing Italy into the affair if the British though it advisable. Derby, the British Foreign Secretary, replied on February 19 that, while appreciating the French offer to co-operate, England would be unable to join in an international control over Egyptian finances. The English had no reason to suppose, Derby explained, that the Khedive desired any system of control by foreign governments.

Meanwhile Decazes, encouraged by a French capitalist group interested in establishing a National Bank of Egypt, proposed that such an institution be formed for the conversion of the Egyptian floating debt. He further suggested that a commission be appointed to report on the operation of the proposed bank and that the English, French, and Italian Governments each select a commissioner to be appointed by the Khedive.[40]

[38] *Annual Register,* 1876, CXVIII, 8-9; Cromer, *Modern Egypt,* pp. 8, 11-12.
[39] Lyons to Derby, Paris, Feb. 14, 1876, *British Foreign and State Papers* (hereinafter cited as *B.S.P.*), LXX, 896-897.
[40] Stanton to Derby, Cairo, March 4, 1876, *B.S.P.*, LXX, 906; Derby to Lyons, London, March 6, 1876, *ibid.,* LXX, 907.

Both France and Italy were eager to participate in this proposed scheme, but Derby insisted that Britain objected to sending a commissioner to take part in the management of a bank. However, if a workable plan for receiving revenues and applying them to the payment of Egyptian debts were proposed, England would be glad to consider it.

Nevertheless, Decazes urged England to appoint a commissioner and explained that the French Government had delayed in taking action in order not to appear out of harmony with England.[41]

The next move by France was a proposal that the Khedive should issue a decree creating a "Caisse d'Amortissement." The substance of this project was communicated to Derby, but he was unwilling to consider it until he had learned more of its details. The British asserted that they would consider participation on a commission but would shrink from the responsibility of being in any way committed to the details of the plan until those details were carefully worked out.[42]

Though very little is known of the details, the British financial agents in Cairo upset the plans of the French capitalists momentarily by persuading the Khedive to issue a decree on April 8 suspending payment on Treasury bills for three months. This caused considerable commotion on the Alexandria Bourse and caused the French Government to seek moral aid from at least one European foreign office. General Stanton wrote hopefully from Cairo that the results would not prove disastrous and that some workable plan might result for the consolidation of the whole of the Egyptian debt on terms which would be satisfactory to the creditors and not too burdensome on the resources of the country.[43] That the British Govern-

[41] Derby to Stanton, March 6, 1876, *ibid.*, LXX, 908; Paget to Derby, Rome, March 5, 1876, *ibid.*, p. 908; Lyons to Derby, Paris, March 23, 1876, *ibid.*, LXX, 911-914.

[42] Derby to Lyons, London, March 25, 1876, *B.S.P.*, LXX, 915; Lyons to Derby, Paris, March 28, 1876, *ibid.*, LXX, 920.

[43] Stanton to Derby, Cairo, April 8, 1876, *ibid.*, p. 927.

ment was pleased by this action is shown by Disraeli's statement in a letter to Lady Bradford on April 7: "There is good news from Egypt."[44]

Decazes, excited at this turn of events, approached Russia on April 9, asking that she bring pressure upon the Khedive to counterbalance the growing influence of England.[45] Le Flô, the French ambassador in St. Petersburg, replied three days later that this move clearly embarrassed Prince Gorchakov, who saw any move in Egypt, where Russia had only indirect interests, as an undesirable blow against England because of the delicate relations growing out of the Near Eastern situation. The matter was apparently so important from the standpoint of France that Le Flô asked that the question of Russian pressure in France's behalf be taken up with the Tsar.[46]

The Khedive's decree of May 2, establishing the Commission of Public Debt, provided that the commissioners would act as representatives of the bondholders. Provision was made for four commissioners, appointed to represent the English, French, Austrian, and Italian Governments respectively.[47] The British, however, refused to appoint a commissioner, but made it clear that any British subject who wished to accept appointment could do so on his own responsibility.[48] On May 7, the Khedive issued a further decree which consolidated the Egyptian debt at £91,000,000. Thus the Cave Report had been completely ignored and the French had been able to establish a European system of control which was independent of England and with which the English Government was in almost complete disagreement.[49]

This divergence of opinion between the French and English

[44] Monypenny and Buckle, *Benjamin Disraeli*, V, 473.

[45] Decazes to Le Flô, Paris, April 9, 1876, *D.D.F.*, 1st ser., II, 47.

[46] Le Flô to Decazes, St. Petersburg, April 12, 1876, *ibid.*, 1st ser., II, 47-48.

[47] *B.S.P.*, LXVII, 1020-1024; Cromer, *Modern Egypt*, pp. 11-12.

[48] Derby to Stanton, London, April 13, 1876, *B.S.P.*, LXX, 926; Stanton to Derby, Alexandria, May 27, 1876, *ibid.*, LXX, 936.

[49] Stanton to Derby, Alexandria, May 27, 1876, *ibid.*, LXX, 936; Cromer, *Modern Egypt*, p. 12.

Governments resulted from several causes. The British hesitated to take any step which might be interpreted as a move
toward the weakening of the Ottoman Empire at a time when
the Near Eastern Question was uppermost in the thoughts of
European statesmen. Lord Salisbury, the Secretary of State for
India, was much more prone to support Egyptian intervention
than his colleagues, Disraeli and Derby, who saw in the crum-
bling of Turkey the greatest danger to European peace.[50] Derby
scrupulously adhered to the principle that the British Government should avoid any direct interference with the Egyptian
finances. As Derby put it several months later: "Russia would
like it [England's taking of Egypt] as making us an accomplice
in her plans."[51] The difference in the attitudes of the French
and English Governments toward the responsibility of government for foreign investments was doubtless a contributing factor. Decazes seemed to be under much greater pressure from
the bondholders and to respond much more readily to it than
the British cabinet.

The arrangement which grew out of the Decrees of May 2
and May 7 were unsatisfactory to both the English Government
and the English bondholders. The question arises as to why
the British Government allowed the French to play such an
important part in the arrangement of the Khedive's finances
during the spring of 1876. Several factors contributed to the
British procedure. It was not lack of support from Germany
at this time, because Bismarck had approached England for
a closer understanding in regard to the Eastern Question on
January 2 and had specifically mentioned his recognition of
Britain's dominant interest in the protection of the road to
India.[52]

---

[50] Salisbury to Mallet, London, Jan. 14, 1876, in Lady Gwendolyn Cecil, *Life
of Robert, Marquis of Salisbury* (4 vols.; London, 1921-1931), II, 80.

[51] Derby to Lyons, London, Dec. 6, 1876, in Newton, *Lord Lyons*, II, 105.

[52] Russell to Derby, Berlin, Jan. 2, 1876, in Winifred Taffs, *Ambassador to
Bismarck: Lord Odo Russell, First Baron Ampthill* (London, 1938), pp. 118-
121; see David Harris, "Bismarck's Advance to England, 1876," *Journal of Modern History*, III (1931), 443-446; Bülow to Münster, Berlin, Jan. 4, 1876, in *Die*

However, the British reaction was far from enthusiastic. Though the Queen urged Derby to enter into a free discussion of the Eastern Question the Government feared that Germany was seeking a quarrel with Russia.[53] Lord Odo Russell, the British ambassador in Berlin, sought to ascertain more clearly Bismarck's views as to an Anglo-German understanding on February 19. The Chancellor was told that England did not wish any change in the territorial status quo in the Ottoman Empire. Bismarck insisted that there were two approaches to the problem: the maintenance of the territorial status quo, and if that should fail and peace became endangered, the powers should seek to maintain peace, not by supporting the status quo, "but by amicably settling what should be done with Turkey to satisfy the powers concerned. . . ."[54] The Chancellor again recognized England's legitimate right to the road to India.[55] A possible reason why Bismarck approached England with the possibility of a partition of the Turkish Empire in the interest of peace was the fact that he felt in early January that England was prepared for a more definite policy in the Near East as a result of the purchase of the Suez Canal shares.[56]

Several factors contributed to a breakdown in the attempted Anglo-German *rapprochement*. Chief among the reasons was fear on England's part that Bismarck desired to fish in troubled waters. For instance there was a rumor current in diplomatic circles in Berlin, St. Petersburg, and Paris at this time that Turkey had offered England a free hand in Egypt in return for

---

Grosse Politik der europäischen Kabinette, 1871-1914, ed. Johannes Lepsius, Albrecht Mendelssohn, and Friedrich Thimme (hereinafter cited as G.P.) (40 vols.; Berlin, 1922-1927), II, 29-31.

[53] Disraeli, the Prime Minister, tended to agree with the Queen. See G. E. Buckle, ed., *The Letters of Queen Victoria* (London, 1926), II, 443-444; Monypenny and Buckle, *Benjamin Disraeli*, VI, 20-21. Lord Lyons wrote "The despatch looks as if Bismarck were preparing for a quarrel with Russia." Newton, *Lord Lyons*, II, 96.

[54] Taffs, *Odo Russell*, pp. 128-131; William L. Langer, *European Alliances and Alignments 1871-1890* (New York, 1931), p. 79.

[55] Russell to Derby, Berlin, Feb. 19, 1876, in Taffs, *Odo Russell*, p. 130.

[56] *Ibid.*, p. 132.

England's noninterference with respect to the Turkish reforms
suggested in the Andrássy note of December 30, 1875.[57] This
rumor caused the British to suspect that there was a conspiracy
on Germany's part to create trouble between England, France,
and Russia.[58]

Disraeli's resentment at the methods used by Germany,
Austria-Hungary, and Russia in preparing and announcing the
Berlin Memorandum (May 12, 1876), along with British opposition to the content of the Memorandum itself, caused the British cabinet to reject the proposal and to adopt an isolated
position in the whole Near Eastern Question.[59] Derby told
Harcourt on May 17: "I regret that England remains isolated
in Europe, but I and my colleagues are unanimous in not being
able to adhere to the Memorandum which is unsatisfactory to
us in almost every point mentioned."[60]

In May, 1876, the English Government had taken a position
against interference in the internal affairs of Turkey which
caused the failure of the Berlin Memorandum and which at
the same time was in complete harmony with the line of action
which had been taken in the Egyptian finances. England's
willingness to take such a firm stand against Europe and resist
all temptation to interfere directly in any part of the Turkish
Empire was probably due to fear that Germany was trying to
cause trouble between England, France, and Russia.

The May settlement soon proved to be very unsatisfac-

[57] Derby to Loftus, London, Jan. 17, 1876, F.O., 65/931, No. 25. The Andrássy
note was addressed to the powers with the approval of Germany and Russia. It
announced their consent in persuading Serbia and Montenegro against warlike
action, but insisted upon reforms in the Balkans. Full religious freedom and
equality before the law for the insurgent Christians, abolition of tax farming, and
measures for the improvement of the lot of the peasants were some of the
suggested reforms. Langer, *European Alliances*, p. 75.

[58] Derby to Loftus, London, Jan. 17, 1876, F.O., 65/936, No. 24.

[59] In a sense the Berlin Memorandum was merely an elaboration of the
Andrássy note. It called for an armistice of two months between the Balkan
insurgents and Turkey and attempted to dictate to the Porte certain reforms.
Langer, *European Alliances*, pp. 81-82; Harcourt to Decazes, London, May 17,
1876, *D.D.F.*, 1st ser., II, 65.

[60] Harcourt to Decazes, London, May 17, 1876, *D.D.F.*, 1st ser., II, 65.

tory, because it favored the holders of the floating debt at
the expense of the holders of the consolidated debt. The
British bondholders, who had considerable holdings in the
consolidated debt, selected G. J. Goschen to represent their
interests and seek means of revising the Decrees of May 2 and
May 7. Goschen was joined by E. J. Joubert as representative
of French interests.[61] In October Goschen and Joubert began
an inquiry into the bonded debt of Egypt. England took the
lead in this inquiry and the French pursued a policy of close
co-operation. The Khedive, in fact, was given to understand
by the French bondholders that, should he refuse to support the
recommendations of Goschen and Joubert, the French would be
forced into even closer co-operation with the British.[62] Consequently, Ismaïl decided to accept the Goschen-Joubert findings
and issued a Decree on November 18 establishing a new system
of financial control and changing the debt structure in such a
way as to give the English bondholders a more equitable position. As a result of these arrangements the capital of the unified debt was reduced from approximately ninety million
pounds to fifty-nine million pounds.[63]

The financial administration of Egypt was placed under the
authority of a French and an English controller. They were
to be named by the Khedive on the authorization or acquiescence of their respective governments.[64] The Controllers-
General appointed were Romaine for England and Malaret for
France. The Commission of Public Debt was composed of
the following membership from the various countries: England,
two; France, two; Italy, one; Germany, one; and Austria, one.[65]

[61] Goschen to Derby, July 28, 1876, *B.S.P.*, LXX, 938; Cromer, *Modern Egypt*, p. 13.

[62] Vivian to Derby, Nov. 10, 1876, F.O., 78/2504, No. 24.

[63] Egyptian Decree, Cairo, Nov. 18, 1876, *B.S.P.*, LXII, 1024-1032; Cromer, *Modern Egypt*, p. 13.

[64] *B.S.P.*, LXVII, 1027-1030; *France affaires étrangères, documents diplomatiques* (hereinafter cited as Livre Jaune), *Affaires d'Égypte*, XVII, 1878-1879, 133.

[65] Edward Dicey, "The Egyptian Liquidation," *Nineteenth Century*, VIII, 458-460; *B.S.P.*, LXVII, 1024.

Despite the refusal of the English to enter into direct
financial control in Egypt at the side of France, the temporary
settlement in the Decree of November 18, 1876, has been called
by Freycinet in his book *La Question d'Égypte* the beginning
of Anglo-French co-operation in Egypt.[66] Goschen wrote of the
results of his mission in Egypt: "When we went to Egypt we
found France and England not united, but struggling for different financial schemes; we have left English influence and French
influence both working together to support the scheme which
we have propounded."[67]   Though Decazes saw weaknesses in
the arrangement, he told Lord Lyons on December 5, 1876, that
the success of Goschen and Joubert could be attributed to the
complete and hearty union of French and English interests, and
French and English influence throughout the negotiations.[68]

Although Goschen had gone to Egypt with the knowledge
and approval of the British cabinet, Derby stood by the position
which he had taken earlier in the year and refused to make any
official recommendation or give approval of British subjects
who assumed positions under the Khedive.[69]   The French Foreign Minister insisted that Derby officially appoint representatives in the interest of closer co-operation. Decazes insisted that
the English and French controllers should hold positions on
exactly the same footing in every respect.   Nevertheless, Lord
Derby refused to give official sanction to the Egyptian financial
arrangement, but expressed satisfaction with the English selections which the Khedive made.[70]

Though the financial difficulties of Egypt were serious during the weeks preceding the Goschen-Joubert settlement, the
chief interest of the powers in Egypt gradually turned to what
that country's fate would be in the event that the Turkish Em-

[66] Charles de Freycinet, *La Question d'Égypte* (Paris, 1905), pp. 154-155.
[67] Langer, *European Alliances*, p. 258.
[68] Lyons to Derby, Paris, Dec. 5, 1876, *B.S.P.*, LXX, 940-941.
[69] Lyons to Derby, Paris, Dec. 5, 1876, *ibid.*, LXX, 940-941.
[70] Vivian to Derby, Dec. 25, 1876, *ibid.*, LXX, 944-945.

pire was partitioned or fell to pieces as a result of a Russo-Turkish war.

Reports of Turkish atrocities in Bulgaria and their effect upon English public opinion and the Reichstadt Agreement (July 8, 1876) between Austria and Russia caused the English Government to give serious consideration to the problem of the eventual intervention and partition of Turkey. On September 4, 1876, Disraeli felt that the policy of nonintervention in Turkey was bankrupt and suggested to Derby the possibility of partitioning Turkey into spheres of influence.[71] Two days later (September 6) Salisbury wrote to Lord Lytton that he did not despair of being told to write to him for his best civilian to govern the new British province of Egypt.[72]

British policy did not take the direction Salisbury had indicated in the letter to Lytton. Disraeli was greatly moved by the reports of Russia's plans to intervene in Bulgaria, for this action, it was felt, would seriously affect England's position on the road to India. However, he came to the conclusion that the occupation of Egypt was not a satisfactory solution to the problem because Russia would be able to menace the Suez Canal from Constantinople by way of Syria.[73]

Disraeli decided that Bismarck might be of aid in reducing the possibility of Russian action. A leading article in the London *Times* (October 16) suggested that one word from Bismarck would keep Russia from going too far.[74] Disraeli considered proposing to Bismarck that England was willing to guarantee German possession of Alsace-Lorraine in return for Bismarck's aid in halting Russia. However, instead of this proposal, Russell merely asked Bismarck for his suggested solution.[75] On October 23 Bismarck told Russell that the whole

[71] Disraeli to Derby, Sept. 4, 1876, in Monypenny and Buckle, *Benjamin Disraeli*, VI, 52.
[72] Salisbury to Lytton, Sept. 6, 1876, in Cecil, *Lord Salisbury*, II, 83.
[73] Monypenny and Buckle, *Benjamin Disraeli*, VI, 84-100.
[74] *Times* (London), Oct. 16, 1876.
[75] Langer, *European Alliances*, pp. 100-101.

of Turkey, including all the various races, was not worth a great war between the powers.[76] Russell's impression of Bismarck's conversation was that the Chancellor was interested in a more lasting settlement of the question than England was willing to sanction. He had hoped for a partition of Turkey with England getting Egypt, but since England was unwilling to pursue such a policy, he was willing to get through Russia what he could not obtain from England—a more nearly permanent solution of the Near Eastern problem.[77] Bismarck's solution went much further than any plans of the British Government. On October 22 Disraeli wrote to Derby: "But what alarms me is that Turkey feeling she is utterly deserted may make some mad compact with Russia, opening the Straits, and giving her complete control over the Asiatic shore. As for compensations to England by having Egypt and Crete, this is moonshine. If Constantinople is Russian, they would only be an expensive encumbrance."[78]

The German Chancellor's views were stated in a memorandum for the German Foreign Office. He was thoroughly convinced that the English should seek compensations in a partition of Turkey rather than endanger European peace by opposing Russia. "If I had to give advice to British policy," he wrote, "I should suggest analogous action with regard to England's weak spot; namely, the Suez Canal and Egypt, and as regards Constantinople, that she should come to an understanding with Russia on the basis of the continuance of Turkish rule there and at Adrianople." England should seek compensations, Bismarck thought, not by war with Russia, but by acquiring Suez and Alexandria.[79]

---

[76] R. W. Seton-Watson, *Disraeli, Gladstone, and the Eastern Question* (London, 1935), p. 98.

[77] Russell to Derby, Berlin, Oct. 23, 1876, in Taffs, *Odo Russell*, pp. 159-160.

[78] Beaconsfield to Derby, London, Oct. 22, 1876, in Monypenny and Buckle, *Benjamin Disraeli*, VI, 83-100.

[79] Memorandum of Bismarck, Oct. 20, 1876, *G.P.*, II, 71-72. Russell reported Bismarck's views as follows: "He was the first to acknowledge the vital interests of England in Egypt, Asia, and India, he could appreciate the wish of England to

When the crisis became more acute in late October, England took the initiative by sending invitations to the Powers to a conference in Constantinople. Salisbury left England on November 20, and visited several European capitals on his way to Constantinople. In Paris, Salisbury reported Decazes as leaning toward a recognition of the possibility of a European occupation. The French Foreign Minister mentioned Bosnia for Austria, Bulgaria for Russia, and Macedonia for England, but admitted, however, that there would be serious difficulty in reaching an agreement to that effect.[80] Salisbury assured the French Foreign Minister that England had not changed her position in the least in regard to Egypt and made it clear that the occupation of that country would not be considered at the Conference.[81] From Paris Salisbury went to Berlin, where he consulted with Bismarck on November 23. He reported that the Chancellor had a gloomy view on the prospects for peace and encouraged the English to take Egypt as their share. If that were not possible, he observed, it would be very beneficial to European civilization that England should occupy Constantinople.[82]

Disraeli's reaction to Bismarck's proposal that England should take Egypt appears in a dispatch to Salisbury, November 29: "I am surprised that Bismarck should go on harping about Egypt. Its occupation by us would embitter France."[83] However, the conference with Bismarck seemed to have convinced Salisbury that the Chancellor really desired peace. Salisbury wrote on November 25, "The result of my visit of Berlin is on

prolong the Sultan's rule on the Bosporus, but he failed to see what interests England had north of the Balkans that could be dearer to her than peace." Taffs, *Odo Russell*, p. 160.

[80] Cecil, *Lord Salisbury*, II, 95-96.

[81] Decazes to Bourgoing and Chaudordy, Versailles, Nov. 19, 1876, *D.D.F.*, 1st ser., II, 117.

[82] Salisbury to Derby, Vienna, Nov. 25, 1876, in Cecil, *Lord Salisbury*, II, 99; Bülow to Münster, Berlin, Nov. 27, 1876, *G.P.*, II, 69-70.

[83] Disraeli to Salisbury, Nov. 29, 1876, in Monypenny and Buckle, *Benjamin Disraeli*, VI, 103-106.

the whole to leave me of Odo Russell's opinion, that Bismarck wishes for peace; not war between us and Russia."[84] During the conversation Bismarck took the greatest pains to impress upon Salisbury that England should not rush hastily into war.[85]

Assuming that the conference in Constantinople would fail and Russia would occupy Bulgaria, Disraeli told Hardy, Secretary of War, at the end of November that "England, on the invitation of the Porte, would send up the fleet and occupy lines behind Constantinople and at Gallipoli," and that he would like to buy a port in the Black Sea from Turkey, but he insisted that what he wanted was a Malta or a Gibraltar which would prevent the Black Sea from becoming a threat to British maritime power in the Mediterranean. He believed that Egypt would be offered, but he still could not see what could be gained by accepting it.[86]

The Constantinople conference, December 11, 1876—January 20, 1877, failed to reach a solution acceptable to the Porte. The Porte put up strong opposition and Germany and Austria-Hungary seemed to waver in their support of the measures agreed upon by Russia, England, and France. This hesitancy on the part of Germany was caused probably by fear that Franco-Russian relations might improve to the detriment of Germany should Franco-Russian co-operation in a few things lead to a more general flirtation.[87]

France had been prepared to support Russia in her claims in Bessarabia, but was opposed to any changes in the Mediterranean.[88] In this Bismarck, doubtless, saw forebodings of a

[84] Salisbury to Derby, Vienna, Nov. 25, 1876, in Cecil, *Lord Salisbury*, p. 99.
[85] Bülow to Münster, Berlin, Nov. 27, 1876, *G.P.*, II, 69-70; Cecil, *Lord Salisbury*, II, 99.
[86] Monypenny and Buckle, *Benjamin Disraeli*, VI, 102.
[87] Russell to Derby, Jan. 16, 1877, in Taffs, *Odo Russell*, p. 174. Bismarck told Russell on Jan. 16: "The Conference has been managed by the Marquis of Salisbury, General Ignatye [*sic*] and Count Chaudordy. He did not complain of neglect since he had no interest in the matter, but he regretted to detect a tendency on the part of the French government to set Russia against Germany, with what object he did not well know. . . ."
[88] Decazes, Nov. 19, 1876, *D.D.F.*, 1st ser., II, 117.

serious upset in the Eastern situation. It is entirely possible that the successful co-operation of Russia, France, and England was primarily the result of the latter's renunciation from the beginning of any designs upon Egypt. In Bismarck's eyes, however, such a course by England gave France a clear path in supporting Russia. Therefore, before the end of the conference, Salisbury, who had been suspicious of the Russian designs at the beginning, had come to believe that Russia wanted peace and that Bismarck was the real trouble maker.[89]

Disraeli also suspected Bismarck's peaceful motives. "Salisbury," he wrote to Lady Bradford, "succeeded in moderating the Russians, and I have done my best to moderate the Turks; but we have found out that Bismarck is resolved that Russia shall go to war."[90]

Decazes did not fail to use to advantage the growing distrust of Bismarck's policy in London and St. Petersburg. Fear that Bismarck intended to lead Russia into war and at the same time isolate and attack France became the chief concern of the French Foreign Office in the early months of 1877. Lord Derby was convinced of the same thing and told the French ambassador in London that all reports tended to prove that Germany regarded war as inevitable and desirable. He went so far as to inform Decazes that Germany had encouraged England to take Egypt, an idea, he explained, about which the British Government had never dreamed.[91]

In the spring of 1877 the question of a partition of Turkey as a means of securing peace in the Near East and eventual annexation of Egypt was revived in some quarters in England. As early as March, Salisbury expressed this point of view. He wrote Lord Lytton, the Governor-General of India, "The object most desirable is if possible, to keep Russia out of war for the present . . . , if things go wrong we may be fighting for Holland

[89] Langer, *European Alliances*, p. 109.

[90] Monypenny and Buckle, *Benjamin Disraeli* (rev. ed., 1929), II, 985.

[91] Bourgoing to Decazes, Pera, Dec. 25, 1876, *D.D.F.*, 1st ser., II, 129; Harcourt to Decazes, London, Jan. 26, 1877, *ibid.*, p. 140.

before two years are out."[92]   By March 9, Salisbury felt that the
policy of defending English interests by supporting Turkey had
become impracticable, and that English interests could be promoted best by a territorial rearrangement.[93]

The visit of Nubar Pasha, Ismaïl's former minister, to
London in April on a private mission for arranging a British
protectorate in Egypt created much speculation as to what
England's intentions might be.   However, Derby gave him no
encouragement, pointing out that if England took Egypt, Russia
could not be blamed for a similar act in some other part of
the Ottoman Empire.   The activities of Nubar were carefully
observed by the German ambassador in London, who reported
that Nubar had informed him that the British cabinet was extremely reserved but that he was well received in many official
quarters.[94]   Evidence of Nubar's influence may be seen in the
active campaign which was begun in the *Nineteenth Century*
for the annexation and control of Egypt by England.   Supplied
by information furnished by Nubar, Edward Dicey built up a
strong case for the idea that England should protect her route
to India.   Dicey said that France would not violently oppose
occupation of Egypt because of the German fear.   The chief
concern England had in the settlement of the Eastern Question,
he maintained, was the bearing it would have on the security
of the Indian possessions.[95]   The increase in English feeling that

[92] Salisbury to Lytton, March 2, 1877, in Cecil, *Lord Salisbury*, II, 29. Rumors
were circulated in March and as late as June that Bismarck's scheme was to
embroil England and Russia in a war and to take Holland. This was denied
on several occasions by the German Foreign Office, but it was seized upon by
the French in an apparent effort to increase English suspicions of Germany and
to restrain England in the event England moved against Russia. Harcourt to
Decazes, London, March 17, 1877, *D.D.F.*, 1st ser., II, 149. In June there were
reports that Bismarck was supporting England in Egypt and Russia's influence
in the East for the purpose of securing Holland for Germany. Münster to
Bülow, London, June 6, 1877, *G.P.*, II, 152.

[93] Salisbury to Lytton, March 9, 1877, in Cecil, *Lord Salisbury*, II, 130.

[94] Münster to Bismarck, London, June 28, 1877, *G.P.*, II, No. 295; Langer,
European Alliances, p. 259; Seton-Watson, *Disraeli and Gladstone*, p. 309.

[95] Edward Dicey, "Our Route to India," *Nineteenth Century*, I (1877), 665,
683-684.

it might be necessary to take measures to protect the route to India is pointed out by Shuvalov, the Russian ambassador to London. On April 18 he wrote Gorchakov that the English were considering the eventuality of occupying the Dardanelles, Gallipoli, and Crete, and transforming Egypt into a tributary state.[96]

At last, on April 24, 1877, the much dreaded Russo-Turkish war began, and the immediate reaction in England was sufficient to indicate that there was fear that Egypt and the Suez Canal might be endangered. The Queen wrote Disraeli on April 25: "We must not submit tamely to Russia's advance and to the dangers in Egypt."[97] The Queen maintained that "to let it be thought that England would submit to Egypt being under Russia would be to abdicate the position of Great Britain as one of the Great Powers."[98] Shuvalov, the Russian ambassador in London, reported on April 24 that he had learned from French sources that Derby intended to ask Russia's intentions concerning Egypt.[99] A telegram from the Tsar to Queen Victoria seemed to have allayed the apprehensions of the British Government. Shuvalov informed Gorchakov that "the neutrality of the Suez Canal, which caused the French much concern, was seriously discussed in England."[100] Gorchakov instructed Shuvalov on May 6 to inform the British that Russia had no intention of making a demonstration at Suez.[101] On the same day Derby clearly outlined England's attitude in a note to Russia. Foremost among the interests mentioned was the neces-

[96] Shuvalov to Gorchakov, 6/18 April, 1877, in R. W. Seton-Watson, ed., "Unprinted Documents, Russo-British Relations during the Eastern Crisis," *Slavonic Review,* V, 414. (*Note*: The double dates reflect the fact that the western calendar was twelve days in advance of the Russian calendar at that time.)

[97] Queen Victoria to Disraeli, April 25, 1877, in Monypenny and Buckle, *Benjamin Disraeli,* VI, 133.

[98] Queen Victoria to Lord Beaconsfield, April 25, 1877, in Monypenny and Buckle, *Benjamin Disraeli,* VI, 133.

[99] Shuvalov to Gorchakov, 12/24 April, 1877, *Slavonic Review,* V, 419.

[100] Shuvalov to Gorchakov, 18/30 April, 1877, *ibid.,* V, 420.

[101] Gorchakov to Shuvalov, April 24/ May 6, 1877, *ibid.,* V, 420.

sity of keeping open, uninjured, and uninterrupted, "the communication between Europe and the East by the Suez Canal."
Derby further pointed out that the interests of European nations were so largely involved in Egypt that a temporary occupation or attack on that country could scarcely be regarded with
unconcern by the neutral powers, certainly not by England.
Russia was strongly warned that the English "were not prepared
to witness the passing of Constantinople into other hands."[102]

Greatly impressed by the possibility of English action,
Shuvalov went to St. Petersburg to make a complete report to
his Government. En route through Berlin he discussed the
situation with the German Chancellor. Bismarck advised that
Russia conclude a moderate peace after a few initial victories.[103]
Shuvalov returned from St. Petersburg on June 8 with satis-
factory assurances to the British in regard to Egypt and the
Suez Canal.[104]

In May and June, 1877, rumors again made the rounds in
England that Bismarck was supporting England in Egypt and
Russia in the East for the purpose of securing Holland for
Germany. According to Münster, German Ambassador to Brit-
tain, both the Queen and the British Foreign Office gave cre-
dence to the rumors.[105]

The appearance of Nubar Pasha again in London late in
June may have been a reason for these renewed suspicions.
That Münster was in touch with Nubar is indicated by the
thorough treatment of the latter's views in his dispatches. According to Münster the former Egyptian minister advocated a
scheme designed to appeal to Disraeli; that England buy Egypt
and indemnify Turkey for the Egyptian tribute which was already held in London as a pledge for the Turkish loan.[106] If

---

[102] Derby to Shuvalov (copy), May 6, 1877, *ibid.*, V, 421-422.
[103] *Ibid.*, X, 464.
[104] *Ibid.*; Le Flô to Decazes, St. Petersburg, June 9, 1877, *D.D.F.*, 1st ser., II,
185-186.
[105] Münster to Bülow, London, June 6, 1877, *G.P.*, II, 152.
[106] Münster to Bismarck, London, June 28, 1877, *G.P.*, II, 158.

the German ambassador's report to Bismarck can be considered as accurate, Russell unsuccessfully sought to convince some of the members of the English cabinet that Egypt should be acquired. He reported the rumor that should France give up Mediterranean influence she might be compensated in Belgium. This, in turn, would carry Germany into Holland.[107] There seems to be some evidence that Decazes took advantage of the English belief in these rumors and suggested an alliance with England for the protection of Holland and Belgium.

That the British cabinet did not intend to take Egypt was made clearly obvious in the debates on the Near Eastern Question in the middle of May. No one went so far as to suggest it. Cross, the Home Secretary, on whom the defense of the government's policy fell most heavily, discounted any immediate fear that Russia would encroach upon the Canal and Egypt, and insisted that the defense of the Suez Canal was not a matter of interest to England alone but of concern to all of Europe.[108] However, Cross did not fail to make it clear that England would go to war in defense not only of Egypt, but even of Constantinople. Though Gladstone did not debate the Government on the question of Egyptian intervention at this time, the Liberal leader became concerned in the matter of Egyptian intervention in the following months. In the August number of *Nineteenth Century* Gladstone discussed the arguments which were current in regard to the annexation of Egypt. "My belief is that the day," he wrote, "which witnesses our occupation of Egypt, will bid a long farewell to all cordiality of political relations between France and England."[109]

The question arises as to what factors influenced the British decision to resist the temptation to take Egypt at this time. A

[107] Münster to Bismarck, London, June 28, 1877, *G.P.*, II, 158; Taffs, *Odo Russell*, p. 201. See Hohenlohe, Fürst Chlodwig zu Hohenlohe-Schillingsfürst, *Denkwürdigkeiten* (2 vols.; Stuttgart, 1907), II, 190, for Russell's views.

[108] Cross on May 7, 1877. Hansard, 3rd ser., CCXXXIV, 467.

[109] W. E. Gladstone, "Aggression on Egypt," *Nineteenth Century*, I (1877), 154-162.

primary cause, no doubt, was the impression that Bismarck sought to cause trouble between France and England.[110] Of considerable importance also was the belief of the English Near Eastern military advisers that, in case Constantinople fell, the right of free navigation for the Russian fleet through the Straits would give Russia the command of the Suez Canal, unless England was prepared not only to annex Egypt, but also to keep at all times a very powerful fleet between the coast of Egypt and the entrance to the Dardanelles. Consequently, as early as December, 1876, the British began a search for possible naval bases as a substitute for the annexation of Egypt. By June, 1877, the British military advisers in Constantinople were warning Beaconsfield against allowing Russia to advance toward North Persia and the Euphrates valley and thus menacing the road to India in that region.[111] Furthermore, the British cabinet found it necessary to consider not only the dangers of embittering France, but also the possibility that such a blow might upset the Republic and restore the Bonapartists to power, an eventuality which would gravely endanger French relations with Germany and probably draw Russia and Germany more closely together.[112] That British annexation of Egypt might possibly throw France into Russia's arms was a contingency that doubtless played some part in the calculations of the cabinet.

Decazes, it seems, feared the consequences of the Russo-Turkish war both upon England proper and upon Anglo-Russian relations. The French Government advised St. Petersburg that France did not wish Russia to take Constantinople.[113]

[110] Lieutenant Col. Robt. Home to Gen. J. A. L. Simmons, Constantinople, Dec. 20, 1876, in Dwight E. Lee, *Great Britain and the Cyprus Convention Policy of 1878* (Cambridge, 1934), p. 171: Layard to Beaconsfield, Therapia, June 20, 1877, *ibid.*, p. 183.

[111] A. H. Layard to Beaconsfield, Private and Secret, Therapia, June 20, 1877, *ibid.*, pp. 171, 183.

[112] Newton, *Lord Lyons*, II, 112; Decazes to Le Flô, Paris, May 28, 1877, *D.D.F.*, 1st ser., II, 181.

[113] Decazes to Michels, Consul-General in Egypt, Paris, April 18, 1877, *D.D.F.*, 1st ser., II, 159: Decazes to Le Flô, Paris, May 17, 1877, *ibid.*, 1st ser., II, 171.

The French feared that if England went to war with Russia, Germany might fall upon them. As a result Decazes used the English suspicions of Bismarck's intentions in regard to Holland to good advantage. On May 18 Lyons complained that Decazes showed no inclination to admit that England had any interests in the East. "His plan seems to be," he concluded, "to involve us in a quarrel with Germany, while he keeps safely aloof; to curry favor with Russia by taking to himself the credit of keeping our forces in the Mediterranean, and to be well with us, but if possible, better with Russia."[114]

The decision of Britain not to take Germany's advice and settle the Near Eastern question by a dismemberment of Turkey, with England taking Egypt as her part, was a great disappointment to Bismarck. France's advances to Russia and the possibility of war between England and Russia caused the Chancellor to fear the future alignments of the powers. Among the possibilities apparently discussed in circles close to the German Foreign Office was a Russian-French-German Alliance, but Bismarck considered this idea too impracticable for serious consideration. On May 13 Count Herbert described his father as desiring an estrangement between England and France, but as not daring to play a part in bringing it about.[115] In a conversation with Russell on the eve of the ambassador's return to England on vacation at the end of May, the Chancellor had insisted on the dismemberment of Turkey if necessary in the interest of peace, and had encouraged Russell to do all in his power to bring about much closer relations between England and Germany. However, Derby's distrust of Bismarck's motives toward France doomed Russell's chances of a sympathetic hearing in London.[116]

Bismarck stated that if only England and Russia would come to an agreement on the basis of the one controlling Egypt and

[114] Lyons to Derby, Paris, May 18, 1877, in Newton, *Lord Lyons,* II, 112.
[115] Herbert von Bismarck to Bülow, Friedricksruh, May 13, 1877, *G.P.,* I, 317.
[116] Russell to Derby, May 27, 1877, in Taffs, *Odo Russell,* pp. 196-197.

the other the Black Sea, both might find it possible to remain content with maintaining the status quo for a long time. As to his purposes in encouraging England to take Egypt, the Chancellor left no doubt. In fact, a quarrel between England and France in the Mediterranean was a pivotal point in his broad plan. The situation which the Chancellor considered as most advantageous to German interest was the gravitation of the interests of Russia and Austria and their mutual rivalries toward the East, the forcing of Russia to take a strong defensive position in the East, and thus stand in need of a German alliance, the establishment of a peaceful status quo between Russia and England which would give them the same interest which Germany had in maintaining that status quo, the separation of England from France, ever hostile to Germany, over the Egyptian and Mediterranean questions, and the bringing about of such relations between Russia and Austria as to make it difficult for both of them to join in an anti-German conspiracy.[117]

When Russell returned to Berlin in July Bismarck attempted to reassure England as to his own motives and those of Russia. He told Russell that Russia was anxious to remain on good terms with Britain and that, in his opinion, any counter-proposal which the British might make would be given a sympathetic hearing. The Chancellor protested that the rumors concerning his designs upon Holland had been pure fabrications. However, he again expressed surprise that England was averse to taking possession of the road to India through Egypt.[118] He explained that, with Turkey defeated, Russia and Austria might divide her European possessions. In this event England should take Egypt, and allow France some concession in the East. The moment was not opportune for England to interfere in the war, Bismarck thought, for the time

[117] Memorandum of Prince Bismarck, Kissingen, June 15, 1877, *G.P.*, II, 153-154.
[118] Taffs, *Odo Russell*, p. 200.

when the war might have been halted had passed.[119] Bismarck told the British ambassador that an Anglo-Austrian alliance was useless and dangerous to the peace.[120]

Tension in the Eastern question relaxed in late July because of reverses suffered by the Russian army. However, the fall of Kars on November 19 caused several of the jingo newspapers in England to call for war before it was too late.[121] The *Times* sought to calm the fears of the public lest England be drawn into the struggle.[122]

Widespread mention of Egypt in the English newspapers and periodicals in December, 1877, and the seriousness of the Near Eastern crisis made Waddington, the new French Foreign Minister, uneasy as to British ambitions in Egypt. Derby undertook to dispel the idea by assuring Harcourt that, in spite of the fact that it was generally believed in France that the English had designs on Egypt, England had no intention of occupying that country.[123]

Russia's rapid advance toward Constantinople in January, 1878, caused great consternation not only in England but throughout Western Europe. The British Cabinet hesitated, and only by a threat of resignation could Disraeli secure support for an aggressive action.[124] On January 19 the Sultan asked the English to be prepared to send a fleet through the Straits, but a misunderstanding on the part of Layard, the British ambassador in Constantinople, as to how the Straits Question was to be settled caused the British fleet to be withdrawn.[125] Faced with

---

[119] Russell to Derby, Berlin, July 9, 1877, F.O., 64/879, No. 283; Taffs, *Odo Russell,* p. 200.

[120] Taffs, *Odo Russell,* pp. 200-201.

[121] W. G. Wirthwein, *Britain and the Balkan Crisis, 1875-1878* (New York, 1935), p. 273.

[122] *Times* (London), Dec. 14, 1877.

[123] Harcourt to Waddington, Dec. 28, 1877, *D.D.F.,* 1st ser., II, 219. Waddington had taken office on December 14 in the Dufaure ministry, which was more liberal and republican than its predecessor.

[124] Taffs, *Odo Russell,* p. 213; Langer, *European Alliances,* p. 130; Monypenny and Buckle, *Benjamin Disraeli,* VI, 227-230.

[125] *D.D.F.,* 1st ser., II, 233; Langer, *European Alliances,* p. 133; Monypenny and Buckle, *Benjamin Disraeli,* VI, 227-230.

a cabinet crisis at home, it was impossible for the British Government gracefully to countermand the orders to the fleet and sail it into the Straits.[126]   On January 26 the terms of Russia's proposed armistice with Turkey were communicated to the powers, and two days later Austria suggested the calling of a conference.   The terms placed the Russian armies so close to Gallipoli and the Straits that the cabinet on February 8 decided to send in the fleet and to invite the other powers to join her. The Sultan, under Russian pressure, was unwilling to grant the British fleet permission to enter the Straits.   After waiting several hours the British admiral withdrew, but on February 15 he was given orders to enter the Straits even by force.   In the meantime the suggested conference had made little headway and the situation seemed to grow more ominous.[127]

Bismarck suggested to the Prince of Wales, who was in Berlin in February, and to Lord Odo Russell that England should seek a compensation by taking Egypt.[128]   On February 25, the Chancellor pointed out to Russell that if England and Austria would attack Russia—though he doubted that Austria would act—the two powers could humiliate the Tsar.   But after that had been done, he added, a redistribution of power in the East would still be necessary.[129]   "For his part," Bismarck said, "he should like to see England, while protesting against Russian aggression and before actually plunging into war, occupy Egypt and the Islands" as a pledge and there concentrate her forces. In the meantime Austria, acting in concert, would occupy Bosnia, Herzegovina, and even Serbia.   The effects of these measures, he believed, would probably render war unnecessary and the Eastern question should cease to threaten the peace of Europe.[130]   Bismarck did not limit his discussion of compen-

[126] Cecil, *Lord Salisbury*, II, 191-192.

[127] Langer, *European Alliances*, pp. 135-137.

[128] Sir Sidney Lee, *King Edward VII* (2 vols.; London, 1925), I, 432; Taffs, *Odo Russell*, p. 218.

[129] Russell to Derby, Berlin, Feb. 25, 1878, F.O., 64/902, No. 142; cf. Taffs, *Odo Russell*, p. 218.

[130] Tafts, *Odo Russell*, p. 218.

sations to England alone, but urged them for Austria, France, and Italy.[131] The Chancellor told Saint-Vallier (March 2), the French ambassador in Berlin, that Gorchakov had taken Germany's advice and compromised with Austria who was going to take a pledge in the shape of Bosnia and Herzegovina instead of fighting. "England was playing a losing game," he thought, "and should take Egypt for a pledge, after that the conference could begin."[132]

Convinced that Bismarck did not propose to block Russia, the almost hopelessly divided British cabinet undertook to chart another course for checking the increase of Russian influence in the Near East. Supported by Lord Cairns and Salisbury, Disraeli launched a plan with a twofold purpose late in February. The cabinet considered the possibility of securing some strong base in the Eastern Mediterranean. In a meeting of March 2, Mytilene, St. Jean d'Acre, and a post on the Persian Gulf were discussed. It was decided that Lyons should be summoned from Paris in order to ascertain his opinions on the French attitude concerning Egypt and other problems.[133] Furthermore, the cabinet considered the question of forming a league of Mediterranean powers in opposition to Russia. The powers which were to be invited to join this combination were Italy, Greece, Austria, and France. Though it doubted that Austria and France would respond favorably, it was hoped that, once the league had been launched, they would join.[134] Disraeli seems to have relied for the success of his scheme upon the confidence that Italy would follow England's lead, and indeed Paget, the English ambassador in Rome, had reported that Depretis, the Italian Foreign Minister, and even the King of

[131] D. E. Lee, "The Proposed Mediterranean League of 1878," *Journal of Modern History*, III, No. 1, 43.

[132] Saint-Vallier to Waddington, Berlin, March 2, 1878, *D.D.F.*, 1st ser., II, 262-263.

[133] Northcote to the Queen, London, March 2, 1878, in Monypenny and Buckle, *Benjamin Disraeli*, VI, 253; Beaconsfield to the Queen, March 2, 1878, *ibid.*, pp. 253-254.

[134] Beaconsfield to the Queen, London, March 8, 1878, *ibid.*, p. 255.

Italy were anti-Russian. "I incline more than I have ever yet
done," Paget wrote on March 1, "to the opinion that Italy
might join an alliance with England and Austria if war should
become necessary in defense of their common interests." When
such reports as this were coupled with Depretis' energetic
declarations concerning the Straits, it is not difficult to see why
Disraeli's hopes were high.[135]

Lyons gave the proposed League disapproval, and found
a ready supporter for his point of view in Derby at the Foreign Office. Egypt as a military base was emphatically ruled
out by Lyons, who felt that it would excite French opinion.[136]
In spite of Lyons' belief that France would not approve the
proposed Mediterranean League, the cabinet decided on March
8 to open negotiations.[137] Depretis eagerly accepted the offer,
and General Menabrea, the Italian ambassador in London, reported on March 9 that he had begun conversations with Lord
Derby on the state of affairs in Egypt, Tripoli, and Tunis. The
British proposal, which carried no mention of Egypt, Tripoli,
or Tunis, was sent on March 13, but in the meantime the
Italian Government had fallen and negotiations came to a
halt.[138] The British proposal merely expressed the desire to
come to an understanding with Italy regarding Mediterranean
questions.[139] On March 28 the new Italian cabinet, with Count
Corti as Minister of Foreign Affairs, rejected the proposal, thus
ending the negotiations for the proposed League.

The proposed Mediterranean League is not without significance in relation to the Egyptian Question. It is suspected
by some that Bismarck contributed to its failure by his strong

[135] D. W. Lee, "The Proposed Mediterranean League," *Journal of Modern
History*, III, No. 1, 38-40.

[136] *Ibid.*, III, No. 1, 42-43.

[137] Beaconsfield to the Queen, March 8, 1878, in Monypenny and Buckle,
Benjamin Disraeli, VI, 255.

[138] Menabrea to Depretis, March 9, 1878, in Crispi, Francesco, *Memoirs* (3
vols.; London, 1912), II, 95-97.

[139] D. E. Lee, "The Proposed Mediterranean League of 1878," *Journal of
Modern History*, III, No. 1, 43.

stand for Russia and by his insistence that the powers seek compensations.[140] Disraeli had expected German opposition, and believed that the fall of the Depretis ministry, in which Francesco Crispi had taken a seat as Minister of Interior, would facilitate negotiations. However, the British Prime Minister showed great zeal for the proposal and the Cairoli ministry which followed rejected it.[141] In another respect the German Chancellor played a part in determining the course of the negotiations. His statement to Saint-Vallier on March 2 that England "should take Egypt for a pledge," had a great effect upon France.[142] Although the French Government had been repeatedly reassured in regard to England's disinterestedness in regard to Egypt, France's suspicion that England had under consideration a scheme for changes in the Eastern Mediterranean caused Waddington to ask the powers in a circular, March 9, that problems of the Eastern Mediterranean, including Egypt and Syria, be excluded from the proposed conference.[143] In St. Petersburg, Le Flô immediately sought and received Russia's support in excluding the Holy Places as well as Egypt and Syria from the agenda of the proposed conference. Russia was emphatic in promising France support on this point. Russia and France were equally united against England's proposal to allow Greece a seat in the conference.[144]

[140] Winifred Taffs believes that Bismarck's efforts may have contributed to the collapse of the negotiations. Taffs, *Odo Russell*, p. 219. Lee sees Bismarck's hand in the Italian desire to discuss Egypt, Tripoli, and Tunis. "Proposed Mediterranean League of 1878," *Journal of Modern History*, III, No. 1, 40-43.

[141] Luigi Chiala, *Pagine de Storia Contemporanea* (Torino-Rome, 1892), I, 295-296. Disraeli believed Crispi would oppose the League.

[142] Saint-Vallier to Waddington, Berlin, March 2, 1878, *D.D.F.*, 1st ser., II, 262-263.

[143] Waddington Circular, Paris, March 7, 1878, *D.D.F.*, 1st ser., II, 269-270; Taffs, *Odo Russell*, p. 220.

[144] Le Flô to Waddington, St. Petersburg, March 9, 1878, *D.D.F.*, 1st ser., II, 272-273; Viel-Castel to Waddington, St. Petersburg, March 13, 1878, *ibid.*, p. 276; Greece was one of the powers which England wished to include in the Mediterranean League. This fact may have some significance in connection with the proposed League.

On March 9 Bülow likewise agreed that only the questions
pertaining to the Russo-Turkish Treaty should be discussed;
"The scope of the congress is already too great," said Bülow
to Saint-Vallier, "to permit the treatment of other problems
such as the Holy Places and Tunis, questions which would open
the door to new conflicts among the Powers."[145] Two days later
Bülow repeated to the French ambassador his agreement with
the French reservations and added that France's wise and
judicious reservations received the support of all the cabinets.[146]
That this statement as to the attitude of the European cabinets
was exaggerated is demonstrated by Bülow's almost frantic dispatch to London on March 17 in which he admitted that the
Porte and Italy had not yet expressed themselves on the congress
and that England was holding out for the principle of bringing
the substance of the entire Russo-Turkish Treaty before the
congress.[147] It seems that Bülow either deceived the French or
changed his mind, between March 11 and March 13, about
the question of bringing Egypt into the congress. On the latter
date Bismarck told Russell that he was willing to agree to the
French proposal, "but he thought it would be inconvenient to
some Powers. For instance, if England had something to say
about Egypt, France might object."[148]

A factor which may help explain the persistence of the German Chancellor in refusing to lose all hope of being able to
inject the Egyptian question into a conference was the financial
situation in Egypt. Possibly the hope to force the question
and get more energetic action in Egypt on the part of the

[145] Saint-Vallier to Waddington, Berlin, March 9, 1878, *D.D.F.*, 1st ser., II, 142.
[146] Saint-Vallier to Waddington, Berlin, March 11, 1878, *D.D.F.*, 1st ser., II,
275.
[147] Bülow to Münster, Berlin, March 17, 1878, *G.P.*, II, 226.
[148] Taffs, *Odo Russell*, p. 221. Bülow wrote Hohenlohe on March 17 that
Prince Bismarck felt the French restriction of the agenda of the conference only
meant Egypt, and that Syria, the Holy Places, and Tunis served merely as a
cloak for his thought; Hohenlohe was told that Germany could not prevent
any power (if they so wished) from bringing up Egypt. Bülow to Hohenlohe,
Berlin, March 17, 1878, *G.P.*, II, 224.

British and French Governments influenced Bismarck. Prince Hohenlohe informed the German Government on March 15 that Waddington's heart was set against English occupation of Egypt.[149] Bismarck believed that the financial problems in Egypt might be used as a means of getting Egypt considered on the agenda of the proposed conference.

To understand the German attitude as expressed by Prince Hohenlohe on March 15 it will be necessary briefly to review the internal development in Egypt in the preceding months and the reactions of the European powers to them. At the close of 1877 the Khedive faced another serious financial crisis. It was felt by a considerable number of the holders of the Egyptian bonds that the Khedive should have an impartial and exhaustive investigation made of his debts, a proposal which the Khedive, hoping to obtain an arbitrary reduction in the interest rate on his debts, opposed. Finally, the Commissioners of the Debt took the initiative and on January 9, 1878, addressed a letter to him in which they urged the necessity of a general inquiry.[150] Although the Khedive declined to institute such an inquiry, he suggested that he was willing to appoint a committee whose duty would be to ascertain the exact amount of the Egyptian revenue. In spite of the remonstrances of the Commissioners of the Debt that such an inquiry would be useless, the Khedive defied their advice and created by decree a Commission of Inquiry, which would investigate the revenue only.

The result of this decree was an explosion of foreign opinion in Egypt against the Khedive's act. At a meeting in Alexandria the more extreme advocates of the interests of foreign creditors condemned the idea of any inquiry and insisted that the Egyptian Government could meet its obligations.[151] The protests

[149] Hohenlohe to Bismarck, Paris, March 15, 1878, *G.P.*, II, 220.

[150] Cromer, *Modern Egypt*, pp. 42-43.

[151] Cromer, *Modern Egypt*, p. 43; Waddington to Harcourt, Paris, Jan. 28, 1878, *Livre Jaune, Affaires d'Égypte, 1878-1880*, I, 5-6. See also Marlowe, *Modern Egypt*, pp. 96, 100.

failed to change the Khedive's mind, and Colonel Gordon, who
was returning from the Sudan at that time, was offered the position to head the inquiry. Because of strong objections on the
part of English interests he refused.[152] The failure of the
Khedive to make any progress with his scheme and his inability
to meet the claims of foreign creditors led the Austrian Government, with Germany's support, to inquire in London on March
5 whether it would be possible for the interested powers to
make energetic representations to the Khedive.[153] Count
Münster represented the feeling of the whole foreign community in Egypt as strong. "Prince Bismarck," he pointed out,
"wishes for united action on the subject by all the powers."[154]

The immediate effect of the German and Austrian move was
a stronger and more co-operative procedure on the part of
the French and English Governments.[155] However, the latter
were reluctant to permit pressure on the Khedive from other
powers but they were forced to join in a collective protest of
the powers on March 28.[156] The initiative in this action was
taken by Austria, but Germany gave her support, urging the
necesssity of collective pressure upon England and France.[157]

The Anglo-French activity and the action of the other
powers in late March at last had their effect for Ismail issued

[152] Cromer, *Modern Egypt,* p. 44.

[153] Memorandum of Count Beust, Austrian ambassador, London, March 5,
1878, *B.S.P.,* LXX, 965-968.

[154] Derby to Russell, London, March 9, 1878, *ibid.,* LXX, 967.

[155] Waddington wrote Michels on March 23: "Co-operate without delay with
Vivian and support him in bringing pressure on the Khedive." Waddington
to Michels, Paris, March 23, 1878, *Livre Jaune, Affaires d'Égypte, 1878-1880,* I,
15.

[156] Michels to Waddington, Cairo, March 26, 1878, *ibid.,* p. 17; for text of
protest see *Documenti Diplomatici; Affari di Egitto, 1878-1879* (hereinafter cited
as *D.D.*), p. 218. Austria, Germany, Italy, England, and France joined in the
protest. Russia, because of her relations with Turkey, had no representative in
Egypt at that time.

[157] Bülow wrote Münster on March 27: "Although England and France appear to us to be justified in taking precedence in this affair, yet the other great
powers are certainly called upon and bound on their side to take part in the
defense of the interests of their subjects." *B.S.P.,* LXX, 974-975.

a decree setting up a Commission of Inquiry suitable to the European powers.[158]   Ferdinand de Lesseps was appointed President, and Derby went so far as to grant Rivers Wilson a leave of absence, at government expense, to serve as Vice-President.[159] Several conclusions may be deduced from this episode during the tense days preceding the Berlin Congress.   In the first place the initiative was taken by Austria, but Germany exercised a restraining influence.   However, the pressure from the powers had a stimulating effect upon Anglo-French action in Egypt.[160]

England continued her search for a military and naval stronghold in the Eastern Mediterranean.   In early April when Salisbury replaced Derby at the British Foreign Office, the British policy became more definite and energetic.   On April 5 Disraeli opened the way by preparing the French Government for other eventualities.   "You know that we have a desire to remain on good terms with France," he told Harcourt, "and even if we found it useful to occupy Egypt we would not do it in view of keeping the friendship of France."   He was obliged, Disraeli told Harcourt, to take certain measures for the protection of British interests and it was hoped that France would not become disturbed and irritated.[161]   However, Waddington was not prepared to admit any change in the Mediterranean situation. That the English reassurances concerning Egypt had not lulled France into a passive attitude with regard to other points in the Near East is revealed in Lyons' interpretation of the French attitude a few weeks later.   "They have been reassured about Egypt," he wrote, "and they think that if England is engaged in hostilities with Russia, she will be less disposed and less able to interfere with France or to separate from her in Egyptian affairs."   They had lost their great fear, he added, which was

[158] *B.S.P.*, LXIX, 662; *D.D.F.*, 1st ser., II, 290.
[159] Waddington to Michels, Versailles, April 5, 1878, *D.D.F.*, 1st ser., II, 290.
[160] Waddington to Michels, Versailles, April 5, 1878, *D.D.F.*, 1st ser., II, 290.
[161] Harcourt to Waddington, London, April 5, 1878, *D.D.F.*, 1st ser., II, 291.

that England, "instead of opposing Russia, would seek a compensation for herself in the annexation of Egypt."[162]

The weeks preceding the meeting of the Congress of Berlin, June 13–July 13, 1878, were filled with tense diplomatic activity. It might be said that Bismarck's advice of two years before had been followed. Both England and Austria-Hungary felt it necessary to seek compensations. The British, in spite of Waddington's attitude, finally signed a secret convention with Turkey on June 4, which provided that England was to be allowed to occupy and administer the island of Cyprus and pay the Sultan annually for this privilege.[163] It was this undertaking which the British finally determined upon in spite of Bismarck's wish that they occupy Egypt.

The Cyprus Convention having been signed, the British cabinet was faced with the possibility of serious opposition to it in France. On the very day on which the Convention was finally signed, Lyons, writing to Salisbury, insisted that public feeling in France would probably be too strong to permit Waddington to acquiesce in any redistribution of territory or influence in favor of England. "I doubt," wrote Lyons, "our logic doing much to reconcile the French to our exercising a separate protection over Turkey in Asia or occupying a Turkish island in the Mediterranean."[164] Salisbury deplored the prospects of a bad reception of the Cyprus Convention. He replied to Lyons: ". . . we must hope for the best."[165]

Therefore, one of the serious problems facing Salisbury when he arrived at the Congress of Berlin was to manage the Cyprus Convention so as to avoid serious difficulties with France and

[162] Lyons to Salisbury, Paris, April 26, 1878, in Newton, *Lord Lyons*, II, 134-135.

[163] Langer, *European Alliances,* p. 148.

[164] Lord Lyons admitted that Salisbury might think him too nervous and displaying the weakness of most ambassadors in overemphasizing the point of view of the country in which he represented the Government. Nevertheless, Lyons insisted that he would hold to his opinion. Lyons to Salisbury, Paris, June 4, 1878, in Newton, *Lord Lyons*, II, 146-147.

[165] Salisbury to Lyons, London, June 5, 1878, *ibid.,* II, 144.

obviate the risk of upsetting any of the bargains which had been concluded prior to the opening of the Congress.

Salisbury waited until July 6, close to the end of the Congress, to inform Waddington of the Cyprus Convention. Resorting to the logic which Lyons had predicted would be of doubtful use, he attempted to remove the sting by explaining that England had been pressed "by advisers of no mean authority to occupy Egypt."[166] It was contended by Salisbury that the occupation of Egypt might have served British interests and would have presented no material difficulties. If the British cabinet had refrained, he wrote, it had done so because such a proceeding would have been unwelcome to the French people. Moreover, England had also been urged to take part of Syria.[167] Thus the English Foreign Secretary implied that the Cyprus Convention was the least of several evils which might have overtaken France, and in order to carry his point, he sought to turn the French wrath toward Germany and, doubtless, he stretched a point by throwing Syria into the bargain.

The public announcement of the Cyprus Convention on July 8 elicited a storm of protest in France. Lyons, on July 16, wrote that the first explosion of French wrath was even more violent than he had expected. "It is well that you had the Minister of Foreign Affairs under your influence," Lyons observed, "and at a distance from excited spirits here."[168]

[166] Salisbury to Waddington, Berlin, July 6, 1878, F.O., 363/769, IV. Salisbury's letter as quoted by Newton (*Lord Lyons*, II, 149-150) differs from the original copy in the Public Record Office. The letter in Newton's version quotes Salisbury as adding to the words "no mean authority to occupy Egypt" the following: "or at least to take the borders of the Suez Canal." Waddington to Harcourt, Paris, July 21, 1878, *D.D.F.*, 1st ser., II, 364.

[167] Salisbury to Waddington, Berlin, July 6, 1878, F.O., 363/769, IV. In Newton there is a somewhat different statement from the Public Record Office copy: "No policy of this kind however, was entertained by Her Majesty's Government." Newton, *Lord Lyons*, II, 149-150.

[168] Lyons to Salisbury, July 16, 1878, in Newton, *Lord Lyons*, II, 153; Lyons to Salisbury, July 11, 1878, Turkey, Berlin Congress Archives, F.O., 78/2908, No. 23. Waddington wrote of the deep shock of the Convention to French public opinion at being faced with an act which his Government had tried to prevent in the terms of its acceptance of the invitation to the Congress. Waddington to Harcourt, Paris, July 21, 1878, *D.D.F.*, 1st ser., II, 364.

During the closing days of the Congress Waddington had a
series of conversations with Salisbury and Disraeli, as well as
with Bismarck, on the question of compensations for France.
These statesmen, on separate occasions, agreed that France
could take Tunis if she wished.[169] Despite the fact that Tunis
is not within the scope of this study it was the outcome of a long
series of diplomatic moves in which the Egyptian Question
played a part. Furthermore, the same reactions and forces
which brought England to offer France a free hand in Tunis,
caused England to make a new promise concerning Egypt.

In a conversation with Waddington at the Congress in which
the communication regarding the Cyprus Convention was the
point of departure, Waddington asked for explicit declarations
on the part of England of such a nature as to assure France
definitely of her intention to maintain the actual state of affairs
in Egypt and Syria. In Egypt at this time, he told Salisbury,
economic and moral interests demanded French concern. "We
are the first to recognize how indispensable it is for England to
maintain her communications to India," Waddington contended, "but in respecting her position as a great Asiatic power
we believe we have a right to a similar respect for our position
as a great Mediterranean power." The French Foreign Minister told Salisbury further that France wished to be assured,
in the future as at present, that the two governments would
proceed in accord to preserve intact the sphere of their respective interests in the Nile valley.[170] That Waddington's
account of the English commitment is substantially true may
be verified in a dispatch from Salisbury to Lyons on July 20,
in which the former said that England offered no objection to
French influence in Egypt and had never taken any step calcu-

---

[169] "Prenez Tunis, si vous voulez, m'a dit Lord Salisbury; l'Angleterre ne s'y
opposera pas et respectera vos decisions." In another interview Salisbury said:
"Vous ne pourez pas laisser *Carthage aux mains des barbares.*" Waddington
to Harcourt, Paris, July 21, 1878, *D.D.F.*, 1st ser., II, 366-367.

[170] Waddington to Harcourt, Paris, July 31, 1878, *D.D.F.*, 1st ser., II, 364.

lated to exclude it.[171] "As to Egypt," Salisbury wrote, "we have
stated distinctly, more than once, that we do not entertain any
intention of occupying it, and that statement we are perfectly
willing to renew." Having done that, he added, and having expressed a desire to work with France in Egypt, he had said as
much as would be seemly or possible.[172] However, Waddington
wished to confirm the substance of his conversations with Salisbury at Berlin and asked the English Government to put it
into the form of an official dispatch. On learning Waddington's
intentions, Salisbury expressed fear that France would make her
request in the form of definite questions which would require
specific answers.[173] For example, Salisbury told Lyons that he
did not object to general promises concerning England's intentions in Egypt, "but any detailed engagements as to questions of administration could not be taken without impru-
dence."[174] When Waddington's proposal reached London, the
British Foreign Secretary objected to stating definitely that
France could take Tunis. The British Government, he insisted, could not give that which did not belong to it.[175]
Though Britain in a moderated form finally gave formal consent for France to proceed as she wished in Tunis, Waddington's insistence on a definite agreement between the two countries in regard to Egypt failed to materialize. Salisbury hesitated to go that far. "It does not seem to me expedient to bind
ourselves formally in this matter," he wrote Disraeli on September 5; "it may suit us at some future period to push ahead,
and then any obligatory engagement could be inconvenient."[176]

In spite of the assurance which had been given France, the
thought still lingered in the minds of English statesmen that the

---

[171] Salisbury to Lyons, July 20, 1878, in Newton, *Lord Lyons*, II, 155-156.
[172] Cecil, *Lord Salisbury*, II, 333.
[173] Waddington to Harcourt, July 21, 1878, *D.D.F.*, 1st ser., II, 364-365.
[174] Salisbury to Lyons, July 20, 1878, in Newton, *Lord Lyons*, II, 156.
[175] Harcourt to Waddington, London, July 24, 1878, *D.D.F.*, 1st ser., II, 369.
[176] James W. Headlam-Morley, *Studies in Diplomatic History* (London,
1930), p. 62; cf. Waddington to Harcourt, July 21, 1878, *D.D.F.*, 1st ser., II, 365;
Waddington to Harcourt, Paris, July 26, 1878, *ibid.*, II, 372.

time might come when it would possibly be convenient and
necessary to take Egypt. Disraeli explained in the debates following the Congress of Berlin how careful the Government had
been to show consideration for France. "We avoided Egypt,"
he said, "knowing how susceptible France is with regard to
Egypt; we avoided Syria; and we avoided availing ourselves of
any part of the *terra firma,* because we would not hurt the
feelings or excite the suspicions of France . . . . We have a
substantial interest in the East; it is a commanding interest,
and its behest must be obeyed. . . ."[177]

Throughout the Near Eastern crisis the British Government
had been faced with the Egyptian question and its bearing upon
Anglo-French relations. In its early phases Decazes had taken
a bold initiative in the settlement of the Egyptian financial
problems, but Derby, urged on by Germany to take Egypt, insisted that the British Government should avoid any direct involvement in the internal affairs of Egypt. The policy of Bismarck was entirely consistent during the whole of the Eastern
crisis. From the beginning, believing that England's purchase
of the Suez shares meant that she intended to take a stronger
stand in Near Eastern affairs, he urged the annexation of
Egypt. There seems to be no doubt that the German Chancellor saw in such a move a plan for a peaceful settlement
through the partition of the Turkish Empire. However, it is
equally clear that Bismarck desired that English annexation
should bring about an estrangement between England and
France. Though there was much discussion of annexation,
both at home and abroad, the British Cabinet, at least partially in deference to French susceptibilities, finally chose another
course. This course, the Cyprus Convention, was not looked
upon favorably in France. The fears of a strong French reaction, therefore, caused Britain to promise Tunis and to renew
promises to France that she had no ulterior motives or designs
upon Egypt. Nevertheless, Disraeli and Salisbury were never

[177] Hansard, 3rd ser., CCXLI, 1170-1171.

willing to agree to a full recognition of French equality. There was a willingness to work with France in solving the Egyptian debt problems, yet the recognition of a difference in the fundamental interests of the two countries in Egypt prevented England from binding herself too closely as to any particular policy in the future.

France, especially under the more conservative policy of Decazes, sought closer relations with Russia and used the Egyptian question at times to promote that end. Waddington, too, sought Russian co-operation in excluding the Egyptian and other Eastern Mediterranean questions from the Berlin Congress. Failing in this because of England's Cyprus Convention, he sought and received a compensation for France, but at the same time attempted to bind Britain more strongly to the principle of Anglo-French equality in Egypt.

BISMARCK AND THE LEGEND OF THE "GLADSTONE MINISTRY"

A Study of the Relations of the Two Potential Chancellors, Stosch and Rickert

Frederic B. M. Hollyday

The history of the German Empire until 1890 is dominated by the personality of Chancellor Otto von Bismarck. He held the center of the foreign and domestic stage, and he was almost invariably the motive force in government. His description of people and events, often expressed in terse epigram or elephantine metaphor, was taken by conservative and liberal opinion alike as true, or as a close approximation of the truth. Historians have generally followed suit, acknowledging that though his version of events is prejudiced, it is substantially correct. During his lifetime, Bismarck spread his views through private conversations, official memoranda, speeches, and the press. They are conveyed to posterity in innumerable memoirs, volumes of correspondence, histories, and, above all, in Bismarck's own *Reflections and Reminiscences*.

These *Reminiscences* describe a "so-called Gladstone Ministry," a "liberal-Catholic" coalition of the later seventies and early eighties, whose purpose was the "negative" one of replacing Bismarck as Chancellor. The members of this coalition are identified with members of the Ministry of State, with Reichstag deputies, and with intimates of the Crown Prince and the Empress Augusta. The names most frequently mentioned are those of Heinrich Rickert, a liberal parliamentarian, and Albrecht von Stosch, Chief of the German Admiralty.[1] The purpose of this study is to investigate the relations between these two men in order to determine the truth behind Bismarck's charges. It is necessary first to examine briefly their characters and careers and to note their early contacts.

Albrecht von Stosch (1818-1896) was reared in the conservative traditions of the Prussian Army, in which he eventually reached the rank of Lieutenant General (*General der Infanterie*). Stosch had early acquired the reputation of being a liberal, a reputation reinforced by his close friendship, dating from 1865, with Frederick William, Crown Prince of Prussia, long the focus of liberal aspirations. Stosch's administrative capacities, his massive common sense, and his genius as a field commander brought him the favor of his sovereign, the conservative William I, and he was employed as a mediator in the bickerings between father and son. His talents secured him the appointment in 1872 of Chief of the Imperial Admiralty, with Bismarck's approval. The motives of the Chancellor in appointing Stosch were apparently to please the aging monarch and conciliate Frederick William, who was expected momentarily to ascend the throne. The independence of mind and temper of the General, soon made an admiral as well, and the jealousy and fears of the Chancellor resulted in heated clashes between the two. Stosch remained in office until 1883, only by virtue of the support of William I. As the conflicts with Stosch grew more violent, Bismarck attempted to dislodge his opponent from the naval post and from the councils of the

[1] Otto, Fürst von Bismarck, *Die Gesammelten Werke* (Berlin, 1924-1932), XV, 338, 373, 378-379.

Crown Prince. Part of his virulent campaign was to link
Stosch with another hated enemy, Heinrich Rickert.[2]
The career of Heinrich Rickert (1833-1902) is in marked
contrast to that of Stosch. Rickert was early identified with the
seaport of Danzig, as a city councilor, as its representative in
the Prussian Chamber and the German Reichstag, and as editor
of the *Danziger Zeitung*. Within the National Liberal party,
he was known as a man of strong convictions, showing especial
devotion to the more advanced liberal causes of women's rights,
popular education, and opposition to anti-Semitism. As a
party leader, he was not considered of the first rank in an age
when many distinguished men were associated with the National Liberals. Some thought him shallow, weak, and overly
ambitious; even the Mayor of Danzig was troubled as early as
1876 by talk of a "Rickert Ministry." Yet Rickert was respected for his industry, moral courage, humanity, and, above
all, for his "instinctive understanding of the undercurrents of
public opinion." His role in the crisis which faced the National Liberals in the late seventies was an important one.[3]
The National Liberal party had been formed under the
impress of the Prussian victory over Austria in 1866 to work
with Bismarck for German unification and to further liberal
aims. As a prominent party leader, Rickert had frequent conversations with the Chancellor and was a frequent guest at his

[2] These statements are based upon the author's unpublished doctoral dissertation, "Albrecht von Stosch: A Political Study of the Bismarckian Period,"
Duke University, 1955.
[3] Julius Heyderhoff and Paul Wentzcke, eds., *Deutscher Liberalismus in
Zeitalter Bismarcks: Eine politische Briefsammlung* (Bonn & Leipzig, 1926), II,
165, 209-210, 274, 327, 328, 342, 369, 481; Theodor Heuss, *Friedrich Naumann:
Der Mann, Das Werk, Die Zeit* (2nd ed.; Stuttgart & Leipzig, 1949), p. 175;
Hermann Pachnicke, *Führende Männer im alten und im neuen Reich* (Berlin,
1930), pp. 34-38; Oscar Klein-Hattingen, *Geschichte der deutschen Liberalismus*
(Berlin-Schöneberg, 1912), II, 433; Theodor Barth, *Politische Porträts* (new ed.;
Berlin, 1923), pp. 77-81; Ernst Müller-Meinigen, *Parlamentarismus* (Berlin &
Leipzig, 1926), p. 189; L. Bergsträsser, *Geschichte der politische Parteien in
Deutschland* (5th ed.; Mannheim, 1928), pp. 106, 124.

convivial *Bierabende*.[4] This co-operation was shattered when, in the seventies, Bismarck began to turn toward the policies of trade protection and paternalism. The National Liberals divided, some following Bismarck, while the left wing, which seceded in 1880, held firm to liberal principles. Eventually in 1884, the "Secessionists," to give them their common title, joined with the old Left Liberal party (*Fortschrittpartei*), from which they had split in 1866, and formed a new and uneasy Left Liberal party (*Freisinnige Partei*). Rickert was prominent as a leader of the National Liberal left wing who tried to compose differences within its ranks, and then as a leader of the "Secessionists" and of the Left Liberals. Firmly defending free trade and laissez faire, he came increasingly under the fire of Bismarck, who attempted to use the appearance of an alliance between Rickert and the Naval Chief to discredit them both.[5]

Rickert's interest in the fleet stemmed partially at least from a liberal predisposition toward the Navy. The short-lived German fleet of 1848 had served to concentrate national liberal sentiment on the Navy as a national institution, and this tradition continued into the following years. In his middle twenties, more than a decade before unification, Rickert had already identified himself with maritime interests, a consequence doubtless of residence in a seaport. He became the authority on naval matters of the "National League" (*Nationalverein*), the liberal organization to unify Germany under Prussia, and was the author of "The German Navy" for its official publication.[6] When he entered the Reichstag in 1874, he was naturally made *rapporteur* on the naval estimates for the Budget Committee. In this capacity, he merely reported to the Reich-

---

[4] Heinrich von Poschinger, *Fürst Bismarck und die Parlamentarier* (Breslau, 1894-1896), I, 19, 94, 99, 101, 170, 187, 242, 257, 264; III, 34.

[5] Hermann Oncken, *Rudolf von Bennigsen: Ein deutscher liberaler Politiker* (Stuttgart & Leipzig, 1910), II, 441-444; Hermann Block, *Die parlamentarische Krisis der nationalliberalen Partei, 1879-1880* (Münster i. W., 1930), pp. 94-95, 97-98.

[6] Oncken, *Bennigsen*, I, 455, 457.

stag the decisions of the committee and its discussions with the
Chief of the Admiralty, with whom he thus came into official
contact. There is no evidence of any closer ties between the
two.

The Chief of the Admiralty's relations with the Reichstag
were cordial, markedly so when Bismarck's breach with the
National Liberals widened. Stosch invariably acted with
especial courtesy toward parliamentarians, if only to secure the
appropriations to carry out his shipbuilding plans. He used
friendly press articles and such publicity devices as a Reichstag
tour of the fleet, until he was denied funds by the Chancellor
for such activities. Bismarck viewed these attempts to win
popularity with a jealous eye, and his distrust was deepened
by the continued cordial support of Stosch by the Emperor and
the Crown Prince. It is not surprising, in view of the official
connection between Rickert and Stosch, that he attempted to
destroy them both by publicly denouncing them as conspira-
tors aiming to supplant him.[7]

The record of the Reichstag debates, in which both Stosch
and Rickert appear in official capacities, sheds little direct light
on their personal relations. Rickert supported various attempts
to cut the naval estimates, measures which found no favor with
Stosch. At the same time, however, Rickert's statements do
show a great concern for the position of the dockyard workers,
for economy, for protection of private enterprise and the interests of Danzig, and for maintenance of co-operation with the
Naval Chief.[8] The apparent public harmony of the two seems
to have aroused Bismarck's suspicions.

[7] Hollyday, "Stosch," chaps. vi & vii.

[8] See especially, *Verhandlungen des Reichstags*, 2 Leg. Per., II Sess. 1874/75,
22 Sitz., Dec. 1, 1874, XXXIV, 416-417; *ibid.*, 30 Sitz., Dec. 14, 1874, XXXIV, 688-
689; *ibid.*, 2 Leg. Per., III Sess. 1875/76, 28 Sitz., Dec. 15, 1875, XXXVIII, 683;
ibid., 3 Leg. Per., I Sess. 1877, 21 Sitz., April 14, 1877, XLIV, 472-476; *ibid.*, 3
Leg. Per., II Sess. 1878, 19 Sitz., March 12, 1878, XLVII, 477; *ibid.*, 4 Leg. Per.,
II Sess. 1879, 22 Sitz., March 19, 1879, LII, 498-500; *ibid.*, 4 Leg. Per., III Sess.
1880, 22 Sitz., March 18, 1880, LVIII, 490.

Fighting a running battle with Stosch, which found a public outlet in an assault in the Reichstag on the Chief of the Admiralty in 1877, but being continually frustrated by the Emperor's support of his rival, Bismarck turned against Rickert, as his program of protection and paternalism met strong parliamentary resistance. The Chancellor vented some of his spleen in 1880-1881 by trying to convince himself and his sycophant Busch that Rickert was a Jew.[9] Rickert, on the other hand, seems to have arrived at the conclusion that Bismark aimed at setting up a dictatorship.[10]

This struggle with Rickert reached its height as new elections approached in 1881. Bismarck was determined to root out all opposition to his policies and concentrated his attention on defeating liberal leaders. He was to use all the machinery at his disposal, the press, public speeches, private conversations, and pressure on governmental subordinates to defeat Rickert in Danzig. Doubtless, his expectations of success were strengthened by the fact that in the previous election Rickert had retained his seat by only twenty-eight votes.[11]

Bismarck predicted on February 4, 1881, in the Prussian Chamber of Deputies that Rickert might be his successor.[12] In April he remarked to future Chancellor Baron von Hertling that "his [Bismarck's] friends" would find it difficult to work with a "Rickert Ministry."[13] A Reichstag debate on the naval estimates on March 23, 1881, perhaps led Bismarck to his first suspicions of a Stosch-Rickert combination against him. Rickert here backed up the Chief of the Admiralty on a technical

[9] Moritz Busch, *Bismarck: Some Secret Pages of His History* (London, 1898), II, 422-424, 436, 453-454.

[10] Poschinger, *Bismarck und die Parlamentarier*, I, 288 n. 1.

[11] Eduard Lasker to Ludwig Bamberger, Berlin, Sept. 16, 1881, in Heyderhoff & Wentzcke, *Deutscher Liberalismus*, II, 384.

[12] Bismarck, *Die Gesammelten Werke*, XII, 163; Horst Kohl, ed., *Die politischen Reden des Fürsten Bismarcks* (Stuttgart, 1892-1905), VIII, 248.

[13] April 7, 1881. Poschinger, *Bismarck und die Parlamentarier*, I, 369. Georg von Hertling, *Erinnerungen aus meinem Leben* (Kempten & Munich, 1920), II, 38, reporting the same conversation, quotes Bismarck as referring to a "Richter-Rickert Ministry."

point and expressed his pleasure with Stosch's willingness to look into the problems of the dockyard worker.[14] Apparently the Chancellor's first mention of a combination between Stosch and Rickert occurred in a conversation with Agricultural Minister Lucius on June 12, 1881. He spoke of a future ministry in which Stosch would be War Minister and went on to threaten a signed attack on the Chief of the Admiralty in the press, because "he allows Rickert to be elected in Danzig by his [naval] dockyard workers." Moreover, he "will tell His Majesty point-blank that he will not serve with such a ———." Lucius noted that Bismarck was ill, and that it was difficult to separate fact and fantasy in his account.[15]

The election drew closer and Bismarck grew more violent in the expression of his anger. He told his officials to work against Rickert in Danzig[16] and (to link the Admiral with his opponents) privately denied Stosch's correct[17] statement that the conservatives had been stronger supporters of the Navy than the liberal parties. He instructed the Admiralty Chief to use all his official powers to insure the election of a conservative in Danzig.[18] The Minister of the Interior used the official *Provinzial-Korrespondenz* to attack Rickert and other radical liberals, even sending such articles postfree to the electorate.[19] The Secessionist leadership was very much disturbed about Rickert's chances in Danzig and even sought to find a safe seat

[14] *Verhandlungen des Reichstags,* 4 Leg. Per., IV Sess. 1881, 20 Sitz., LXII, 464-466.

[15] Freiherr Lucius von Ballhausen, *Bismarck-Erinnerungen* (Stuttgart & Berlin, 1921), pp. 209-210.

[16] Stosch, "Denkwürdigkeiten," II, 223. The first (and only published) volume is Ulrich von Stosch, ed., *Denkwürdigkeiten des Generals und Admirals Albrecht von Stosch: Briefe und Tagebuchblätter* (2nd ed.; Stuttgart & Leipzig, 1904). The two unpublished volumes are used here with the kind permission of Herr Ulrich von Stosch.

[17] This is a conclusion based upon a close examination of the *Verhandlungen des Reichstags* from 1872 to 1883.

[18] Bismarck to Minister of the Interior von Puttkammer, July 29, 1881, in Bismarck, *Die Gesammelten Werke,* VIc, 220.

[19] Eugen Richter, *Im alten Reichstag: Erinnerungen* (Berlin, 1894-1896), II, 235.

for him in the second elections, should he be defeated in the first.[20] Governmental pressures extended beyond administrative orders and official press attacks. The Emperor himself was brought into the struggle. On September 9, 1881, in Danzig for a meeting and review of the fleet with Tsar Alexander III, William I said to the Mayor of Danzig that "he saw the re-election of Rickert as directed personally against himself."[21] Stosch used all the influence of the Admiralty on its officials and employees to secure the return of a Conservative.[22] Nonetheless, these extraordinary measures failed.

The news of the result of the elections reached Bismarck at his estate of Varzin on October 28. The Left Liberal victory, including the re-election of Rickert, was greeted with "calm and humor."[23] Yet the result rankled, as the events of the following years demonstrate. The victory of Rickert, according to Stosch, was the result of the Reichstag deputy's use of his power as *rapporteur* on naval estimates to further the interests of the dock workers and lesser naval officials. The Chief of the Admiralty noted that Rickert had secured an unjustified upgrading in the rank of dock engineers, "against the reasons I repeatedly presented." As a result, Rickert was re-elected by a great majority with the support of a "number of dock officials and the greatest part of the dock workers," while the "dutiful countermeasures of the dockyard authorities were entirely unsuccessful."[24]

The first action of the Chancellor was to initiate a disciplinary prosecution against the "political [dock] engineers." This resulted in two acquittals and a new bill of indictment, which was dropped immediately after Stosch left office in 1883.

[20] Eduard Lasker to Ludwig Bamberger, Berlin, Sept. 16, 1881, in Heyderhoff & Wentzcke, *Deutscher Liberalismus*, II, 384.

[21] Stosch, "Denkwürdigkeiten," II, 222. Cf. Poschinger, *Bismarck und die Parlamentarier*, III, 34.

[22] Stosch, "Denkwürdigkeiten," II, 223.

[23] Wilhelm v. Schweinitz, ed., *Denkwürdigkeiten des Botschafters General v. Schweinitz* (Berlin, 1927), II, 173.

[24] Stosch, "Denkwürdigkeiten," II, 222-223.

The purpose of the prosecutions, according to the Chief of the Admiralty, was to compromise him as responsible for Rickert's election, "although I was not even there."[25] Even in 1883 a "highly qualified jurist" was not permitted to hold an office in the Agricultural Ministry, because he had *voted* for Rickert, and Bismarck refused to show his support of a "Gladstone Ministry."[26]

The Reichstag budget debates on naval matters which followed the election of 1881 did nothing to lessen the Chancelor's ire. Rickert, on December 7, 1881, expressed his satisfaction that Stosch had made a special effort to meet the problems of ill dock workers. Rickert's further statement that he regretted he could not make as *rapporteur* a personal remark on the problems of the dock worker, concerning which he had conferred many times with Stosch, doubtless reinforced Bismarck's belief in an alliance between the deputy and the Naval Chief.[27] In the last naval debate before Stosch was dismissed, Rickert praised his completion of his original shipbuilding plan, and his respect for the financial desires of the Reichstag. He also defended Stosch on a technical matter.[28] The first debate following Stosch's dismissal brought Rickert's tribute to "the naval administration, with whose earlier Chief the parliament has always worked in harmony for the development of this national institution," and additional statements of appreciation for the economy, decision, and energy with which the former Chief of the Admiralty had exercised his functions.[29]

Meanwhile, Bismarck was nursing his hatred of the imagined Stosch-Rickert alliance. He instructed the Vice Presi-

[25] *Ibid.*, p. 223.

[26] Lucius, *Bismarck-Erinnerungen*, pp. 255-256; Erich Eyck, *Bismarck: Leben und Werk* (Erlenbach-Zürich, 1941-1944), III, 310.

[27] *Verhandlungen des Reichstags*, 5 Leg. Per., I Sess. 1881/82, 12 Sitz., Dec. 7, 1882, LXVI, 257, 261.

[28] *Ibid.*, II Sess. 1882/83, 37 Sitz., Jan. 23, 1883, LXIX, 1028-1029, 1229.

[29] *Ibid.*, IV Sess. 1884, 8 Sitz., March 18, 1884, LXXV, 119. Cf. the tribute of the National Liberal Robert von Benda, a personal friend of Stosch, p. 122.

dent of the State Ministry in April, 1884, to be on the alert for attacks on the royal prerogative by such parliamentarians as Rickert.[30] The increasing age of William I strengthened his fears that a "Gladstone Ministry" would be formed, when Crown Prince Frederick William should become Emperor. He attempted therefore to separate him from any advisers suspected of "liberalism," either by transferring them elsewhere or by direct attack. He succeeded in persuading Karl von Normann, the intimate counselor of the Crown Prince for more than two decades and perhaps the closest friend of Stosch, to accept a minor diplomatic post away from Berlin.[31] He then turned to a public attack on Rickert and Stosch in the Reichstag debate of June 26, 1884.

The immediate occasion for this attack was Rickert's defense of himself against the charge of one of the Chancellor's followers that he and the Left Liberals had "expensive inclinations for ironclad frigates." The deputy from Danzig said that he and his followers had based their vote for the naval estimates on Stosch's "expert judgment."[32] Bismarck, in reply, noted that with the opposition "the Navy is more popular than the land forces," and he hoped its popularity would continue even under Stosch's successor. He also stated that he had "frequently heard talk"—he did not know "whether with or without the consent" of his earlier colleague from the naval administration —that his colleague "Herr von Stosch was publicly viewed as his successor." With English understatement, he admitted:

[30] Bismarck to State Minister von Puttkammer, Berlin, April 26, 1884, in Bismarck, *Die Gesammelten Werke,* VIc, 296.

[31] Sir Frederick Ponsonby, *Letters of the Empress Frederick* (London, 1929), pp. 192-193; Norman Rich and M. H. Fisher, eds., *The Holstein Papers* (New York, 1955–), II, 146, 148, 150. Cf. Gustav Freytag to Stosch, Siebleben bei Gotha, July 7, 1884, in Hans F. Helmolt, ed., *Gustav Freytags Briefe an Albrecht von Stosch* (Stuttgart & Berlin, 1913), p. 151, and Freiherr Franz von Roggenbach to Stosch, Segenhaus, Feb. 3, 1884, in Julius Heyderhoff, ed., *Im Ring der Gegner Bismarck: Denkschriften und Politischer Briefwechsel Franz v. Roggenbachs mit Kaiserin Augusta und Albrecht v. Stosch, 1865-1896* (2nd ed.; Leipzig, 1943), p. 225.

[32] *Verhandlungen des Reichstags,* 5 Leg. Per., IV Sess. 1884, 42 Sitz., June 26, 1884, LXXVI, 1059.

"On this account, I have always regarded this gentleman with particular interest," and he had only feared that the opposition, "at whose head Deputy Rickert stands," would not support the fleet after Stosch's departure. He was pleased that this had not happened. He asseverated in conclusion that "Deputy Rickert has been the essential prop of Minister von Stosch."[33]

In rebuttal, the Left Liberal orator Eugen Richter claimed that the Navy had needed more parliamentary support than had the Army, which had "its powerful prop in high places." He asserted that, if the money had been refused for the Navy, the Left Liberals would have been denounced for their "enmity" and "mistrust" of the Chancellor. He stated that this was the first time he had ever heard of the possibility of Stosch becoming Chancellor. In any case, Bismarck's capabilities were too great for any one successor; a ministry responsible to the Reichstag should follow him.[34] The Chancellor countered with the statement that Richter had not been included in the proposed "Stosch Ministry" and therefore had not been consulted. Bismarck was certain, however, that the supporters of such a ministry, whether with or without the Admiralty Chief's knowledge, had counted on Stosch's "participation, his power, and his connections."[35] Heinrich Rickert concluded this debate by stating that he had supported the War Minister just as much as he had Stosch. He had "absolutely no knowledge" of an attempt to make Stosch Chancellor,[36] a denial he repeated in the *Danziger Zeitung*[37] and in private.[38] The Chancellor was not content to let the matter rest there.

[33] *Ibid.* p. 1077; Kohl, *Bismarcks Reden*, X, 209-210; Bismarck, *Die Gesammelten Werke*, XII, 486-487. Cf. Lucius, *Bismarck-Erinnerungen*, p. 298.

[34] *Verhandlungen des Reichstags*, 5 Leg. Per., IV Sess. 1884, 42 Sitz., LXXVI, 1079.

[35] *Ibid.*, p. 1080; Kohl, *Bismarcks Reden*, X, 212-213.

[36] *Verhandlungen des Reichstags*, 5 Leg. Per., IV Sess. 1884, 42 Sitz., LXXVI, 1083.

[37] Helmolt, *Freytags Briefe*, p. 326.

[38] Pachnicke, *Führende Männer*, p. 35.

Bismarck's attack stimulated a lively press agitation in which the principal protagonists were the National Liberal *Magdeburger Zeitung* and the officially inspired *Norddeutsche Allgemeine Zeitung*.[39] The *Magdeburger Zeitung* of June 30, 1884, maintained that the antagonism between Bismarck and Stosch stemmed not from liberal support of the Naval Chief, but "originated from the basic differences in the natures of both statesmen." The Admiral was not the candidate of the liberal parties for the Chancellor's post, but the choice of the conservatives. The article confessed that the liberals had worked in harmony with Stosch, because "he was a very competent man, who was always open to practical suggestion and to whom the German Navy owes great thanks." The liberals "never proposed" Stosch as future Chancellor, because they knew Bismarck preferred the National Liberal leader Rudolf von Bennigsen to a "Lieutenant General, who, with great services to the Empire, had yet grown old in one-sided conservative ideas."[40]

The officially inspired *Norddeutsche Allgemeine Zeitung* of July 5, 1884, took a strong stand against this "first attempt" to create a legend. It termed as "characteristic" the implication of the *Magdeburger Zeitung* that the liberals would never propose a general as Chancellor, which might indeed be the attitude of the Left Liberals in 1884. The *Norddeutsche Allgemeine Zeitung* asked: "How does one become a Reichstag Deputy in Danzig?" The answer to this question showed that the "former Chief of the Admiralty was influenced at least enough by liberalism to wish to see it represented in parliament." It continued: "'Herr von Stosch not only associated with the so-called Court Liberals, Rickert . . . etc. . . . , he supported them in the political sphere. He was ready to place his relations at

[39] The articles are reprinted in [Dr. Robolsky], *Unsere Minister seit 1862,* pp. 238-245, Helmolt, *Freytags Briefe,* pp. 326-332, and, in part, in Heinrich von Poschinger, *Fürst Bismarck und der Bundesrat* (Stuttgart & Leipzig, 1897-1901), II, 128-129.

[40] Quoted in the *Norddeutsche Allgemeine Zeitung,* July 5, 1884, Helmolt, *Freytags Briefe,* pp. 326-327.

Court at their disposal." It claimed that the "heterogeneous
elements, the National Liberals, Left Liberals, the Secessionists,
and the Ultramontanes" had allied to form a ministry to replace
the existing one, just as the coalition of diverse elements led
by Gladstone had assumed office from the Tories. In this ministry, the "Chief of the Admiralty was intended for the role of
Mr. Gladstone." The journal chided the Left Liberals for
abandoning "their candidate" after they considered him as
"politically dead," and for accusing him of being a conservative,
unfit to be Chancellor because he was a general. The press
attacks continued; replying to another article of the National
Liberal *Magdeburger Zeitung,* which had termed the references to a "Gladstone Ministry," a "bandit's tale"; Bismarck's
organ, the *Norddeutsche Allgemeine Zeitung,* returned to the
charge on July 14, 1884, and reiterated the denials and assertions of the article of July 5.[41]

Albrecht von Stosch was no man to accept tamely the im-
putation that he had aspired to be a "Gladstone" for the liberals. He felt that he had become the target of the Chancellor
and his press because of his opposition to the separation of
Karl von Normann from the Crown Prince; the purpose of the
articles in the *Norddeutsche Allgemeine Zeitung* (he wrote)
was "to kill me morally" before Frederick William ascended
the throne; he was determined to fight back.[42] His close friend,
the distinguished writer and publicist Gustav Freytag, considered the articles of the *Norddeutsche Allgemeine Zeitung*
an attack on Stosch's honor which justified either legal action
or, at least, a complaint to the editor. Freytag suggested that
Stosch, as a general, could call upon a military court of honor
to protect his position with the Emperor and Crown Prince.
He could complain to the Minister of Interior and ask him to

[41] *Ibid.,* pp. 326-332.
[42] To Gustav Freytag, Oestrich, July 8, 1884, in Stosch, "Denkwürdigkeiten,"
III, 12.

use his influence on the editor, or he could seek the support of William I and his heir.[43]

Stosch now took measures to defend himself. He wrote the War Minister on July 15, 1884, complaining of the attack of the "official newspaper on me, an old General." The journal sought to establish his "connection with the parties in enmity to the Government," and he asked the War Minister to take steps to prevent any further attacks "on a general."[44]   A copy of this letter was sent to the Crown Prince.[45]   Stosch wrote Freytag of his appreciation for his advice. Not only had he informed Frederick William of the measures to defend an "old general, flooded with honors by His Majesty," against the charge of being "revolutionary and an opponent of the Government," but he had also asked the Chief of the Military Cabinet to give a copy of his letter to the Emperor. These expressions, are conclusive proof that Stosch did not favor Rickert and the Left Liberals and even considered their moderate program, demanding as its chief point a ministry responsible to the Reichstag, "revolutionary." Stosch wrote further to Freytag that the Crown Prince agreed with everything he stated, but believed that Stosch was "only the cloak" for Bismarck's attacks; "it is the Crown Prince who is meant." The General complained: ". . . that may be quite right, but it only makes the Prince's weakness, in letting it all fall on me, more marked."[46]   Frederick William was "very angered" by the attacks.[47]

The efforts to silence the official gazette were finally successful. The War Minister stated that since the *Norddeutsche Allgemeine Zeitung* was not an official journal he could do

[43] To Stosch, Siebleben, July 9, 1884, in Helmolt, *Freytags Briefe*, pp. 151-152.
[44] To Paul Bronsart von Schellendorf, in Stosch, "Denkwürdigkeiten," III, 14.
[45] Stosch to the Crown Prince, Oestrich, July 16, 1884, *ibid.*, III, 14.
[46] Oestrich, July 17, 1884, *ibid.*, III, 14-15.
[47] Crown Prince to Stosch, Potsdam, July 20, 1884, *ibid.*, III, 19.

nothing. Stosch retorted that it was "accessible to ministerial approaches." The War Minister then expressed his regret at the attack, but still felt he could take no action. The Chief of the Military Cabinet wrote Stosch that since William I knew nothing of the affair, it would be better for Stosch to present his case in person. Although a letter to the editor produced no reply, Stosch felt it "still must have reached the right address, for since then all has been quiet."[48] The attacks of 1884 ceased, but were to have their echoes in the following years.

These echoes persisted throughout the eighties. In the Reichstag debate of November 26, 1884, Rickert denied that the Left Liberals had tried to replace Bismarck with Stosch. The Chancellor, shifting his ground, replied that he had heard of other colleagues, besides Stosch, who had aimed at supplanting him.[49] In the following years, Bismarck attacked Rickert continually. His entire speech on grain duties of February 16, 1885, was directed at Rickert.[50] In a speech in the Prussian Chamber of Deputies early in 1886 he spoke once again of a "Gladstone Ministry," in which Rickert was to have a post, but Stosch was not mentioned.[51] A few days later he complimented a deputy on a speech against Rickert.[52] The following January he once again declared that Rickert had supported Stosch as head of the Navy.[53]

The fall of Bismarck did not lessen his hatred of Rickert,[54] who became more and more nationalistic as time passed, sup-

---

[48] To Freytag, Oestrich, July 30, 1884, *ibid.,* III, 19-20.

[49] *Verhandlungen des Reichstags,* 6 Leg. Per., I Sess. 1884/85, 3 Sitz., LXXVI, 36-37; Kohl, *Bismarcks Reden,* X, 264-265.

[50] Kohl, *Bismarcks Reden,* XI, 20, 25, 26, 28-40; Heinrich von Poschinger, *Fürst Bismarck als Volkswirth* (Berlin, 1889-1891), III, 68-74.

[51] Jan. 26, 1886. Bismarck, *Die Gesammelten Werke,* XIII, 177; Kohl, *Bismarcks Reden,* X, 473-474.

[52] Feb. 10, 1886. Heinrich von Poschinger, *Fürst Bismarck: Neue Tischgespräche und Interviews* (Stuttgart & Berlin, 1895-1899), II, 133.

[53] Jan. 11, 1887. Bismarck, *Die Gesammelten Werke,* XIII, 227; Kohl, *Bismarcks Reden,* XII, 214.

[54] But cf. Bismarck's remark of March 25, 1895, in Poschinger, *Bismarcks Tischgespräche,* II, 223.

porting energetically increases in the naval and army budgets, and co-operation with the new Chancellor, General von Caprivi.[55] In a Reichstag speech of December 2, 1892, Rickert praised Stosch as a "protector of the economic interests of the country" and as a man who respected "the constitutional rights of the people's representatives and who also gave this respect practical expression," actions which had aroused Bismarck's distrust.[56] The Bismarck-inspired *Hamburger Nachrichten* of December 6, 1892, launched a bitter attack on Rickert and accused him of ambitions to become a colleague of Caprivi.[57]

The belief that Rickert and Stosch were close political collaborators seemed publicly confirmed in 1894. The Prussian Government introduced a bill in the Prussian Diet to give control over religious legislation to the General Synod of the Evangelical State Church. Stosch emerged from retirement to speak in opposition to the measure on March 15, 1894. As a member for life of the Chamber of Peers, he had a public platform open to him. Despite his arguments, the bill was passed, but encountered strong opposition in the Chamber of Deputies. Rickert proclaimed that his faction of Left Liberals were in complete agreement with Stosch's views. Nevertheless, the Chamber of Deputies also passed the measure.[58]

However, it is clear that the relations between Albrecht von Stosch and Heinrich Rickert were entirely fortuitous. The Chief of the Imperial Admiralty, faced with the continued opposition of the Chancellor, naturally attempted to establish and maintain rapport with the Reichstag, in order to obtain appropriations for the fleet. His political views were not liberal in any party sense—he even viewed a responsible ministry as

[55] Klein-Hattingen, *Geschichte Liberalismus*, II, 434, 476.

[56] *Verhandlungen des Reichstags*, 8 Leg. Per., II Sess. 1892/93, 7 Sitz., CXXVII, 106c.

[57] Johannes Penzler, *Fürst Bismarck nach seiner Entlassung* (Leipzig, 1897-1898), IV, 273. Cf. V, 164.

[58] *Deutscher Geschichtskalender*, 1894, I, 239, 241-248; Vice Admiral Batsch, "Erinnerungen an Stosch," *Deutsche Revue*, XXII (1896), 362-366.

revolutionary, but he co-operated with all parties, including the liberal factions, which dominated German parliamentary life during his term of office. His duties brought him into touch with a prominent liberal leader, Heinrich Rickert, who, as representative of Danzig, took a strong interest in maritime affairs and served as *rapporteur* on naval estimates for the Budget Committee. The contacts between the two men were entirely official, but, in Bismarck's eyes, this apparent co-operation of opponents was ominous. He came to view Stosch, known as a friend of the Crown Prince and supposedly supported by Rickert, as the key figure in a "Gladstone Ministry," a miscellaneous amalgam of all his opponents who, he believed, formed a shadow cabinet in anticipation of the death of William I. He concentrated his fire on the two, whom he thought the central figures in the conspiracy to replace him.

The election of Rickert by the dock workers and minor naval bureaucrats of Danzig in 1881 led the Chancellor to conclude, quite erroneously, that the Chief of the Admiralty had used his influence to secure the defeat of the conservative candidate. The return of the liberal leader, coming as it did after direct orders to Stosch to work against Rickert, great activity on the part of the official press, and the exercise of pressure by the Emperor, festered in Bismarck's mind, already inflamed by the fear of losing office when the Crown Prince should come to the throne. He attempted to separate his future sovereign from antagonistic influences. A faithful adviser was given a minor diplomatic post, while Rickert and Stosch were attacked publicly in the Reichstag and in the official press. The depth of the Chancellor's hatred is shown by the repetition of his charges in the *Reflections and Reminiscences.*

The legend of a "Gladstone Ministry" to be backed by Stosch and Rickert was spread by Bismarck through the organs of public opinion during his lifetime and in his memoirs after his death. By not assigning a precise date to such a combination, by varying its composition, and by describing its aims as a political alliance to displace him, he painted a picture which was superficially plausible and difficult to disprove. In fact, Bismarck was totally in error. Neither Heinrich Rickert nor Albrecht von Stosch had any plans for forming a "Gladstone Ministry."

BELGIAN NEUTRALITY
AND THE BRITISH PRESS, 1887

Mary Elizabeth Thomas

The question of Great Britain and her guarantee of Belgian neutrality was raised and considered briefly in 1887, then put aside without any real decision. Although Britain had long been interested in the Low Countries, her position as a protector of Belgium stemmed from international efforts to solve the problems arising from the Belgian movement for independence. At the time of the Belgian revolt against the Dutch (1830), Great Britain and the other Great Powers (Russia, Prussia, Austria, and France) tried to arrive at a solution which not only would recognize the independence of those provinces, but would assure the continuation of such a status. Hence the five powers imposed "Perpetual Neutrality" upon the region—by treaty with Belgium they confined her to prescribed territorial limits; provided that within those limits she should form an independent and perpetually neutral state; guaranteed to her these rights; and required her to observe the same neutrality toward all other states.[1] These provisions they reaffirmed eight years later when Holland recognized Belgian independence and neutrality.[2] Inviolability of Belgium and Antwerp apparently

[1] November 15, 1831. Edward Hertslet, *Map of Europe by Treaty* (3 vols.; London, 1875), II, 858-871, No. 153.

[2] *British Foreign and State Papers*, 1832-1839 (hereinafter cited as *B.S.P.*), XXVII, 990-991, 1000-1002; Hertslet, *Europe*, II, 994-995, No. 184.

was accomplished by the simple device of obtaining from the Great Powers the promise to respect and guarantee the neutrality of Belgium, and of requiring that small country to accept the neutrality imposed on her.[3]

Great Britain occasionally felt the need of further assurance. Although both France and Prussia in 1870 gave assurance of respect for Belgian neutrality, Britain negotiated treaties with them by which each pledged anew "fixed determination to respect the neutrality of Belgium"; these treaties provided that if either nation should violate that neutrality in the course of a war, Great Britain and the nonaggressor would co-operate (but not beyond the limits of Belgium). These treaties were to continue in force until one year after the ratification of any peace treaty, when "the Independence and Neutrality of Belgium will, so far as the High Contracting parties are respectively concerned, continue to rest, as heretofore, on Article I, Quintuple Treaty of 19th April, 1839."[4]

In 1886-1887 the protection of Belgium did not seem as grave a problem to Great Britain as the Eastern Question, France and colonial affairs, or the Irish Question. At two points Russia's interests were in conflict with those of Britain—in Afghanistan and in the Straits. Further complications resulted from the abdication of the Bulgarian prince, Alexander of Battenburg, whose kidnapping reportedly was the work of Russian agents. In France, army bills that would provide additional recruits and improved weapons seemed to indicate that that country continued to plan revenge for her defeat of 1871. On the other hand, the British believed that they had no insurmountable difficulties with Germany. In fact, late in

---

[3] Prior to 1907 the meaning of "neutrality" varied. In this work the term will be used as it was popularly applied to Belgium prior to 1914: abstinence from military alliances and from any participation in war, unless actually attacked, but with independence and territorial integrity guaranteed by other powers.

[4] Hertslet, *Europe*, III, 1887-1888, No. 437, Articles I, II; 1890-1891, No. 426, Articles I, II, III; No. 427, Article III.

1886, their interests were drawing them closer to Germany and Austria than to Russia and France.[5]

The general European tension was heightened by the efforts of the German Government to force a new army bill through the Reichstag.[6] The speech from the throne asserted that in view of the development of the armies of her neighbors, Germany could no longer refrain from increasing her own defensive power, and left no doubt that France and Russia were the neighbors.[7] The Minister of War, speaking before the Reichstag, implied that it would be difficult to maintain peace, and indicated France as the chief danger.[8]

The *Times,* which had noted the Reichstag speeches, suspected a political motive, and called attention to the conspicuous absence of any reference to the armaments of Russia.[9] When the moderate-led Government of France was defeated on a domestic issue, the same journal reported that German and Austrian newspapers were taking a gloomy view of the situation and were prophesying that the government might fall into the hands of the chauvinists. Furthermore, rumors suggested a Franco-Russian understanding, and Great Britain did not pretend to have an effective military force with which to strike against a Continental combination. In fact, Salisbury regarded the army as unfit for war against even a second-class power.[10] The *Times* modified its tone, and recognized that a combination of the two naval powers, France and Russia, might become as dangerous to Britain by sea as to Germany by land.[11] A few days later it blamed those two states for the general tension and

[5] Salisbury to Wolff, May 3, 1887, in Harold Temperley and Lillian M. Penson, *Foundations of British Foreign Policy from Pitt (1792) to Salisbury (1902)* (Cambridge, 1938), pp. 453-454.

[6] *Times* (London), Nov. 20, 1886. Note: To give the information then available to the British public, the writer follows the crisis as given in the *Times.*

[7] *Times,* Nov. 26, 1886.

[8] *Times,* Dec. 4, 1886.

[9] *Times,* Dec. 4, 1886.

[10] Salisbury to the Queen, Aug. 29, 1886, in George Earle Buckle, ed., *The Letters of Queen Victoria,* 3rd ser. (3 vols.; London, 1930), I, 194.

[11] *Times,* Dec. 7, 1886.

predicted that the storm would burst unless some means were found to relieve the apprehension.[12] Meanwhile, there were frequent press dispatches relating to Belgium's strength of defense and her proposed changes in military service and in military expenditures—and all of these suggest that the British public was interested in the subject or that editors regarded it as important.

In the midst of this international tension, a startled public learned of the resignation of Randolph Churchill as Chancellor of the Exchequer. It is the effect of his resignation rather than his motives that is of importance for purposes of this study. The press was disposed to condemn his insistence upon reduction in expenditures for the army and navy, especially when the other members of the cabinet, and European statesmen as well, took a gloomy view of the possibility of maintaining peace. Queen Victoria noted in her diary that the newspapers were "full of anger and indignation" at him.[13] The cabinet was badly shaken, Parliament was postponed, and the Prime Minister, Lord Salisbury, was busy reorganizing his ministry.

Such was the situation when the *Fortnightly Review* published the first of the series of unsigned articles on "The Present Position of European Politics," and Britain—already protesting that the time was not ripe for reducing military expenditures—was confronted with the question: What would be her attitude should Belgian neutrality be violated? It might be said, however, that the author was discussing "the recent development of the reign of force in Europe," and for the January issue made Germany the subject. This was broadened to include Franco-German relations, which inevitably turned to "Belgian neutrality."[14] All told, less than one-seventh of the space was given to Belgium or to Anglo-Belgian relations, but for a brief time Belgian neutrality became a matter of concern to both Britain and Belgium.

[12] *Times,* Dec. 14, 1886.
[13] Windsor, Dec. 24, 1886. *Letters of Queen Victoria,* 3rd ser., I, 233.
[14] *Fortnightly Review,* Jan. 1, 1887, pp. 1-31.

The *Fortnightly* article contended that Europe had become an armed camp which could mobilize quickly, but that the two great rivals on the Continent were each too strongly fortified for either to attack the other directly. After describing the strong fortifications of the French frontier, the author stated that the real problem for Britain was whether or not the Germans would pass through Belgium. He felt that it was time to discuss the question seriously and to determine in advance the British position in case Belgian neutrality should be violated. But he suggested that if Belgium would seriously prepare for self-defense, her neutrality would be secure. He doubted that Germany would attack France by way of Belgium, yet he considered it highly probable that France would take a route through Belgium in order to attack Germany, if the Belgians were content to rely upon so small an army as they then had. If Belgium was to be safeguarded, it had to be done at Liége and upon the upper Meuse; until this region was made secure, it might be a temptation to the German staff.

The writer agreed that some might say that Belgium's position was guaranteed by all of the Great Powers; but he asked whether it was certain that in a Franco-German duel any of the powers except Great Britain would come to her assistance. In the event of war, fresh treaties would have to be made if there was to be no likelihood of the violation of Belgium. Under such circumstances, "delays would take place in the consultations of the Powers during which the neutrality itself would be at an end."[15] As to whether or not British interests required the defense of Belgium, the author thought there would be little more danger in Germany holding Antwerp than in France having Cherbourg, and thus doubted that Britain would intervene alone. Should Belgium acquiesce in the occupation of a portion of her territory, British opinion would not permit intervention unless the other powers co-operated, which they were not likely to do. He intimated, however, that if

[15] *Fortnightly Review*, Jan. 1, 1887, pp. 23-25.

"certain statesmen" were in actual rather than nominal power at the time, Britain would be committed to war in defense of Belgian neutrality as soon as it was threatened, but if other statesmen, "such as Lord Randolph or Chamberlain" were at the helm, they would take notice of the tone of public opinion before plunging into war. To prevent action in such a contingency from depending upon the individuals in power at the moment, a policy should be determined in advance. He added:

. . . . That England is bound by treaty to defend Belgium, and must maintain her treaty obligation . . . would hardly be a sufficient argument to induce the British Parliament to contemplate an isolated intervention. The public law of Europe is an important matter, but people would be inclined to answer that we ought not to stand forward by ourselves to be its guardians.[16]

If Britain meant to fight for Belgium, there would be less possiblity of having to do so if she could induce Belgium to maintain a suitable army for defending herself. "If the Belgians could be counted upon not to fall back at once upon Antwerp, but to fight sufficiently to force the hand of a possibly unwilling Government in England, Germany would not make their country a battlefield."[17]

Although the article was unsigned, Sir Charles Wentworth Dilke was soon confirmed as the author. In view of the discussion that ensued, the reason for this article by a prominent member of the Opposition will bear speculation. It has been suggested that Dilke himself favored British support of Belgium, but that he was convinced the public did not. It is difficult to reconcile this interpretation with the views expressed in the first *Fortnightly* article. Internal evidence would suggest that the article was written some time after Salisbury's Guildhall speech (November 9), in which he suggested that Great Britain

[16] *Fortnightly Review,* Jan. 1, 1887, p. 26.
[17] *Fortnightly Review,* Jan. 1, 1887, p. 27.

could not intervene alone to maintain the Treaty of Berlin.[18] It may be wondered if Dilke was trying to call attention to a similar problem closer to home waters.

Dilke's background made him thoroughly conversant with foreign problems. A widely-traveled man, he had served as Under-Secretary of State for Foreign Affairs under Gladstone; but, through no choice of his own, he was currently on the political sidelines. It is known that he was irritated by the Belgian King's Congo policies, and he was alarmed by the growing armaments of Europe. He seems to have been convinced that a government under Chamberlain or Churchill (both of them close personal friends of his) would be slow to enter a fray over Belgium. Since the Liberals were not in control of the cabinet, and since Churchill was not Prime Minister, may Dilke have hoped to arouse public opinion sufficiently to influence an unsteady ministry? Further explanation may lie in the author's concern about the inadequacy of the British army, for he wrote that "England, unless she turns over a new leaf in military matters and adopts a system more in accordance with modern war than her present old-fashioned military organization" could not place forces in Antwerp quickly enough to be of consequence.[19] Belgian defense plans emphasized Antwerp, far to the side of the probable route of invasion, and seemed to do little to strengthen her forts near Liége or the Upper Meuse. Perhaps he hoped to jar Belgium into a different type of planning for defense.

Another possible explanation may be offered for the publication of the article. James Thomas ("Frank") Harris was then the editor of the *Fortnightly Review*. Men of prominence contributed to the periodical while it was under his editorship, but Harris was one of those helping to turn British journalism along more sensational lines—a policy calculated to increase

[18] *Letters of Queen Victoria*, 3rd ser., I, 222 n.
[19] *Fortnightly Review*, Jan. 1, 1887, p. 24.

circulation. Whatever the motive for the article, the question of Belgian neturality was thrust upon the public.

The *Times,* a Conservative journal, lost no time in commenting on the problem presented by the "Reviewer," and devoted a leader to it on New Year's day. It did not profess to examine the grounds on which the "Reviewer" based his belief that France and Germany were each too strong for the other, but held that if this judgment was sound, it was "of the utmost consequence not only to Germany and France but also to England." Recalling that even though Belgium was under a guarantee to which Great Britain was a party, and repeating Dilke's statement that statesmen had never discussed British action in the event of violation of Belgian neutrality, the *Times* noted that not Britain alone, but the Great Powers together were parties to the guarantee. Posing the question of what Britain would do if obliged to act alone, the writer suggested that the answer would depend upon a variety of circumstances, including such uncertainties as the action of Belgium herself, the view of the Government in office in England, and the state of public opinion at the time. Agreeing that if Belgium prepared for her own defense there was less chance that Britain would be forced to defend her, the *Times* added that if Belgium did not thus prepare, no other power could be expected to defend her, "unless the interests of that Power as well as its former obligations require it to do so . . . . We cannot refrain from expressing our satisfaction that the conclusions reached by so well-informed a critic coincide in the main with our own. . . ."[20] The Liberal *Pall Mall Gazette,* on the other hand, gave little attention to the *Fortnightly* except to affirm a general conclusion that no war was imminent.[21]

The *Standard,* the organ of the Salisbury administration, considered that Franco-German relations were more critical than at any time since 1878. The journal may have been in-

[20] *Times,* Jan. 1, 1887.
[21] *Pall Mall Gazette,* Jan. 3, 1887.

dicating Government irritation with the report that France
would revive the Egyptian question. It warned that when all
were arming as if for battle, it was difficult to pay much attention to protestations of pacific purpose.[22] Although, like the
Pall Mall Gazette, it suggested Belgium as the only route by
which Germany could attack France, it did not discuss the
eventuality of a German invasion as a problem for Great Britain. Turning to Eastern Europe, the *Standard* confirmed
Britain's friendliness toward Austria by suggesting that if Russia
should attack Austria, the latter would have the support of the
Balkan peoples, and "assistance from England would not be far
off."[23]

Since Salisbury's strength was uncertain, the newspaper may
have been putting aside deliberately the embarrassing Belgian
question. Great Britain was drawing closer to members of the
Triple Alliance, and a policy of co-operation with Austria in
Balkan matters had been announced publicly in the Guildhall
speech of November 9.[24] As Germany was considered the more
probable trespasser in Belgium, Salisbury may well have been
reluctant to oppose the one country (Germany) likely to check
France. Yet for the Prime Minister to announce publicly that
Britain would not uphold a treaty which she had helped to
make would be embarrassing—especially at the very time when
he was talking about the "sacredness" of treaties relative to the
Balkans.

The German Reichstag reassembled on January 4, but refused to pass the army bill in the form desired by Bismarck.
Again, there was fear of war unless the bill was passed. Bismarck made his famous speech in which he said that Germany
was far from a quarrel with Austria or Russia, and that
Germany did not intend to attack France, but that he was convinced she was in danger of war from that power—whether in
"ten days or ten years" was the question.[25] On January 14 the

[22] *Standard,* Jan. 3, 1887.   [23] *Standard,* Jan. 10, 1887.
[24] *Times,* Nov. 10, 1886.   [25] *Times,* Jan. 12, 1887.

Reichstag was dissolved, and elections were fixed for February 21.[26]

The English press thereupon became more concerned about the situation in Western Europe, and, except for the *Manchester Guardian,* gave it considerable attention. The *Standard* consistently took a gloomy view: Bismarck probably had ulterior motives in his civil tone toward Russia; the Chancellor had thrown little fresh light on the situation; and it would be impossible to exaggerate the perils that threatened European peace. With Germany asking more men and France demanding fresh credits, where, it asked, was the security for peace, and how long would it last?[27] Two days later the same newspaper observed that so long as there were two well-armed Great Powers contemplating war it was impossible to believe in the preservation of peace.[28] Less gloomy was the *Pall Mall Gazette,* which felt that Bismarck had exaggerated the dangers of war, but added that the stock exchange was depressed on the day following Bismarck's speech.[29]

The *Saturday Review* (Conservative) believed that the war scare was promoted by Bismarck to force the passage of the army bill and felt that if threatening conditions existed, the cause might be found wherever Bismarck was at the moment.[30] The *Spectator* (Unionist) considered that Bismarck's certainty of war in itself made hope of peace impossible, and that the Chancellor was not unmindful of this.[31] The *Times,* disposed to regard the scare as an electioneering scheme on the part of the German Conservatives, was not alarmed. Meanwhile, from Paris there were persistent rumors of a Russo-German agreement.[32]

For more than a year before this crisis, Belgium had been worried about her own security. Her army was not well pre-

[26] *Times,* Jan. 15, 1887.   [27] *Standard,* Jan. 12, 1887.
[28] *Standard,* Jan. 14, 1887.
[29] *Pall Mall Gazette,* Jan. 12, 13, 1887.
[30] *Saturday Review,* Jan. 15, 1887.
[31] *Spectator,* Jan. 15, 1887.   [32] *Times,* Jan. 13, 1887.

pared, she had not kept her forts in good condition, and she
feared that the Meuse Valley might serve as a highway for
German operations against France. Her plans for defense—
adopted some years before the Franco-Prussian war—were in
need of revision. Hitherto the plans had been to make Antwerp
sufficiently strong to withstand a siege and thus enable a "sus-
taining" force from England or elsewhere to land. The *Fortnightly Review* article apparently caused Belgium to feel that
in this crisis she must keep up her courage. A Brussels correspondent of the *Times* attempted to show that Belgium was
secure, but he based his arguments on the premise that Germany, regardless of French fortifications, would take the most
direct route into the heart of France. Belgium, he asserted, had
no fear of invasion by Germany.[33] Yet in reality, the small
country was more worried than she cared to admit, for Bismarck was pressing the Belgian Government to declare how,
what, where, and by what means Belgium intended to defend
her neutrality.[34]

Great Britain learned that "The Present Position of European Politics" of the *Fortnightly Review* had attracted much
attention in Brussels, with most of the newspapers publishing
excerpts from it. The *Journal de Bruxelles* did not agree that
for strategic reasons Germany would probably be the invader,
but it rationalized that the maintenance of a neutral barrier
would be advantageous to both belligerents. The two political
parties in Belgium, it maintained, had always recognized the
country's international obligation of making its neutrality respected; it admitted, however, that there was room for improvement in Belgium's military organization, "which ought to
be perfected without delay." It would appear as if the country had taken stock of her military resources, for a high army

[33] *Times,* Jan. 12, 1887.
[34] Instructions of Bismarck to Count von Brandenburg, Jan. 4, Jan. 13, 1887,
in unpublished documents as cited by Heinz Trütschler von Falkenstein, *Bismarck und die Kriegsgefahr des Jahres 1887* (Berlin, 1924), p. 53.

officer assured Lord Vivian[35] that Belgium could put at least 100,000 well-armed troops into the field "at very short notice"; but he warned that the condition of the forts at Namur and Liége was such that they could not be expected to hold an enemy in check for more than forty-eight hours.[36]

Vivian, however, was not optimistic, Belgian assurances notwithstanding. He reported a week later that the unsettled outlook of foreign affairs, the increasing armaments of France and Germany, and the warning notes in the speeches of Bismarck and Moltke had seemingly impressed the Belgians with the necessity of turning their attention to the condition of their defenses. Nonetheless, Vivian was skeptical of their accomplishing anything concrete. It would take years to build adequate fortifications for the valley of the Meuse and to increase the army sufficiently for it to withstand a strong invading force; apart from this, a further handicap lay in the attitude of the political parties, which would probably prevent Parliament's granting the necessary supplies. The Government was trying, therefore, to perfect the army with the resources at hand, and to put the country in a better state of defense without attracting too much attention or creating unnecessary alarm.[37] The forts covering the valley of the Meuse admittedly were obsolete, but the Belgians were making surveys to determine where earthworks could be built.

Despite the Belgians' contemplation of military reform, there remained the impression that they relied heavily upon receiving outside help should the country need it. If there was any doubt that the Belgians were depending upon British backing, that doubt was removed when the Belgian Foreign Minister, Prince de Chimay, told Vivian emphatically that the policy and plans of Belgium rested entirely upon the assumption that she could rely on the support of England in the event

[35] British Minister to Belgium.
[36] Vivian to Iddlesleigh, Brussels, Jan. 7, 1887, F.O., 10/498, No. 7.
[37] Vivian to Salisbury, Brussels, Jan. 15, 1887, F.O., 10/498, No. 16, confidential.

of her neutrality being seriously threatened; if assurance of
that support was not given, a complete change of policy by
Belgium would be necessary. Seemingly, if her territory were
violated, Belgium would actively take the side of the other
belligerent.[38]

Belgium persistently sought reassurance of Great Britain's
willingness to assist her. Two days after Bismarck's Reichstag
speech, Count de Jonghe d'Ardoye, Belgian minister to Austria-
Hungary, discussed the *Fortnightly Review* article with Sir
August Paget in Vienna.[39] The latter seems to have said that
Great Britain, if she did not want to give up the influence she
had so far exerted in Europe, would have to defend Belgian
neutrality under all circumstances, just as in 1870.[40] This was
the position of the first Salisbury administration, and it was so
stated by Sir Philip Currie (then Assistant Under-Secretary of
State for Foreign Affairs for Great Britain). Asked by Bismarck
whether England would fight if Belgium were attacked, Currie
had replied that ever since he had been in the Foreign Office,
Belgium and Constantinople had been regarded as places his
country would fight to defend.[41] Sir August, in replying to
d'Ardoye, merely assumed that the views of the earlier Salisbury Government were still in effect.

The British press, however, continued to question whether—
or to what extent—Britain was obligated to Belgium. The *Pall
Mall Gazette*[42] admired the Chancellor's boldness in speaking

[38] Vivian to Salisbury, Brussels, Jan. 18, 1887, F.O., 10/498, No. 37, confidential.

[39] Ambassador to Austria-Hungary.

[40] Conversation of the Belgian minister with the English ambassador in
Vienna, Jan. 13, 1887, German translation in *Die Belgischen Dokumente zur
Vorgeschichte des Weltskrieges 1885-1914*, Bernhard Schwertfeger, ed. (9 vols.;
Berlin, 1925), IX, zweiter Kommentarband, 123.

[41] Summary of a memorandum by Sir Philip Currie of his conversations with
Prince Bismarck, Sept. 28-30, 1885, in Lady Gwendolyn Cecil, *Life of Robert,
Marquis of Salisbury* (4 vols.; London, 1931), III, 259. Hereinafter cited as
Salisbury.

[42] The editor, William Thomas Stead, served as assistant editor while John
Morley was editor, 1880-1883. When Morley, a Gladstonian Liberal, went into
politics, 1883, Stead succeeded him as editor, a position which he held until

out and proposed that after Britain had ceased discussing the bearing of his speech upon questions of peace and war, it might consider the moral to be drawn. The majority of Englishmen, it believed, felt that Belgium would have to work out her own salvation. The people should require Bismarckian frankness from the Foreign Secretary, who was a responsible official; it suggested that a Foreign Minister who would proclaim that Britain had no vital interests outside her own dominions would be a truly great man. Perhaps the purpose was to sting Salisbury into some commitment, for the writer asked:

Will he [Salisbury] . . . take heart and proclaim the pax Britannica to Europe? The Minister who shall first declare that the English people have no vital interest anywhere outside the dominions of the Queen . . . will be the first Chancellor of Great Britain.[43]

During the interval preceding the elections, Bismarck did not permit fear of war to abate. The *Daily News* (Liberal) took a different view and proclaimed: "There is imminent risk of almost immediate war between France and Germany. The Cabinet met on Saturday, and its members know that what we say is true."[44] Despite the alarmist note of the *Daily News*, the British press tended to regard the Franco-German situation as serious but not critical. In discussions of Belgian neutrality, it questioned, "What would England do if war *should* break out between France and Germany, and Belgium be violated?" rather than "What will England do with regard to Belgium when war does break out between France and Germany?"

The *Pall Mall Gazette* acknowledged the *Daily News* article on the day of its appearance, but denied that war was imminent. It warned—as had the "Reviewer"—that Englishmen should look ahead and determine what position they would take in the event of war between "the two giants." It reasoned: Con-

1889. Albert Shaw, "William T. Stead," *Review of Reviews*, XLV (June, 1912), 689-695.
[43] *Pall Mall Gazette*, Jan. 19, 1887.
[44] *Daily News*, Jan. 24, 1887.

trary to general impression, Great Britain had no obligation to
Belgium from the Treaty of 1870, which had been made to insure an ally for Britain if she should have to intervene on behalf
of Belgium. With the Treaties of 1870 at an end, Britain was
held bound by the 1839 treaty to go to war with "either France
or Germany or both, with or without allies, if either or both
should violate the neutral territory of Belgium." Thus the
country was left alone with Belgium on her hands. It might
be its duty to try to keep the powers out of the old cockpit of
Europe, but it was not bound to undertake an impossibility.

And it is quite impossible [the article went on] for England to hurl
back French or German armies from the Belgian frontier if they
choose to take that road. All that we can do is to declare war
against the Power that first violates that neutrality of Belgium. In
other words, we can do as Mr. Gladstone undertook to do in 1870.
Will Lord Salisbury follow suit?[45]

Salisbury's hands were still tied. Until Parliament met he
could not be certain of his strength as head of a coalition cabinet and was therefore in no position to take a firm stand with
regard to conditions in western Europe. He wrote to the
Queen that the prospect was very gloomy abroad, but that Great
Britain, because of domestic and Balkan affairs, could not
brighten it.

The highest interests would be risked here at home, while nothing
effective could be done by us to keep peace on the Continent. We
have absolutely no power to restrain either France or Germany,
while all the power and influence we have will be needed to defend
our influence in the South-East of Europe.[46]

When Parliament convened (January 27), the speech from
the throne was of no particular significance, merely stating that
"My relations with all foreign Powers continue to be friend-

[45] *Pall Mall Gazette,* Jan. 24, 1887.
[46] Salisbury to the Queen, Jan. 24, 1887, in *Letters of Queen Victoria,* 3rd ser.,
I, 262.

ly."[47] Salisbury, on the other hand, said that nothing had occurred during the last few weeks to make the danger seem more acute, and the ambassadors at Berlin and Paris believed that conditions were not warlike but peaceful. He did admit, however, there was danger to peace from the growth of armaments.[48]

For the next few weeks the British press in general regarded the situation as grave, a point of view reflected in two widely discussed problems—the reduction of the Royal Horse Artillery[49] and the relation of Great Britain to France, Germany, and Belgium. Parliament discussed the condition of the army; many quarters gave thought to home defense; the *Saturday Review* became agitated over the army, saying that if England should send two army corps to Antwerp she would be nearly "denuded" of troops.[50] The *Pall Mall Gazette* considered that the surest safeguard to Belgian and Swiss neutrality would be their ability to defend themselves against invasion.[51]

In Brussels, meanwhile, rumors foretold the outbreak of war on the Belgian frontier in May or June, and no less an authority than "a recent Council of Belgian generals" was credited as being the source of this information.[52] In the Chambers there was much talk of improving the army and fortifications. Enlarging an army and strengthening fortifications would have been appropriate defense measures had sufficient time been available, but if Bismarck's pronouncements were well founded, a strong protector would be the surer means of defense. Belgium seems to have felt that, in the light of British press discussion, it needed further assurance of support. Another conference between representatives of the two Governments was

---

[47] T. C. Hansard, *Parliamentary Debates of Great Britain*, 3d ser. (hereinafter cited as Hansard), 1887, CCCX, 3.

[48] Hansard, 3rd ser., CCCX, 37.

[49] First notice of this was given by an "Order from the War Office," of Jan. 21, 1887. *Times*, Jan. 22, 1887.

[50] *Saturday Review*, Jan. 29, 1887.

[51] *Pall Mall Gazette*, Jan. 31, 1887.

[52] *Times*, Jan. 20, 1887; *Pall Mall Gazette*, Jan. 21, 1887.

held in Brussels on January 27, but British and Belgian accounts of the meeting are not entirely in agreement. According to the Belgian version, Vivian said that in case of war
Belgium could count upon England, though the English forces
on hand were not large and in the beginning Belgium would
have to defend herself.[53] Although such a statement of British
policy agrees with that given by Paget in Vienna on January
13, it is not in agreement with the report of Vivian. The
Belgian Prime Minister, he wrote, dined with him on the evening of January 27, and "significantly repeated what Prince de
Chimay had previously said . . . that the King's Government
confidently assumed that they might rely, in case of need, on
the support and help of England in resisting any violation of
the neutrality of Belgium." The dispatch does not indicate
that any reply was given.[54]

A few days later there was again a conversation between
Beernaert and Vivian, when the former inquired as to the possibility of Britain's renewing the special engagements of 1870 for
the defense of Belgian neutrality. Vivian said that he was not
in a position to answer, but he believed that the policy had
been questioned even at the time it was made.[55] Salisbury made
no reply.[56] The diplomatic corps was given no notice of a
change in the Government's policy toward Belgium.

While the problem continued to receive attention from the
British press, the *Fortnightly Review*, with its series of articles
entitled "The Present Position of European Politics," next gave
emphasis to France and devoted only one paragraph to the
Belgian problem. The author merely advised those who believed in the value of the neutralization of Belgium to read the

[53] Letter (Jan. 27, 1887) found among the papers of Baron Lambermont, in
German translation, *Belg. D.*, II, 120-121.
[54] Vivian to Salisbury, Brussels, Jan. 28, 1887, F.O., 10/498, No. 26, confidential.
[55] Vivian to Salisbury, Brussels, Jan. 31, 1887, F.O., 10/498, No. 29, confidential.
[56] Temperley and Penson, *Foreign Policy*, p. 445.

correspondence of 1870 when Austria and Russia refused to support Great Britain in defense of that country.[57] In short, he renewed his warning that should Britain intervene on behalf of Belgium she would find herself acting alone.

A writer in the *National Review* believed that as the Franco-German border was so strongly fortified, Bismarck would not observe a treaty too scrupulously if his military leaders advised against it. Belgian territory might thus be violated with or without the consent of the cabinet at Brussels, for the Belgian army was in no condition to protect the country.[58] In its reviews of "Politics at Home and Abroad," this periodical supported its contributor. It should be possible, it concluded, to obtain from Germany a guarantee that the territory of Belgium would not be violated permanently, and that at the end of the struggle Belgian neutrality and independence "would be rigorously respected. . . . If Bismarck gave this assurance England would be idiotic to damage her own interests to forbid a temporary use of a right of way."[59] It counseled Great Britain to avoid aiding her time-honored enemy, France, and to conserve her forces; should Germany violate her promise, Belgium would be in the hands of a country without a navy, and the small British army would not have been decimated by a struggle against Germany.

On the opening day of Parliament, the *Standard* surveyed foreign affairs: Great Britain was at peace with all of the powers; her relations with Germany were excellent; her bonds with France were not quite so close as with Germany, while with Italy and Austria there was a community of interest.[60] It enlarged upon the thesis propounded by the *National Review* when it published a letter to the editor on "The Neutrality of Belgium" by "Diplomaticus." Presenting the picture of the

---

[57] *Fortnightly Review,* Feb. 1, 1887, p. 171.
[58] A. Hilliard Atteridge, "The Military Frontier of France," *National Review,* Feb., 1887, p. 846.
[59] *National Review,* Feb., 1887, p. 856.
[60] *Standard,* Jan. 27, 1887.

Franco-German border as so well fortified that the easier way
for either of the two to invade the other was by way of Belgium,
the writer raised the question of Britain's attitude in such an
eventuality, and suggested that the temporary use of a right of
way was different from permanent occupation and that the
British people should decide in advance what their attitude
would be. In answer to the question, "Must not England honour its signature and be faithful to its public pledges?" "Diplomaticus" offered this solution:

. . . your Foreign Minister ought to be equal to the task of meeting
this objection without committing England to war. The temporary
use of a right of way is something different from a permanent and
wrongful possession of territory; and surely England would easily
be able to obtain from Prince Bismarck ample and adequate
guarantee that, at the close of the conflict, the territory of Belgium
should remain intact as before.
You will see, Sir, that I raise in a very few words an exceedingly
important question. It is for the English people to perpend and
pronounce. But it is high time they reflected on it.[61]

Much significance was attached to the "Diplomaticus" letter
because it was attributed to Alfred Austin. Editor of the
National Review, friend of Salisbury, and author of many leading articles for the *Standard,* Austin sometimes tried to call
attention anonymously to phases of Salisbury's policy upon
which the Prime Minister himself preferred not to comment.[62]
Moreover, Austin was a close friend of Churchill's successor as
Chancellor of the Exchequer and became his official secretary.
To what extent—if at all—the Conservative leader was consulted
with regard to the "Diplomaticus" letter is not known,[63] but it
may safely be assumed that Austin would not publicly propose
a policy distasteful to his friends in high government positions.
Certainly Salisbury in November had defined Britain's Continental policy as "action in concert with the other Powers," but

[61] *Ibid.,* Feb. 4, 1887.
[62] Cecil, *Salisbury,* IV, 55-57.
[63] *Ibid.,* IV, 58-59, 61.

not the fulfilment of obligations to those who did not think it necessary to protect themselves.[64] The policy suggested by "Diplomaticus" would seem to be in accord with that of the Prime Minister.

Great Britain had foreign problems of greater magnitude than that of Belgium, and Salisbury was then drawing closer to the Central Powers. There were discussions with Austria-Hungary and with Italy, and the result was that (on February 12) Salisbury and the Italian ambassador exchanged nonidentic notes pertaining to the maintenance of the status quo in the Mediterranean. The Austro-Hungarian Government, when informed of the agreement, proposed a similar exchange of ideas between Austria and Great Britain. This was done (March 24) and on the same day notes were exchanged relative to Austria's adherence to the Anglo-Italian agreement.[65] Since British interests could best be furthered by co-operation with these two powers, Salisbury preferred not to impair that relationship by committing the country to close co-operation with France, which protection of Belgium against Germany might do. The "Diplomaticus" letter was generally regarded as anticipating Salisbury's policy.

What the cabinet could do in any circumstances would be conditioned by public opinion. That Parliament did not oppose the "Diplomaticus" policy may be inferred from the lack of Parliamentary discussion of the subject. There was discussion of the state of the military and naval forces, but Belgian neutrality passed unnoticed. Prompted by the "Diplomaticus" letter, the press did take up the Belgian problem and by devious routes reached the same conclusion as "Diplomaticus."

[64] Salisbury's speech at the Guildhall, Nov. 9, 1886. *Times*, Nov. 10, 1886.

[65] Salisbury to the Queen, Feb. 2, 5, 1887, in Cecil, *Salisbury*, IV, 20-22; Salisbury to the Queen, Feb. 10, 26, 1887, *Letters of Queen Victoria*, 3rd ser., I, 272-273, 276; Salisbury to Corti, Feb. 12, 1887. Quoted in *British Documents on the Origins of the War, 1898-1914* (hereinafter cited as *B.D.*), G. P. Gooch and H. Templerley, eds. (11 vols.; London, 1933), VIII, 2, No. 1 (b); Corti to Karolyi, London, March 24, 1887, *B.D.*, VIII, 6-7, No. 1, annex iii, editor's note, *B.D.*, VIII, 2.

The decision against intervention was not restricted by party affiliation. The *Morning Post* (Conservative) felt that Great Britain should not allow treaties to be violated without a protest. The dignified and natural course would be to protest against the violation and take steps to insure that at the end of the conflict Belgian territory would remain intact.[66] The *Morning Post* would take no risks to protect Belgium.

The *Pall Mall Gazette,* in an article entitled "England and Belgium, Are We Bound to Intervene, There Is No Guarantee," went even further and argued that the "Diplomaticus" letter could be summed up by two statements: (1) England was under treaty obligation to defend Belgian neutrality, but (2) because of altered circumstances (since 1839), England must "pocket her pledges"—against Germany at any rate. The *Gazette* feared that the "Diplomaticus" pronouncement would be misinterpreted abroad—that Germany would consider it as official permission to invade Belgium, and that France would view it as admission of an obligation which Britain lacked the daring to fulfil. The *Standard*'s argument, it continued, rested upon the false assumption that Great Britain was bound to defend Belgium. The *Gazette* insisted that the 1839 treaty was not a guarantee of Belgian neutrality, but rather a five-power guarantee to the Netherlands of the treaty contracted between that country and Belgium.[67]

On the following day the same newspaper took issue with the *Morning Post* for having said that "the treaty of the 15th November, 1831, was canceled by the treaties of the 19th April, 1839, *but the provisions regarding the neutrality of Belgium remained intact.*"[68] Reaffirming that by the 1839 treaty the guarantee disappeared, the *Pall Mall Gazette* expressed surprise

[66] *Morning Post,* Feb. 4, 1887. Quoted in J. S. Ewart, *Roots and Causes of the War, 1914-1918* (New York, 1926), p. 436.

[67] In so reasoning, the journal was ignoring Article I of the treaty between the five powers and Belgium, and Article II of the treaty between the five powers and the Netherlands, 1839. For these treaties see Hertslet, *Europe,* II; and *B.S.P.,* XXVII.

[68] Quoted from the *Morning Post* by the *Pall Mall Gazette,* Feb. 5, 1887.

that the *Morning Post* went to such pains to prove that a guarantee existed, since it would recommend no action save a protest. "To construct a non-existent guarantee in order to have the privilege of uttering an unavailing protest is surely the very superfluity of futility." The *Gazette* was even more critical of the *Standard*, which it said "constructed" a guarantee, but would not have Britain fulfil it. The *Standard* (charged the *Gazette*) would assert the guarantee against every one in general, but would withdraw it against anyone in particular. Again it denied the existence of a guarantee, concluding that "with such absurdities staring them in the face, it is surprising that our contemporaries do not take the trouble to ascertain that the guarantee which they are so ingeniously but unheroically whittling down does not in fact exist at all.[69]

On the day after the publication of the "Diplomaticus" letter, the *Spectator* believed that the probabilities were "in favor of a speedy war." Arguing that the guarantee did not bind Great Britain to fight alone, it predicted that she "would take out her opera glasses in order to play better the role of an interested spectator watching thrusts in a duel." Certain that public opinion opposed British participation in war, that journal continued:

Our guarantee for her [Belgium] is not a solitary one, and would not bind us to fight alone; but there are general interests to be considered. The probability is that we shall insist on her not becoming a theatre of war, but shall not bar—as indeed we can not bar—the traversing of her soil.[70]

The *Spectator* was convinced that Great Britain would not intervene.

The *Saturday Review* was of the opinion that if France and Germany really intended war, they would not have talked so much about it, but would have talked of peace. The "next war," when it came, would be general, and Britain would prob-

[69] *Pall Mall Gazette*, Feb. 5, 1887.
[70] *Spectator*, Feb. 5, 1887.

ably be drawn into it. Should she ignore an attack on Belgian neutrality, such inaction would bring its own punishment:

The victorious party, or in the event of a general *mêlée,* some party feeling the temptation and seeing the opportunity, would certainly presume still further on the pusillanimity of Great Britain, and Englishmen, if they could not be honourably challenged into fighting, would be kicked and plundered into it.[71]

This journal's advocacy of protection stood practically apart from the remainder of the press.

The press was pleased with reports of the Chamber's discussion of improving the Belgian defenses and the army. Observing these with satisfaction, the *Standard* considered it certain that the neutrality of the country would be respected "in proportion" as other states were convinced of Belgium's ability to defend herself.[72] The *Manchester Guardian* was not quite so well pleased. It already doubted that Britain was in a position to stretch out a strong arm of defense if her honor or her interests should be assailed in the immediate future. The best soldiers and best sailors, it said, agreed that the country was not properly prepared for defense either at home or on the ocean and that a reform was needed in the army. The journal was inclined to regard Belgium's having to increase its army as casting doubt upon the character of the guaranteeing powers:

It seems like a satire on the character of the Great Powers that a state whose neutrality was agreed to and guaranteed some fifty years ago should be able to place so little faith in treaties as to be preparing to defend itself. This is perhaps to the student of European affairs a fact of far greater significance than any modification in Belgian armaments. . . .[73]

All civilized people, it argued, were peaceful, yet were devoting their energies to warlike preparations. Germany seemed to be responsible.

[71] "Continental Complications," *Saturday Review,* Feb. 12, 1887.
[72] *Standard,* Feb. 14, 1887.
[73] *Manchester Guardian,* Feb. 12, 1887.

The Reichstag elections had not yet been held, and the atmosphere remained tense. Whatever comfort Belgium may have received in January from Vivian and Paget was dispelled by the "Diplomaticus" letter, which had been copied by the Belgian press. Through its Foreign Minister the Belgian Government again approached Great Britain. De Chimay, who repeated that their plans and preparations were based on the assumption that the country could rely on British support to make her neutrality respected, stated that failure of such support would involve a complete change of plans by his country. Vivian advised de Chimay that it was a mistake to suppose that the *Standard* or any other paper was the official or even the inspired organ of Her Majesty's Government. The Belgian Foreign Minister was disappointed, however, that Salisbury had made no observation on Belgium's plans to defend her neutrality.[74] The tone of the British newspapers continued to arouse uneasiness in Belgium, but Vivian reported that he was in no position to allay it. Perhaps for that reason the Belgians continued to assert their determination to employ "all the means in their power" to enforce respect for their neutrality.[75]

Meanwhile, Paget and de Jonghe d'Ardoye reportedly held another conversation in Vienna. Paget, too, advised that newspaper articles were generally without importance. He gave Belgium little comfort, however, for he added the unwelcome view that Britain was obligated jointly with the other guaranteeing powers, and that she was not bound to defend Belgian neutrality if the other powers remained inactive. Belgium would do well to prepare as though she might have to act alone. This statement differed radically from the assurances given in January, but was so nearly in accord with the view of "Diplomaticus" that the Belgians concluded that the *Standard* had had the task of inspiring public opinion on the question.[76]

[74] Vivian to Salisbury, Brussels, Feb. 5, 1887, F.O., 10/498, No. 33, confidential.
[75] Vivian to Salisbury, Brussels, Feb. 12, 1887, F.O., 10/148, No. 39.
[76] From the German translation of Count de Jonghe d'Ardoye's account of his conversation with Sir August Paget, Feb. 12, 1887, *Belg. D.*, IX, 123.

The Brussels correspondent of the *Times* reported much surprise and some bitterness because of the attitude of "certain
English journals."[77] The Belgian King's alarm is shown by his
letter saying that it was futile to expect a new treaty of guarantee with Great Britain. He hoped, however, that France might
be induced to make a declaration in favor of Belgian neutrality,
and as soon as that had been accomplished, similar promises
would be asked from Germany.[78]

The Belgian Government apparently continued to ask for
definite assurance of British assistance in case of violation, for
on February 20 Vivian wrote that the only crumb of comfort
he had been able to offer de Chimay was an assurance that
Salisbury had disclaimed responsibility of the Government for
the views expressed in "newspaper articles."[79] Such information afforded little cheer to a small nation desirous of promises
of actual aid in time of need. But there was no word from
Salisbury.[80] A few days later Vivian wrote interpreting this
silence as evidence that Her Majesty's Government considered
it inopportune or inexpedient to express any opinion on the
validity of the treaty guaranteeing Belgian neutrality, or to
make commitments as to future policy.[81]

In the week preceding the Reichstag elections there were
frequent assertions and denials of diplomatic efforts on the part
of Belgium to protect herself. The *Standard*'s Berlin correspondent reported a rumor that if France should try to pass
through Belgium, Germany would send troops to assist the
Belgians. The *Pall Mall Gazette* wondered if the story was

[77] *Times,* Feb. 9, 14, 1887.

[78] From the German translation, Leopold to Lambermont, Feb. 13, 1887,
Belg. D., IX, 122.

[79] Vivian to Salisbury, Brussels, Feb. 20, 1887, F.O., 10/498, No. 54, confidential.

[80] Salisbury's daughter says of this ". . . his silence was, in fact, as definite
in its refusal to repudiate the guarantee of neutrality as it was in its tacit
admission that circumstances might make it impossible for a parliamentary
minister to honour it." Cecil, *Salisbury,* IV, 62.

[81] Vivian to Salisbury, Brussels, Feb. 26, 1887, F.O., 10/498, No. 60, confidential.

true that Germany would enter Belgium, if at all, as the protector, not invader, and believed it not improbable.[82] There were rumors that Belgium and Holland were negotiating a defensive alliance; the *Times* published a Brussels dispatch denying the allegation and asserting that Belgian policy was still in strict conformity with the Treaty of 1839.[83] Also from Brussels came news of official denial of the report (originating in Paris) that the Belgian Government had asked the European powers to determine anew its rights and duties as a neutral.[84]

The *Times,* which had ignored the "Diplomaticus" letter, conceded that the guarantee of Belgian neutrality might be collective, but felt that there was "neither policy nor dignity in repudiating beforehand a duty which, if contingent on events unlikely to happen, is nevertheless definitely embodied in a solemn international instrument. . . ." It asserted that the best evidence of a small state's willingness to defend itself was definite improvement in its defenses and army. Belgium's efforts to increase her own defense increased the assumption that her neutrality would be respected.[85] Three days later the same journal devoted practically two pages (with maps) to a discussion of the Franco-German frontier. After indicating the strategic importance and strength of the fortifications there, it suggested that should Germany invade France through Belgium, she might by agreement retain a permanent protectorate over it. The outlook was not so grave as in the past, it concluded, but the British Foreign Office should decide in advance what course the interest of the Empire demanded in the event of hostile action by Germany.[86]

The cause of Belgium's alarm was disappearing. Bismarck secured an undisputed majority in the Reichstag with the elections of February 21, and the war scare that had gripped Europe for more than two months began to abate. Both France and

[82] *Pall Mall Gazette,* Feb. 16, 1887.
[83] Times, *Feb.* 17, 1887.
[85] *Times,* Feb. 15, 1887.
[84] *Times,* Feb. 18, 1887.
[86] *Times,* Feb. 18, 1887.

Germany assured Belgium that her territory would not be violated. The French Minister to Brussels officially promised de Chimay that France would not violate Belgian neutrality; and de Chimay in his turn said that Belgium would resist invasion and, should Germany attempt to pass through her territory to attack France, her troops would "form the advance guard of the French army."[87] A few days later the German Minister to Belgium gave assurance that his Government intended to respect the neutrality of Belgium as stipulated by treaties—a declaration verified from Berlin.[88] The time for acute anxiety on the part of Belgium had passed, and she could discuss in an unhurried fashion the means of strengthening her defense.

By the close of February, it was generally agreed that Great Britain would not intervene on behalf of Belgium. The very lack of dissent indicates that the decision was virtually unanimous, irrespective of politics. So true was this that an attack made on behalf of the opposition was chiefly related to the Eastern situation, and Belgium passed unmentioned.[89] Commenting on the attack, the Saturday Review said, "The Foreign Policy of the Government could hardly have received a greater compliment than the fact that Mr. Labouchere [considered an especially dangerous critic in foreign affairs] had to be selected to head an attack on it."[90] Apparently public opinion so strongly supported the Government's policy on the Belgian question that the Opposition thought it unprofitable to mention it.

[87] Vivian to Salisbury, Brussels, Feb. 26, 1887, F.O., 10/498, No. 60, confidential; Bourée to Flourens, Brussels, Feb. 20, 1887, Documents Diplomatiques Français, 1871-1914, 1st ser. (Paris, 1934), VI (supplement), 61.

[88] Vivian to Salisbury, Brussels, March 5, 1887, F.O., 10/498, No. 74; report of the German Minister to Brussels, Count von Brandenburg, Feb. 23, 1887; instructions of Count Bismarck to Brussels, Feb. 27, 1887 (unpublished), as given in Trützschler von Falkenstein, Bismarck und die Kriegsgefahr, pp. 53-54; report of Count von Straten Pontzhog, Minister to Berlin, March 18, 1887, Belg. D., I, 179-181.

[89] Hansard, 3rd ser., CCCXI, 48-87.

[90] Saturday Review, Feb. 26, 1887.

Though the line of reasoning followed by the press varied, the conclusions were similar. To summarize, it might be said that by the end of February only the *Saturday Review* felt that Britain should intervene. The press in general, except for the *Pall Mall Gazette,* recognized the existence of a guarantee to Belgium, but considered that it was collective. The general conclusion was that Great Britain should not intervene. The *Manchester Guardian* doubted the country's ability to defend Belgium. The *Times,* the *Standard,* and the *Fortnightly Review* agreed on the possibility of the violation of Belgium, and of that country's acquiescence, but they questioned whether Great Britain was bound by the 1839 Treaty, or at any rate would act alone. The *Standard* and the *Manchester Guardian* agreed that Great Britain would be unable without assistance to protect Belgium. The *Times* intimated that violation of Belgium would probably leave Germany with a permanent protectorate over it, but did not seem to consider that an alarming possibility. All—either by actual statement or by implication—agreed that Britain should decide her policy in advance of any conflict. With the publicizing by Belgium of official and semiofficial assurances that Belgian neutrality would have nothing to fear from Germany, and with the sudden cessation of the Franco-German war scare, the press tended to drop the question. It had ceased to be newsworthy.

Dilke believed that the death knell of intervention for the preservation of Belgian neutrality had been sounded when the British horse artillery was reduced in early February.[91] His article of June dealt primarily with "The United Kingdom," but concluded that two factors deterred Britain from fighting for Belgium unless seriously provoked: (1) her admitted military unreadiness, which would prevent rapid mobilization; and (2) a strong desire for peace because of her interest in acquiring wealth and trade. The realities of the Belgian question might not be pleasant to the Belgians or to the British, but the truth

[91] *Fortnightly Review,* March 1, 1887, p. 354.

was seldom palatable to those concerned. Great Britain, he wrote, in 1870 was committed to the necessity of saving Belgium, but by 1887 she had given up that idea, and had done so "in public with much demonstrative earnestness by many of the same men who but a few years ago were strongly urging upon their countrymen the exactly opposite view." It had become clear that Belgium was not to be saved by Great Britain.[92] *Blackwood's,* basing its opinion on the last two elections in "several" London constituencies, concluded that Londoners had rejected Gladstone's foreign policy, and tried to show that Germany would not march through Belgium. It agreed with Dilke, however, that Belgium should arm if she would protect her liberties, for Great Britain was under no obligation to protect her if she would do nothing for herself.[93] Perhaps the best summary of the whole discussion was in these words of Dilke:

The response to my first article has been virtually unanimous, and it is clear that my question whether we intend to fight for Belgium according to our treaty obligations, or to throw treaty obligations to the winds under some convenient pretext, is already answered.[94]

Great Britain's attitude on the Belgian question had been determined by various factors. In all the discussions of possible violation of Belgian neutrality, Germany was considered to be the probable aggressor. British intervention on behalf of Belgium would mean alliance with France—and an alignment distasteful to Britain because of national interests and tradition. Although the British had no desire to see France annihilated, they rejoiced privately when concern over the European situation prevented her from devoting undivided attention to questions which annoyed them. The best Continental counterweight to France was Germany, whose colonial ambitions

[92] *Fortnightly Review,* June 1, 1887, pp. 785-834.
[93] "The Defence of Military Power in Europe," *Blackwood's,* Sept., 1887, pp. 309-313.
[94] *Fortnightly Review,* June 1, 1887, p. 812.

Britain did not yet regard as a major problem, and for whose sovereigns she had a real affection. Primary interest lay in the Queen's Dominions, and, in 1887, the gravest problem was that of Ireland and Home Rule, beside which other questions paled into insignificance. The *Saturday Review*, surveying the session of Parliament, remarked that there had been no real debate on foreign affairs; from beginning to end it had been Ireland.[95] Unanimity of Government, Opposition, and public in opposing intervention on behalf of Belgium is to be concluded from the lack of literature to the contrary. There was no official decision, however, and with the passing of the war scare Britain put aside the problem.[96]

[95] *Saturday Review*, Sept. 17, 1887, p. 381.

[96] Mr. Seton-Watson, who does not refer to the Belgian problem, believes that Salisbury in 1887 was so concerned with probable Russian aggression in the Near East that he was unwilling to risk offending Germany, who might restrain Russia. R. W. Seton-Watson, *Britain in Europe, 1789-1914: A Survey of Foreign Policy* (Cambridge, 1937), p. 560.

FOREIGN POLICY
DEBATED
Sir Edward Grey and His Critics,
1911-1912

John A. Murray

From the summer of 1911 until March, 1912, significant segments of articulate British opinion waged an increasingly virulent campaign against both the conduct and trend of British
foreign policy as directed by Sir Edward Grey. And while
historians have microscopically combed through reams of diplomatic correspondence relative to the outbreak of war in 1914,
and subsequently belabored the matter of "responsibility,"
there has been thus far insufficient examination, especially of
a biographical nature, of the leading figures of that era. Of
Sir Edward Grey we know relatively little. And yet this quiet,
kindly man, an authority on birds, fish, and fishing, a true lover
of the outdoor life, served as British Foreign Secretary from
December, 1905, until December, 1916, a period in that responsible office exceeded only by Lord Palmerston and Lord
Salisbury. Aside from his two volumes of *Memoirs* and a sympathetic biography by George Macaulay Trevelyan, there is
available little primary material on Grey. He remains a relatively obscure statesman in pre-1914 diplomatic history.

At the time of the Agadir crisis during the summer of 1911, British and German subjects, for the first time since the advent of their twentieth-century rivalry, became aware of the frightful possibility of warring against each other. Reaction to this fear, to accumulated grievances against Russian incursions against Persia's integrity and independence, as well as to Grey's apparent anti-German predilections and his "secretiveness" in the administration of the nation's foreign affairs, all were lumped together into the chorus of dissatisfaction which rang out against him during this seven-month period. An examination of the origins and development of this opposition to Grey, as well as its results, provides the historian with deeper insights into this enigmatic figure of British diplomacy, and also into the impact and growing importance of popular opinion and propaganda. British diplomacy was not unaffected by this clamor, which reached its high-water mark in February, 1912; the Haldane Mission, Grey's resistance to Russian advances in Persia, along with his less strenuous efforts to instruct the Parliament and the public about his foreign policy, are vitally linked to the opposition which gradually mounted against him.

Historians are aware of Grey's failure to educate his colleagues in the Asquith cabinet and in Parliament, as well as the public, about foreign affairs. Consequently, British subjects received most of their information on international affairs from the newspaper and periodical press. Since 1890 the British press had experienced a revolution of its own with the advent of the halfpenny newspaper and a concomitant meteoric rise in circulation. Publicity given to foreign affairs and politics increased proportionately. And while a coal miner from Wales or a wharf hand at Liverpool might never look behind the headlines, he was being conditioned, to some extent, to the significance of international issues. Still the direction of foreign affairs remained the prerogative of a select few. Continuity of policy, moreover, remained the vogue during Grey's tenure, as the Conservative Opposition looked askance at a public debate

on policies initiated by the former Conservative Foreign Secre-
taries, Lord Salisbury and Lord Landsdowne, and carried on by
the Liberal Foreign Secretary.

Although the British public generally considered the direction of foreign policy as a kind of esoteric science, still from
the time of the debate on the Anglo-Russian Convention of
1907 sporadic murmurings of dissent against Grey's policy were
raised. Initially there was disagreement over the Persian "bargain," whereby that ancient land was divided into British, Russian, and neutral spheres of influence. Later, Radical-Liberal
and Labor opposition to firmer Anglo-Russian ties crystallized
at the time of a Keir Hardie-inspired parliamentary division
over the meeting of King Edward VII and Tsar Nicholas II
at Reval in the summer of 1908. The subsequent phase of
opposition to Grey was less clearly defined. Primarily it was
an "attitude" which expressed itself mainly through the press,
and to a lesser degree in Parliament, where debate on foreign
affairs was discouraged, against any entanglement in the Balkans
where British interests were not directly involved. The Bosnian
crisis of 1908-1909 engendered this attitude and it remained
a constant though secondary factor in the anti-Grey feeling.
With David Lloyd George's fulminating declaration to the
bankers of London at Mansion House in July, 1911, which was
considered abroad as an expression of ministerial policy, the
stage was set for prolonged and bitter debate over Sir Edward
Grey's administration of British foreign policy.

It was primarily the unrest over Agadir that transformed
the sniping at Grey into a full-fledged barrage. There was
mounting concern over the obvious deterioration in Anglo-
German relations. One faction in Parliament, representing
what A. J. P. Taylor labels "the New Radicalism," was anxious
about Britain's "treaty obligations," to which Asquith and the
London *Times* made reference during the troublesome July

days.[1] What especially disturbed such Radical-Liberals as
Arthur Ponsonby, E. D. Morel, and the like, was that Britain
was not free to act as it saw fit, but rather was pledged to support France against Germany. Supported by Labor, certain
Irish Nationalist members, and a few Liberals, they would draw
back the veil that shrouded the conduct of foreign affairs. The
matter of secrecy was, of course, interwoven with criticism of
Grey's policy in Persia and his attitude toward Germany; attack on one issue was tantamount to an attack on all. British
desire to see relations with Germany improved was due to dissatisfaction with Grey's apparent determination to maintain
the traditional balance of power, alarm over growing armaments, and other factors, rather than, as M. R. D. Foot has
pointed out in his study on British foreign policy, to any
especial liking for Germany.[2]

Also the Persian pot again began to bubble. There was
already a considerable backlog of grievances over Persia. The
former Viceroy of India, now Lord Curzon, as well as many
former colonial officials and friends of Persia, had not been
reconciled to the terms of the 1907 Convention with Russia.
On the other hand, Radical-Liberals and Laborites delighted in
pointing out repeated Russian violations of the "spirit" of the
agreement. Persistent penetration of Russian influence toward
the British sphere in the southeast of Persia prompted many of
Grey's hitherto staunchest supporters to urge him to abandon
the role of a passive spectator. Persia excited considerably
more interest in the summer of 1911 as British subjects were
treated to a generous coverage in the press of the efforts of a
young, idealistic American, W. Morgan Shuster, to salvage the

---

[1] A. J. P. Taylor, *The Trouble Makers* (London, 1957), pp. 95-131. On July
6, 1911, the *Times* insisted the British ministry "act up to the letter of our
treaty obligations with France. . . ." Questions on this matter were raised in
Parliament, and, on July 6, Asquith spoke of "the fulfillment of our treaty obligations to France." Great Britain, *Parliamentary Debates* (hereinafter cited as
Parl. Debs.), 5th ser., XXVII, 1341.

[2] M. R. D. Foot, *British Foreign Policy since 1898* (London, 1956), p. 47.

sinking Persian ship of state. But by October Shuster had run
afoul of the Russians. In Britain the radical press, supported
by the many ever-present Russophobes, protested that Persia
and Shuster were slowly being crushed beneath Cossack heels.
Grey, they argued, was supporting this intolerable action. Stimulus to the still amorphous opposition to Grey was lent by
Shuster's tactic of appealing to the British public for support.
Pleading his case through the press—notably in a series of interviews with the Teheran correspondent of the *Times*—he criticized Grey for seconding Russia on the matter of the appointment of one Major Stokes, a British military attaché, as com-
mandant of a Treasury gendarmerie. Shuster pressed his fight
in an open letter published in the *Times,* on November 10-11.
In it he charged that documents in his possession proved that
the British and Russian legations in Persia were in agreement to
defeat his program of financial reforms. It was incompre-
hensible to him that Grey would connive with Russia in inter-
fering with Persia's internal affairs.

By mid-November the direct attack on Grey was well under
way. In the *Nation,* a Radical-Liberal weekly, editor Herbert
Massingham wrote a series of articles critical of Grey under
the general title "Our Secret Diplomacy." C. P. Scott, editor
of the *Manchester Guardian,* and sometimes referred to as
"the keeper of the Liberal conscience," argued in a series of
leaders that Grey's policy in Persia as well as his hostility to
Germany needed "cabinet re-examination." A. G. Gardiner,
editor of the Liberal *Daily News,* followed much the same line
in a series of articles entitled "The Perils of Secret Diplomacy."[3]
In a talk to the Reform Club on November 14, which attracted
considerable attention, Arthur Ponsonby, M.P., reminded his
listeners that Grey had made but one speech on foreign affairs
outside of Parliament during the last six months—that (in May)
on Anglo-American relations. And yet those six months had

[3] See the *Nation,* Nov. 11, 18, 1911; *Manchester Guardian,* Nov. 18, 20, 1911;
Daily News, Nov. 16, 20, 1911.

been filled with "the simultaneous occurrence of an unprece-
dented number of events of the very gravest and most critical
importance all over the world."[4]

Lord Curzon, an acknowledged authority on the Middle
East, told the members of the Persia Society at their Inaugural
Dinner on November 15 that it was incumbent upon those who
believed in an independent Persia to admit that Anglo-Russian
diplomacy there had not been wise. Though avoiding personal
criticism of Grey, Curzon made it perfectly clear that the British Foreign Office had failed in its trust. As was the case after
the debate on the Anglo-Russia Convention in 1908, the former
Viceroy received his most generous support from his political
adversaries, the Radical-Liberals; the *Manchester Guardian,* the
Nation, the *Daily News,* even the *Labour Leader* hailed his
talk as a triumph. On November 18, the Teheran correspondent of the *Times* reported that in the British colony the speech
had awakened a sympathetic echo. The general sentiment there
was: "At least someone has spoken." Reflecting the opinion
of those interested in Persia, A. G. Gardiner claimed that Grey
could now be called to task, "for he is not flouting Liberal
opinion only, but the opinion of all parties in this country who
believe that our word is our bond."[5] On the other hand, the
Conservative press ignored Curzon's speech. On November 21
the *Morning Post* offered this laconic observation: "Refrain
from all gossip on foreign policy. The impression should not
be let abroad that Grey does not enjoy the support of the nation as a whole."

[4] Ponsonby's address was published in pamphlet form under the title
Democracy and the Control of Foreign Affairs (London, 1912). He expanded
his views in a book, *Democracy and Diplomacy: A Plea for Popular Control
of Foreign Policy* (London, 1915).

[5] *Daily News,* Nov. 16, 1911. While it is true that the editorials in the
majority of the leading London journals were unsigned, it is also true that there
was little chance of an editorial's appearing without the approval of the chief
editors. For this reason the name of the editor will be used throughout this
study as the one "responsible" for the editorial.

A number of Grey's colleagues in the cabinet and in Parliament also evidenced signs of discomfort because of his administration of foreign affairs. Working in the rarified atmosphere of the Foreign Office, the Foreign Secretary tended to draw more and more away from any outside influence, even of his fellow cabinet members. Well after Agadir, Lord Loreburn, Lord Chancellor in the Asquith Government, hearing, during a casual conversation with Alfred Lyttleton at his home, of the war preparations which had taken place at that critical time, expressed his indignation at such subterfuge. Loreburn, John Morley, and Lewis Harcourt agreed to make a protest in the cabinet against such secrecy. The question was raised by Morley at a meeting in October, and a resolution was passed by the cabinet that "no military conversations in the future would be held with any foreign power without the knowledge of the cabinet."[6] This protest also led to the formation of a cabinet or "watch-dog" committee composed of Asquith, Lloyd George, John Morley, Lord Crewe, and Walter Runciman, which from October, 1911, was to assist and guide the Foreign Secretary in Britain's relations with Germany.[7] Still Grey's secretiveness persisted. As Lloyd George recalled in his *Memoirs:* "There was a reticence and secrecy [at the Foreign Office] which practically ruled out three-fourths of the Cabinet from the chance of making any genuine contribution to the momentous questions then fermenting on the Continent of Europe."[8] In addition, the cabinet's preoccupation with turbulent domestic issues left them with little time to keep adequately informed on the

[6] John L. Hammond, *C. P. Scott of the Manchester Guardian* (London, 1934), p. 144.
[7] See Nicholson to Hardinge, March 2, 1911, in G. P. Gooch and Harold W. V. Temperley, *British Documents on the Origins of the War, 1898-1914* (hereinafter cited as *B.D.*) (London, 1927-1938), VI, 590.
[8] David Lloyd George, *The War Memoirs of David Lloyd George* (London, 1933), I, 47. Grey wrote that all matters of importance regarding foreign affairs were regularly treated in the "confidential print" circulated to all the members of the cabinet. Viscount Grey of Fallodon, *Twenty-Five Years, 1892-1916* (London, 1935), II, 259.

equally complex matter of foreign affairs. Consequently Grey continued in his isolation until such time as a crisis once more turned heads in his direction.

The possibility of a parliamentary foreign affairs committee to consider ways and means of effecting some form of control over foreign affairs, however slight, was raised in the House of Commons shortly after the Agadir crisis. Proposed by Arthur Ponsonby and Noel Buxton, this committee would serve primarily as a study group to strengthen contact between the Foreign Secretary and Parliament. Specifically it would strive to improve Anglo-German relations. However, neither Asquith nor Grey gave this request serious consideration. Still the move to set up such a committee was symptomatic.[9]

As the news from Persia grew increasingly ominous, and as reaction to Grey's seemingly inflexible attitude toward Germany increased, more direct action was taken in Parliament. On November 13, 16, and 20, there were requests for a full policy statement from Sir Edward Grey and for an opportunity for adequate debate on his statement and on foreign policy in general.[10] Radical-Liberal journals along with the *Labour Leader,* the *Economist,* and the Conservative *Daily Telegraph* seconded this request. Almost overnight foreign affairs became the leading topic of the day in the newspapers, in the clubs, wherever public opinion might find a medium for expression. While British public opinion had seldom been organized or vigorous enough to effect a ministerial reaction concerning foreign affairs, in November, 1911, it showed such strength that it could not be safely ignored.[11] Hard pressed, the Prime Min-

---

[9] See T. P. Conwell-Evans, *Foreign Policy from a Back Bench* (Oxford, 1932), pp. 81-82. Also see Ponsonby, *Democracy and Diplomacy,* pp. 83-92. On Dec. 11, 1911, the *Morning Post* wrote that "the formation of a Radical caucus to watch over foreign affairs is not a pleasant symptom. It is a sign of a party which does not trust its own ministers."

[10] *Parl. Debs.,* 5th ser., XXXI, 22, 511, 816.

[11] Henry Noel Brailsford observed, "It is only within modest limits, and then only when a section of Conservative opinion was with them, as it was in the later phases of the Persian question, that the Radical-Liberal press seemed to

ister finally agreed that November 27 would be set aside for a debate on foreign policy. This announcement immediately lent new enthusiasm to those critical of Grey, though it would be inaccurate to call it, as yet, an "anti-Grey movement."

The press was excited over the prospects of the debate. There were daily editorials and leaders in the *Manchester Guardian* and in the *Daily News* which warned, however, that discussion alone would not suffice but only a thorough inquiry into the basic components of British foreign policy. The *Economist*, an important Liberal financial weekly, carried the attack to the Foreign Secretary on similar lines. Its editor, Francis Hirst, also pointed out that British policy in Persia lacked imagination and had done little more than support Russian aggressions. Taking its cue from this sentiment, the *Labour Leader*, unofficial organ of the Parliamentary Labor party, scorched Grey "for alienating Germany and for playing upon Persia the old game of exploitation." Its fiery editor, A. Fenner Brockway, urged Labor party members to tackle Grey effectively in the forthcoming debate. "This autocratic ruler of the foreign office must be stopped."[12]   In a series of articles in his "F. O. Bag" in the *Illustrated Graphic,* Lucien Wolf pointed out that Grey had been consistently outwitted in Persia. Russia was eager to move ahead in every quarter, he warned, and Grey should awaken to the new threat of Russia in the revival of the question of the Dardanelles.[13]

Grey was not unaware of this attempted encroachment upon his foreign policy preserve. And while he did not enjoy publicity—he repeatedly asserted that it was "forced" upon him— he was very much alive to the danger of a parliamentary

---

deflect his [Grey's] course of action." *The War of Steel and Gold* (London, 1914), p. 136. Also see E. Malcolm Carroll, *Germany and the Great Powers, 1866-1914* (New York, 1938), p. viii.

[12] *Economist,* Nov. 22, 1911; *Labour Leader,* Nov. 27, 1911.

[13] *Graphic,* Nov. 18; Dec. 2, 9, 16, 1911. Wolf was referring to what has been called "the Charykov kite." See Grey to O'Beirne, Oct. 23, 1911, *B.D.,* IX, (1), 313.

setback which could conceivably bring about a dissolution of
Britain's ententes with France and Russia. Therefore he sought
to fortify his position. On November 24, the Foreign Office
published the complete text of the 1904 agreements with France,
including the heretofore unpublished secret articles.[14]   Although Lillian Penson and Harold Temperley have accurately
judged that, according to the Bluebook standard, "Grey took
the public into his confidence very much less than his predecessors," his publication of the articles constituting the basis for
the *entente cordiale* was timely.   As initiative for their publication came from the Government and not from an adverse action
by the Parliament, Grey had stolen a march on his critics.   Moreover, as the Agadir crisis had been resolved peaceably, with a
concomitant strengthening of the French entente, his advantage
in the parliamentary test was impressive.

Rather it was the secondary matter, that of Persia, which
had grown increasingly thorny and which was, at that time,
Grey's most vulnerable point. He admitted later in his *Memoirs*
that "Persia tried my patience more than any other subject."[15]
And though he repeatedly warned A. A. Neratov, who was acting as Foreign Minister for the ailing Sazonov, against further
Russian advances in northern Persia, Russian agents and Cossacks continued to play fast and loose with Persia's integrity.
Particularly did they seek to thwart Shuster on every possible
occasion, attempting to force him to recognize Russia's special
interests in Persia. This Shuster would not do. Even the concerted pressure which forced him to give way in the Stokes
controversy did not sway him from his decision to ignore
British-Russian privileges. By November the situation had
grown tense, with Russia strengthening its position at Teheran
and throughout the north; Grey struggled to preserve the entente. To achieve this end he would sacrifice Shuster.[16]

[14] See Great Britain, Foreign Office, *Treaty Series*, 1911 (Cd. 5659); B.D., II,
374-407.

[15] Grey, *Twenty-Five Years*, I, 169.

[16] Fortunately the twentieth-century story of Persia is now being studied

With Grey's motion "That the foreign policy of this country be now considered," debate was formally opened before an overflow crowd in the House of Commons on November 27. But as predicted by the more discerning writers, Grey's motion was misleading. He was not there to debate the substance of his policy; it was "out of the question," as the *Times's* foreign editor, Valentine Chirol, wrote, for Grey to announce any change in the direction of British policy or that the ententes themselves should be altered. Grey was there to explain the Government's action in the recent crisis with Germany and to discuss what he considered pertinent questions. Still the tall, thin, melancholy squire of Fallodon did not unilaterally limit the discussion to Agadir. He replied to questions on Persia, and, as regards secrecy, assured the members that "No British Government could embark upon a war without public opinion behind it, and such engagements as there are which really commit Parliament to anything of that kind are contained in treaties . . . which have been laid before this House." For an hour and a half he once more wove his spell, or what A. G. Gardiner liked to term "his hypnotic influence," over the House. It was a typical Grey talk, without a jest, hardly eloquent, nearly dull. Nevertheless, what the *Times* labeled "Grey's transparent sincerity," was well received with every conciliatory phrase drawing an earnest cheer from the bulk of the Liberals. Again and again the Tory benches broke into an expression of good will with a fervent "Hear, Hear!"[17]

Grey was followed by the new and relatively unknown Conservative leader, Andrew Bonar Law. Amid "loud cheers" from his own side and from the Liberal front benches, he stated

---

from many angles. Shuster's own record, *The Strangling of Persia* (London, 1912), is essential reading. There is a scholarly unpublished doctoral dissertation by Hossein Nazem, "Russia and Great Britain in Iran, 1900-1914" (Columbia Univ., 1954), which examines both the Persian and Russian documents extensively. John A. Murray, "British Policy and Opinion on the Anglo-Russian Entente, 1907-1914," unpublished doctoral dissertation (Duke University, 1956), deals with both the Persian and European aspects of the Anglo-Russian entente.

[17] *Parl. Debs.*, 5th ser., XXXII, 43-165.

that a change in his party's leadership implied no change in its attitude toward foreign policy. He would strive as had others before him "to keep foreign affairs out of the scope of party politics." He was satisfied with Grey's résumé of the Government's action in the recent "unpleasantness" with Germany. He did not comment on Persian affairs. Grey's critics were less friendly and their remarks ranged far and wide over the field of British foreign policy. Leading off, the colorful Scot, Ramsay MacDonald, sarcastically proclaimed that, unlike Bonar Law, he was something of a heretic "in respect to the pious views in favour of continuity of foreign policy." If policies inherited from one's predecessors were bad—he considered the ententes bad for Britain—then there was no advantage to be gained in carrying them out. Persia presented a particularly dismal picture of the working out of the Russian entente. MacDonald charged that to pledge oneself "to protect the sovereignty of a country and then deliberately trample upon it was a crime against all the basic principles of the Liberal party." What the Laborites feared most of all was that Grey intended to change, or already had changed, the ententes into alliances. It would be horrible, he exclaimed, to come into a war on account of such alliances with only a small faction in the Government knowing of such commitments. Asquith immediately rose to Grey's defense, vigorously denying that the Government had any agreements beyond those known to the House.

Representing the dissenters among the Irish Nationalists, John Dillon pointed out that never in the history of Parliament had its members received so little information on the state of the nation's foreign policy. "We must read in our newspapers of the horrible depredations made by Russia on the Persian people with the apparent approval of the British foreign secretary." The British public was concerned and demanded an explanation from Grey: "For Sir Edward Grey has convinced the people that England is a party to Russian aggression and consented practically to the partition of Persia." There was loud applause from the back benches. Several of the Tories cried "Shame!"

Dillon was followed by an impressive list of speakers; prominent among them were Noel Buxton, a founder of the Balkan Committee and one of Grey's more influential critics, Colonel E. Yate, an old Persia hand, and Keir Hardie and Arthur Henderson of the Labor party. The white-bearded Hardie was bitterly disappointed with Grey's remarks, which he pointed out, were obviously cool toward Germany. As for Persia, he denounced the Foreign Secretary for serving as a cat's-paw for Russia and for "invading Persia and destroying its independence."[18] Dillon's remarks, and spirited and extended comments by others on Persia, brought Grey to his feet, though, as he had said from the outset, he did not intend to treat the matter exhaustively. The kernel of his argument, which he had stressed since the initial debate on the Anglo-Russian Convention in January, 1908, was that this agreement "had put an end to the continual squabbles of Russia and Britain in Central Asia." And Morgan Shuster, Russia's target of the moment, had persistently violated the "spirit" of the Convention. He would have to go. Then, giving Persian integrity and independence a strange twist, Grey showed his Liberal-Imperialist colors by declaring:

It is absolutely essential that that independence should be an independence which does take account of the respective interests of Russia and Great Britain in the parts adjoining the frontiers. We ourselves could not possibly allow the part of Persia adjoining the Indian frontier to be in a condition which threatens the security of that frontier. The independence of a country like Persia must take account of the interests of its neighbours.[19]

[18] George G. Murray, an apologist for Grey, states that "only a very small number of jingoes at one end and of Radicals at the other took different views." *The Foreign Policy of Sir Edward Grey, 1906-1915* (Oxford, 1915), p. 48. This estimate is an oversimplification.

[19] *Parl. Debs.*, 5th ser., XXXII, 152-165. Grey was more explicit on this point when he wrote O'Beirne, his minister at St. Petersburg, on Oct. 26, 1911: "Persia's independence cannot, I agree, be allowed to be marked by unfriendli-

Reiterating what he, Spender in the *Westminster Gazette*, Chirol in the *Times*, Leo Maxse in the *National Review*, and others had so often declared, he asked: "What would it have been like in Persia without any Anglo-Russian Agreement?" Before his critics could question him the Speaker adjourned the debate for the evening.

On the following day the debate was taken up in the House of Lords. After the exciting spectacle of the debate in Commons, it was reasonable to anticipate that the Lords could contribute only a feast of surplus scraps. Such was not the case. And while the number of speakers and the Lords in attendance were few, the quality of the debate was high. Traditionally, of course, the House of Lords was the national arena where foreign affairs received more learned attention. This debate was especially enlivened by Lord Courtney of Penwith, who contributed a fresh and stimulating approach by challenging the policy of entangling alliances and continental commitments. Plowing his lonely furrow across a field of opposition, Courtney was heard in "frigid silence." Turning to Persia he excoriated the Asquith Government, giving chapter and verse, for its betrayal of that nation's basic liberties. Other Lords, less effective, nonetheless made their points against the Government, particularly against Grey's policy in Persia. Lord Lansdowne, speaking for the Conservative Opposition, dissociated himself and his party from Courtney's remarks, but was still unable to indorse wholeheartedly the present course of British diplomacy in Persia. Lord Morley then spoke "unenthusiastically" for the Government. Again he chastised Shuster and the Persian Government for failing to respect special British-Russian interests there.[20]

On November 29 Poklewski-Koziel, Russian minister at Teheran, presented the Persian Foreign Minister, Vosuk-ed-

---

ness either to Great Britain or to Russia." Great Britain, *Accounts and Papers* (hereinafter cited as *A & P.*), CXXII, 306.

[20] *Parl. Debs.*, HL, 5th ser., X, 362-377. Also see G. P. Gooch, *Life of Lord Courtney* (London, 1920), p. 547; A. G. Gardiner, *Pillars of Society* (London, 1913), p. 66.

Dowleh, the second Russian ultimatum of the month formally demanding the dismissal of Morgan Shuster as Treasurer-General of Persia. Unless the demands of the ultimatum were met within forty-eight hours, Russian troops stationed at Kazvin, seventy-five miles to the north, would proceed to the capital. In presenting the ultimatum the name of the British Government was used, implying its approval.[21] Queried on this point in the House of Commons on November 30, Grey replied that Shuster had made things impossible in Persia and that the British Foreign Office was in agreement with the terms of the Russian ultimatum, save where it demanded an indemnity.[22] Here Grey was telling half-truths; in fact, the inspiration for the second ultimatum demanding Shuster's ouster came from the British Foreign Office. It was suggested at the very time when the anti-Grey forces were gathering in Britain. Grey had informed his ambassador at St. Petersburg, Sir George Buchanan, on November 17, that "although I [Grey] do not suggest it," he could make it quite clear to Neratov that "any demand on Russia's part for Shuster's dismissal will be met with no objections by His Majesty's Government."[23] But though he connived to force Shuster out, he warned the Russian ambassador at London, Count Benckendorff, that "an occupation of Northern Persia or even a military expedition would end the independence of Persia and entail a revision of the Anglo-Russian agreement about Persia." Obviously he could not defend new Russian demands as being consistent with the agreement.[24]

[21] Barclay to Grey, Dec. 24, 1911, *A & P.*, CXXII, 477-479. Also see Shuster, *Persia*, pp. 164, 165.

[22] *Parl. Debs*, 5th ser., XXXII, 562.

[23] Grey to Buchanan, Nov. 17, 1911, *A & P.*, CXXII, 328. Grey wrote O'Beirne on Nov. 16: "The real and substantial difficulty seems to be Shuster's anti-Russian policy in Northern Persia, and the Russian government should, I think, make public their own case against it. Could they not formulate their complaints against Shuster and make a formal demand respecting them?" *Ibid.*, CXXII, 321.

[24] Grey to Buchanan, Dec. 2, 1911, *B.D.*, X, (1), 815, 816. Also see Benckendorff to Neratov, Dec. 2, 1911, in B. De Siebert, *Entente Diplomacy and the World* (New York 1921), p. 130.

"Sir Edward Grey's default in the Persian trust is now complete," read the headlines in the December 1 number of the *Manchester Guardian.* The effects of Grey's action was constituted a denial "of the most elementary rights of an independent country." "What is Grey doing at this critical hour?" asked the *Daily News.* Whatever course he was following could never be reconciled "with England's honour or England's interests." In editorial after editorial the *Daily News* thundered its disgust with Grey's betrayal of Persia. Grey's support of Russia in the Shuster matter, charged Gardiner, was the more deadly because it would also silence the United States Government which otherwise might have made representations on Shuster's behalf.[25] "We have suffered the suppliant to be torn from our knees; we have joined in violating his rights," concluded the *Nation.* Even the staunchly pro-Grey *Spectator* admitted that "A Russian protectorate of Northern Persia seems to be approaching." The *Spectator* agreed with the *Daily Telegraph* that such a move by Russia would not fit into the framework of the Anglo-Russian agreement.[26] In the *Westminster Gazette,* often considered as Grey's "unofficial organ," J. A. Spender agreed that the most pressing problem in foreign affairs was the tangled mess in Persia. Public opinion was decidedly uneasy, and while "Persia must submit to correction," Liberals did not want to see Persia punished. Grey must be on his guard, Spender warned, to see that the agreement with Russia did not make Britain a party to any action which might injure Persia's integrity or independence, or lead to its partition.[27]

The foreign policy debate was resumed in the House of Commons on December 14, though Lord Curzon had risen

[25] There was no likelihood of American intervention on Shuster's behalf. Indeed Neratov was informed that the United States disapproved of Shuster's actions. Grey to Buchanan, Nov. 21, 1911, *B.D.,* X, (1), 834. Also see Abraham Yeselson, *United States-Persian Diplomatic Relations, 1883-1921* (New Brunswick, 1956), pp. 118, 119, 124.

[26] *Daily News,* Dec. 1, 2, 1911; *Spectator,* Dec. 9; *Nation,* Dec. 9, 1911.

[27] *Westminster Gazette,* Dec. 1, 2, 1911.

again in the Lords on December 7 to protest against Russia's continued violations of Persia's rights. Widespread reaction throughout the country, particularly in the press, to the second Russian ultimatum provided a convenient wedge for Grey's critics. Again a lengthy and impressive list of members spoke out against his mishandling of the Persian situation. Starting off, Sir Henry Norman, a Conservative member, pointed out that in spite of Grey's many assurances it was obvious that the British public was dissatisfied with his "collusion" with Russia in trampling on Persia's sovereignty. While his constituents understood little about Persia, he declared that they were distressed that Grey had failed to live up to his word to Persia as set forth in the Preamble to the Convention and in the Spring Rice explanatory note to the Persian Government.[28] Swift MacNeil, an Irish member, demanded that Grey either abide by Britain's obligations or explain to the members when and why the policy of maintaining Persia's independence had been abandoned. "Only the Russians appear to know what our policy is," he protested, "and we in England are led to suspect that we have no policy at all in Persia." Stung by the many bitter and telling criticisms, Grey replied at length, but actually revealed little about the course of British diplomacy in Persia. To the dismay of his critics he declared that "Russia had played perfectly fair with the Anglo-Russian Agreement." Further startling his audience, Grey explained that nothing could be done until the present crisis was over, "and the crisis would not be over until the Russian demands had been met." Then British policy would have to be constructive. Above all, neither Russia nor Great Britain could have "the spirit and intention" of the Anglo-Russian Convention upset. He would have the British public remember "that there is much more in the Persian question than the Persian question." Greater

[28] In part the Preamble stated that the two powers "mutually engaged themselves to respect the integrity and independence of Persia. . . ." *B.D.*, IV, Appendix 1, 618-620. The Spring Rice communication to the Persian Government of Sept. 4, 1907, may be found in Shuster, *Persia*, pp. 28-30.

issues were at stake than Persia's integrity. Furthermore, Shuster's determination to ignore British-Russian interests was the primary cause of the crisis, and without the Convention and British-Russian co-operation things would have been a great deal worse.

Then, indicating for the first time what his future policy in Persia might be, Grey laid down six propositions which had been submitted to the Russian Government as defining British policy. In substance they were tantamount to a British-Russian protectorate over Persia. The most important article asserted that the outcome of the current crisis would have to be a Persian Government which would not disregard the special interests of the two powers and which would conform to the "spirit" of the Convention, to which, one may recall, Persia was not a signatory. Shuster would have to be succeeded without delay by an adviser acceptable to both Governments. When the Russian ultimatum was complied with, and these British propositions agreed to, then a joint British-Russian loan would be made available to the Persian Government. Grey also stated that he understood the Russian military measures in the north to be "provisional and not permanent," and would cease when the Russian ultimatum was accepted.[29]

Grey's explanations were received with obvious disappointment. Liberals and Radical-Liberals were particularly distressed that Grey evinced no understanding of or sympathy for "the Liberal tradition in foreign policy." The impression Grey created was that he alone carried on the foreign policy of the nation. Even Conservative members were not convinced that the exigencies of larger issues explained away serious mistakes in Persia. The consensus of parliamentary opinion, from which Bonar Law did not trouble to dissociate himself, was that the Anglo-Russian Convention, despite Grey's contrary claim, contained what approximated a guarantee of Persia's integrity and

[29] *Parl. Debs.*, 5th ser., XXII, 2543-2661.

independence. And in supporting Russia in its aggressions in Persia, Grey had violated that pledge.

Nor was the press satisfied with Grey's accounting. What was regarded as his questionable diplomacy continued to supply headline and editorial material for British journals. The degenerating Persian picture with the "knight in shining armor, Morgan Shuster, being evicted by the ruthless Russian barbarians," as well as Grey's failure to effect some form of an Anglo-German *rapprochement,* kept the press preoccupied over what had hitherto been a relatively dormant and unintelligible issue for Britishers. The debate in Parliament and subsequently in the press clearly demonstrated that the Foreign Secretary was losing ground. Spender, a leading oracle for the Liberals, agreed that there was neither sufficient prominence given to foreign affairs in Parliament nor adequate information about them afforded the general public. While supporting the main lines of Grey's policies, Spender—the only journalist with whom the Foreign Secretary deigned to discuss foreign affairs—agreed with Grey's critics that nothing ought to be done that might impair the sovereignty of Persia. Sounding a warning that must have troubled his good friend, Spender wrote that "Grey must guard against our agreement making us parties to any action against Persia which could lead to its partition."[30] Even the *Times,* which had been consistently anti-Shuster and in full support of Grey, now backed away from Russia's forward policy in Persia. Summing up its own views, the *Times* wrote that "possibly the frank and full exchange of views between London and St. Petersburg might with advantage have been initiated at an earlier date."[31]

Elsewhere Grey's critics were more belligerent. Long ago many of the Radical-Liberal journals had disembarked from his ship of state; they were now prepared to sink him. Strongest criticism continued to emanate from the Liberal *Daily News,*

[30] *Westminster Gazette,* Dec. 15, 1911.
[31] *Times,* Dec. 1, 4, 8, 19, 1911.

the *Manchester Guardian,* the *Nation,* and the *Labour Leader.* These were reinforced by growing anti-Grey sentiment voiced in the *Economist,* the *Near East,* by Lucien Wolf in the *Graphic,* as well as by articles by Henry Noel Brailsford, E. D. Morel, and others. Not a day passed without England's largest Liberal daily, the *Daily News,* carrying the attack to Grey. It was not a jot impressed by Grey's effort to mend his parliamentary fences. The role played by Britain in Persia was "most humiliating." Drawing a sharper arrow from its quiver, the *Daily News* let fly with a more direct shot: "We cannot see a fair possibility of improvement unless it is sought in a bolder spirit than Sir Edward Grey's. We do not believe that either the cabinet or the party feel happy within his policy." The *Daily News* contended that Grey would have to go.[32] G. P. Scott, who Trevelyan called "the most well-informed and intelligent of Grey's critics," spoke for those "who neither liked nor understood Grey's foreign policy." Since 1904, Scott had gravitated toward an isolationist position, attracting to his cause a sizable Liberal following. In editorials following the November-December debates, the *Manchester Guardian* found Grey's explanations "incomplete and lacking in clearness." The British public, it wrote, was forced to believe that if Britain was on the brink of war with Germany in the summer of 1911, "it could only have been for reasons which were and still are a mystery." Until Grey clarified Britain's "obligations," there was no validity to his assertion that the Parliament had control over his foreign policy. Hitting out where Grey was likely to be most sensitive, Scott depicted Grey's Persia policy as an "outrage on justice" which violated the most sacred tenets of the Liberal creed regarding foreign policy.[33]

In the *Nation* both Herbert Massingham and Brailsford attacked Grey's "ingrained Germanophobia," his secrecy, and

[32] *Daily News,* Nov. 28, 30; Dec. 1, 2, 8, 26, 1911.

[33] *Manchester Guardian,* Nov. 28; Dec. 4, 5, 6, 15, 16, 1911. Also see George M. Trevelyan, *Grey of Fallodon* (Boston, 1937), p. 227; Hammond, *Scott of the Guardian,* pp. 152-155.

his Persian policy which had erased Persian independence. "Germany is the great Grey bogey," Brailsford insisted, "the power which is always to be feared, always suspected." In his editorial sharply entitled, "Grey Must Be Stopped," Massingham declared that "public opinion has not authorized the government which acts in its name to follow a policy so mean and weak as this." Grey's parliamentary efforts were most unsatisfactory, and he only hoped that his policies might yet be reversed.[34] Brockway in the *Labour Leader* wrote without any circumlocution that the reception of Grey's speech "proves that Great Britain must adopt a new foreign policy before anything like permanent peace can be assured."[35] Lucien Wolf, whose anti-Russian prejudices often colored his writings, saw only two possible courses left to British diplomacy: either to return to isolation, which he, like C. P. Scott, preferred, or to convert the ententes into real alliances which would then bring some stability by making clear where all the powers stood.[36] In the *Economist,* Hirst pointed out that "if anything were required to convince the British public that something is fundamentally wrong with the foreign office, it would be the course of events in Persia."[37]

What had been accomplished thus far by Grey's opponents? The debate itself had been confusing, with three larger issues—Germany, Persia, and Foreign Office secrecy—being discussed simultaneously. For one thing, the Russians were carefully

[34] *Nation,* Dec. 2, 9, 16, 1911.

[35] *Labour Leader,* Dec. 1, 8, 1911. The *Manchester Guardian* on Dec. 8 reported that the German press evidenced disappointment at the coolness of Grey's remarks, especially as he did not make a more cordial response to an earlier overture by the German Chancellor. Also see Carroll, *Germany and the Powers,* pp. 695, 696.

[36] *Graphic,* Dec. 2, 9, 16, 1911. Wolf's special concern was the persecution of the Jews in Russia. In January, 1912, he began publication of a four-page journal, *Darkest Russia: A Weekly Record of the Struggle for Freedom.* In it, as Max Beloff writes, "the polemic against the entente with Russia could be carried on by giving full publicity to the repressive policies of the existing regime." Beloff, *Lucien Wolf and the Anglo-Russian Entente* (London, 1951), p. 29.

[37] *Economist,* Dec. 2, 9, 16, 1911.

absorbing the headlines. Alexander Izvolski, former Russian Foreign Minister, now ambassador at Paris, observed that Grey no longer carried with him the over-all support of his own party. He cautioned Neratov: "While Grey will go a long way with us, it is dangerous to stretch the bow too tight. Matters will be put to the crucial test if we march to Teheran."[38] In London, Count Benckendorff was fully alive to the dangers in the attack on Grey. Repeatedly he warned his Government to refrain from sending troops to the Persian capital: British reaction to the Shuster matter was robust enough. Should Russia persist it would make it almost impossible to maintain the entente. Furthermore, unless this Government "strictly adhere to the agreements in the Anglo-Russian Convention . . . Grey would have to resign." This would be a critical setback for Russia "as it would most certainly involve the complete reorientation of English policy."[39] And while Neratov repeatedly threatened to enforce the second ultimatum, the Russian Cossacks were held at Kazvin. When pressed, Russia too prized the entente! The matter of Anglo-German relations was still unresolved. Yet the Kaiser, taking advantage of Grey's admission to Parliament on November 27 that he did not wish to stand in the way of German African expansion, instructed Count Metternich, his ambassador at London, to examine with Grey the possibilities of an Anglo-German colonial agreement. In truth, the Kaiser was striving for greater things: primarily an Anglo-German political and naval understanding.[40] Grey was evasive, but British opinion was having its impact. His agreement to initiate discussions after the Christmas holidays afforded him time to discuss the matter fully with his colleagues. The most significant result of the debate, therefore,

[38] Dec. 7, 1911. René Marchand, *Un Livre Noir* (Paris, 1922), I, 168.

[39] Benckendorff to Neratov, Dec. 4, 1911, in Siebert, *Entente Diplomacy*, pp. 132, 133. Also see Benckendorff to Sazonov, Feb. 9, 1911, in Siebert, *Graf Benckendorffs Diplomatischer Schriftwechsel* (Berlin, 1928), II, 249, 250, 251-256.

[40] See Bernadotte E. Schmitt, "Lord Haldane's Mission to Berlin in 1912" in Louis J. Paetow, ed., *The Crusades and Other Historical Essays* (New York, 1928), pp. 247-249.

was that British reaction had apparently saved Persia from Russian occupation, even though Persia had been partly stripped of its integrity and independence. Secondly, the matter of a possible Anglo-German *rapprochement* had been raised, and Grey had not vetoed this approach.

After a period of uneasy truce during Christmastide, a many-sided assault on Grey broke out in January and, until mid-April, the Foreign Secretary was to experience some of the darkest days of his political career. Several books, pamphlets in abundance, periodical articles, editorials and leader articles, resolutions by societies and associations, memorials by political, social, and cultural organizations, along with public demonstrations, speeches, debates, and questions in Parliament, concentrated on Sir Edward Grey and the current course of British foreign policy. Suddenly it appeared as if Grey were buffeted from every quarter. Many foes were especially bitter that Grey had callously seconded Russia in evicting Shuster at the very moment when his Persia policy was supposedly under examination. And the news from Persia had quickly worsened as reports of Russian atrocities at Tabriz trickled into Britain from Constantinople.[41] On January 7, Lord Lamington, a former Governor-General of Bombay, speaking on behalf of the Persia Committee at Edinburgh, charged that Grey had by no means exhausted the resources of diplomacy in Persia. Alluding to the reports for Tabriz, he contended that it seemed very certain that the province of Azerbaijan was being lost to Russia.

Grey had more reason to be alarmed at the speech by the Liberal party's elder statesman (Grey's former chief at the Foreign Office), Lord Rosebery, to a meeting in Glasgow on January 13. He spoke of Grey's "closed-down" approach to foreign policy, and pointed out the dangers incurred by Grey in his secretive handling of the Agadir crisis. "What is seen on

[41] These reports were later verified. See E. G. Browne, "The Reign of Terror at Tabriz," *Persia Committee* (London, 1912); Barclay to Grey, Jan. 22, 1912, *A & P.*, CXXII, 526; *Manchester Guardian*, Feb. 9, 13, 1912.

the stage of foreign policy is but a small part of the whole," he declared, "but no Glasgow merchant would do what we do in foreign affairs—that is, to engage in vast and unknown liabilities and affix his signature to them without knowing their nature and extent." The Radical press warmly welcomed the former Prime Minister's speech. Scott wrote in the *Manchester Guardian* that Rosebery had made it clear that Grey's policies were wholly unacceptable. The *Daily News,* the *Nation,* and the *Economist* joined Scott in proclaiming that Grey's usefulness was at an end; as Gardiner put it in the *Daily News:* "Sir Edward Grey as Foreign Secretary is impossible."[42]

The prospects for Grey continued to be cloudy. On January 16 an impressive public demonstration against him and his Persia policy was held in the new London Opera House with Sir Thomas Barclay in the chair. Conducted under the auspices of the Persia Committee, the spectacle of a full complement of ladies and gentlemen in evening dress applauding perorations by Ramsay MacDonald, Professor E. G. Browne, H. F. B. Lynch, Arthur Ponsonby, and others was a memorable sight. Browne, whose reputation as a Persian scholar was firmly established, contributed an exciting summary of his most recent pamphlet, "The Persian Crisis of December 1911: How It Arose and Whither It May Lead Us."[43] It constituted a carefully reasoned assault on Grey's diplomacy in Persia. He was followed by Ponsonby, Philip Morrell, and Sylvester Horne, who expressed general Radical sentiment. Finally, a resolution "that this meeting expresses its deep concern at the continued disregard of the undertaking jointly given by Great Britain and Russia in 1907 to preserve Persian integrity and independence" was unanimously adopted and sent to Grey. A similar meeting took place in Manchester on January 25. Large financial interests were represented. Speaking on behalf of those who had

[42] *Daily News,* Jan. 10; *Nation,* Jan. 17; *Manchester Guardian,* Jan. 14; *Economist,* Jan. 14, 1912.

[43] Published under the name of the Persia Committee, Jan. 1912. Also see E. G. Browne, *The Persian Revolution of 1905-1909* (Cambridge, 1910).

been "injured" on account of the disturbed situation in Persia, Sir Arthur Haworth, M.P., declared that a memorial was being sent to Grey directing his attention to their "troubles" which in round numbers amounted to a loss of over five hundred thousand pounds for every three months that exports to Persia were disrupted. About the same time Grey received another resolution adopted by the Labor Party Conference meeting at Birmingham, which requested him to seek some form of armament agreement with Germany. Other resolutions, not sent to Grey, dealt with criticism of his Persia policy and his "secret diplomacy."

Before the end of the month Morgan Shuster had arrived in London. Wined and dined, he was accorded a hero's welcome, for the occasion of his visit fitted in neatly with the over-all movement against Grey. On January 29 a testimonial dinner was held in his honor at the Savoy. After a lengthy oration by H. F. B. Lynch on the history of the Anglo-Russian Convention, Shuster delivered a tempered but telling narration of his recent experiences in Persia. The overflow audience received his words with enthusiasm. But, judged the *Daily News*, "they make lamentable reading for this country." Even the *Times* was moved to sympathize with Shuster, observing that his flavor of bitterness was not wholly without justification. J. A. Spender's editorials and leaders in the *Westminster Gazette* indicated that he was torn between his friendship for Grey and Grey's somewhat below-standard management of the Foreign Office. Devoted to the traditions of the Liberal party, Spender could not approve Grey's repeated failure to discuss foreign affairs in Parliament. The fragmentation of Persia's integrity and independence was equally troublesome. He believed that it would be necessary for Grey to devote more time to explaining his policies to the British public, which some day could conceivably be called upon to defend them.[44]

[44] *Daily News*, Jan. 30, 31; *Times*, Jan. 31; *Manchester Guardian*, Jan. 30, 31; *Westminster Gazette*, Jan. 31, 1912.

From November, 1911, until late in 1912 a flurry of periodical articles on foreign affairs appeared in British journals. The number of pieces critical of Grey far outnumbered those supporting him. Both Philip Morrell's "Our Persian Policy," and Sidney James Low's "The Foreign Office Autocracy" were frontal assaults on Grey. Another by H. F. B. Lynch, "Sir Edward Grey on Persia," upbraided Grey for his desertion of the British investor in the Middle East. This discussion continued in the British periodicals throughout 1912, even after the storm against Grey had blown over.[45]

There was also much ado at this time about the formation of a short-lived "Foreign Policy Committee," founded by Professor L. T. Hobhouse. Its platform called for greater publicity of foreign affairs and fuller parliamentary control over the main lines of policy. At its inaugural meeting in late January, Lord Courtney, the first president, called upon Members of Parliament and the public to press Grey for action toward improving Anglo-German relations. Grey should also make a concerted effort to check Russia in Persia.[46] This organization, however, lacked dynamic leadership and, as will be seen, was barely under way when Grey took the wind out of its sails. Of far greater importance was the revival by Noel Buxton and Arthur Ponsonby of a foreign affairs committee within the framework of the parliamentary Liberal party. Over seventy members of Parliament joined this group whose primary function was to secure greater parliamentary consultation in foreign affairs. Emphasis was upon improving Anglo-German relations and on safeguarding Persia's sovereignty. Although it failed in effectiveness "for want of knowledge and lack of vigour," its formation and initial vitality in early 1912 dem-

[45] Philip Morrell, "Our Persian Policy," *Nineteenth Century,* LXXI (Jan., 1912), 40-47. Robert Machray, "The Fate of Persia," *Fortnightly Review,* XCVII (Feb., 1912), 291-302; Sidney James Low, "The Foreign Office Autocracy," *ibid.,* XCI (Jan., 1912), 1-10; H. F. B. Lynch, "Sir Edward Grey on Persia," *Contemporary Review,* CI (Jan., 1912), 642-651.
[46] Gooch, *Life of Lord Courtney,* pp. 572-573.

onstrated that the opposition to the Foreign Secretary had reached alarming proportions within the ranks of his own party.[47]

There was also continued disagreement among the members of the Asquith cabinet over Grey's policies. While Lloyd George's Mansion House declaration in the summer of 1911 had served to demonstrate to the German Government apparent unity of purpose within the Government, there were dissenters who gradually came to be heard. John Burns, Lord Morley, and Lord Loreburn were seldom comfortable with Grey's administration at the Foreign Office. Even Lloyd George was growing restive; ever the opportunist, he could hardly ignore the tempest over foreign policy. Once before, in August, 1908, Lloyd George had trenched upon Grey's territory; now, in February, 1912, he moved one step from Asquith and Grey when he pointed out to the London Liberal Club that fear and jealousy must be removed from Anglo-German relations. Equally disturbing were Lord Lansdowne's remarks on Persia in the House of Lords on February 14. Questioning Grey's Persian policy for the first time, Landsdowne declared that he was "profoundly disturbed" at the course of events in Persia. "At the present time," he said, "Persian independence is a very shadowy independence, and the difficulty of maintaining its integrity is rapidly increasing." He hoped Grey might soon be able to reassure the Conservative opposition about their concern for Persia.[48]

But the movement against Grey appeared now to be losing headway. Although Persian affairs were reviewed again in Parliament on February 21, with a strong indictment being made out against Russia by Ponsonby and Morrell, there was little enthusiasm, and a full-scale attack on Grey could not be mounted. Grey's defense was his well-worn dictum that with-

[47] Conwell-Evans, *Foreign Policy*, p. 83. In his chapter "The New Radicalism before 1914," A. J. P. Taylor (*The Troublemakers*, pp. 95-131) fails to examine Grey's vital role in checkmating "the dissenters."

[48] *Parl. Debs.*, HL, 5th ser., XI, 19, 20.

out the Russian Convention Persia would be in chaos.[49] In reality, there was very little chance of bringing about Grey's downfall. While criticism against him had grown steadily since September, 1911, and had attracted considerable support from his own party, the Liberals in Parliament had no intention of bringing about the downfall of their own Government on a matter of foreign policy. If Grey fell the Asquith Government would necessarily fall with him. But in 1911 and 1912, the Liberal party was still united on all-important domestic issues. And because the Liberals had lost their overall majority in the 1910 elections, and were now dependent on Irish and Labor as well as Radical-Liberal support, a division within the ranks of the party on foreign policy would have led to disaster.

Nevertheless, Grey had been forced from his Whitehall isolation. Privately he had resisted further Russian advances in Persia. Taking the hint, Neratov was content with Shuster's ouster and with Russian predominance in the north.[50] Grey also took to the public podium. He spoke to his Northumberland constituents on January 19, and though he told them he was so busy that he knew little of the current criticisms being flung at him, he managed to discuss each point at length. Twice on February 15 he made major foreign policy talks in Manchester, the hotbed of anti-Grey opposition. Both talks were remarkable for the warmth of their references to Germany, and for his personal optimism regarding Persia. But Persia was already a secondary matter, as Britons believed the game there lost. It was now on the crucial matter of Anglo-German relations that Grey's opposition concentrated. And it was here that Grey was most successful in meeting the demands of his critics,

[49] *Parl. Debs.*, 5th ser., XXXIV, 628-695.
[50] Persia was still to provide excellent bargaining material for Russia. As Persian oil became essential for British ships, British interest in the oil-rich neutral zone of Persia was intensified. In 1915, an agreement was finally reached whereby Russia would annex both the Straits and Constantinople after victory in the war; Britain would absorb the neutral zone.

temporarily at least. The announcement of Lord Haldane's mission to Berlin served as a sop to his critics and Germanophiles, and also furnished proof that the Government was actively seeking to lessen tensions.

Grey himself had declined to lead the mission to Berlin, selecting instead Lord Haldane, a known admirer of Germany, yet an unfortunate choice. An "unofficial" visit, it was nonetheless an open secret, widely reported in the press. Grey had agreed to the visit "without demur and with good will," but actually "he had no great hope that anything would come of it."[51] The truth of the matter was that there was no room in Grey's diplomatic armory for an Anglo-German political or naval understanding. But the visit, made at the moment when pacifist and anti-Grey sentiments were at their prewar peak in Britain, would serve to suspend certain severe and powerful elements of criticism. Accordingly the over-all effort against him weakened. While Liberal and Radical-Liberal journals waxed enthusiastic over the possibilities of the visit, the Conservative journals, and such chauvinist writers as Leo Maxse, John St. Loe Strachey, and H. W. Gwynne, opposed it. It would seem reasonable to give an affirmative answer to Professor Bernadotte Schmitt's provocative question: "Was Sir Edward Grey half-hearted about the whole business?"[52] The evidence suggests that Grey was using the mission to silence criticism, to shift the focus of attention and burden of proof to Berlin. He was supporting what he had already evaluated as an abortive effort. The mission was little more than a gesture on Grey's part.[53]

[51] Grey, *Twenty-Five Years,* I, 251-252. Asquith wrote that "it was an effort not to arrive at a final arrangement, but to examine the ground with the object of finding out whether there was a road by which such an arrangement could be reached." H. H. Asquith, *The Genesis of the War* (London, 1923), p. 98.
[52] Schmitt, "Haldane Mission," in Paetow, ed., *Essays,* p. 275.
[53] Grey reassured both the Russian and French ambassadors that the mission was little more than a gesture. Benckendorff wrote Neratov that Grey had told him that "on several occasions an exchange of views between the two governments had taken place, without having, however, led to any practical result."

Proof that the campaign against him was failing was demonstrated during the parliamentary debate of February 21, when criticism emanated solely from the back benches, and the debate, for the most part, was relatively lifeless. From this point on, in spite of the failure to obtain a naval understanding with Germany, foreign affairs in Britain were overshadowed by explosive domestic issues. Grey himself soon was preoccupied, indeed his star shone most brightly, with the disruptive wars in the Balkans. Though criticism of him persisted, it was sporadic and lacked the purpose and determination that had characterized it during the latter months of 1911 and early 1912.[54] This writer, however, cannot accept A. J. P. Taylor's thesis that "the dissenters won. Grey adopted their policy."[55] For while Grey was practically coerced into standing up to Russia after Shuster's dismissal, his concern for Persia was only momentary. His support of Winston Churchill's "Persian oil for British ships" in the summer of 1914, in which little or no concern was paid to Persia's rights and privileges, hardly fits into the Liberal scheme of things. Nor did the eventual absorption of the neutral zone reflect a devotion to Liberal traditions. And while Grey permitted the Haldane mission and later joined Germany in negotiations over the Bagdad Railway and the proposed division of the Portuguese colonies, these bargains had little or no bearing on his rigid maintenance of Britain's ententes, which were secretly expanded into quasi-military and naval alliances during the period from 1912 to 1914. As regards Persia, it was recognized that little could be done. Shuster was gone; the spark of reform had been extinguished. But here Grey also had made amends. Russian troops were held

---

Siebert, *Entente Diplomacy*, pp. 622, 623. Also see Cambon to Poincaré, Feb. 28, 1912. *Documents diplomatiques français, 1871-1914*, 3rd ser., II, 113-114.

[54] In October a brief but formidable attack was made on Grey by Sir John Brunner, the president of the National Liberal Federation. In a remarkable letter to all the chairmen of British Liberal associations, he urged them to stand "in frank opposition" to the existing policy of the government and to Grey in particular." See the *Nation*, Oct. 19, 1912.

[55] Taylor, *Trouble Makers*, p. 125.

back from occupation. Grey had also made an effort to inform the Parliament and public of the essentials of his Persian policy. Also government papers on Persia were, from 1912 on, published with unusual regularity, though they were, for the most part, trackless miles of verbiage. Moreover, attention was now focused on domestic problems of awesome proportions. Home Rule, Church disestablishment in Wales, and later the Curragh Mutiny overshadowed protests against the Foreign Secretary.

The prolonged criticism of Grey in Parliament, in the press, and wherever opinion might find a medium for expression, demonstrated that, while willing to debate the merits and demerits of Grey's policies, relatively few were willing to bring about the downfall of the Liberal Government. At no time could Grey's critics muster a majority or a near majority. Primarily the demand had been for reform, not for the dissolution of the Government. The most significant result, however, was that at last foreign affairs had a hearing. Especially in the Parliament and in the press, many men hitherto unfamiliar with the field of foreign affairs had, of necessity, ventured into this unknown area. And while in the remaining prewar years foreign affairs were not specially before the public eye, representatives of the Liberal, Radical-Liberal and Labor press, proved that they would not permit foreign affairs to be withdrawn from public debate or political discussion. Reaction to Foreign Office secretiveness and continuity in foreign affairs would manifest itself more actively after World War I.

Moreover, this extended criticism of Grey demonstrated that the British public was more informed—with the risk of being more misinformed—of international issues. And while little interest was taken by the average citizen in these matters, a real likelihood was that German leaders misinterpreted criticism in the British press and in Parliament, and based much of their hope for British neutrality during the 1914 crisis on the 1911-1912 reaction to Grey.

For the most part, Sir Edward Grey had emerged relatively unscathed. The ententes remained intact; the balance of power in Europe was maintained. He could return to his Whitehall sanctuary secure in the knowledge that, unless some unanticipated catastrophe befell him, the Foreign Office was still safe from prying eyes. Only a slight lifting of the veil had been necessary thus far to appease the majority of his critics. Foreign developments, also, had helped to relax the pressure against him. The Kaiser had demonstrated that Germany was still intransigent in demanding a political understanding as a basis for a naval agreement. Russia was willing to bide its time in Persia to save the entente and the balance of power. In addition, domestic affairs in Britain diverted the attention of those dissatisfied with Grey. The most surprising aspect of the foreign policy debate, in spite of so concentrated an attack, was that Grey revealed so little. Even the Haldane mission had an unreal quality about it. An examination of Grey himself during this troubled time tells little about the man. He remains still very much an enigma in pre-1914 diplomatic history.

THE AUSTRO—
ITALIAN ANTAGONISM,
1896-1914

William C. Askew

If great international antagonisms have an element of mystery, unreality, and irrationality which defies the historian and if they can be comprehended fully only by those who experience them, they have, nevertheless, a solid, tangible, and rational basis as well. Their very essence, of course, is a combination of mistrust and fear. They are the stuff out of which diplomatic crises and wars are created.

While history records many such antagonisms, that between Italy and the Dual Monarchy from 1896 to 1914 was in some respects unique. These nations had been allies since 1882. Press, cabinet ministers, and ambassadors made thousands of professions of loyalty and declarations that relations were cordial or becoming intimate. One often heard that agreement was perfect. But Barrère, the great French Ambassador to Italy, summed it all up in March, 1908, by describing them as "enemy-allies."[1] He did not exaggerate.

This essay has a restricted objective. It makes no attempt to trace the diplomatic relations of the two powers in the period under survey. That is a task for another time and

---

[1] Barrère to Pichon, March 19, 1908, *Documents diplomatiques français* (hereinafter cited as *D.D.F.*) (Paris, 1929–), 2d ser., XI, 526, 527.

place. The writer rather seeks, on the basis of an examination of the most pertinent diplomatic documents in the archives in Rome and Vienna, to describe those factors which fomented an enduring antagonism, to analyze the mistrust and fears which existed, and to draw some conclusions concerning the role, obviously great, which this antagonism played in European diplomacy before World War I.[2]

It should be pointed out in the beginning that Italian diplomacy was not the evil and dishonest thing which German and Austrian historians have pictured it as being. Italy, as the weakest of the great, could not afford diplomatic failure. Her diplomats, mostly aristocrats, were, with a few significant exceptions, among the finest in the world. The Foreign Office followed the practice of leaving its ambassadors and ministers in the capitals of Europe for a long enough period to learn the language and customs of a country, and to build up contacts and friendships. They were well informed. If Italy had any slogan which summarized her diplomacy it was that coined by Visconti Venosta: "Independent ever, isolated never." Italy's greatest concerns in the period under survey were with Tripoli, the other shore of the Adriatic, and an equal voice with other powers in the Eastern Question. East Africa bordering on the Red Sea was also an absorbing interest. Negotiation of successful trade treaties was a matter of supreme importance which occupied much of the time and skill of the *Consulta*. Defense of Italian immigrants in foreign lands and maintenance of their *Italianità* also caused serious concern. Unlike other great powers, Italy had no large amount of surplus capital to invest abroad. When investments were made for political reasons, it was the Government that pushed the bankers, rather than the

[2] The writer is grateful for the opportunity to spend some 34 months in the archives in Rome, Vienna, and London and to the Haus-, Hof-und Staatsarchiv in Vienna for copies of many documents. The names of people to whom a great obligation is due would fill this page. The author is grateful also for a John Simon Guggenheim Memorial Fellowship, a Fulbright grant, and for a grant through the Colgate Research Committee of Lucius N. Littauer Foundation funds for work in Italy in the summer of 1956.

bankers' pushing the Government. But the economy was expanding and there were markets to be gained.

Italian policy was unusually responsive to public opinion but public opinion was divided on what Italy's policy should be. One group of Italians, dazed by the frightening manifestations of German power, advocated close alignment with Germany even at the price of alliance also with the traditional enemy, Austria. Another group of Italians, impressed by the close cultural affinity with the "Latin Sister," demanded alignment with France. Practically all Italians could agree on close relations with England although they felt at times that England did not reciprocate. In an age when imperialism was considered normal and healthy, Italian opinion was also divided about colonies. One part of the nation felt that imperialism was a luxury which Italy could not yet afford. Italy must wait until she had gained inner strength and solved her pressing problems of poverty and illiteracy at home. But other Italians advocated a policy of calculated risk. Italy must seek colonies while still weak, in order to gain resources with which to build herself up at home. The apparent oscillations of Italian policy are largely to be explained in terms of these divisions.[3]

[3] For an excellent discussion of the bases of Italian policy see Volume I of the monumental work of Federico Chabod, *Storia della politica estera italiana dal 1870 al 1896: Le premesse* (Bari, 1951). See also Walter Schinner, *Der Österreichisch-italienische Gegensatz auf dem Balkan und an der Adria von Seiner Anfangen bis zur Dreibundkrise 1875-1896* (Stuttgart, 1936). Luigi Salvatorelli, *La triplice alleanza: Storia diplomatica 1877-1912* (Milan, 1939), is an able study of the alliance negotiations. Professor Augusto Torre has contributed many excellent articles to the study of pre-1914 diplomacy, some of which are collected in his *Alla vigilia della guerra mondiale 1914-1918* (Milan, 1942). Gaetano Salvemini, *La politica estera dell'Italia dal 1871 al 1915* (2nd ed.; Florence, 1950) is a penetrating essay. Francesco Tommasini, *L'Italia alla vigilia della guerra: La politica estera di Tommaso Tittoni* (5 vols.; Bologna, 1934-1941), is based on study in the archives by a diplomat who was active in the period. S. Cilibrizzi, *Storia parlamentare politica e diplomatica d'Italia da Novara a Vittorio Veneto* (8 vols.; Rome, no date), contains an analysis of many parliamentary debates. Luigi Albertini, *The Origins of the War of 1914,* Isabella M. Massey, trans. and ed. (3 vols.; Oxford, 1952-1957), is an impressive work. Extremely useful on Austrian foreign policy is A. J. May, *The Hapsburg Monarchy, 1867-1914* (Cambridge, Mass., 1951).

One cannot escape the conclusion also that foreign policy, as in many parliamentary states, became at times a kind of political football, a means of attacking the Government in power. How often did the radicals and republicans attack Austria, not only because they mistrusted her but also because they could thus inflame opinion against the Government? Lack of adequate funds for the military weakened Italy's voice among the great powers. Frequent cabinet crises alarmed Italy's neighbors, and successive premiers and foreign ministers did cause some alterations in the conduct of foreign policy. Physical weakness and internal dissension over objectives left Italian diplomacy unusually sensitive to threats to the national honor and prestige and to alleged slights and insults which stronger powers might well have ignored. Italy had an intense desire to belong to the truly great.

Aside from such factors as the weight of history and differences in national temperament, a number of more concrete issues promoted tensions at times bordering on hostility between Italy and Austria-Hungary. Almost constant debate on the validity and meaning of the Triple Alliance reflected the currents of hostility and at the same time did much to inflame passions. The Albanian rivalry was an acute issue, but Irredentism excited more popular passion. The Adriatic was the great zone of rivalry, but there were fundamental divergences in Balkan policy outside the Adriatic zone. The military mistrusted each other and there was a serious armament race between the two allies. Relations between the two ruling families were strained. Of minor but growing importance was the commercial rivalry.

Obviously these factors cannot be separated into compartments. They existed simultaneously, interacting. But for convenience' sake they will be discussed separately and wherever possible in summary fashion with the hope that a fair picture of the antagonism will emerge.

I. *Allies or Enemies: Currents of Opinion*

As the tragic year of Adowa opened, the Italians were profoundly disappointed with lack of support from the Triple Alliance as they faced defeat by the Ethiopians. The *Tribuna* probably reflected prevailing opinion when it declared on January 1, 1896, that, while the Triple Alliance existed on paper, it had ceased to be the Polar Star by which the political navigator determined his course. Saddened by England's failure to do anything to rescue Italy from the catastrophe which Crispi's failure to balance means and ends was causing, Blanc, the Italian Foreign Minister, was bitter toward Germany and Austria for leaving Italy alone against France and Russia, who were backing Ethiopia.[4] On January 12 Blanc complained to Nigra, Italy's great ambassador at Vienna, that Italy's allies had allowed France to secure preponderance in the western Mediterranean and Russia in the eastern half of that sea. The Triple Alliance had also failed to protect the hinterlands of Tripoli and Eritrea. Austria, he charged, had initiated negotiations with France for a commercial treaty with Tunisia without even informing Italy and had shown disinterest in the vital matter of preventing French arms and munitions from going to Ethiopia via Obock and Djibuti. Austrian disinterest in Africa might be better defined as community of interest with France. Blanc made substantially the same complaint to Pasetti, the Austrian ambassador in Rome.[5] Nigra sought to calm the nervous Foreign Minister by showing the limits of Austria's obligations and

[4] Blanc to Lanza (Berlin), secret letter, Jan. 7, 1896, and dispatch 3, Feb. 2, 1896, Cassette verdi, II (hereinafter cited as C.V.). Only two classifications are used in this study. *Riservato* and *confidenziale* Italian documents are described as confidential. The secret designation remains unchanged.

[5] Blanc to Nigra, secret dispatch 1199/17 and secret letter, Jan. 12, 1896, C.V., II, IX, also Nigra Papers. The widely held view that arms were flowing to Ethiopia with the blessing of the French Government is denied in the French documents. See *D.D.F.*, 1st ser., XII, 468, 469. Tornielli, the Italian ambassador in Paris, believed that France had acted correctly since the end of 1894. Tornielli to Caetani, March 12, 1896, *I documenti diplomatici italiani* (hereinafter cited as *D.D.I.*) (Rome, 1952–), 3rd ser., I, 4-9.

the loyalty and correctness of her actions both with regard to the arms question and the Tunisian treaty. Austria, he later wrote Foreign Minister Visconti Venosta, would follow the lead of Italy and England in Mediterranean questions and felt no obligation to aid Italy in Africa. Crispi and Blanc continued to complain to their allies that their lack of support made France feel that she could offend Italy with impunity.[6] What the Italians feared most of all was that Austria might move in Macedonia or elsewhere in the Balkans at a time when Italy was tied down in East Africa and that France might in turn seize Tripoli. Blanc even threatened to go to the side of France and Russia and suggested that Germany join Italy in an approach to these powers. In any event, Blanc was determined to demand Tripoli if the status quo in the Near East were disturbed.[7] The Germans did their best to persuade Blanc that there was nothing to fear as long as Italy was loyal to Germany and Austria-Hungary.[8] But shortly after Adowa radical deputy Imbriani blamed the Triple Alliance for the ruin of Italy.[9]

While there was some doubt in the Austrian Foreign Office that Italy could be relied upon as an ally,[10] Foreign Minister Goluchowski became genuinely alarmed after Adowa at the danger of republicanism in Italy and its influence on the South Tyrol and Trieste. He sought German co-operation in support of a strong Italy which would not experience additional fail-

[6] Crispi to Lanza, secret, Feb. 9, 1896; Blanc to Berlin, London, Vienna, March 1, 1896; Nigra to Blanc, report 127/40, Jan. 17, 1896, *C.V.*, II; Nigra to Visconti Venosta, personal letter, July 22, 1896, *D.D.I.*, 3rd ser., I, 90. Visconti Venosta was displeased when Austria signed the Tunisian commercial treaty. Visconti Venosta to Nigra, personal letter, Aug. 1, 1896, *ibid.*, 3rd ser., I, 98, 99.

[7] Blanc to Nigra, dispatch 2166/26, Jan. 16, 1896, Nigra Papers; Bülow to Hohenlohe, Jan. 15, 1896, *Die grosse Politik der europäischen Kabinette, 1871-1914* (hereinafter cited as *G. P.*), J. Lepsius, A. M. Bartholdy, F. Thimme, eds., (Berlin, 1922-1927), XI, 77-80; Pasetti to Goluchowski, report 7B, Jan. 25, 1896, Politisches Archiv (Vienna) (hereinafter cited as P.A.), Italien 1896, XI/114.

[8] Hohenlohe to Bülow, Jan. 23, 1896; Bülow, to F.O., Jan. 23, 27, 1896, *G.P.*, XI, 88, 89, 97, 98.

[9] *Atti parlamentari, Camera, Discussioni*, March 17, 1896, pp. 3432, 3433.

[10] Lichnowsky's memo., Feb. 29, 1896, *G.P.*, XI, 116-118.

ures.[11] Goluchowski not only sought a revival and expansion of the Mediterranean agreements between Italy, Austria-Hungary, and England but also a renewal of close ties between Italy and Spain.[12]

The Italians were slow to forget that the alliance had been of no real help in their darkest moment and it is probably not stretching the point too far to see the genesis of Italy's special agreements with France and England in the tragic experience of 1896.[13] In 1897 Adolfo Frassati, vice-director of the *Stampa* of Turin, called for the formation of a dual alliance between Italy and England which, he said, would be the arbiter of Europe. His main grievance was with Germany for sacrificing the interests of both Italy and Austria to Russia.[14] Outbursts of violence occurred in 1898 against Italians at Trieste, Nabresina, and other towns in Austria, in reprisal for the assassination of the Empress of Austria by an Italian. Barzilai, Italy's most untiring opponent of the Triple Alliance, used this occasion to make a severe attack on Austria in the Chamber on December 14. San Giuliano, later to become one of Italy's most competent foreign ministers, took vigorous issue with him on the ground that Russia sought universal hegemony and that France sought either to annex Tripoli or to take away a great part of its value.[15]

Opposition to the Triple Alliance was by no means confined to Italy. In the Hungarian Delegation in January, 1900, there were charges that the alliance did not safeguard Hungarian interests and had a bad effect on Austro-Hungarian relations with the Holy See. Finance Minister Kállay rebutted these

[11] Eulenburg to Hohenlohe, March 6, 1896, *ibid.*, XI, 126-129.

[12] Hohenlohe memo., March 15, 1896, *ibid.*, XI, 130-132.

[13] For able studies of these agreements, see Enrico Serra, *Camille Barrère e l'intesa italo-francese* (Milan, 1950) and *L'intesa Mediterranea del 1902* (Milan, 1957).

[14] Adolfo Frassati, "La politica estera dell'Italia e l'alleanza franco-russa," *Nuova Antologia*, 4th ser., LXXI (Oct. 16, 1897), 712-736.

[15] Barzilai demanded the end of the Triple Alliance. *Atti parlamentari, Camera, Discussioni*, Dec. 14, 15, 1898, pp. 971-977; 988-996.

charges, and Goluchowski made a brilliant and warm defense of the Triple Alliance.[16]

Relations, which had remained fairly normal, definitely worsened after Prinetti became Foreign Minister in a Zanardelli cabinet in 1901. Both Prinetti and De Martino, his Undersecretary of State for Foreign Affairs, were known to have been somewhat unfavorable to the Triple Alliance in the past. When Prinetti responded to an interrogation by radical deputy Guerci by denying that he had spoken of the renewal of the alliance, the *Neue Freie Presse* on March 12 found his declaration extraordinarily cold and warned that there would be war if Italy joined the Franco-Russian alliance. The *Neues Pester Journal* and the *Budapesti Naplo* were also fearful that Italy might join France and Russia.[17] Nigra warned Prinetti that war would result if Italy abandoned the Triple Alliance and joined France.[18] Even the inexperienced and impulsive Foreign Minister was impressed by this warning.[19] Pasetti was alarmed at the growing intimacy between France and Italy and believed quite correctly that they had exchanged notes on Tripoli. He found Prinetti weak and without foresight in dealing with the press and blamed Prinetti for inspiring Italian press declarations that Italy's continued membership in the Triple Alliance depended upon favorable commercial treaties with Austria-Hungary and Germany.[20]

[16] Cusani (*chargé* at Vienna) to Visconti Venosta, tel. 89, Jan. 12, 1900, Reg. 243; *Tribuna*, Jan. 18, 1900. There was another Hungarian attack on the Triple Alliance in the same month.

[17] Tommasini, *L'Italia alla vigilia della guerra*, I, 79, 80; Nigra to Prinetti, report 358/183, March 12 and consular report 408/33 from Budapest, March 14, 1901, P68/349.

[18] Nigra to Prinetti, report 396/207, March 18, 1901, P15.

[19] Prinetti to Nigra, personal tel. 736, March 25, 1901, Reg. 249. I have not found the confidential letter to Nigra mentioned in this telegram.

[20] Pasetti to Goluchowski, reports 11C, 11E, Feb. 26, 1901, P.A., Italien 1901, XI/123. The Germans thought that Prinetti and the cabinet were less able to oppose the pro-French currents in Italy than their predecessors. Szögyény to Goluchowski, report 11D, March 13, 1901, P.A., Berlin 1901, III/153.

Prime Minister Zanardelli's interview in the New York
Herald on March 25 alarmed his allies. Zanardelli declared
that Italy would not bind herself anew to the Triple Alliance
until after ripe reflection and observed that commercial relations influenced political relations. The Triple Alliance would
expire before the treaties of commerce, "but we shall know
long in advance what decision to take with regard to both
one and the other." He spoke in glowing terms of France and
of the coming visit of the Italian squadron to Toulon. Pasetti
protested to Prinetti against an implication in the interview
that the Triple Alliance was hostile to France and contested
the attempt to link the renewal of the alliance with the conclusion of commercial treaties. Prinetti indicated that the
interview came as a surprise and that he had complained to
the King.[21]

Zanardelli gave Chancellor Bülow the most definite assurances of Italian loyalty to the Triple Alliance when they met
at Verona on April 2 and declared that he had been misquoted.
Lanza, the Italian ambassador to Berlin, now on leave, spoke
reassuring words to Pasetti about Prinetti and about the intentions of Victor Emmanuel III. While the Austrians did
denounce the commercial treaty at the end of 1902, to take
effect at the end of 1903, they negotiated provisional arrangements until a new treaty was concluded.[22]

Prinetti did little to improve relations with Austria by his
warning to Pasetti in May that agitation against the Triple
Alliance from the Italian Left with the support of the French

[21] Pasetti to Goluchowski, conf. reports 16B, 17, March 26, 28, 1901, P.A.,
Italien 1901, XI/123. A copy of the interview appears in Italy's Vienna Embassy
file. Zanardelli was known to be an ardent Irredentist. See E. Ondei, *Giuseppe
Zanardelli* (Brescia, 1954), p. 167.

[22] Szögyény to Goluchowski, tel. 5385, April 3, 1901, P.A., Berlin 1901, III/153;
Pasetti to Goluchowski, reports 19 A-B, April 6, 10, 1901, P.A., Italien 1901,
XI/123, 124. Bülow professed no apprehensions concerning the *rapprochement*
of Italy and France. Lanza to Prinetti, tel. 979, April 18, 1901, Reg. 250. For the
commercial negotiations, see Tommasini, *L'Italia alla vigilia della guerra*, I, 279-
283.

radicals might become so strong that the Government would be powerless to fight against it.[23] Goluchowski in turn spoke with some heat to the Delegations about attempts to subordinate the Triple Alliance to the commercial treaties. Prinetti expressed his displeasure, but a later declaration by Goluchowski denying that relations with Italy were cooling won Prinetti's praise.[24]

Actually the doubts which Victor Emmanuel had about sending the Third Army to the German front in the event of war, as agreed in 1888, weighed heavily on relations between the allies after the King expressed his doubts to Germany in February, 1901, and after the Austrians learned of his views in April.[25]

[23] Pasetti to Goluchowski, reports 24C, 29 A-E, May 7, 1901, P.A., Italien 1901, XI/123. Prinetti indicated that he had taken steps to prevent a meeting of Socialists and radicals of the *Unione lombarda della pace* from giving offense to the Dual Monarchy. Pasetti concluded early in 1902 that the only serious opposition to the alliance came from the extreme left to which republicans and Irredentists belonged and found that the *Secolo* was the only important paper in opposition. Pasetti to Goluchowski, report 3C, Jan. 14, 1902, P.A., Italien 1902, XI/125.

[24] Nigra to Prinetti, tel. 1335, May 25, 1901, Reg. 250; Prinetti to Nigra, tel. 1263, May 25, 1901, Reg. 249. See also Nigra's tels. 1316, 1317 of May 22 and Prinetti's tel. 1247 of May 23.

[25] F. Cognasso, "Osservazioni sulla politica estera del ministro Prinetti secondo le recenti pubblicazioni documentarie," *Atti della R. Accademia delle Scienze di Torino* (Turin, 1936), p. 300; Salvatorelli, *La triplice alleanza*, pp. 239, 240; *G.P.*, XVIII, 683-708; Pasetti to Goluchowski, Secret, April 20, 1901, P.A., Italien 1901, XI/124. Italy formally withdrew her pledge to send the Third Army to the Rhine on December 21, 1912, but pledged offensive action against France across the Alps. In 1913 Italy concluded a new naval convention with Germany and Austria-Hungary designed to cut France off from North Africa. In November, 1913, Chief of the General Staff Pollio offered to send two cavalry divisions to Germany. The last military agreement of March 11, 1914, provided that the Third Army would be sent to Germany and would include 200,000 soldiers of which 150,000 would be combatants. François Charles-Roux, "Les Conventions militaires Italo-Allemandes sous la Triple-Alliance," *Revue de Paris*, XXXIII.₄ (Aug. 1, 1926), 608-631; *G.P.*, XXX (II), 576; Wolfgang Foerster, "Die deutsch-italienische Militärkonvention," *Die Kriegsschuldfrage*, V (May, 1927), 395-416; Graf Waldersee, "Von Deutschlands militärpolitischen Beziehungen zu Italien," *Berliner Monatshefte*, VII (July, 1929), 636-664; Angelo Gatti, "La rottura militare della Triplice Alleanza," *Rassegna Italiana*, XII (Dec., 1923), 755-767; A. F. Pribram, *The Secret Treaties of Austria-Hungary, 1879-1914* (Cambridge, Mass., 1920), I, 283-305; Albertini, *Origins of the War of 1914*, I,

The debates in the Italian Chamber in June reflected the deterioriation in Austro-Italian relations. Radical deputy Guerci declared on June 11 that Italy would be preparing for her saddest days if she did not abandon the Triple Alliance. Luzzatti, Italy's tariff expert, felt that Italy could live with Austria without the Triple Alliance but could not maintain good neighborly relations without a treaty of commerce and navigation. Pasetti found Prinetti's declarations on June 14 correct about the peaceful character of the Triple Alliance and about the probable lessening of military burdens because of the alliance but was impressed with the thought that Visconti Venosta would have given a different tone to the debate and that Prinetti had gained no personal success even if the Triple Alliance had emerged victorious.[26]

The Italian press echoed a new feeling of independence. The *Tribuna* rejoiced on April 11 that Italy was no longer humble and that now her friendship and alliance were being sought. The *Secolo* of Milan took a strong stand against the Triple Alliance on July 22 because it required Italy to guarantee territory to her allies which did not rightfully belong to them.[27] The *Corriere della Sera* (August 23) judged all Italians myopic who wished to desert Germany and Austria and to form a new triple alliance with Russia and France and warned that Pan-Slavism was no less a danger than Pan-Germanism; nevertheless, it carried an article by Ugo Ojetti on September 16 which declared that Russian support was a hundred times more useful for Italy in the Balkans than Austrian support. The *Deutsche Revue* on September 1 published an article by "An Italian Diplomat" to the effect that the Triple Alliance

---

555-565. General Pollio even spoke of the possibility of sending Italian troops to help Austria.

[26] *Atti parlamentari, Camera, Discussioni,* June 11, 14, 1901, pp. 5002, 5003, 5011, 5162-5171; Pasetti to Goluchowski, reports 36 A-G, 36B, June 18, 1901, P.A., Italien 1901, XI/123.

[27] Kuhn (*chargé* at Rome) to Goluchowski, report 46F, July 30, 1901, P.A., Italien 1901, XI/123.

was less important for Italy than when concluded and that it would be useless to renew it unless accords advantageous to Italian agriculture were also reached.[28] Guicciardini, who later became Foreign Minister, echoed the same idea that the Triple Alliance had lost some of its importance for Italy to the Chamber on May 23, 1902. On August 11 of the same year the *Tribuna* proudly concluded that Italy had become a kind of arbiter of the Triple Alliance, capable of denying victory to Germany and Austria. The *Reichswehr* of Vienna replied that the loss of Italy as an ally would not be serious and denied that Italy could determine the outcome of a war by Germany and Austria against France and Russia.[29] The *Corriere della Sera* (August 22) affirmed that Italy's mission was one of conciliation between the Triple Alliance and the Franco-Russian alliance.

The story of the negotiations for the renewal of the Triple Alliance has been told too many times to need repetition here. Prinetti's efforts to secure a formal pledge to work for autonomy in the Balkans if the status quo could not be maintained, to limit the new term of the Triple Alliance to three years, and to provide for adequate compensation for any changes made in the existing trade treaties were defeated. The Austrians manifested good will concerning a trade treaty and were willing to exchange ideas regarding Macedonia. They gave a pledge of disinterest in the Tripolitan question.[30] It is to be doubted that the long negotiation improved Austro-Italian relations.

While Tittoni, who was Foreign Minister for most of the time between late 1903 and 1909, was a partisan of the Triple Alliance and of better relations with Austria, he met with very

[28] Imperiali to Prinetti, report 1479/504, Sept. 2, 1901, P68/349.

[29] *Atti parlamentari, Camera, Discussioni*, May 23, 1902, p. 2020; *Tribuna*, Aug. 22, 24, 1902.

[30] Tommasini, *L'Italia alla vigilia della guerra*, I, 123-140; Salvatorelli, *La triplice alleanza*, pp. 215-261; *G.P.*, XVIII, 501-610; A. F. Pribram, *The Secret Treaties of Austria-Hungary* (Cambridge, Mass., 1921), II, 114-142. The pertinent Italian documents appear in *C.V.*, I.

limited success in changing the atmosphere between Rome and
Vienna. In some respects tensions were probably greater when
he left office to become Ambassador to France. It did not
escape Austrian and German attention that the Italian reaction
to the visit of President Loubet to Rome in 1904 was more
cordial than any manifestation toward Italy's allies in years.[31]

Malagodi in the *Tribuna* on May 1, 1904, spoke of an
Anglo-French-Italian alliance as the ideal alliance of three
powers who were sisters in democracy and liberty. The authoritative observer for the *Nuova Antologia* concluded that the
Triple Alliance was nothing but a guarantee against war, also
between allies.[32] While the *Corriere della Sera* on May 3 recognized the utility and necessity of the Triple Alliance, it was
also impressed on May 7 that Italy had it within her power to
disrupt the equilibrium of military force between Triple Alliance and Franco-Russian alliance.

There appeared to be rising dissatisfaction with the Italian
alliance in Hungary. On August 27 the *Eti Ujság* of Budapest
spoke of the alliance as unnatural while the semi-official *Pester
Lloyd* asked next day if Italy was tired of the alliance and indicated that an open adversary would be preferred to a discontented ally. At the Consulta, Fusinato, the under-secretary,
discussed this article with Austrian *chargé* Somssich and won
the impression, later confirmed by Goluchowski, that there was
no official inspiration. Fusinato in turn promised a friendly
article in the *Popolo Romano*.[33] By August 31 the *Pester
Lloyd* excluded war but still insisted that the alliance had been
compromised.[34]

---

[31] For German concern, see *G.P.*, XVIII, 613-647; XX, (1), 37-102.

[32] XXX, "Il presidente Loubet a Roma," *Nuova Antologia*, 4 ser., CXI (May
1, 1904), 149-156.

[33] Fusinato's memo., Aug. 30, 1904; Bordonaro (Budapest) to Tittoni, report
1466/234, Aug. 28, 1904, P68/350; Somssich to Goluchowski, tel. 109, Aug. 30,
1904, P.A., Italien 1904, XI/131; *Corriere della Sera*, Aug. 30, 1904. The *Popolo
Romano* article appeared on August 31. Somssich to Goluchowski, tel. 111, Aug.
31, 1904, P.A., Italien 1904, XI/134.

[34] Bordonaro to Tittoni, tel. 1897, Aug. 31, 1904, Reg. 265.

To a suggestion from Italian Minister Guiccioli at Belgrade that Italy follow a *do ut des* policy toward Austria, Tittoni agreed that this policy or an outright anti-Austrian policy were the only ones possible. He favored an intimate union between Serbia, Bulgaria, and Montenegro and advised Guiccioli to "see all, hear much, speak little, promise nothing."[35] The *Nuova Antologia* called Italy and Austria "enemy-allies."[36]

That Austria felt it necessary to conclude a treaty of neutrality with Russia on October 15, 1904, to apply in the event of an unprovoked war with a third power, an agreement largely aimed at Italy, is eloquent testimony to the bad state of relations between Austria and Italy.[37] Barzini, one of Italy's top journalists, in an article in the *Corriere della Sera* on October 30, demanded an accord between Italy, France, and England for the Near East to counterbalance Russia and Austria.

Lützow, now ambassador at Rome, recalling that Luzzati had once said to him that between Italy and Austria only two things were possible, alliance or war, urged his Government to pay more attention to small acts of courtesy toward Italy and to focus Italian attention on regions where Austria had no interests. He recalled that Deák had once said that a bad marriage was better than no marriage at all.[38]

Obviously disturbed, Bülow was ready in 1905 to work for conciliation between Italy and Austria. Tittoni and Prime Minister Giolitti authorized Lanza to inform Germany of the substance of Prinetti's agreement of 1902 with France as it concerned neutrality in the event of aggression or provocation directed against France by another power.[39]

[35] Guiccioli to Tittoni, private letter, Sept. 1, 1904; Tittoni to Guiccioli, private letter, Sept. 19, 1904, C.V., XXI/3.

[36] XXX, "Punto ed a capo," *Nuova Antologia*, 4th ser., CXIII (Sept. 16, 1904), 320-326.

[37] Tommasini, *L'Italia alla vigilia della guerra*, I, 433-441.

[38] Lützow to Goluchowski, conf. report 90C, Dec. 13, 1904. P.A., Italien 1904, XI/132.

[39] Lanza to Tittoni, conf. tels., March 3, 4, 1905; Giolitti and Tittoni to Lanza, Feb. 25, 1905, C.V., III/2/91, 92, 93. Bülow appeared to be favorably impressed.

When William II visited Italy in April, 1905, Victor Emmanuel made no mention of Austria in his toast, a fact which the *Neue Freie Presse* was quick to report. The *Deutsche Zeitung* welcomed the idea of a revival of the Alliance of the Three Emperors. Then Austria could remain indifferent to the policies of France and Italy.[40] In September at Baden-Baden Bülow warned Tittoni that Italy and Austria must either be allies or enemies and that war would come if the alliance were not renewed.[41]

Italy's relations with Germany deteriorated in 1906 because of German criticism of Italian conduct at Algeciras but Austro-Italian relations appear actually to have improved. The action of Visconti Venosta, Italy's representative at Algeciras, was a model of caution which won the praise of Bülow. But the Kaiser told Szögyény that he would turn his whole armed force against Italy with enthusiasm if Italy became hostile to Austria-Hungary. He complained of Italian double dealing.[42]

Lützow concluded in March, 1906, that Italy's alliance with Austria had never been sounder or with deeper roots. He thought the elite of the Italian nation were convinced that hostility toward Austria was short-sighted and that Italy had little more chance to get Trieste than to get Hamburg and Rotterdam. Most of the agitation, he found, came from Austrian citizens; hostility toward the Triple Alliance was now directed more toward Germany than Austria.[43] Lützow was most favorably impressed with Guicciardini, who had succeeded Tittoni as Foreign Minister. He was a gentleman in the full

[40] Avarna to Tittoni, report 669/372, April 7, 1905, P68/350. See also *Corriere della Sera*, April 8, 1905. Tittoni told Lützow that he would have included mention of Austria if he had foreseen the reaction of a part of the European press. Lützow to Goluchowski, April 18, 1905, P.A., Italien 1905, XI/134.

[41] Tittoni's memo., Sept., 1905, C.V., XVI/7/2.

[42] Szögyény to Goluchowski, conf. letter, April 10, 1906, P.A., Geheimakten, Liasse XXXIII/38, Fasz. rot 477.

[43] Lützow to Goluchowski, conf. reports 24E, 26, March 20, 24, 1906, P.A., Italien 1906, XI/135. Monts, the German ambassador, expressed doubt that Italy was worth anything as an ally.

meaning of the term and impressed Lützow as being the most truth-loving Italian he had met.[44]

A part of the Austro-Hungarian press refused to agree with Lützow's optimistic views. Eugene Rákosi's *Budapesti Hirlap* (April 19) designated the Italian ally as the only potential enemy of Austria-Hungary.[45] While the *Neues Wiener Journal* thought that Italo-Austrian relations were improving[46] and the *Pester Lloyd* rejected English and French reports that the end of the Triple Alliance was near, describing the idea of a four-power alliance of France, England, Russia, and Italy as absurd,[47] the *Deutsches Volksblatt,* organ of Austria's German Progressive party, declared on April 19 that Italy had no diplomatic value for Germany; Italy's demands for expansion on Austrian coasts made her alliance with Austria a burden. It predicted that the policy followed by Italy recently would lead her out of the Triple alliance.[48] The *Corriere della Sera* replied on April 24 that Austria and Italy must be either friends or enemies and called upon Germany to aid in settling differences.

Lützow continued to report an improvement of relations and a growing realization that the Dual Monarchy was the surest protection against both Pan-Germanism and Pan-Slavism. Luzzatti told him that the King was now a sure friend and ally of Austria-Hungary.[49] Even the appearance of the book *Verso la guerra* by Battista Pellegrini, Zanardelli's former secretary, in June failed to provoke much excitement in the press.

[44] Lützow to Goluchowski, conf. report 28B, April 4, 1906, P.A., Italien 1906, XI/135.

[45] Bordonaro to Guicciardini, report 577/71, April 19, 1906, P68/350.

[46] *Corriere della Sera,* April 20, 1906.

[47] *Ibid.,* April 21, 1906.

[48] Avarna to Guicciardini, report 883/456, April 21, 1906, P68/350.

[49] Lützow to Goluchowski, conf. report 30C, reports 37B, 38B, April 17, May 7, 15, 1906, P.A., Italien 1906, XI/135. An article by Primo Levi denying Italian territorial aspirations in the Balkans, asserting that Italy and Austria complemented each other economically, and assuring that Irredentism was no longer a reality impressed Lützow. See XXX, "Italia e Austria," *Nuova Antologia,* 4th ser., CXXIII (May 1, 1906), 155-162.

Pellegrini argued that sooner or later war must come between Italy and Austria.[50]

At least two leading Italian Socialists advocated close relations with Austria but were opposed to the Triple Alliance. Arturo Labriola argued in the *Avanti* in May that Italy should leave the Triple Alliance and draw close to France and Austria-Hungary.[51] Bissolati came out in the *Tempo* on July 29, 1907, for closer relations between Italy and Austria-Hungary so that both could be liberated from German domination.[52]

Goluchowski's declaration to the Delegations in June, 1906, that relations with Italy were good failed to convince Kramář, the Young Czech leader, who said that the Triple Alliance was not adapted to world politics and was now only of a ceremonial nature.[53]

From the Italian side came several calls in 1906 for better relations with Austria. The *Esercito Italiano* spoke out for the Italian Army on November 25 against efforts of the French press to sow discord in the Triple Alliance and especially between Italy and Austria. Italy's alliance was not a forced matrimony but a marriage of interest and convenience.[54] *Chargé* Carlotti worked in Vienna to have the *Neue Freie Presse* adopt a more friendly tone toward Italy.[55] Luzzatti gave an interview on December 8, declaring that Italy and Austria-Hungary, as the weakest of the Great Powers, needed each other. Rudini appealed in the same paper for new life for the Triple Alli-

[50] Gsiller (Venice) to Goluchowski, report 33, July 24, 1906, P.A., Venedig 1906, XXXVIII/284.

[51] Flotow (*chargé*) to Goluchowski, report 40C, May 29, 1906, P.A., Italien 1906, XI/135.

[52] Somssich to Aehrenthal, report 34D, Aug. 6, 1907, P.A., Italien 1907, XI/137. See also *Corriere della Sera*, July 30, 1907.

[53] Avarna to Guicciardini, tel. 1525, June 11 and report 1339/674, June 13, 1906, Reg. 273; P15/93.

[54] Lützow to Aehrenthal, conf. report 73H, Nov. 27, 1906, P.A., Italien 1906, XI/136.

[55] Carlotti to Tittoni, tel. 3055, Dec. 7, 1906, Reg. 276.

ance.[56] But Lützow concluded in the spring of 1907 that the progress which had been made was largely on the governmental level and that Tittoni was mainly responsible. He foresaw no such friendship developing as that between Italy and France.[57]

Official Italo-Austrian relations probably reached their high point of intimacy and cordiality in the decade before 1914 as a result of Aehrenthal's visit to Tittoni at Desio and to Victor Emmanuel at Racconigi in July, 1907, and Tittoni's visit to Aehrenthal at Semmering and to Francis Joseph at Ischl in August. There was for the moment no point of disagreement between the two statesmen, as the *Tribuna* pointed out on July 15. The *Corriere della Sera*, at first skeptical, concluded on August 23 that reciprocal trust had been achieved. Tittoni urged the *Popolo Romano*, the *Tribuna*, and the *Giornale d'Italia* to respond with greater warmth to articles in the Austrian press.[58]

Avarna worked secretly and indirectly and with the knowledge of Aehrenthal to promote private efforts by Moneta of Italy and Plener of Austria to organize Austro-Italian friendship committees. These efforts were finally successful in August, 1908. Baroness von Suttner of Austria and Moneta of Italy headed the movement. But there was little enthusiasm in the press. Leopold von Chlumecký, one of Italy's most effective opponents, had already concluded in the *Österreichische Rundschau* that there was not the necessary cordiality between the two peoples for a real entente. The *Zeit* (December 27, 1907) deplored that a majority of Italians were still hostile to Austria and concluded (August 11, 1908) that the antagonism

---

[56] Carlotti to Tittoni, report 2552/1296, Dec. 8, 1906, P68/350. See also *Corriere della Sera*, Dec. 9; *Tribuna*, Dec. 10.

[57] Lützow to Aehrenthal, conf. report 20, April 30, 1907, P.A., Italien 1907, XI/137.

[58] Tittoni to Tommasini, tel., Aug. 26, 1907, Tommasini Papers. Even the *Zeit* concluded that the Balkans had ceased to be an apple of discord between Rome and Vienna. Avarna to Tittoni, report 1647/750, Aug. 5, 1907, P68/351.

could be eliminated only by war or by positive accords. The *Münchner Allgemeine Zeitung* judged (December 30, 1907) that efforts to bring the Italian and Austrian peoples together had failed and doubted the value of alliances supported only by Governments and not by peoples. The *Corriere della Sera* was optimistic when it concluded (September 15, 1908) that cordiality had been re-established between Italy and Austria and that German mediation was no longer needed. A part of the press in Italy remained hostile, but the attacks were probably more against Tittoni than his policy.[59]

Even before the Bosnian crisis Aehrenthal regarded Italy with suspicion. In peace Italy would be a very sensitive neighbor but with little feeling for others. In war Italy would be an unreliable ally.[60] Lützow agreed but pointed to the progress Tittoni had made in popularizing the alliance and felt that it prevented Italy from being a neighbor ready to drive a dagger into the Austrian neck.[61]

Italian diplomacy in the crisis will not be discussed in this paper. But a reading of the Italian documents leads this writer to conclude that Italian criticism of Tittoni's diplomacy in this period is largely unjustified. Struggling against an irrational outburst of popular passion, he showed considerable skill and an acute awareness of the realities of the situation. Neverthe-

[59] Avarna to Tittoni, private letters, May 7, July 26, 1907, Archivio Riservato (hereinafter cited as A.R.), I/7/96, 108; reports 2052/956, 2598/1242, 2609/1250, Oct. 7, Dec. 28, 31, 1907, P68/351; report 1568/900, Aug. 4, 1908, P68/351; Tommasini to Tittoni, conf. report 1741/965, Aug. 15, 1908, P68/351; Somssich to Aehrenthal, conf. reports, 39B, 39E, 41C, Aug. 18, Sept. 1, 1908, P.A., Italien 1908, XI/140. For a typical Chlumecký performance see "Politische Dramen—dramatische Politik," *Österreichische Rundschau*, XIV (Feb. 15, 1908), 239-244. A copy went to Tittoni. Avarna to Tittoni, report 370/188, Feb. 17, 1908, P15/95. See also Leopold von Chlumecký, *Österreich-Ungarn und Italien* (Vienna, 1907).

[60] Aehrenthal to Lützow, private and conf., June 27, 1908, P.A., Italien 1908, XI/141.

[61] Lützow to Aehrenthal, secret letter 2, July 7, 1908, P.A., Italien 1908, XI/141. Avarna noticed that Austrian political circles felt that most Italians were hostile. Avarna to Tittoni, private letter, Dec. 30, 1907, A.R., I/7/45.

less, with the Bosnian crisis[62] Italian opinion turned against Tittoni and hatred for Austria flared up anew. French *Chargé* Legrand reported a feeling of delusion and humiliation which recalled the days after France occupied Tunisia. Luzzatti threatened to break with Tittoni if he did not give Italian policy an orientation toward Paris and London.[63] Lt. Col. Jullian, the French military *attaché*, reported from Rome that Austria had wounded Italian national sentiment and that for the Italian people only one war was possible, that with Austria. He pointed to almost 100 millions in extraordinary credits to build up Italy's eastern defenses and concluded that in war France would need only covering troops on her Alpine frontier.[64] Tittoni told Muraviev, the Russian ambassador, in November that Italy would remain neutral in any war between France and Germany. If Russia and Austria were at war, Italy would remain neutral for the present, but it could be otherwise in three years after Italy reorganized her military forces.[65]

Aehrenthal expressed doubt to Bülow on December 8 that Italy would be a capable ally in case of need and proposed conversations between von Moltke and Conrad on the assumption of Italian neutrality.[66] Lützow did not believe that Italy would be of military help and saw the danger of a volunteer force on the side of Austria's enemies in the event of a Balkan war.[67]

[62] For excellent accounts of the crisis, see B. E. Schmitt, *The Annexation of Bosnia, 1908-1909* (Cambridge, 1937); M. Nintchitch, *La Crise bosniaque (1908-1909) et les puissances européennes* (2 vols.; Paris, 1937); Tommasini, *L'Italia alla vigilia della guerra*, IV, V. Tommasini was involved in the crisis and used the Italian documents. See also Albertini, *The Origins of the War of 1914*, I, 190-300 and his *Venti anni di vita politica* (Bologna, 1950-1953), I, 373-501.

[63] Legrand to Pichon, secret tel., Oct. 8, 1908. *D.D.F.*, 2nd ser., XI, 825-826.

[64] Jullian to Picquart, Oct. 26, 1908, *ibid.*, 2nd ser., XI, 860-863.

[65] Barrère to Pichon, secret, Nov. 19, 1908, *ibid.*, 2nd ser., XI, 938-940.

[66] Aehrenthal to Bülow, private letter, Dec. 8, 1908, in *Österreich-Ungarns Aussenpolitik von der bosnischen Krise 1908 bis zum Kriegsausbruch 1914: Diplomatische Aktenstücke des österreichisch-ungarischen Ministeriums des Äussern* (hereinafter cited as *O.U.A.*), L. Bittner, A. F. Pribram, H. Srbik, H. Uebersberger, eds. (Vienna, 1930), I, 558-563.

[67] Monts to Bülow, Dec. 9, 1908, *G.P.*, XXVI, 327.

Bülow felt that Germany should play down the Italian danger
and try to iron out difficulties. He reasoned that a war with
Italy would be more popular among the Austrian clericals and
aristocrats and the Czechs and other Slavs than a war with
Russia. There was danger that Austria would throw too many
troops against Italy and not enough against Russia. Germany
wanted Austrian strength thrown against Russia, and the Italian
frontier defensively held. Von Moltke was ready to talk with
Conrad. Bülow believed that Italy would remain neutral in
the event of war.[68]

Cartwright, the new British ambassador in Vienna, who had
an Italian wife, blamed Lützow in large part for bad Austro-
Italian relations, declaring that he had no standing in Italy.[69]
But Tittoni told Monts on December 2 that the anti-Austrian
movement went much deeper than the press indicated and expressed a desire for a change in the leading statesmen in Vienna.
Aehrenthal in turn remained critical of Tittoni, who, he said,
had listened more to St. Petersburg than to Berlin and Vienna.[70]

When, on December 7, Tittoni once again urged that
Austria attend the forthcoming Turin and Rome expositions,
Aehrenthal declared that it was the memory, not of past events,
but of recent events that prevented attendance. He reminded
the Italian representative that sentiment in Italy was not friendly toward Austria; Fortis had recently been applauded by the
whole Chamber when he announced that the Dual Monarchy
was Italy's only possible enemy; Italy's behavior was viewed in
Austria as not that of a friend and ally; his re-examination of
the question would depend on future Italian opinion toward
Austria.[71] Austria finally accepted the invitation to the expositions.

[68] Bülow to Monts, private letter, Dec. 14, 1908; Bülow to Tschirschky, Dec.
15, 1908, ibid., XXVI, 336-339.
[69] Tschirschky to Bülow, Dec. 21, 1908, ibid., XXVI, 347-350.
[70] Monts to F.O., Dec. 2, 1908, ibid., XXVI, 455. See also Aehrenthal to
Bülow, private letter, Feb. 20, 1909, ibid., XXVI, 610-616.
[71] Tittoni to Avarna, private letter, Dec. 7, 1908, A.R., II/91/183; Pro
Memoria, Dec. 20, 1908, A.R., II/91/182.

From Stockholm, Costa, the Italian minister, argued that the best way to get along with Austria was to be strong and show one's teeth. Tittoni agreed.[72]

Luzzatti told Barrère in November, 1908, that no one in Italy wanted the Triple Alliance; it was dead; Italy must arm so that she could leave the Triple Alliance in two years; Austria had violated international treaties, threatened and duped Italy, and outraged Italian sentiment; there was nothing in common between Italy and Austria-Hungary.[73] Barrère was impressed with the precautions necessary to protect the two Austrian embassies in Rome.[74] Jullian reported a new mobilization plan under study for a war with Austria.[75] Realizing that in three years Italy would no longer be negligible militarily, Barrère took strong issue with the British view that Italy should be kept in the Triple Alliance.[76] Aehrenthal believed that the Quai d'Orsay was identified with Barrère's efforts to disrupt the Triple Alliance but concluded by February, 1909, that reason had gained the upper hand at the Consulta. He still was under no illusions about the worth of Italy as an ally, so he wrote Lützow.[77] Full of sympathy for Tittoni, who was then endangering his career to promote better relations with Austria, Lützow still held that thinking Italians wanted friendship and were opposed to a policy of adventure. He reported assurances by Fortis that he wanted no war with Austria.[78]

After the Bosnian crisis, Aehrenthal expressed pleasure that

[72] Costa to Tittoni, conf. letter, Dec. 12, 1908, A.R., II/96/462; Tittoni to Costa, conf. letter, Dec. 27, 1908, A.R., II/96/339.

[73] Barrère to Pichon, Nov. 24, 1908, *D.D.F.*, 2nd ser., XI, 942, 943.

[74] Barrère to Pichon, Nov. 29, 1908, *ibid.*, 2nd ser., XI, 953-956.

[75] Jullian to Picquart, Dec. 6, 1908, *ibid.*, 2nd ser., XI, 975-977.

[76] P. Cambon to Pichon, Dec. 3; Barrère to Pichon, Dec. 20, 1908, *ibid.*, 2nd ser., XI, 974, 975, 999-1002. See also Lützow to Aehrenthal, tel. 235, Dec. 6, 1908, P.A., Italien 1908, XI/141.

[77] Aehrenthal to Lützow, 533, Feb. 10, 1909, P. A., Italien 1909, XI/143. Tittoni told Lützow that France had incited opinion against him. Lützow to Aehrenthal, Feb. 1, 1909, *O.U.A.*, I, 789.

[78] Lützow to Aehrenthal, Feb. 16, 1909. *O.U.A.*, I, 833, 834. Fortis blamed most of the difficulty on the Masons, who controlled the Italian press and favored anticlerical France.

Italo-Austrian relations had emerged undamaged. He was too optimistic. Tittoni found a sense of painful irritation persisting in Italy at Aehrenthal's methods and a demand that Italy come to terms with Russia. The British were impressed with the fact in October, 1909, that the relations of Italy and Austria could not be worse. There was a strong note of mistrust in the Hungarian press. Avarna reported that poltical circles felt that Italy had vacillated for a second time as at Algeciras. If this happened a third time, Italy's allies would lose faith in her. Aehrenthal had influenced the Austrian press; Italy should enlighten her public opinion.[79] Lützow tended to minimize hostile press comments and quoted Giolitti to the effect that public opinion could not be learned from newspapers. He was certain that German and Austrian power would hold Italy in the alliance and urged his Government to be unsparing with small attentions and kind words.[80]

Lützow ended his mission in Rome in March, 1910, with a sense of pride at what had been accomplished in six years. Avarna believed that Austro-Italian relations were better than when Goluchowski left office.[81] All Vienna papers except the *Zeit* reacted favorably to the new Luzzatti ministry, formed on March 31 with San Giuliano as Foreign Minister.[82]

[79] Durrazo (Budapest) to Tittoni, conf. report 517/74, April 5, 1909, P1129/-734; Avarna to Tittoni, tel. 1249, April 6 and private letter, April 14, report 1056/413, April 26, 1909, Reg. 294; A.R., III/121/74; P68/351bis. The *Fremdenblatt* praised Italian policy on April 25. For British views, see Hardinge to Bax-Ironside, Oct. 28, 1909, *British Documents on the Origins of the War, 1898-1914* (hereinafter cited as B.D.). G. P. Gooch and H. Temperley, eds. (London, 1926-1938), IX, (1), 80, 81. For Tittoni's views see Tittoni to Avarna, personal, Oct. 18, 1909, A.R., III/119. Jagow, the German ambassador, detected fears in Italy of Austrian attack. Lützow to Aehrenthal, conf. letter, June 22, 1909, P.A., Italien 1909, XI/143.

[80] Lützow to Aehrenthal, conf. letter 34A, May 26, 1909, P.A., Italien 1909, XI/142. For evidence that anti-Austrian feeling was still strong at Venice, see Baum to Aehrenthal, reports 7, 16, May 2, 30, 1909, P.A., Venedig 1909, XXXVIII/293.

[81] Lützow to Aehrenthal, conf. report 14B, March 17, 1910, P.A., Italien 1910, XI/143; Avarna to San Giuliano, private letter, April 25, 1910, A.R., V/179/109.

[82] Cerruti (*chargé* at Vienna) to San Giuliano, tel. 1004, April 2, 1910, Reg. 300.

Efforts were made on both sides to create better understanding and better feeling. Avarna found that the Italian press was confused on questions of foreign policy and that Italian journalists lacked a perfect knowledge of languages and of conditions in other countries. There was too much sentiment. Language toward Austria was intemperate and the handling of Balkan questions was not objective. The *Tribuna* and the *Giornale d'Italia* maintained correspondents at Vienna who were of Austrian origin and Irredentist. He urged a reorganization of the press office and recommended that Dr. Andrea Cantalupi, an Italian journalist, be employed in Vienna in the interest of better press relations. San Giuliano agreed that he should be employed with secret funds from the Ministry of Interior, and he performed valuable service.[83] The *Neue Freie Presse* addressed an open letter to Luzzatti, and Baroness von Suttner and a number of artists and intellectuals made an appeal in the same paper for a *rapprochement*.[84] San Giuliano, who had concluded that much of Italy's trouble came from the imperfect knowledge which Austria and Germany had of her,[85] worked earnestly to improve relations with Austria or at least for what *Chargé* Ambrózy called a truce of God. The minister warned that Italians often spoke in exaggerated terms and that Austria placed too much emphasis on some of these extreme statements. It was not true that every Italian hated Austria. Italians also held the erroneous view that Austria awaited the suitable moment to fall on Italy. Yet there was no fundamental clash of the vital interests of the two powers. On the

[83] Avarna to San Giuliano, private letter, July 18; San Giuliano to Luzzatti, July 28, 1910, Gab. XXI/138, also Luzzatti Papers in the Archivio Centrale dello Stato (Rome). San Giuliano proposed sharp increases in the budget for foreign affairs with much more money for secret funds to influence the press and to counteract Austrian propaganda in Albania. San Giuliano to Luzzatti, personal letter, Aug. 6, 1910, Luzzatti Papers.

[84] Mérey to Aehrenthal, report 32G, July 5, 1910, P.A., Italien 1910, XI/144; Avarna to San Giuliano, report 1305/609, June 26, 1910, P68/351bis. The Italian press reacted rather coldly.

[85] San Giuliano to Tittoni, conf. report 2055/709, Dec. 30, 1908, P68/351bis.

contrary, the Dual Monarchy was Italy's bulwark against Slavism and Germanism. Irredentism, he said, had lost all significance.[86]

Unfortunately, Mérey, the new Austrian Ambassador to Italy, shared many of the erroneous Austrian ideas about Italy.[87] He appears to have been an unwise choice. He was much impressed soon after he came to Italy by a publication of the *Lega navale,* headed by retired Vice-Admiral Gualtieri, which expressed real doubt that Italy would ever fight on the side of Austria[88] and never appears to have trusted the Italians. San Giuliano eventually came to prefer to carry on negotiations at Vienna rather than with Mérey in Rome.

San Giuliano made an excellent impression on Aehrenthal when they visited at Salzburg and Ischl from August 30 to September 2, 1910. Perhaps the outstanding result of their conversations was a conviction by both men that there should be less emphasis on petty incidents. But San Giuliano was not entirely reassured. He instructed Avarna and all consuls in Austria-Hungary to report all incidents and proposed to make counterclaims whenever Austria made remonstrances on minor incidents.[89]

To the warm *Tribuna* appeal to the press (August 30) to promote a meeting of minds in Italy and Austria *Danzers Armee Zeitung* responded on September 8 with a demand for military increases to make Italy fear if not love Austria and with the charge that the House of Savoy had been unfaithful to its alliances for centuries. Aehrenthal deplored this article but

[86] Jagow thought that Italy feared Russian preponderance in the Balkans as much as Austrian. Ambrózy to Aehrenthal, conf. report 39C, Aug. 27 and tels. 120, 121, Aug. 29, 1910, P.A., Italien 1910, XI/144. Fritz Telmann made an appeal in the *Morgen* (June 13) to Austrians to get rid of their erroneous views about Italy. Avarna to San Giuliano, report 1183/543, June 14, 1910, P68/351 bis.

[87] Avarna to San Giuliano, private letter, April 23, 1910, A.R., V/179/108.

[88] Mérey to Aehrenthal, report 35L, July 27, 1910, P.A., Italien 1910, XI/144.

[89] See P.A., Geheimakten, Liasse XXXV/10, Fasz. rot 481; Ambrózy to Aehrenthal, report 41B, Sept. 9, 1910, P.A., Italien 1910, XI/144; San Giuliano's circular, tel. 4088, Sept. 5, 1910, Gab. II.

he reminded Avarna that Italian papers had made insulting remarks to Francis Joseph on his eightieth birthday.[90] Aehrenthal's visit to Turin was hailed by the *Tribuna* (October 2) as a new affirmation of the Triple Alliance, but Ambrózy was impressed three days later with the depth of the mistrust and fear of Austria.[91] Fortunately, Germany was working actively to promote better relations between her allies.[92]

Italo-Austrian relations came through the stress and strain of the Libyan war rather well. Italy did not forget, however, that Russia had been a warmer supporter and that the Austrian press had probably encouraged Turkish resistance even though Aehrenthal tried to restrain it.[93] Undoubtedly the clericals and a part of the Austrian military favored an Austro-German-Russian alliance, and even Avarna admitted that a breach of the status quo would reveal the superficiality of the Triple Alliance.[94] But the alliance held firm through the heated negotiations for an extension of Italian operations. Berchtold yielded on the Dodecanese occupation but he was firm that Italy must not occupy Chios. Although he realized that a rigid interpretation of Article VII of the alliance might be useful for Italy in the future, San Giuliano did not hesitate to threaten that Austrian opposition to Italian liberty of action would render the alliance impossible.[95]

False reports that Italy had made an accord with France and England led to the usual outburst of alarm in the Austrian

[90] Avarna to San Giuliano, conf. report 1851/817, Sept. 14, 1910.

[91] Ambrózy to Aehrenthal, report 44D, Oct. 5, 1910, P.A., Italien 1910, XI/144.

[92] San Giuliano to Pansa and Avarna, most conf. tel. 3042, Nov. 3, 1910, A.R., V.

[93] Avarna to San Giuliano, conf. tel., 8318, Dec. 23, 1911, Reg. 323. Many of the points of friction in this period are discussed in my *Europe and Italy's Acquisition of Libya, 1911-1912* (Durham, 1942).

[94] Avarna to San Giuliano, Aug. 12, 1911, C.V., IV/2. Avarna was a strong exponent of the idea that Italy should have the Isonzo valley and the Trentino if Austria expanded in the Balkans. He felt that the alliance needed to be reinforced by a positive accord on compensation before rather than after a crisis developed.

[95] San Giuliano to Avarna and Pansa, secret tels. 494, 495, 992, April 4, June 4, 1912; San Giuliano to Avarna, secret tel. 990, June 3, 1912, Gab. 341.

press in July and August, 1912.[96] Perhaps the sanest words
came from the *Arbeiter Zeitung* on August 8 when it blamed
Austria for Italy's "extra waltz" because she had wounded
Italian sentiment over the Adriatic and the Tyrol.[97] In a long
conversation with Mérey which he felt should win him a post
in Paradise, Bollati, Secretary-General of the Foreign Office,
denied such an accord but also affirmed that it would not be in
contradiction with the Triple Alliance.[98]

Berchtold's reception at Pisa in October, 1912, was said to
be the warmest accorded an Austrian Foreign Minister in
twenty-five years.[99] When the Triple Alliance was renewed
in December after long negotiations, only Barzilai and Bissolati
raised their voices in opposition, but Torre reported in the
Corriere della Sera that a majority of the deputies were unfavorable.[100] Balkan questions, especially the Albanian problem, and Irredentism now put the Austro-Italian alliance to a
severe test in the coming months before Europe was engulfed
in war.

II. *The Albanian Rivalry*

Italy and Austria agreed on a common policy in Albania
as early as 1897 but official agreement did not end the struggle
for influence in this troubled region nor did it quiet the fears
of the Governments and peoples. Both nations subsidized leading Albanians. Both sought economic advantages. Both were
developing schools and seeking to influence the clergy. The
Austrian claim to protect the Albanian Catholics was deeply
resented by Italy. Consular officials on both sides were over-
zealous in their activities and often made alarmist reports to

[96] Avarna to San Giuliano, reports 1453/570, 1667/677, 1683/683, July 11,
Aug. 12, 1912, P121/493; P17/138; P9/60.
[97] Avarna to San Giuliano, tel. 4949, Aug. 8, 1912, Reg. 335.
[98] Bollati to San Giuliano, July 12, 1912, Gab. IX/58bis.
[99] Mérey to Berchtold, Nov. 4, 1912, *O.U.A.*, IV, 770.
[100] Mérey to Berchtold, tel. 243, report 89A-S, Dec. 10, 1912, *ibid.*, V, 88;
P.A., Italien 1912, XI/147; Györgyey (Milan) to Berchtold, report 58, Dec. 19,
1912, P.A., Mailand, XXXVIII/303.

their Governments. Each nation believed that the other intended to gain control of Albania and thus make itself supreme in the Adriatic. Neither Italy nor Austria would allow this to happen without a struggle.[101]

The Austrians feared the activities of between 150,000 and 200,000 Albanians in South Italy who began to organize in 1895 under the intellectual leadership of Girolamo da Rada. Their organizations and meetings grew in number and they began publishing newspapers. They received small subsidies from the Italian Government. The Austrians believed that the Italo-Albanians were working for an Italian protectorate over Albania. Da Rada, in fact, felt that under certain conditions most of Albania might be federated with Italy and the rest with Greece.[102] With the possible exception of Millelire, the active Italian consul at Janina, there appears to have been no serious Italian advocate of a protectorate in 1896. Millelire reported that the Albanians wanted autonomy under Italian protection and reminded his Government that Valona was the key to the Adriatic.[103] There was a very definite Austrian fear that Italian prestige and influence were increasing while Austrian influence was declining[104] just as there was an Italian fear that Austria was penetrating Albania through the Catholic clergy and that Italian influence was waning.[105]

Another Austrian fear was that Italy would be closely associated with Montenegro, a state with boundless ambitions, after the marriage of the Prince of Naples to Montenegrin Princess

[101] Space does not allow the citation of a vast number of consular and foreign office documents which substantiate these conclusions.

[102] Pisko (Janina) to Goluchowski, report 9, April 11, 1896, P.A., Albanien 1896, XXXVIII/326.

[103] Millelire to Bianchini, Sept. 30, 1896, *D.D.I.*, 3rd ser., I, 160-164.

[104] Szommer (Durazzo) to Goluchowski, report 6, June 20, 1896, P.A., Albanien 1896, XXXVIII/324; Meichsner (Janina) to Goluchowski, report 28, July 10, 1896, P.A., Albanien 1896, XXXVIII/326.

[105] Leoni (Scutari) to Visconti Venosta, report 286/144, Nov. 30, 1896, P15. For proof that Austria sought to use the clergy in order to build up her influence, see Pisko's memo., July, 1896, P.A., Albanien 1896, XXXVIII/326.

Elena in 1896.[106] In fact, Nicholas, Prince of Montenegro, proposed to Italy on December 8 that Montenegro should have northern Albania and Italy should have all of southern Albania except a part of the vilayet of Janina, which should go to Greece. Austria could in turn annex Bosnia-Herzegovina. Next day the modest Prince had a proposal for the division of practically all of the Balkan Peninsula between Italy, Montenegro, Serbia, Bulgaria, and Greece.[107]

Believing that the break-up of the Turkish Empire was only a matter of time, Goluchowski began planning on November 17, 1896, for a protectorate over an independent north and central Albania. The Greek parts could fall to Greece. Pisko at Üsküb recommended the expenditure of 100,000 francs a year in subsidies in addition to grants to the clergy. He found that many chiefs in north and central Albania favored an Austrian occupation or an Austrian protectorate but that a number of Beys in the south were pro-Italian.[108]

Goluchowski was alarmed by reports from Berlin that Nigra regarded an Austro-Italian intervention in the western Balkans as almost inevitable and that Italy was preparing two army corps for such a project, by Salisbury's information that when Greek troops entered Macedonia Italy intended to occupy Albania,[109] and by the fact that one of four Albanian papers published in Italy, the *Nazione Albanese,* worked for an Italian protectorate over Albania.[110] The Italians were equally alarmed at Austrian intentions. The *Secolo* and the *Tribuna* accused

---

[106] Kuczynski (Cetinje) to Goluchowski, conf. report 73B, Nov. 20, 1896, P.A., Montenegro 1896, XVII/18.

[107] Bianchi (Cetinje), conf. letters Dec. 8, 9, 1896, *D.D.I.,* 3rd ser., I, 218-220. Pasetti found that the Italian press was encouraging Greater Serbia ideas. Pasetti to Goluchowski, report 66B, Oct. 31, 1896, P.A., Italien 1896, XI/115.

[108] Goluchowski's memos., Nov. 17, Dec. 8, 23, 1896, P.A., Geheimakten, XXXI/A, Albanien 1896-1906, Fasz. rot 480; Pisko's memo., Jan., 1897, P.A., Geheimakten, Liasse XXXI, Albanien, Fasz. rot 473.

[109] Szögyény to Goluchowski, conf. tels. 56, 57, Feb. 21, 1897, P.A., Preussen 1897, XII/246; Deym to Goluchowski, conf. report 9B, Feb. 23, 1897, P.A., Liasse Türkei XXVIII, Fasz. XII/246.

[110] Pisko to Goluchowski, report 81, April 16, 1897, P.A., Üsküb 1897, XXXVIII/359.

Austria, in April, 1897, of wishing to create unrest in Albania as a pretext for occupying it, and both papers saw Russia and Austria agreeing over the division of Turkey to the exclusion of Italy.[111] Nigra, however, discounted reports from Consul Leoni at Scutari and believed assurances from Goluchowski and Kálnoky that Austria had no ambitions in Albania.[112]

When Goluchowski visited Prime Minister Rudinì, Visconti Venosta, and the King at Milan and Monza on November 5 and 6, full agreement was reached to work for autonomy if the status quo could not be maintained in the Near East. If Turkey lost Macedonia, Albania should have either a privileged status under Turkish sovereignty or become independent. Visconti Venosta complained to Goluchowski that Austrian consuls encouraged the clergy to oppose Italian schools. Goluchowski promised that he would force this practice to stop if it was happening, but on condition that Italian schools refrain from propaganda for annexation to Italy. These oral assurances laid the basis for the written exchange of notes of December 20, 1900, and February 9, 1901, pledging to maintain the status quo in Albania as long as circumstances permitted but to work for autonomy if the status quo could not be preserved. There was also a pledge to conciliate and safeguard the reciprocal interests of the two powers in Albania.[113]

The significant fact is that formal assurances of a secret nature failed to convince consular officials or public opinion.

[111] Pasetti to Goluchowski, tel. 74, April 24; report 24C, April 29, 1897, P.A., Italien 1897, XI/116; Türkei, Liasse XXX/Albanien, Fasz. XII/259.

[112] Nigra to Visconti Venosta, conf. report 1448/380, May 4, 1897, P15. The *Politische Correspondenz* on April 27 denied that Austria caused trouble in Albania. Nigra to Visconti Venosta, report 1372/354, April 27, 1897, P15. An unfounded report reached the Ministry of Interior that Austria had secretly ordered an army corps to invade Albania and thus to present Italy with another Tunisia. Minister of Interior to Visconti Venosta, conf., May 5, 1897, P15.

[113] The pertinent documents are in P.A., Geheimakten, Liasse XXXV/1, Fasz. rot 481. See also Alfred Rappaport, "Albaniens Werdegang," *Die Kriegsschuldfrage*, V (Sept., 1927), 815-844. Pasetti was pleased with the Italian press reaction to the Monza meeting except for the radical and Irredentist press. Pasetti to Goluchowski, report 59, Nov. 11, 1897, P.A., Italien 1897, XI/116.

Charges and countercharges continued to flow into the two Foreign Offices. The Albanian notables were in the happy situation of playing off one power against the other.[114] Perhaps the
most sensible suggestion came from Guicciardini, who passed
for an expert on Albania and later became Foreign Minister.
He proposed a temporary protectorate by the concert of Europe
if the status quo became impossible.[115] The Germans were
fearful that the Albanian question would affect the solidarity
of the Triple Alliance.[116] Ugo Ojetti sounded an ominous note
in a series of articles in the *Corriere della Sera* in July and
August. After a visit to Albania, he insisted on the Italian right
to be concerned and perhaps one day to occupy Albania.[117]
Foreign Minister Prinetti appealed to Austria for an end of
the press polemic over Albania. He indicated government influence on the press in that sense and assured Austria that Italy
would not support Montenegrin aspirations which were out of
harmony with the Triple Alliance.[118]

   The Italians left few stones unturned to spread their influence in Albania. They had schools at Durazzo, Valona, Janina,
and Scutari. Important Italian centers for training Albanians
were S. Adriano in S. Demetrio Corone, the Oriental Institute
at Naples, and Palermo. Post Offices were established at Scutari, Durazzo, and Janina in 1902. The Puglia and Bojana ship
lines were important. Italian merchants were not idle. The

   [114] Even the semi-official *Pester Lloyd* sounded a note of alarm on May 9,
1901, concerning Italian intentions in Albania. Bollati to Prinetti, report 862/73,
May 18, 1901, P844/664. In the Italian Chamber on June 8 Deputy De Marinis
declared that Austria was preparing to annex Albania. *Atti parlamentari,
Camera, Discussioni,* June 8, 1901, pp. 4907-4913. Pasetti attributed the increasing Italian agitation over Albania in part to the King. Pasetti to Goluchowski, report 36B, June 18, 1901, P.A., Italien 1901, XI/123.

   [115] F. Guicciardini, "Impressioni d'Albania," *Nuova Antologia,* 4th ser.,
XCIII (June 16, 1901), 577-611; Kuhn to Goluchowski, report 46E, July 30, 1901,
P.A., Italien 1901, XI/123.

   [116] Lanza to Prinetti, report 1257/412, July 28, 1901, P844/664.

   [117] *Corriere della Sera,* Aug. 3, 1901; Kuhn to Informationsbureau, report
33/J.B., Aug. 13, 1901, P.A., Italien 1901, XI/124.

   [118] Kuhn to Goluchowski, report 49B, Aug. 28, 1901, P.A., Italien 1901,
XI/124.

Austrians feared Italian colonization plans and activity with the clergy. The *Consiglio Albanese d'Italia* was formed in 1904 with General Ricciotti Garibaldi as president and with a newspaper, the *Gazzetta Albanese*. The Austrians were competing with the Italians at every turn and were even converting some Orthodox to Roman Catholicism.[119]

At Abbazia in April, 1904, Goluchowski and Tittoni discussed Albania. Goluchowski asserted that Austria was only seeking to arouse Albanian national feeling in preparation for autonomy but complained that Italy was making pro-Italian propaganda. Tittoni denied the charge. The two statesmen impressed each other favorably and press reaction in the two countries was good.[120] But tension mounted in May when Deputies Cirmeni, Barzilai, Sommi-Picenardi, and Chimirri pointed up the danger of Austrian domination of the Adriatic. Chimirri predicted that Venice would become German if Austria controlled Albania.[121] Both Tittoni and Goluchowski sought to reassure opinion. Tittoni on May 18 pronounced the principle of autonomy on the basis of nationality if the status quo could not be maintained in Turkey.[122]

After Ficher, editor of the *Politische Correspondenz,* and an editor of the *Neue Freie Presse* spoke to Avarna of rumors of war over Albania and other Balkan questions, Avarna worked both privately and officially to put an end to the polemic and with noticeable effect.[123] General Türr, who was friendly to

[119] Kral's memo., April, 1905; Zwiedinek's memos., Jan. 11, 1898, Jan., 1902, P.A., Geheimakten, XXXI/B, Albanien 1896-1906, Fasz. rot. 480; Nigra to Prinetti, June 19, 1902, P844/665. There was considerable alarm in Austria at Garibaldi's efforts to organize a volunteer force.

[120] Goluchowski's memo., April, 1904, P.A. Geheimakten, Liasse XXXV/2, Fasz. rot 481; Tittoni's circular, tel. 721, April 12, 1904, Reg. 261; Avarna to Tittoni, report 450/138, April 11, 1904, P68/350; XXX, "Il convegno d'Abbazia," *Nuova Antologia,* 4th ser., CX (April 16, 1904), 732-739.

[121] *Atti parlamentari, Camera, Discussioni,* May 13, 14, 17, 1904, pp. 12519-12521, 12615-12630.

[122] *Ibid.,* May 18, 1904, pp. 12649-12651.

[123] Avarna to Tittoni, private letter, Aug. 28, report 1305/599, Aug. 31, tels., 1898, 1899, 1910, Aug. 31, Sept. 1, 1904, P68/350; Reg. 265; Bordonaro to Tittoni, tel. 1897, Aug. 31, 1904, Reg. 265.

Italy, proposed autonomy for both Albania and Macedonia in
the *Magyar Hirlap* on September 8.[124]   Commenting on V.
Mantegazza's anti-Austrian book, *L'altra sponda,* Lützow minimized the danger of an armed expedition by Ricciotti Garibaldi but expressed fear of Italy's peaceful penetration.[125]

When Tittoni and Goluchowski met at Venice, April 29
and 30, 1905, they confirmed that Albania must be a *noli me
tangere* for both powers and agreed that at some future date
when an administrative reorganization of Macedonia took place,
the Albania parts should be added to the vilayets of Scutari and
Janina.   Both recognized the desirability of preparing Albania
for autonomy and of using their schools for this purpose.[126]
Aehrenthal and Tittoni reaffirmed their agreement on Albania
on their visits in July and August, 1907.[127]

During the Bosnian crisis Tittoni worked to have Turkey
insist that Austria renounce her protection of the Albanian
Catholics, which he considered one of Austria's most powerful
weapons for exerting influence.   His efforts were not successful, and this question caused irritation up to the outbreak of
war.[128]

From Primo Levi at Salonika came the sound warning in
1910 that Italians talked too much about Albania. Austria was
only trying to separate the Albanians from Italy, not to win
them for herself.   Austrian expenditures, he found, were less
than reported.   He concluded that the Albanians had no love
either for the Italians or the Austrians.[129]   They were, in fact,

    [124] Bordonaro to Tittoni, report 1524/243, Sept. 8, 1904, P68/350.
    [125] Lützow to Goluchowski, conf. report 14C, March 8, 1905, P.A., Italien
1905, XI/133.
    [126] Goluchowski's memo., May, 1905, P.A., Geheimakten, Fasz. rot 480; Tittoni's
memo., May 2, 1905, P68/350.
    [127] Tittoni's memo., July 15, 1907, and résumé of Desio meeting, Aug., 1907,
A.R., I/5/4; Aehrenthal's memo., July 15, 1907, P.A., Geheimakten, Liasse
XXXV/3, Fasz., rot 481.
    [128] Tittoni to Imperiali, tel. 3432, Dec. 7, 1908, Reg. 289. There were several
exchanges on this subject. The Austrians made elaborate preparations for an
Albanian rising against Montenegro during the Bosnian crisis. P.A., Geheimakten, Liasse XXXIX/g, Karton rot 486.
    [129] Levi to Guicciardini, March 7, 1910, Gab., XXXV/475.

opposed to one of Italy's most cherished projects, the Danube-Adriatic railway, on the ground that it would promote the spread of Slavism. One of their leading spokesmen, Deputy Ismail Kemal Bey, sought to promote English and Italian support for a railroad from Valona to Monastir.[130]

By 1911 the Italians were in first place in export and import trade with Albania.[131] General Garibaldi remained a disturbing factor with his numerous threats to send volunteers to fight in Albania. On the other hand, Italians suspected that Austria was aiding the Albanian revolt and planned to reoccupy the Sanjak. Actually Austria and Italy were both working to restrain Montenegro and to urge conciliation on Turkey. Italy took firm measures to prevent the departure of volunteers and to send home Italians suspected of participation in the insurrection.[132]

Aehrenthal expressed sharp dissatisfaction when San Giuliano acted on an alarmist report from Consul Labia at Durazzo and sent the *Varese* in June, without Austrian approval. Aehrenthal asked that the ship be recalled and Italy complied.[133] When a group of Albanian leaders planned a meeting in Bari in August to raise money to acquire arms, the Italian Government placed the leaders under surveillance and

[130] San Giuliano to Tittoni, conf. report, 1388/537, Oct. 21, 1909; Imperiali to Guicciardini, conf. report 440/153, March 12, 1910, P844/669. On the Danube-Adriatic, see A. J. May, "Trans-Balkan Railway Schemes," *Journal of Modern History*, XXIV (Dec., 1952), 352-367; W. S. Vucinich, *Serbia between East and West: The Events of 1903-1908* (Stanford, 1954), pp. 210-230.

[131] Biliński (Janina) to Aehrenthal, report 23, May 26, 1911, P.A., Janina, XXXVIII/328.

[132] Mérey to Aehrenthal, report 1B, Jan. 4, 1911, P.A., Italien 1911, XI/145; San Giuliano to Giolitti, April 1, 3, 25, 1911, P844/670; Gab. XXI/138; San Giuliano's circular, tel. 1677, May 8, 1911, Reg. 309; Giolitti to San Giuliano, April 26, 1911, P844/670; Anselmo Lorecchio, "La rivoluzione nell'Albania e nel Yemen," *Nuova Antologia*, 4th ser., CLII (April 16, 1911), 699-713.

[133] Aehrenthal to Mérey, conf. private letter, June 16, 1911, P.A., Albanien, Liasse XXXIV, Fasz. XIV/34; Avarna to San Giuliano, tels. 2550, 2570, 2625, 2626, June 7, 8, 10, 1911, Reg. 313; Labia to San Giuliano, tels. 2538, 2563, 2615, June 6, 7, 10, 1911, Reg. 313; San Giuliano to Avarna, tel. 2043, June 7, 1911, Reg. 309.

prohibited the meeting.[134]   With the Tripolitan action pending, Italy wished to avoid offending Austria.

If Aehrenthal assumed a threatening tone toward Italy in order to force a suspension of operations in the Adriatic and Ionian Seas after the outbreak of the Turco-Italian War, one of his main fears was that Italy was denying Turkey the means to prevent arms from being smuggled into Albania.   San Giuliano complied and promised energetic measures to prevent Italian weapons from entering.[135]   Aehrenthal even blamed the Italian consuls at Scutari and Valona for a part in fomenting Albanian unrest before they left.   San Giuliano denied the charge.[136]   So serious did tension with Austria appear that San Giuliano called for the friendly intervention of Germany, a maneuver which he was to repeat many times before the outbreak of war in 1914.[137]

When an independent Albania began to emerge from the fires of the Balkan wars Austro-Italian tension increased.   Italy and Austria agreed on the principle of absolute parity, except that Italy excluded her forest concessions.   San Giuliano was greatly alarmed at the end of 1912 lest Montenegro cede Mount Lovčen to Austria in order to obtain Scutari.   He favored Montenegro's wishes to have Scutari in order to limit the number of Catholics in Albania under the influence of Austria[138] but

[134] San Giuliano's circular, tel. 3205, Aug. 20, 1911, Reg. 311.

[135] Avarna to San Giuliano, secret tels. 5100, 5121, Oct. 1, 2, 1911, Reg. 317; San Giuliano to Avarna, tel. 3840, Oct. 2, 1911, Reg. 316. Aehrenthal feared also that Italy might provoke Greek and Montenegrin action against Turkey and he was under pressure from the Austrian military circles and Francis Ferdinand. Avarna to San Giuliano, tels. 5403, 5585, Oct. 7, 11, 1911, Reg. 317.

[136] Avarna to San Giuliano, tel. 5872, Oct. 18, 1911, Reg. 319; San Giuliano to Avarna, tel. 4316, Oct. 18, 1911, Reg. 318.

[137] San Giuliano to Pansa, secret tel. 3844, Oct. 2, 1911, Reg. 316.

[138] San Giuliano to Imperiali, tel. 2566, Dec. 28, 1912, Gab. 345. For excellent discussions of the questions arising out of the Balkan wars, including the Albanian question, see E. C. Helmreich, *The Diplomacy of the Balkan Wars, 1912-1913* (Cambridge, Mass., 1938); Albertini, *The Origins of the War of 1914*, I, 364-539; Augusto Torre, "Italia e Albania durante le guerre balcaniche (1912-1913)," *Rivista d'Albania*, I (1940), 213-254; Albertini, *Venti anni di vita politica*, II, 313-444.

not at the expense of a cession of Lovčen to Austria. Berchtold denied that he had asked for Lovčen but told the Italians that Article VII of the Triple Alliance did not give Italy the right to compensation if Austria acquired territory from an independent Balkan state.[139] Then San Giuliano threatened to make special accords with other powers within the limits of the Triple Alliance if Italian interests were not safeguarded by the alliance.[140] He pressed for European control of Albania so that Italy would not face Austria alone there.[141]

Faced with the grave danger that Berchtold would use force to exclude Montenegro from Scutari, Italy reserved full freedom of action to move into southern Albania,[142] worked on Serbia to give Austria no excuse for action in Albania, and urged that any naval demonstration be by all powers or at least that England join Italy and Austria. San Giuliano was willing to act jointly with Austria on the mandate of Europe and Giolitti agreed, although neither preferred such a solution.[143] That Italian opinion was strongly on the side of Montenegro is indicated by the large number of anti-Austrian and pro-Montenegrin demonstrations in April.[144]

[139] Avarna to San Giuliano, tel. 2613, Dec. 30, 1912, Gab. 344; Berchtold to Mérey, Dec. 29, 30, 1912, *O.U.A.*, V, 267, 275, 276, 358. For evidence that Berchtold had tried unsuccessfully in November to obtain Lovčen, see *ibid.*, IV, 906, 907, and Torre in *Rivista d'Albania*, I, 237.

[140] San Giuliano to Vienna, Berlin, London, tel. 220, Jan. 9, 1913, Reg. 347.

[141] San Giuliano to Vienna, Berlin, London, tel. 22, Jan. 13, 1913, Gab. 369.

[142] San Giuliano's circular, tel. 82, Feb. 8, 1913, Gab. 369. Pansa spoke to Jagow of Italian action at Valona. Pansa to San Giuliano, tel. 1352, Feb. 17, 1913, Reg. 348; San Giuliano to Avarna, tel. 1088, Feb. 19, 1913, Reg. 347; Macchio's memo., Feb. 22, 1913, *O.U.A.*, V, 801.

[143] San Giuliano's circulars, tels. 1499, 1648, 1746, 1848, 1919, March 13, 20, 24, 28, April 1 and tels. 1507, 1508, 1509 of March 14, 1913, to Squitti, Torretta, Avarna, and Bollati, Regs. 347, 349. Giolitti was opposed to any naval demonstration on March 20 but agreed that Italy and Austria might act on the mandate of Europe on March 22. Giolitti to San Giuliano, March 20, 22, 1913, Giolitti Papers in Archivio Centrale dello Stato (Rome), XIX/45.

[144] Minister of Interior to San Giuliano, 8373, 8271, 8485, 9223, 9073, 8557, 9214, 8273, 9088, 9073, 9140, April 11, 15, 27, 29, 30, 1913, P109/483. The prefects were ordered to take measures against the demonstrations.

While pressing to have Montenegro cease the bombardment of Scutari, San Giuliano sent two ships to join the Austrian division at Antivari. Germany, England, and France each sent a ship.[145] After the fall of Scutari, San Giuliano sought to have the powers take it over and Germany restrain Austria. He proposed the occupation of Antivari by a European force but now refused to join Austria under a European mandate unless England participated. He told Berchtold that Article VII of the Triple Alliance did not permit Austria to act without Italian consent. If Austria acted, Italy would move at Valona. If Italy participated in any operation, there must be no attack on Montenegro. Fortunately, Montenegro yielded in the matter of Scutari on May 5, 1913, and the powers took control.[146]

By the second half of 1913 Avarna had concluded that Austrian secret action in Albania would not cease as long as the weak Berchtold was directing foreign affairs. San Giuliano was likewise deeply impressed with this secret activity and suspected that there was a move behind Berchtold's back for a separatist movement. He sought to influence leading Albanians to pull together.[147]

Irritated over a dispute with Austria concerning the construction of a bridge near Scutari, San Giuliano once more threatened in October to turn to the Triple Entente to prevent Austrian preponderance in Albania and the Balkans. Avarna was authorized to warn Berchtold that if Austria embarked on a policy of antagonism to Italy in Albania, Italy could count on the support of three powers while Austria could count on only one. Bollati could inform the Germans that Italy would prefer that Albania go to Serbia rather than to Austria

[145] San Giuliano's circular, tel. 1704, March 22; San Giuliano to Avarna, tel. 1898, April 4, 1913, Reg. 349; Squitti to San Giuliano, tel. 2860, April 5, 1913, Reg. 352.
[146] In addition to the published documents of the great powers, this summary is based on Regs. 351, 356 and Gab. 368, 369 of the Italian documents.
[147] Avarna to San Giuliano, tel. 5956, June 22, 1913, Reg. 360; San Giuliano to Avarna, tel. 5515, Aug. 6, and to de Facendis (Valona), tel. 5516, Aug. 6, 1913, Reg. 357.

and that Lovčen should be kept by Montenegro. He was ready to turn to Austria's adversaries for support.[148]

Austrian threats to move against Serbia in 1913 were certainly not pleasing to Italy who worked to restrain Austria. San Giuliano sought to have Serbia withdraw her troops from Albania, but he told Berchtold that Greece was a worse offender. After Serbia yielded to Austria's eight-day ultimatum in October, San Giuliano criticized Berchtold for acting without Italian consent.[149]

The story of developments in Albania in 1914 is too involved for adequate summation here. Trust between the two Governments broke down, and tension over Albania was one of the important factors which influenced Italian decisions in 1914. Tension mounted after *Chargé* Ambrózy accused Italy of bad faith with regard to furnishing arms to Albania on April 10. San Giuliano refused to do business with him until his words were withdrawn on April 11.[150] At the Abbazia meeting of the two Foreign Ministers they reached general agreement, April 14-18, on Albania, but Berchtold entered complaints against Aliotti, the Italian minister at Durazzo.[151] Matters became much worse after the arrest of Essad Pasha, a pro-Italian member of the cabinet, on May 19. Italy blamed Austria but Austria denied the charge. By June 24 Berchtold was threatening a separate course, even suggesting that there might be a union of Albania with Greece.[152] Austro-Italian collaboration

[148] San Giuliano to Bollati and Avarna, tels. 6834, 6868, Oct. 7, 8, 1913, and tel. 6874 of Oct. 8 to Bollati, Reg. 359. Bollati warned against an accord with France. Bollati to San Giuliano, private letter, Oct. 12, 1913, Gab. XXV/315.

[149] See Regs. 359, 361, 365. For the best statement of the Italian position when faced with the threat of an Austrian attack on Serbia in July, 1913, see Augusto Torre, "Il progettato attaco austro-ungarico alla Serbia del Luglio 1913," in *Studi storici in onore di Gioacchino Volpe* (Florence, 1958), pp. 999-1018.

[150] San Giuliano to Avarna, tels. 496, 500, 501, 505, 506, April 10, 11, 12, 1914, Gab. XXIX/380.

[151] San Giuliano's memos., April 14, 15, 1914. Gab. LXII. See also Berchtold's memo., April 18, 1914. *O.U.A.*, VII, 1063-1069.

[152] Berchtold to Mérey, June 24, 1914; Mérey to Berchtold, June 26, 1914, *O.U.A.*, VIII, 184, 185, 203, 204; San Giuliano to Bollati and Avarna, tels. 695, 696, June 26, 1914, Gab. 391.

was threatening to break up as the cannon went off in 1914. San Giuliano agreed with the Austrians that Aliotti was not the man for the Albanian post but refused to be rushed in replacing him. Barrère, in fact, reported on June 20 that Aliotti was more popular in Italy than San Giuliano and that he could not be touched.[153] So bad did matters become that Mérey told San Giulano on July 18 that proof of Italian disloyalty in Albania would fill a 500-page book.[154] San Giuliano sought to reach three goals: restoration of co-operation with Austria; involvement of Europe to the limit as the Albanian Government faced collapse; the counteracting of Austria's anti-Italian propaganda by exerting influence on leading Albanians.

III. *The Divergences in Balkan Policy Outside the Adriatic*

Italy and Austria consistently declared for the status quo and denied territorial aspirations in the Balkans, but here agreement ended. Italy supported the principle of nationality if the status quo could not be maintained. "The Balkans for the Balkan Peoples" became a slogan at the Consulta. Certainly after 1906 Austria no longer supported such a principle. Italy sought to pull the Balkan states together and was consistently friendly with all of them, except that relations with Greece became strained over Albanian boundaries. Austria sought to keep the Balkan states divided.

Italy realized that a strong Austria-Hungary was a bulwark against the Slavic and Germanic floods and played a delicate game to keep Austria reasonably content with her Balkan position so that she would not commit aggression and yet to oppose any advantage which could lead to Austrian preponderance. Italy insisted on an equal voice with Russia and Austria in the Balkans and resented the close collaboration and special position of these states after the 1897 and Mürzsteg agreements. A

[153] Barrère to Viviani, June 20, 1914, *D.D.F.*, 3rd ser., X, 593, 594.
[154] San Giuliano to Vienna and Berlin, tels. 727, 747, July 18, 22, 1914. Mérey refused to produce the proof.

major aim of Italian policy was to return the Macedonian reform program to the concert of Europe. With the help of England it was successful. Italy's 1909 accord with Austria not
only promised compensation if Austria reoccupied the Sanjak
but also made it less likely that Austria would make separate
agreements with other states about the Balkans. Likewise, the
Racconigi agreement of 1909 with Russia not only secured
Russia's blessing for the Tripolitan enterprise but also pledged
the two states not to make separate agreements on the Balkans
with other states. Italy consistently opposed any special position for Austria in the economic or political field, but there was
nothing in her policy which aimed at building up Russian
power to a preponderant position.

No nation worked more earnestly than Italy to restrain the
small Balkan states and Austria from action which would endanger the peace. Her favorite project was a Balkan accord
between Italy, Russia, and Austria which Austrian objections
always defeated. But was not such an accord the surest guarantee of Balkan peace?

Italy insisted that Article VII of the Triple Alliance covered the whole Balkan peninsula and pledged Austria not to
move without prior agreement with Italy based on suitable
compensation. This interpretation would have given Italy a
kind of veto on Austrian moves. Austria-Hungary insisted that
Article VII applied to the nonindependent parts of the Balkan
peninsula but not to the independent states. Only at the last
minute, and under German pressure, did Berchtold accept the
Italian and German interpretation, but by that time the world
was in flames and an Italian veto was meaningless.

One cannot escape the conclusion that public opinion in
both countries accepted the wildest Balkan rumors and was in
general badly informed as to the true national interest. Tittoni appears to have been more nearly correct than the Italian
public when he felt that Austrian renunciation of the Sanjak
and of her special position in Montenegro was a greater gain

for Italy than the annexation of Bosnia was for Austria. Likewise Austro-Hungarian opinion appears to have been blind to
the advantages of a little kindness and courtesy in dealing with
the Balkan peoples.

IV. *Irredentism*

One cannot escape the conclusion that Italians felt deeply
about the Trentino and Trieste and in general had a strong
spiritual and cultural bond with the Italians living in Austria-
Hungary. There appears to have been a general Italian belief
that these Italians were being mistreated and that the Slavs
and Germans were being favored over them, just as there was
a general Austrian belief that Italy only awaited the opportune
moment to add these people to the Italian state. Irredentism
did play a major role in the Austro-Italian antagonism. How
important was the movement?

Irredentism assumed various forms from cultural affinity to
movements to prepare for an invasion of Austria. There were
many organizations but their membership was not large. Many
Irredentist manifestations made much noise and attracted great
attention in the Austrian press but were otherwise quite harm-
less, a welcome excuse for university students to have a holiday.
The movement was more intense in the North than in the
South. Its strongest supporters were the radicals and republicans. It assumed serious proportions only when the Government failed to curb it or even sympathized with it. Italians on
both sides of the frontier participated in it. All Irredentists
seemed to be able to agree on two demands in the period under
survey: autonomy for the Trentino and an Italian university at
Trieste.[155] Many observers felt that the grant of these demands
would have caused the virtual death of Irredentism.

[155] For a history of the question to 1896 see Augusto Sandonà, *L'irredentismo
nelle lotte politiche e nelle contese diplomatiche italo-austriache* (3 vols.; Bologna,
1932-1938). Good for much of the period under survey is Tommasini, *L'Italia
alla vigilia della guerra*. For a very biased Austrian account see M. Mayr,
Der italienische Irredentismus (2nd ed.; Innsbruck, 1917).

After a period of relative quiet, Irredentism began to manifest itself in small ways in 1899. On April 18 the *Independente* published a summary of a letter written by Zanardelli, president of the Chamber of Deputies, to Dompieri, the mayor of Trieste, praising those Italians who were defending the name of Italy against the new barbarians who sought to wipe out the last traces of Rome in the Giulian territory. Malvano, the Secretary-General at the Consulta, expressed regret, as did Foreign Minister Canevaro, who asked that there be no publicity. One of Canevaro's last acts as Foreign Minister was to request copies of the *Independente* for use in making it impossible for Zanardelli to enter a new cabinet. Goluchowski was happy to comply.[156]

When Zanardelli became Prime Minister in 1901, Irredentism seemed to become stronger. In part this was probably due to Zanardelli's sympathy for the movement and in part because of the growing agitation in the Tyrol for autonomy. From Venice, Consul Gsiller reported that he had never seen Irredentism so strong and that the Albanian question was closely connected.[157] He was impressed with the fact that the geography text used in the elementary schools indicated that Austria ruled Italian territory. In 1902 Consul Úrényi at Milan blamed Irredentist agitation in part on the national characteristics of the Italian people, charging them with megalomania, disloyalty, and indolence, but he also found that the French inspired Irredentism. Most of this activity ended in bombastic phrases. The Socialists, he found, were opponents of Irredentism.[158]

[156] Pasetti to Goluchowski, reports 23B, 24C, 26, April 18, 24, 29 and conf. tel. 1283, May 1, 1899. P.A., Italien 1899, XI/119; Goluchowski to Pasetti, conf. tel. 13, May 2, 1899, P.A., Italien 1899, XI/120; Lambertenghi (Trieste) to Canevaro, tel. 1035, April 19, 1899, Reg. 239; Canevaro to Lambertenghi, tel. 1100, May 2, 1899, Reg. 238.

[157] Gsiller to Goluchowski, report 43, Aug. 4, 1901, P.A., Venedig 1901, XXXVIII/271.

[158] Úrényi to Goluchowski, conf. report 7, report 9, July 25, 26, 1902, P.A., Mailand 1902, XXXVIII/272.

Most of the major demonstrations in Italy after 1896 seem
to have been caused by students and generally in response to
some outbreak of violence in Austria-Hungary. The 1903 and
1904 demonstrations were in response to troubles over the university at Innsbruck. Italian maneuvers held near the frontier
in 1903 appear to have stimulated Irredentism.

Lt. Colonel Zucculin, the Austrian military *attaché*, made
an illuminating report on Irredentism on December 14, 1903.
He found few Irredentists in the Senate but some 60 to 70 in the
Chamber. The most important organizations, he found, were
the *Dante Alighieri*, with 18,500 members, the *Trento e Trieste*, the *Italia* of Padua, the *Patria* of Milan, and the student
association *Corda Fratres*. There were a large number of anti-
Austrian associations. Ricciotti Garibaldi represented the
sharpest anti-Austrian standpoint.[159]

By the middle of 1904 the Irredentist movement appears to
have become a guerrilla war instead of a frontal attack as under
Zanardelli.[160] Lützow reported that no person took Ricciotti
Garibaldi seriously. He was a source of embarrassment to the
Government. Garibaldi approached the Austrian embassy in
May, 1905, with an appeal for mercy for four youths implicated
in smuggling bombs from Italy to Trieste. He denied any
thought of leading armed volunteers against Austria, indicated
that he was for the status quo, and asserted that the only enemy
was Pan-Germanism. He appealed for an Italian university at
Trieste, autonomy for the Trentino, and safeguards for Italian
interests elsewhere. He was even ready to recognize Austrian
supremacy in the Balkans. Lützow informed Tittoni, who
assured him that the Government had Garibaldi well in hand.
Lützow even suggested paying Garibaldi to moderate the Irredentist press, but Goluchowski vetoed the idea.[161]

[159] P.A., Innere Behörden, XL/155.
[160] Gsiller to Goluchowski, report 17, June 10, 1904, P.A., Venedig 1904,
XXXVIII/277.
[161] Lützow to Goluchowski, reports 48E, 52, June 16, 23, 1904, P.A., Albanien,
Liasse XIX/3, Fasz. XIV/27; Italien 1904, XI/131; Lützow to Goluchowski, conf.

A crisis of some magnitude developed in August, 1905, when Marcora, president of the Chamber of Deputies, referred to "Trento nostro." The long argument over a formula for an expression of regret strained Austro-Italian relations almost to the breaking point. Tittoni even threatened to resign and sought German mediation, which Goluchowski opposed. Not until August 24 was a compromise formula found.[162]

Attacks early in September, 1906, by Croats at Fiume, Zara, and Sušak against Italians not only dimmed any hopes of co-operation of Italians and Slavs in Dalmatia but also led to attempted demonstrations at Bari, Rome, and Taranto. Some windows of the Austrian consulate at Taranto were broken. Goluchowski expressed regret for the Croat attacks and promised that the guilty would be punished. The Hungarian Government paid a small indemnity.[163]

The Austrian military seem to have been the most nervous group in the country about Irredentism. They were alarmed in 1907 about reports from confidants of Italian military men that there was an intention to have a partial mobilization and to take the South Tyrol upon the death of Francis Joseph.[164] Section Chief Jettel spent his vacation in the South Tyrol in August, 1907, and from the preparations on both sides of the border gained the impression that Italy and Austria stood on the threshold of war. He concluded that the Trentino was the Achilles' heel of Austro-Italian relations.[165] Rumors circulated late in 1909 and in 1910 that the Trentino would go to Italy upon the death of Francis Joseph. Conrad became

reports 37B, 38A-B, 39B, 42B, May 26, 30, June 13, 27, 1905; Goluchowski to Lützow, conf. 714, June 21, 1905, P.A. Italien 1905, XI/133, 134.

[162] For the Italian telegrams, see Regs. 266, 268. See also Tommasini, *L'Italia alla vigilia della guerra*, II, 174-190.

[163] See Reg. 274 and P68/350 for the Italian documents. See also P.A., Italien 1906, XI/136; Venedig 1906, XXXVIII/284; Bari 1906, XXXVIII/282; Tommasini, *L'Italia alla vigilia della guerra*, III, 75-102; XXX, "La tela di Penelope," *Nuova Antologia*, 4th ser., CXXV (Sept. 16, 1906), 319-326.

[164] P.A., Interna, Informationsbureau 1907, Fasz. 682.

[165] Jettel to Aehrenthal, Aug. 10, 1907. P.A., Interna 1907, XL/163.

alarmed at a report of an influx of Italian citizens into the Trentino.[166] The Italians blamed the Austrian military for preventing contacts between Italians of Italy and Austria and for efforts to keep Italians out of the unredeemed territories.[167]

The Austrian military continued to cite many manifestations of hatred against Austria in the years before the war, as, for example, assertions of soldiers during the Turko-Italian war that they would next march on Vienna. When Mérey discussed the matter with San Giuliano in January, 1912, the latter declared that he was doing all legally possible to curb Irredentist outbursts, which he frankly judged as unimportant.[168]

The university question remained serious throughout the period, and without solution because of Austrian internal politics. It became serious in Italy at the time of the Bosnian crisis as a result of demonstrations by students, some armed with pistols, at Vienna and Graz. Numerous demonstrations followed in Italy. Austrian flags were burned in Rome and Florence. Stones were thrown at the embassy. Tittoni came to regard the Bosnian question as secondary to a concession on the university question. He suggested Trent as the best location. But he quickly shifted to Trieste. So serious did the tension become early in 1909 that Tittoni ordered Avarna briefly to limit his relations with Aehrenthal to a minimum. To Lützow he threatened resignation. Aehrenthal favored, but Francis Ferdinand opposed, at least for a time, an Italian university at Trieste.[169]

[166] P.A., Interna 1909, XL/172, 173; Italien, Liasse VII/14, Fasz. XI/163.

[167] Avarna to San Giuliano, conf. private letter, Sept. 8, 1910; San Giuliano to Avarna, conf. dispatch 210, Oct. 3, 1910, P166/538.

[168] Aehrenthal to Mérey, Jan. 6; Mérey to Aehrenthal, report 2K, Jan. 8; Auffenberg to Aehrenthal, 525, Jan. 26, 1912; General Staff memo., 4100, 1912, P.A., Italien, Liasse VII/7, 13, Fasz. XI/163, 164.

[169] Tommasini, L'Italia alla vigilia della guerra, IV, 469-491; Tittoni to Lützow, Nov. 26, 1908, A.R., II/90/169; Tribuna, Nov. 27; Avarna to Tittoni, tels. 3862, 3890, Nov. 26, 28, 1908, Reg. 290; Tittoni to Avarna, tels. 3308, 3345, 3364, Nov. 26, 28, 29, 1908 and tels. of Jan. 22, 25, 1909, Vienna Embassy files; Avarna to Tittoni, conf. and private letter, Jan. 7, 1909, A.R., III/114/3. A provisional solution (1911) provided for law courses at Vienna.

Perhaps no single act by the Austrians in the period under survey disturbed the Italians more profoundly than the Hohenlohe decrees of August, 1913, ordering Italian citizens to be dismissed from public jobs in Trieste. San Giuliano postponed his October trip to Salzburg, threatened to take reprisals, and thought of turning to France. He appealed to Germany, who finally intervened. Not until November 20 did Avarna send the welcome news that for an indefinite period Italian citizens would not be dismissed and that Francis Joseph disapproved of the decrees. How deeply they wounded Italy may be seen from Consul Crippa's report from Bologna of September 10.[170]

There were serious demonstrations in Italy on May 4 and 5, 1914, in retaliation for violence at the beginning of the month against Italians at Trieste. The Italian Government dismissed the prefect at Naples and gave rigid instructions to officials for the future but objected to the apology Berchtold desired. San Giuliano indicated that there was a general feeling of exasperation at Austrian conduct. These events were another cloud on the horizon of Italo-Austrian relations as the war came.[171]

v. *Pressures from the Military*

Military records available are of a fragmentary nature and the last word cannot be said about the military rivalry. But a few generalizations are perhaps in order. The military tended to be more pessimistic than the diplomats about Austro-Italian relations. There was a military group which favored a preventive war with Italy, and Conrad, the Austrian Chief of Staff, headed it. No more effective means perhaps existed to secure military appropriations than to play up the antagonism between the two countries. Italy and Austria were in an arma-

[170] See Regs. 357, 359, 364, Gab. 368, 369 for the numerous Italian telegrams. Ambrózy to Berchtold and enclosure, report 54E, Sept. 13, 1913, P.A., Italien XVI, Fasz. XI/173.

[171] See Regs. 375, 378, Gab. 391, 395; Mérey to Berchtold, reports 22/P, 23/P, May 8, 10, 1914, P.A., Italien 1914, XI/173; Barrère to Doumergue, May 10, 1914, *D.D.F.*, 3rd ser., X, 346-348; *G.P.*, XXXIX, 402-409.

ment race both on land and sea. Both were increasing the military personnel and defenses on their border. But there was
increasing demand for naval co-operation after France shifted
her fleet to the Mediterranean in 1912.

A cry that Italy was reducing her military budget while
Austria was making increases was raised by Deputy Maurigi in
the Chamber in 1901. Sonnino rebutted this assertion and
indicated that Italy was spending 387 million lire, or 40.69 per
cent of the state budget, for military purposes.[172] But by 1904
Tittoni and the cabinet were alarmed at Austrian armaments,
and Goluchowski denied in the *Fremdenblatt* and *Politische
Correspondenz* that extraordinary credits were being asked because of friction with Italy.[173] This Italian fear continued in
1905. Luzzatti expressed such a fear of Austrian attack, and
there was some belief that Austria might seek a diversion from
her internal problems by attacking Italy. Avarna, however,
found no indication of offensive intentions even though a part
of the army officers would view a war with Italy as desirable.
Austria, he recognized, was devoting special attention to the
frontier.[174] From Vienna the French ambassador reported that
for Austria the enemy was Italy.[175] The British learned in 1906
that Austrian army and navy people believed war with Italy was
probable and at no distant date.[176]

Conrad concluded as early as April, 1907, that Italy was the
state with which war was most likely and the sooner it came
the better. He estimated Italian expenditures on the Austrian
front from 1900 to 1917 would run to 177,000,000 lire and believed that Italy would attack as soon as Austria was involved

---

[172] *Atti parlamentari, Camera, Discussioni,* March 26, 1901, pp. 2888-2891.

[173] Barrère to Delcassé, June 10, 1904, *D.D.F.*, 2nd ser., V, 244-247; Avarna
to Tittoni, tel. 1252, report 703/269, May 24, 25, 1904, Reg. 264; P15; von Chelius
to Schlieffen, Dec. 18, 1904, *G.P.*, XX, (1), 89-92.

[174] Barrère to Delcassé, Feb. 3, 8, 1905, *D.D.F.*, 2nd ser., VI, 86, 87, 97;
Avarna to Tittoni, personal letter and conf. report, del Maestro to Avarna, May
6, 1905, C.V., III/2/94, 94bis.

[175] Reverseaux to Delcassé, Feb. 10, 1905, *D.D.F.*, 2nd ser., VI, 107.

[176] Boothby to Grey, Oct. 19, 1906, *B.D.*, VIII, 29, 30.

in inner or foreign complications. He favored action when Italy went to war with Turkey. He was relieved as Chief of Staff on November 30, 1911.[177] The Italians were not idle. The French reported that they were spending 400 millions to arm against the Austrian ally.[178] In 1908 Austria was reported to have moved the equivalent of an army corps from her northeastern to her southern front.[179] The Italian naval debates in 1907 were so sharply directed against Austria that Aehrenthal complained.[180] The Italian military concluded that between 1904 and 1908 Austria had not only increased the army corps on her frontier from two to three but also added a division each to the Innsbruck and Graz corps.[181] Italy was faced with the construction of four new Austrian battleships announced in 1909 and her navy had already been reduced from the ideal of double that of the Austrian fleet to 1.60 to 1.[182] Yet Admiral Chiari, president of the Austrian Naval League, could declare in 1910 that Italy had a three-to-one advantage.[183]

The renaming of Conrad as Chief of Staff in December, 1912, made a bad impression in Italy, but he appears to have moderated his earlier views. He was named on condition that he not concern himelf with politics.[184]

Perhaps Szeptycki, the Austrian military *attaché* in Rome, represented the feeling of quite a large part of the military

[177] Conrad von Hötzendorf, *Aus meiner Dienstzeit* (Vienna, 1921-1922), I, 509, 510; II, 14, 77, 172-174, 218-284, 429-452; R. A. v. Urbanski, "Conrad v. Hötzendorf und der Präventiv-Krieg gegen Italien," *Berliner Monatshefte*, VIII (1930), 248-258.

[178] Laroche to Pichon, Aug. 29, 1907, *D.D.F.*, 2nd ser., XI, 260-262; Barrère to Pichon, April 21, 1908, *ibid.*, 2nd ser., XI, 574-576.

[179] Crozier (Vienna) to Pichon, April 10, 1908, *ibid.*, 2nd ser., XI, 560-562.

[180] Avarna to Tittoni, June 23, and conf. and private letter, July 6, 1907, *C.V.*, III/3/50, 58; Tittoni to Avarna, conf. tel., July 2, 1907, *A.R.*, I/7.

[181] Minister of War to Tittoni, Feb. 21, April 4, 1908, *A.R.II/95/19*, 25.

[182] Saint-Pair to Thomson, May 20, 1909, *D.D.F.*, 2nd ser., XII, 256-258.

[183] *Reichspost* (Oct. 21), quoted by *Tribuna*, Nov. 14, 1910.

[184] Rodd to Grey, Dec. 15, 1912, *B.D.*, IX, (II), 287, 288; Conrad, *Aus meiner Dienstzeit*, II, 373-375; *O.U.A.*, V, 93, 162-164, 176.

when he reported in 1913 that Italy would be friendly for six more years—until her army was ready to attack Austria.[185]

VI. *Other Causes for Tension*

Two other factors of some importance remain to be mentioned. There was a growing economic rivalry between Italy and Austria. Both countries were pushing for markets in the Balkans. Both were jealous rivals for railroad advantages. Both were seeking spheres of influence around Adalia, and negotiations were in progress for a division of zones. But the economic factor was secondary. The great sources of antagonism were political and psychological.

One psychological factor was the strained relationship between the rulers. The Italians keenly resented the fact that Francis Joseph had never returned the visit which Humbert made to Vienna in October, 1881. The opposition of the Pope prevented a visit to Rome and the Italians would not receive Francis Joseph elsewhere. William II was much concerned with this matter but no solution was found. Still more important was the Italian fear, perhaps somewhat exaggerated, of Francis Ferdinand, who had the reputation of being anti-Italian and at one time of being against the Triple Alliance.

VII. *Conclusion*

What did Austro-Italian antagonism mean to Great Power relationships before 1914? One important effect was to make Austria's position appear less secure in Europe and to encourage the desperate gamble to restore her fading prestige and influence which created the tragedy of 1914. Another effect, perhaps, was to give the Triple Entente a feeling of strength which it really did not possess.

This antagonism led Italy to fight back with the weapons at her disposal. These were really two in number. She sought

[185] Szeptycki to Conrad, March 29, 1913, *O.U.A.*, V, 1100.

to invoke German pressure and mediation at Vienna, much to the annoyance of the Austrians. She also turned to the Triple Entente for support. There was nothing immoral or dishonest about these tactics.

Above all, this antagonism made of Italian diplomacy a kind of shoring-up operation to prevent matters from coming to a head, to postpone the evil day when the status quo would be shattered. Feeling in Italy ran too deep to make Italian support in an aggressive war possible.

Contrary to much that has been written, Italy had a kind of master plan to prevent the war. She sought to force acceptance of her interpretation of Article VII of the Triple Alliance, which would have given her a kind of veto on violent Austrian action. At the same time she favored complete acceptance of the Austrian ultimatum by Serbia, but with Great-Power supervision of its execution. There appears to have been nothing necessarily inconsistent in these two moves if they were both directed toward preserving the peace. That the Italian peace plan failed is evident. But it was the best plan offered to prevent the tragedy of 1914.[186]

[186] See Mario Toscano's excellent study, *L'Italia e la crisi europea del Luglio 1914* (Milan, 1940) and the penetrating appraisals by Augusto Torre, "Ricordi di Antonio di San Giuliano," *Nuova Antologia,* 463, CDLXIII (Jan., 1955), 29-42 and "Il marchese Di San Giuliano fra la neutralità e l'intervento," *Nova Historia,* (June, 1954), Nos. 22-25, 104-119. For a severe attack on Italian policy, see Albertini, *The Origins of the War of 1914,* III, 254-295.

LLOYD GEORGE:

LEADER OR LED IN BRITISH WAR AIMS,

1916-1918

Rodney O. Davis

David Lloyd George was widely hailed as the man of the hour when he became Britain's Prime Minister in December, 1916. In him, many felt, had been found the man to give positive direction to the tremendous war effort which was under way. No more would Britain "wait and see"; now she would act. At the helm was the author of the knock-out-blow theory. Only three months earlier Lloyd George had given his famous interview to an American newspaperman in which he had said that Britain would fight to a finish—to a knock-out. The Northcliffe press and others had seized upon the then Minister of War as the forceful personality necessary to lead Britain on to victory. Lloyd George's predecessor as Prime Minister, H. H. Asquith, and many of his colleagues had been castigated for dilatory tactics or no tactics at all and even accused of being willing to make a compromise peace. At the moment of destiny, just before Germany and Woodrow Wilson took steps concerning an end to the great struggle, Lloyd George assumed command.

Was Lloyd George a man to give positive direction in a time of crisis? Perhaps he was an astute politician who followed, although with considerable success, the maxim: "There go my followers. I am their leader. I must follow them." During the Boer War this young Welsh Radical had opposed war. In the earlier period of the Liberal ministry he had also opposed war. He had had a passion for social reform, and any expenditures for the armed forces meant that much less for the Radical program. That he was a fighter was evidenced by the budget crisis of 1909-1910, but his preference was clearly for the political and social battlefield and not the military one. As late as August 2, 1914, Lloyd George was still not among those committed to war. According to Walter Runciman, he was ready on that date, if war came, to retire temporarily to Criccieth since he had had enough of "standing out against a war-inflamed populace."[1] The German invasion of Belgium, however, strengthened many faint hearts and brought a united Britain into the conflict. Notable among these last-minute conversions was that of Britain's Chancellor of the Exchequer, David Lloyd George.

Whatever his own disposition might have been in December, 1916, and after, Lloyd George had to work from a foundation that had been laid previously. Britain had been at war for over two years and she was closely involved with other powers. Britain, France, and Russia (and later Japan) signed in September, 1914, a pact not to make separate peace and to reach agreement prior to declaring peace terms. Britain thus was tied to such war aims as might suggest themselves to the other powers. Secret treaties were soon forthcoming to implement the Declaration of London. Notable among them was the agreement on Constantinople and the Straits as Russian fruits of victory. The apparent necessity for other allies also led to secret treaties with Italy and Romania which guaranteed to these powers extensive gains. Lloyd George wrote later of the Treaty of London by which Italian adherence was gained:

[1] Arthur C. Murray, *Master and Brother; Murrays of Elibank* (London, 1945), p. 120.

I have no recollection that the details of the agreement were ever given to the Cabinet. We were only too well pleased to secure the adhesion of another Ally to scrutinise closely the proposed territorial re-adjustments which were the conditions of the bargain. War plays havoc with the refinements of conscience.[2]

The aims envisaged in secret treaties were not, however, the public pronouncements as to aims to which Lloyd George fell heir. The multitude of men and women who bear the brunt of modern warfare at home and in the trenches, particularly in a democratic country like Britain, are not usually motivated by narrow or selfish aspirations for territorial gain. They need a full measure of idealism to arouse their passions. In Britain's case it could be said that "the cup runneth over." Belgium was the cornerstone upon which the rest of the structure was built. Restitution, reparation, and guarantees began with Belgium, but were soon applied all over Europe and even beyond. Definitive statements of what such aims would mean if applied in a practical sense were not forthcoming. The generalities were simply accepted and believed; they were not argued. In a journal entry of August 11, 1916, Viscount Esher noted that Lloyd George himself admitted that no one in Britain was really aware of what the aims or objectives should be, "apart from vague generalities."[3]

Lloyd George attempted to unite the "vague generalities" into one word—"knock-out"—in his famous interview. He did not ask if such a conclusion was desirable or even possible. Asquith, however, asked the cabinet members to express their views. A. J. Balfour, First Lord of the Admiralty, wrote a memorandum under the explicit assumption that Germany would be forced to accept dictated terms. Lord Lansdowne, Minister without Portfolio and Unionist leader in the House of Lords, was not, however, convinced that dictation of terms

[2] David Lloyd George, *Memoirs of the Peace Conference* (New Haven, 1939), II, 501.

[3] Reginald Viscount Esher, *Journals and Letters of Reginald Viscount Esher* (London, 1934-1938), IV, 47-48.

was a closed question. As a result, in the words of Lloyd George, "The British Cabinet was brought by the intervention of one of its most respected members to a searching and considered examination of the question."[4] The merits of Lansdowne's arguments are not germane to this paper. The significant point is that there is fairly general agreement that the memorandum led to discussions which made the participants aware that not all of the cabinet members were as convinced as Lloyd George of the desirability and possibility of inflicting a complete defeat on the German army in the field. Within a month Lloyd George had replaced Asquith, who retired from the Government along with the others who had fainter hearts.

Lloyd George had just become captain of the ship of state when Germany announced her peace note of December 12, 1916. Within a week Woodrow Wilson had requested from each of the belligerents a statement of the terms upon which it would be willing to end the conflict. France and Russia had already answered Germany negatively when the new Prime Minister spoke to the House of Commons on December 19. He acknowledged their replies and added that he stood there "on behalf of the Government to give a clear and definite support to the statement which they have already made." After noting the lack of any proposals on the part of Germany, he continued that Britain would put her "trust in an unbroken Army rather than in a broken faith."[5] The official Entente reply to the German note did not contain any detailed statement of aims, but the reply to Wilson, on January 10, 1917, went far in that direction. The generalities of restitution, reparation, and guarantees were followed by a list of specifics which, while not exhausting all possibilities, were to be included in any final negotiations. Britain's public aims now included Alsace-Lorraine for France, Poland for the Tsar, the ex-

[4] David Lloyd George, *War Memoirs of David Lloyd George* (Boston, 1933-1936), II, 287. For Lansdowne memorandum, see *ibid.,* pp. 288-296.

[5] Great Britain, *Parliamentary Debates of Great Britain,* 5th ser. (1916), LXXXVIII, 1333-1338.

pulsion of the Turks from Europe in addition to the enfranchisement of their subject populations, and the liberation of
Italians, Slavs, Romanians, and Czecho-Slovaks. Lord Robert
Cecil, Minister of Blockade and Under-Secretary of State for
Foreign Affairs, collaborated in the drafting of the note to Wilson. He indicated in his autobiography the road that Britain
was traveling: "I say to my shame it was then that I first became
conscious of the existence of Czecho-slovakia—the French Government claiming, with our concurrence, its independence as
one of the objects for which we were fighting."[6]

The Lloyd George Government received much favorable
publicity during December, 1916, and January, 1917, particularly from the Northcliffe and the Conservative press. The
position it took in respect to the German note and Wilson's
request for a statement of aims found support also among many
Liberal journals. Such support was needed, for Lloyd George's
strength lay in an appeal to the popular imagination through
the press rather than in the Commons or in the Government.
Lloyd George was perhaps the first British politician who used
to full advantage the popular press and its close associate, public
opinion. J. A. Spender, one-time editor of the *Westminster
Gazette,* wrote of him:

In yet another respect he was the child of the hour: he intuitively
understood the modern Press which was so painful a stumbling-
block to his more solemn colleagues. He was, in the jargon of the
day, the supreme propagandist. His mind leapt with that of Fleet
Street; he seemed to deal with public affairs as if he was editing a
popular newspaper with its 'splash' for everyday, its headlines, its
pictures.[7]

The recorders of the history *No. 10 Downing Street* went even
a step further: "It could be said that he let No. 10, and his
security there, stand by the Press alone."[8]

      [6] Viscount Cecil of Chelwood, *All the Way* (London, 1949), p. 141.
      [7] John A. Spender, *The Public Life* (London, 1925), I, 120-121.
      [8] Basil Fuller and John Cornes, *No. 10 Downing Street* (New York, 1936),
pp. 254-255.

That there was a close alliance between Lloyd George and the press cannot be disputed. Many claimed that Lloyd George was actually put into power by Northcliffe while others added that Max Aitken, another newspaper magnate, was partially responsible. In any event, Lloyd George did receive favorable publicity at the same time that newspaper personalities were receiving honors and even peerages at a rate unheard of before this time. Later the *Daily Chronicle* was purchased by friends of Lloyd George in order that he might have a dependable organ amongst the Liberal press. Less dramatic but seemingly quite effective was the direction given to the press from time to time as to the coverage the Government would like in certain cases. Citing that there was a relationship does not, however, answer the question as to which of the parties was the senior partner and it leaves wide open the possibility that a third party—public opinion—might be stronger than either.

The origin of public opinion in any given situation is as difficult to explain as the term itself is to define in a really meaningful way for the period covered herein. Such things as the results of public opinion polls are not available. During the war there was no general election and even the by-elections are not particularly helpful since they were conducted under a more or less effective party truce. The proceedings of Parliament are less helpful than they might be because of the lack of any division on the question of war aims. One has, therefore, to look to a multitude of sources, most of which are somewhat indirect, and then to arrive at a somewhat tenuous conclusion as to what public opinion really was. The popular press is helpful because it both supplied the "facts" which people used in their thinking and it also had to reflect the thinking of the people to some extent in order to remain popular. There are limitations, however, such as the responsibilty the editor may feel toward truth as well as his duty to party, to proprietor, and to advertiser. Nevertheless, public opinion, despite its difficulties, remains a useful and necessary concept.

The public's view of Lloyd George's position on war aims is, moreover, but one part of a very complex whole. Much of the support and/or opposition which he received was undoubtedly predicated on other factors—some of which will be cited herein, but none of which will be exhaustively treated. His "knock-out" speech had earned him the enmity of many who would have preferred a peace by negotiation and who felt that such a peace could be secured only if Lloyd George were unseated. The same speech had, of course, gained him followers amongst those who shared his views on victory. His replacement of Asquith and the way in which it came about likewise led to support and to opposition. He was still a Liberal in a land where politics was never completely forgotten. He was involved in the struggle between Easterners and Westerners as well as the struggle between the advocates of civilian control and the advocates of military control of policy in wartime. He represented the rank commoner to some who wanted aristocratic control of government and represented the monarchy to some who wanted a republic. He had taken stands on social reform, disestablishment, the drink question, taxes, tariffs, and unified command of the Allied forces—all of which were controversial issues. Nevertheless, he was Prime Minister and he either led or was led in respect to war aims.

The British public was basically prowar late in 1916 and early in 1917. There was a segment of it which was willing to make peace at a price and another segment which was anxious to make peace at almost any price, but Lloyd George seems to have had the majority with him—or to have been with the majority. Then came the March revolution in Russia. Two groups were competing for power: the Provisional Government, which attempted to carry out Russia's commitments to the Allies, and the Soviet, which called for an early peace of no annexations and no indemnities. Lloyd George seems to have recognized the struggle, but not to have taken sides. Like the Provisional Government, he seems to have been willing to accept what victory might bring. He told the representatives of the Dominions on the Imperial War Cabinet, on March 20, to remember that the German colonies were only a part of the larger question and that the amount of such territory which they would be able to keep was dependent mainly on how much over-all success they gained in the war.[9] W. A. S. Hewins, a Unionist and Under-Secretary of State for Colonies, substantiated in his diary the opportunism of the Prime Minister. After quoting Lloyd George as wanting territory, Hewins added that Lloyd George hoped for a revolution in Germany which would end the war, and a subsequent arrangement with the Germans. He concluded:

One felt that there was no rationality in the man, that he has only vague sense impressions as it were, and if we went again he might say something quite different. But I think he is not friendly to France, wishes for an arrangement with Germany if the Kaiser can be overthrown, does not really mean a national and Imperial policy, is prepared for a deal with regard to the German colonies, and has been giving pledges to U. S. A.[10]

Lloyd George was not, however, completely oblivious to the influence of the Soviet in Russia despite his desire for territory. The Laborites and Socialists in Britain took the new Russian Government much more seriously. When the Soviet suggested a conference of representatives of all belligerent Socialists in Stockholm, many British Laborites and Socialists wanted to attend. Lloyd George, in a telegram to the French Socialist Albert Thomas, recognized the wisdom of allowing British representation provided that the individuals were not extremists.

As far as war aims are concerned [the Prime Minister contended], I do not think there is any great difference between those of France and England and those of Russia. We could accept declaration of new Russian Government to the effect that re-establishment of a

[9] Lloyd George, *War Memoirs*, IV, 40-45.
[10] Diary entry of April 11, 1917. W. A. S. Hewins, *The Apologia of an Imperialist* (London, 1929), II, 132-135.

general peace should not tend towards either domination over other nations or seizure of their national possessions, or violent usurpation of their territories, and that it should be a peace without annexations or indemnities and based on rights of nations to decide their own affairs, provided that by these phrases it was not intended that French and British should be bound to restore to Turkey or German misgovernment populations in Africa or Mesopotamia which they have rescued from it, and also that it was understood that provinces which have been torn from France by German militarism should be restored to her.[11]

A passport was even issued to J. Ramsay MacDonald to allow him to go to Russia, but not to Stockholm. MacDonald was unable to make the trip because of the opposition of the seamen's union, but Arthur Henderson, Labor member of the War Cabinet, did visit Russia. Thus far Lloyd George was in accord with the masses of the people, but not his Conservative supporters in the Government. Henderson, on his return, recommended attendance at the Labor party meeting in Stockholm and lost his seat in the War Cabinet in the process. After Labor had voted to attend Stockholm on a consultative basis, the Government announced its decision against issuing passports. The more conservative elements in Britain had their way, but Labor moved to the left and found its leadership outside the Government.

Lloyd George on June 29 spoke at Glasgow, which was a center of labor discontent. He contended that Britain's aims had not changed from what they were when the conflict began. Those aims, he said, were the same as those Woodrow Wilson had expressed earlier in the month. Britain was fighting for liberty, equality, and fraternity—for international right and international justice. Mesopotamia and Armenia were not, therefore, to be returned to the Turks and the future of the German colonies was to be decided by the peace conference. "The wishes, the desires, and the interests of the peoples of

[11] Received May 22, 1917. Mary A. Hamilton, *Arthur Henderson: A Biography* (London, 1938), pp. 130-132.

these countries themselves must be the dominant factor in settling their future government. That is the principle upon which we are proceeding."[12] Labor could not seriously quarrel with such aims and neither could the Russians. Were such, however, the aims to which Britain was committed?

Secret agreements and secret commitments are usually secret for a purpose—for one reason or another, they are not fit for public consumption. Almost simultaneously with the Glasgow speech, Lloyd George's Government approved a further secret partition of the Turkish dominions which guaranteed Italy a share of the spoils. A month previous the Imperial War Cabinet had decided that the British representative to the peace conference should be guided by the thought that all of the German colonies as well as Mesopotamia should remain in the hands of the British Empire. Meanwhile, the alleged attempt of the Emperor Karl of Austria to try to make peace had run aground, at least in part, over Italian demands for non-Italian territory. In the summer and fall of 1917 there were other attempts at peace, with someone's desire for territory looming large in the failure of each. The destruction of German militarism, an openly avowed aim of the Allies, also awaited accomplishment.

In November Lloyd George participated in a decision which he was convinced brought the destruction of German militarism and victory itself a step closer—the organizing of the inter-allied Supreme War Council. In conjunction with this Rapallo Agreement, he made a speech in Paris which was highly critical of British military commanders. Thereby he succeeded in inciting against himself a host of people who respected and admired Britain's military leaders. The opposition was voiced across the country in the press and in the halls of Parliament. Lt. Colonel Repington, a military correspondent for the *Times* and then the *Morning Post*, wrote on November 19: "It is too delicious

[12] James B. Scott, ed., *Official Statements of War Aims and Peace Proposals, December 1916 to November 1918* (Washington, 1921), pp. 107-114.

to compare the Paris speech and this one [in the House of Commons] with L. G.'s past speeches at the Albert Hall, Carnarvon, etc. They are absolutely contradictory, and everything that he said was true then, he now says is untrue. What a game of hanky-panky politics are!"[13] Within ten days another form of opposition was forthcoming which was to lead to drastic changes.

The *Daily Telegraph* of November 29, 1917, carried an open letter from Lord Lansdowne under the title "Coordination of Allies' War Aims." The day also marked the opening of the inter-allied conference at Paris to discuss strategy so that both Lloyd George and the Foreign Secretary, A. J. Balfour, were absent from the scene. Lansdowne was too important a personage to be ignored and the subject he dealt with was at best controversial—so much so that the editor of the *Times* had refused to publish the letter. The reaction varied from all-out support to its rejection as a surrender document. Generally speaking, the London Conservative papers, along with the *Times*, opposed it; the Liberal and Labor papers gave it varying support; and the provincial papers were more noncommittal. The Government, through the office of the ministerial whip, disavowed any connection with the letter. After Bonar Law, the Government's chief officer in the Commons and the leader of the Conservatives, had condemned the letter, Lord Burnham, editor of the *Daily Telegraph*, objected on the grounds that Balfour had not opposed the publishing of the letter in principle and that Lord Hardinge, Permanent Under-Secretary of State for Foreign Affairs, had even examined it for detail on Balfour's recommendation. Law requested that Burnham not put this information in print and not inform Lloyd George of it in order to avoid trouble.[14]

[13] Lt. Col C. à Court Repington, *The First World War, 1914-1918* (Boston, 1920), II, 139.

[14] December 3, 1917. Baron George A. Riddell of Walton Heath, *Lord Riddell's War Diary, 1914-1918* (London, 1933), p. 297.

Lloyd George, with or without the above information, damned the Lansdowne letter with faint praise both publicly and privately in December, 1917. Two years later, however, while admitting disagreement with Lansdowne, he expressed admiration for the latter's courage and his willingness to sacrifice so much for something in which he believed.[15] Was Lloyd George as committed to principles? Publicly he spoke of the war again and again as a war for principles. Privately, he does not seem to have been quite so willing to be a leader. C. P. Scott reported conversations with Lloyd George in December, 1917, in which the latter said that he dared not meet the demand for a statement of aims because it would be likely to alienate his Conservative supporters and it might not gain him the support of the Liberal opposition.[16] Colonel Edward M. House, Woodrow Wilson's right hand man, found also that commitment to the Conservatives deterred Lloyd George from a liberal restatement of war aims and that the opposition to such in France and Italy was also a factor.[17] Lord Riddell added another reason: "We talked of peace terms. L. G. said we should have to secure some territory to compensate us for what we had expended."[18]

Lloyd George was in a quandary. He dared not move positively in any direction for fear of alienating someone. His hand, however, was being forced. The followers were moving and the leader had to follow. Lord Lansdowne was the first public figure of acknowledged stature to seek openly a liberal restatement of aims. Labor followed in December by drawing up such a statement. The program was prepared and the leadership also seemed to be available. Lansdowne was a Con-

[15] September 1, 1919. Baron George A. Riddell of Walton Heath, *Lord Riddell's Intimate Diary of the Peace Conference and After, 1918-1923* (London, 1933), p. 119.

[16] John L. Hammond, *C. P. Scott of the Manchester Guardian* (2nd ed.; New York, 1934), pp. 219-221.

[17] December, 1917. Charles Seymour, *The Intimate Papers of Colonel House* (Boston, 1926-1928), III, 280.

[18] December 9, 1917. Riddell, *War Diary*, p. 298.

servative; Asquith, now leader of the opposition Liberals, seemed available; Henderson, Labor's former member of the War Cabinet, was of a similar frame of mind. The followers were also available. Labor was agitating in a menacing way and it had shown its position in its December memorandum. The Bolshevik revolution, the publication of the secret treaties, and the Russian demand for an immediate armistice had all had their effect on Laborites and Socialists. They had also affected the extreme Right—the old aristocratic families. Many of these people, fearful of the spread of the Bolshevik contagion, were thinking of compensating the Germans in the East in return for concessions in the West. Lloyd George was also among those who appear to have considered such a possibility for ending the conflict.

The manpower shortage was what really made Labor the leader and Lloyd George the led. The Government, early in the war, had made certain pledges to the Labor leaders from which it now felt that it must be released. In an attempt to appease Labor, the Prime Minister, on December 23, 1917, addressed a letter to a special conference of the Trades Union Congress and the Labor party. In respect to war aims it contained only generalities such as the liberty of oppressed nationalities and respect for laws and treaties. Labor was not satisfied. As Balfour cabled to Colonel House on January 5, 1918, when requesting a further public statement by Wilson:

Finally the negotiations arrived at a point at which their successful issue depended mainly on the immediate publication by the British Government of a statement setting forth their war aims. This statement has now been made by the Prime Minister.[19]

Lloyd George's memoirs are not quite so revealing:

It was therefore deemed desirable to make a full, carefully prepared and authentic statement of Allied war aims so as to reassure the public, and at the same time to enable the Government to ascer-

[19] Seymour, *House*, III, 340.

tain definitely whether the nation was behind them in the prosecution of the War until those aims were achieved.[20]

Lloyd George had moved far from the position he had accepted a year earlier in the Entente reply to Wilson of January 10, 1917. His speech of January 5, 1918, was less vindictive in tone. Moreover, there were significant changes in detail. A united Poland, which was previously to have been a prize for the Tsar, was now to be independent. The destruction of German militarism, which often was explained as the democratization of Germany, was replaced by the recognition that the German people would have to determine their own future government. Restoration and indemnities for Belgium, Serbia, and Montenegro became restoration and reparation for Belgium alone. The other two along with the occupied parts of France, Italy, and Romania were to be restored, but reparations for them were not mentioned. Russia was excluded except for the comment that she would have to fend for herself if she continued to take independent action. The 1917 restitution clause for Alsace and Lorraine now appeared as: "We mean to stand by the French Democracy to the death in the demand they make for *reconsideration* [my italics] of the great wrong of 1871. . . ." Less than three months earlier Lloyd George had publicly stated: "However long the war may last, this country intends to stand by her gallant ally, France, until she redeems her oppressed children from the degradation of a foreign yoke."[21] The breakup of the Austro-Hungarian Empire was softened to "self-government on true democratic principles." Italy and Romania were now limited to legitimate claims for union with people of their own race and tongue. Turkey could now keep Constantinople, with the Straits internationalized and neutralized. Instead of "enfranchisement of populations subject to the bloody tyranny of the Turks," we have: "Arabia, Armenia, Mesopotamia, Syria and Palestine are

[20] Lloyd George, *Peace Conference,* I, 34-35.
[21] Scott, *War Aims,* p. 161.

in our judgment entitled to a recognition of their separate national condition." The German colonies, not mentioned in January, 1917, were now to be "at the disposal of a conference whose decisions must have primary regard to the wishes and interests of the native inhabitants of such colonies." Another new inclusion was "the creation of some international organization to limit the burden of armaments and diminish the probability of war."[22]

Lloyd George informed Lord Riddell on the day of the speech: "*I went as near peace as I could. It was the right moment. The time had come to speak out definitely.*" Contrary to what Balfour had cabled House and to what he himself later wrote, Lloyd George told Riddell that the speech "was a counter-offensive against the German peace terms with a view to appealing to the German people and detaching the Austrians."[23] Whatever the cause of the speech, the Prime Minister apparently lacked confidence in the effect that it might have. Within the hour of its completion he sent for H. Wickham Steed, foreign editor of the *Times*. After impressing Steed with the significance of the speech, he stated that "for tactical reasons it is important that it should not be opposed by the Press."[24] At that point the *Times* began to discuss war aims, and, along with all except the strongly nationalistic papers, it gave Lloyd George favorable coverage.

Lloyd George's speech was more reasonable and more conciliatory in tone than anything yet expressed by any Allied leader—Woodrow Wilson excepted. Nevertheless, he did not win the whole-hearted support of the proponents of peace. They continued to attempt to marshal their forces and there was talk of a Lansdowne-Asquith or a Lansdowne-Asquith-Henderson ministry. Part of the Prime Minister's failure to

[22] For texts, see *ibid.*, pp. 35-38, 225-233.

[23] Riddell, *War Diary*, p. 304.

[24] *Times* (London), *The History of the Times* (New York, 1935-1952), IV, 347.

receive more support can be attributed to the close relationship he maintained with many of the press lords. This problem was even discussed in Parliament, but with neither heat nor light. The war was moving too fast for domestic issues to evoke much interest.

The treaty of Brest-Litovsk was signed by the Russians on March 3. The British viewed the terms as exemplifying what they could expect if they made a treaty before defeating the German armies. Moreover, the great German offensive in the West began on March 21. Talk of peace evaporated once Britain was in danger of being defeated. All sides rallied to the cause of the nation. The long and arduous spadework done by the proponents for peace—a clean peace or a peace without victory to use Woodrow Wilson's phrase—was lost in the surge of patriotism. There were not even murmurs of peace while Germany was advancing. The German threat was not ended until the second battle of the Marne was fought, July 15 to August 7. August 8, when the British attacked at Amiens with tanks, was, as aptly called by General Ludendorff, the black day of the German army. Germany was now in retreat. The war was over in all except name, but only the German High Command really understood it.

Attempts were then made by the more pacific elements in England to revive the efforts for a reasonable peace and to effect some sort of organization. Time, however, was on the other side. Bulgaria signed an armistice on September 30, Turkey on October 30, Austria on November 3; and on November 11, with the signing of Germany, the war was over.

Britain soon faced the khaki election—the first general election since 1910. The two most famous slogans of the campaign were "Hang the Kaiser" and "We shall squeeze the orange until the pips squeak." Lloyd George prepared a double defense for himself on this score. He disavowed using the phrases and then accused the opposition of using them also so that they could hardly have affected the fortunes of the election. Win-

ston Churchill, however, contended—in incomparable language
—that Lloyd George was, in principle at least, in favor of
hanging the Kaiser:

Mr. Lloyd George, himself an actor although a man of action,
would, if he had had his way, have deprived us of this invaluable
exposure in order to gratify the passions of victorious crowds. He
would have redraped this melancholy exile in the somber robes of
more than mortal guilt and of superhuman responsibility, and led
him forth to a scaffold of vicarious expiation. Upon the brow from
which the diadem of empire had been smitten, he would have set
a crown of martydom; and Death, with an all effacing gesture, would
have re-founded the dynasty of the Hohenzollerns upon a victim's
tomb.[25]

Britain's chief representative in the drama at Versailles was
David Lloyd George. He and his supporters had won by an
overwhelming majority in the election and he could be said to
have the mandate to hang the Kaiser and to squeeze the orange
until the pips squeaked. The peace itself was negotiated, in
a sense, but Germany was not involved in the negotiations. The
victorious powers settled amongst themselves, often with much
difficulty, what share each should have of the spoils of war
and how extensive those spoils should be. Britain, that country which was not fighting for territory, together with the
Dominions reaped the most extensive harvest.

Lloyd George was the spokesman for the majority of his
countrymen when he gave his knock-out interview. He held a
similar position on January 5, 1918, when he addressed the special conference of the Trades Union Congress and the Labor
party. Finally, he appeared for the people and seemed to express
their convictions at Versailles. What he said, however, on each
of these occasions—as well as on many others—was not consistent.
Nor could it be said that he was among the first to arrive at the
varying convictions which he expressed from time to time.
Was he, then, a Machiavellian politician who felt that holding

[25] Winston S. Churchill, *Great Contemporaries* (New York, 1937), p. 29.

office was an end in itself? Were there principles by which he lived which could make him a leader of men?

Much has been written about Britain's victorious Prime Minister by his associates and contemporaries which helps to answer the above questions. Sir Charles Mallet, biographer of Lloyd George and holder of minor governmental posts, wrote:

Wherever one looks in Mr. Lloyd George's record the same qualities appear: the large plans, the abundant energy, the variable judgment, depending so often upon public opinion, the love of talk, the love of scheming and the noticeable lack of thoroughness and grip.[26]

C. P. Scott of the *Manchester Guardian* must have been similarly impressed when he wrote that Lloyd George "was unstable, had no real hold on political principles, was swayed by his surroundings . . . and would make no heroic sacrifice."[27] Leopold Amery, assistant secretary of the War Cabinet and the Imperial War Cabinet in 1917, did not differ. He did not find Lloyd George deliberately inconsistent or untruthful. Instead, being one who lived "entirely in response to the immediate stimulus, he had no clear memory either of past events or of his own former motives."[28] Austen Chamberlain, one-time member of the War Cabinet, after noting a comment of A. J. Balfour on the amazingly accurate conclusions that Lloyd George reached at times by instinctive judgment, wrote: "This instinctive judgment, more like a woman's than a man's, accounts for some of his greatest successes—and no small part of his failures."[29] Bonar Law added a new quality. On the eve of the formation of the second coalition, he did not question Lloyd George's ability at the War Office. However, he feared that Lloyd George "was out for his own honour and glory, and

[26] Sir Charles Mallet, *Mr. Lloyd George: A Study* (London, 1930), p. 121.
[27] Hammond, *Scott*, p. 243.
[28] Leopold S. Amery, *My Political Life* (London, 1953), II, 95.
[29] Sir J. Austen Chamberlain, *Down the Years* (London, 1937), pp. 244-245. See also Esher, *Journals*, IV, 230.

that he was not a person to be trusted when national and personal interests happened to clash."[30] H. Wickham Steed, in a sense, extended Bonar Law's comments:

The outstanding merit of Mr. Lloyd George was his perception that, for him and for Great Britain, there could be no evasion of the issue, that there was no way out or round or under, but only a way through—to victory. Though this perception sometimes became obscured, it guided him in the main. His great demerit was that, when the war had been won, he allowed his old skill as a parliamentary tactician to get the better of his finer qualities, and to beguile him into treating the Allied and Associated governments like so many pieces in a game, to be played against each other and manoeuvred in accordance with his own political or personal predilections.[31]

Two final quotations of contemporaries help summarize the views. The first is by Winston Churchill, at that time a Liberal, who served in Lloyd George's Government. The second is by J. A. Hobson, also a Liberal, but an author who had no governmental responsibilities. Churchill was favorably impressed:

The new Prime Minister possessed two characteristics which were in harmony with this period of convulsion. First, a power of living in the present, without taking short views. Every day for him was filled with the hope and impulse of a fresh beginning. He surveyed the problems of each morning with an eye unobstructed by preconceived opinions, past utterances, or previous disappointments and defeats. In times of peace such a mood is not always admirable, nor often successful for long. But in the intense crisis when the world was a kaleidoscope, when every month all the values and relations were changed by some prodigious event and its measureless reactions, this inexhaustible mental agility, guided by the main purpose of Victory, was a rare advantage. His intuition fitted the crisis better than the logical reasoning of more rigid minds.

The quality of living in the present and starting afresh each day led directly to a second and invaluable aptitude. Mr. Lloyd George

[30] Lord Beaverbrook, *Politicians and the War* (London, 1932), II, 128.
[31] Henry Wickam Steed, *Through Thirty Years, 1892-1922* (New York, 1924), II, 133.

in this period seemed to have a peculiar power of drawing from misfortune itself the means of future success.[32]

Hobson's view was more critical:

> The case of Mr. Lloyd George's war-idealism is different. Mr. George never took these or any other principles very seriously. He is not an unprincipled, but rather a non-principled man. Principles, apart from the useful enthusiasm they evoke in others, have no meaning for him in politics. Politics is a game of short-range expedients, coloured and directed by sympathetic tact. This applies to high as well as low politics. History has taught him no lessons about the evolution of society or general tendencies in human affairs. He must deal with each issue that arises on its own merits and by calculations of present expediency. There is for him no other way. His personality is a powerhouse of flickering ideals and evanescent enthusiasms. These ideals and enthusiasms are not for realization, but for evoking energy which shall be applied to the matter in hand. So the loftiest rhetoric of war-ideals flowed from his lips when the immediate need was the appeasement of labour troubles and the stimulation of the people to intense production of war materials. He felt these glowing phrases as he spoke them, but he did not mean them, at least in any serious sense of the term 'meaning.' The elevated sentiments of liberty and justice, the bright images of a land fit for heroes and a world living in amity, touched his sympathy and stirred his imagination as he painted them, but they carried neither intellectual nor moral conviction and no lasting will towards their fulfilment. They were true for him at the moment with such measure of sincerity as his facile and changeable mind was capable of entertaining. . . .[33]

There is, then, fairly general agreement on many of Lloyd George's characteristics. He was an intuitive rather than a reasoned thinker, which led to inconsistency time and again in his utterances. He had a genius for ferreting out public opinion and then saying what would be most acceptable to his listeners. He seldom, if ever, forgot himself or his own interests in the service of a cause which he followed on its merits

---

[32] Winston S. Churchill, *The World Crisis* (London, 1923-1931), III, 256-257.
[33] J. A. Hobson, *Problems of a New World* (New York, 1921), pp. 120-121.

alone. He was an organizer, a director, a good public-relations man, and he did get things done. His final defense, of course, would be that Germany was defeated and Britain was victorious while he was Prime Minister.

Britain did win the war, but there are many who contend—with more than a little justification—that the settlement which followed laid the groundwork, directly and indirectly, for subsequent events in Germany and for World War II. Was there another way out? The historian should occasionally—*qua* man —be willing to evaluate his evidence and attempt an educated guess concerning the "world of might have been." Many individuals have contended that a reasonable and lasting peace could have been made at the end of 1916, that Lansdowne was more perceptive at that time than Lloyd George. The advantages of such a contention are obvious. In particular, the Bolshevik revolution might have been averted. From a strictly British vantage point, however, peace does not seem to have been likely at that time. The weight of evidence is on the side of Lloyd George. His intuition was more discerning of the temper of public opinion than Lansdowne's reasoning. Moreover, there is little indication that Germany would have been willing to make a peace at that time which the Allies could in any sense have called reasonable.

There is, however, another possibility—the war, instead of being too long, may have been too short. British public opinion had reached a state late in 1917 and early in 1918 where it favored a reasonable peace. Movements were under way which may well have made that opinion a decisive factor. Lloyd George did give his Trades Union speech on January 5, 1918, but Brest-Litovsk and the German March offensive dealt the movement a mortal blow. Germany exhausted herself and the war was over before any revival could take place. Efforts, however, were again being made to enlist supporters for a reasonable peace in the summer of 1918. Here comes the big "if." If the German army had been willing and able to retreat to its own borders and then make a stand, the war would have had all the prospects of continuing on into 1919. The German people seemed ready to support a peace without victory. Time would have been available in Britain either to insure Lloyd George's support or to replace him with someone more amenable to the idea of peace without victory. His career was such, however, that he very likely would have said: "There go my followers. I am their leader. I must follow them."

It is not likely that a peace without victory would have introduced the world to a universal reign of blessing or that World War I would have been "the war to end all wars." Nevertheless, this writer, for one, would be more than willing to try living in a world where a reasoned and reasonable effort was made by men to live harmoniously with their fellow-men.

HITLER
REMILITARIZES THE
RHINELAND

C. Waldron Bolen

The chief architects of Germany's foreign policy in the two decades between the First and Second World Wars were Gustav Stresemann, Foreign Minister of the Weimar Republic, and Adolf Hitler, Chancellor of the Third Reich. Under the guise of fulfilling the terms of the Treaty of Versailles, the former regained for his country a position of "respectability" among the nations and removed many of the restrictions which the Allies had imposed.[1] Employing more drastic methods—a combination of power politics, propaganda, and the *fait accompli*— Hitler carried Stresemann's doctrine of equality and full sovereignty to its logical conclusion. This is not to say that the two leaders differed only in method. Stresemann undoubtedly hoped to secure advantages for Germany while working within the existing European state system. Hitler, on the other hand, had more ambitious goals, the incorporation of all Germans in a great Reich and the acquisition of more space in eastern Europe.[2]

[1] Hans Gatzke, *Stresemann and the Rearmament of Germany* (Baltimore, 1954), pp. 46-71, 107-16. The writer wishes to thank the Kress Committee of Clemson College for funds granted to make the research for this essay possible.

[2] Norman Baynes, *The Speeches of Adolf Hitler, April 1922–August 1939* (London, 1942), I, 103; Hossbach's memorandum, Nov. 10, 1937, Germany,

Although the National Socialist party consistently denounced the policy of fulfilment and came to power by defeating the coalition of parties which had supported this view,[3] Stresemann's diplomacy redounded to Hitler's advantage. First, it afforded a screen for the secret rearmament of Germany,[4] and, second, it brought the withdrawal of the French soldiers from the Rhineland five years before the time specified in the Treaty of Versailles.[5] Thereafter western Germany was a military vacuum, for Articles 42 and 43 of the Treaty had banned fortifications and military forces in a zone extending from France and Belgium to a line drawn fifty kilometers east of the Rhine River. One cannot say that Stresemann would have accepted this limitation as final, but, in the Locarno Treaty of 1925, he put the demilitarized zone on a better legal basis. Freely negotiated by Germany, France, and Belgium, and guaranteed by Britain and Italy, the pact insured Germany against any military action by France comparable to the invasion of the Ruhr in 1923 and, conversely, France and Belgium were insured against a German attack. To the Nazis, however, the Locarno Treaty was a monstrous deed,[6] for the exposed frontier was a permanent handicap in the management of Germany's foreign policy. Neurath, the Reich Foreign Minister, revealed after the German reoccupation that it was the policy of his Government to do nothing active, especially in Austria and Czechoslovakia, until the Rhineland had

---

Documents on German Foreign Policy, 1918-1945 (Washington, 1949), ser. D, I, 29-35.

[3] Otto Abetz, *Das offene Problem: Ein Rückblick auf zwei Jahrzehnte deutscher Frankreichpolitik* (Cologne, 1951), p. 11; *Völkischer Beobachter*, April 19, 1928; Gordon Prange, *Hitler's Words: Two Decades of National Socialism, 1923-1943* (Washington, 1944), pp. 59-61.

[4] Gerald Freund, *Unholy Alliance: Russian-German Relations from the Treaty of Brest-Litovsk to the Treaty of Berlin* (New York, 1957), pp. 201-212; Gatzke, *Stresemann*, pp. 7-15.

[5] The last French soldiers left the vicinity of Mainz in June, 1930.

[6] *Völkischer Beobachter*, April 19, 1928.

been "digested."[7]   The pursuit of a revisionist policy also dictated withdrawal from the League of Nations and the World Disarmament Conference.   But Hitler was cautious until the Saar was safely in his grasp,[8] whereupon he boldly repudiated all restrictions on German armaments.   The new army, the instrument for the remilitarization of the Rhineland and for the support of more ambitious ventures, was now in the making.

The earliest document among the captured military records[9] dealing with the reoccupation of the Rhineland is an order from General von Blomberg, Minister of Defense, to the commanders-in-chief of the army, navy, and air force—Fritsch, Raeder, and Göring.   The order gave the code name, operation "*Schulung*"—meaning schooling or training, and stated that it was to be executed as a surprise blow at lightning speed. Strictest secrecy was to be observed during the planning stage, with the smallest possible number of officers employed in the work.   Supported by the air force, the operation was to be carried out by units at their peacetime strength and with their peacetime equipment, with the navy providing safe transport for the East Prussian troops if transport by land was impossible.[10]   Significantly, this order was issued on May 2, 1935, the day of the signing of the Franco-Russian Treaty of Mutual Assistance.   This pact, later extended to include Czechoslovakia, was to be the pretext for the Rhineland action.

The details for operation "*Schulung*" were prepared in the working committee of the Reich Defense Council.   Although few records were kept, on June 26, 1935, Colonel Jodl reported to the working committee of the Council that weapons, insignia, and field gray uniforms were being stored in the demilitarized

[7] Bullitt's memorandum, May 18, 1936, United States, *Nazi Conspiracy and Aggression* (Washington, 1946-1948), VII, 890.

[8] The transfer was made on March 1, 1935.

[9] Records of the Foreign Ministry for this period are not available.

[10] *Nazi Conspiracy and Aggression*, I, 440-441, and VI, 951-952; His Majesty's Stationery Office, *The Trial of German Major War Criminals, Proceedings of the International Military Tribunal Sitting at Nuremberg, Germany* (hereinafter cited as *I.M.T.*) (London, 1946), Part 1, 207-208, Part 15, 382-383.

zone under conditions of the greatest secrecy. Since plans for mobilization were discussed at this meeting, the committee decided that written directives should be kept at a minimum, being used only to insure the smooth execution of the march. Without exception such documents were to be kept in safes.[11]

Until the time was ripe for executing the move, Hitler applied his talents in sowing confusion among the former Allies. The League's condemnation of Germany for rearming and the challenge from Stresa provided an opening.[12] In a Reichstag speech on May 21, he defended Germany's right to rearm, proposed an arms agreement, and promised to observe every treaty voluntarily signed, including the Locarno obligation, as long as other nations would do the same.[13] At the same time he announced that the recently contracted Franco-Soviet Treaty was incompatible with the Locarno Pact. Four days later he informed the other signatories of Locarno— Britain, Italy, and Belgium—of this interpretation.[14] When these powers replied that they did not take this view,[15] the German Government announced that the matter was not closed.[16]

Of more importance to the success of his Rhineland plan was Hitler's discovery that the Stresa front was not solid. The

[11] Nuremberg doc. EC-405, *I.M.T.*, Part 9, pp. 241-242, and Part 15, pp. 382-383; *Nazi Conspiracy and Aggression*, Supplement A, p. 80.

[12] Britain, France, and Italy announced at Stresa (April 14) the formation of a common front against any unilateral repudiation of treaties. Winston Churchill, *The Gathering Storm* (Boston, 1948), p. 133.

[13] Germany, *Verhandlungen des Reichstags*, IX Wahlperiode 1933 (Berlin, 1936), Vol. 458, 43-47, and 53-54; Baynes, *Speeches of Hitler*, II, 1227, 1241. André François-Poncet calls Hitler's proposals bait for Britain. *The Fateful Years, Memoirs of a French Ambassador in Berlin, 1931-1938* (New York, 1949), p. 177.

[14] Article I of the Locarno Treaty guaranteed the frontiers of Germany and France and Germany and Belgium, including the provision for the demilitarized zone. The inconsistency alleged by Germany was based on a technicality: under the Franco-Soviet Pact, if either power submitted a dispute to the Council of the League of Nations without that body arriving at a decision, the ally was still bound to come to the aid of her friend. In a Russo-German war, France would be expected to attack Germany through the exposed Rhineland. Werner Frauendienst, ed., *Weltgeschichte der Gegenwart in Dokumenten 1935-1936, International Politik* (3rd ed.; Essen, 1944), III, 296-299.

[15] *Ibid.*, III, 303-306.   [16] *Ibid.*, III, 306.

good will of the British enabled him to weaken the relationship between London and Paris, the Anglo-German Naval
Agreement being the means,[17] while Mussolini's Ethiopian
venture opened a gap between London and Rome.[18] At this
point, with Britain pressing for sanctions against Italy for aggression, Hitler revived an old fear, the fear of encirclement.
When the French ambassador reported this to his Government,
after a conversation with the Chancellor in November,[19] he
warned that the dictator intended to move into the Rhineland
and that his sole hesitancy was due to consideration for the
appropriate time. The observant ambassador advised his Government to forestall Hitler by sounding him on his intentions.
Once the cards were on the table, possibly he could be induced
to pledge not to erect any fortifications in the Rhineland, in
return for French approval of the stationing of a limited number of German garrisons there. Should this proposal be rejected by the Chancellor, the alternative was to threaten with
armed force a German move into the area. Premier Laval's
Government, however, took no action on the recommendation,
for they believed that tampering with the Locarno Pact might
cause the whole arrangment to crumble. Britain would then
regain her freedom of action and Italy, absorbed in Ethiopia,
would lose interest in the Rhineland.[20]

According to Friedrich Hossbach, Hitler's adjutant, the decision to reoccupy the Rhineland was made by the *Führer* in
south Germany during the second week in February, 1936.
From the Winter Olympic Games at Garmisch-Partenkirchen,
Hitler had gone to Schwerin for the burial of a Nazi leader.

---

[17] For Churchill's criticism, see *Gathering Storm*, pp. 137-141.

[18] François-Poncet, *Fateful Years*, pp. 177-178; J. W. Wheeler-Bennett, *Munich,
Prologue to Tragedy* (New York, 1948), p. 252.

[19] Otto Meissner, *Staatssekretär unter Ebert-Hindenburg-Hitler* (Hamburg,
1950), p. 409; François-Poncet, *Fateful Years*, p. 188.   William E. Dodd con-
firms this revival of the fear of encirclement. To State Dept., Feb. 12, 1936, U.S.,
Foreign Relations of the United States, Diplomatic Papers, 1936 (hereinafter
cited as *U.S. For. Rel.*) (Washington, 1953), I, 195-196.

[20] François-Poncet, *Fateful Years*, pp. 189-190.

While returning to south Germany he stopped in Berlin for a conference with General von Fritsch, commander-in-chief of the army. Since the army leaders had always insisted that remilitarization of the zone was a necessity from the point of view of national defense, Hitler apparently convinced Fritsch that the step could now be taken without a war. General von Blomberg was informed on the following day.[21] The generals accepted Hitler's decision but warned against any test of strength with the French army, for their old and new elements were not yet mixed.[22] On returning to Munich, Hitler summoned von Hassell from Rome in order to get his opinion on the attitude Italy would be expected to take relative to the move. The Chancellor was evidently convinced that Italy would not intervene.[23] Threatened with an oil embargo, Mussolini was actually showing signs of wanting a *rapprochement* with Germany.[24]

The chief officials in the Wilhelmstrasse were soon informed of the Chancellor's decision, but, without the dispatches, one could only guess when this information was transmitted to the embassies abroad.[25] And, from the evidence available, one can conclude that the army generals were the only high officials who questioned the operation or warned against it.[26] The top

[21] F. Hossbach, *Zwischen Wehrmacht und Hitler, 1924-1938* (Hannover, 1949), p. 97; Max Braubach, *Der Einmarsch deutscher Truppen in die entmilitarisierte Zone am Rhein im Marz 1936* (cited hereinafter as *Der Einmarsch deutscher Truppen*) (Cologne, 1956), pp. 11-14.

[22] John W. Wheeler-Bennett, *The Nemesis of Power* (New York, 1954), p. 349.

[23] Hossbach, *Zwischen Wehrmacht und Hitler*, p. 97.

[24] Erich Kordt, *Nicht aus den Akten, die Wilhelmstrasse in Frieden und Krieg* (cited hereinafter as *Nicht aus den Akten*) (Stuttgart, 1950), p. 128. Von Hassell's frequent trips were noted by the correspondent of *Figaro*, Feb. 21.

[25] At various times Dr. Forster, counselor of the embassy in Paris, was summoned for consultation. Braubach, *Der Einmarsch deutscher Truppen*, p. 15. Von Hoesch, in London, was informed late in the game. Geyr von Schweppenburg, *The Critical Years* (London, 1952), pp. 54-55.

[26] General von Manstein's testimony at Nuremberg. International Military Tribunal, *Trial of the Major War Criminals before the International Military Tribunal* (Nuremberg, 1948), XX, 603.

political advisers, Neurath and Ribbentrop, were optimistic,[27] but their subordinates, Bülow, Schmidt, and Kordt had misgivings about the undertaking.[28]

Because of the need for secrecy, Hitler initiated no war of nerves prior to the execution of *"Schulung."* But he did make an effort to influence foreign opinion to adopt a more favorable attitude toward Germany. A few days before the move the German press adopted a softer line toward France and Russia. William E. Dodd reported on February 16 that German newspaper comment on the Franco-Russian Treaty, which would soon be presented for ratification in the Chamber of Deputies, had been suppressed. The ambassador expected some nonofficial comment after ratification. With tongue in cheek, he stated that "no one in Germany is thinking of taking action" on the Rhineland question.[29] Further evidence of this effort to influence foreign opinion is attested by the two peace-feelers put out by Hitler on the eve of the debate in the Chamber of Deputies. The first conciliatory gesture was made in a communiqué released in Berlin on February 21,[30] and the second was made in an interview with Bertrand de Jouvenel, correspondent of the *Paris Soir*. Hitler may have expected to turn some French parliamentarians against the Treaty, thereby embarrassing Premier Sarraut's new Government,[31] but it is possible, too, that he desired to influence French and British

---

[27] According to Paul Schmidt, Neurath was the only government official consulted by Hitler who felt confident that the Rhineland could be remilitarized without opposition from France and Britain. *Nazi Conspiracy and Aggression,* V, 1102. The cabinet as such was not informed until after the march began.

[28] Kordt, *Nicht aus den Akten,* pp. 129-131; *I.M.T.,* Part 10, pp. 149-150; Lutz von Schwerin-Krosigk, *Es geschah in Deutschland* (Stuttgart, 1951), p. 310.

[29] The quotes are Dodd's. To State Department, Feb. 15. *U.S. For. Rel.,* I, 199. In an earlier dispatch (Feb. 8) Dodd stated that Germany was more dangerous than in 1914. The New York *Times* (March 1) correspondent noted the lull in the press.

[30] The brief statement followed the official line: that the Franco-Russian Treaty would, if ratified, violate the Locarno Pact. *Figaro,* Feb. 22.

[31] Laval's cabinet fell on January 22. Sarraut's ministry held the reins until the Popular Front coalition won the May election.

opinion favorably.[32]   In any case, the interview had little effect
on the debate in the Chamber, since it did not appear until
February 28, the morning after the Treaty was ratified.[33]   On
receiving this news, Hitler accused the French Government of
delaying the publication of the interview.[34]   And, when François-Poncet visited the chancellery on March 2 in order to
continue the earlier talks and to examine the views expressed
in the newspaper interview, the Chancellor showed no desire to
explore the ground for a *rapprochement*.[35]

Hitler's order to execute *"Schulung"* was delivered to the
commanders-in-chief of the army, navy, and air force on March
2. March-day or Z-day was not given, but General von Fritsch
was ordered to move units of the VI, IX, and V army corps
into permanent garrisons in the territory east of the Rhine.
Then three infantry battalions were to be transferred across
the Rhine, one each to the cities of Aachen, Trier, and Saarbrücken. The regional police in the entire zone were to be
incorporated into the new army. Air Minister Göring was
ordered to transfer one fighter squadron to Cologne and one
to Coblenz, and antiaircraft units to the most important
bridges on the lower and middle Rhine. Beginning at 0800
on Z-day those battalions assigned to the Aachen, Trier, and
Saarbrücken garrisons, the AA units assigned to the bridge-
heads, and the first fighter squadron were to move toward the
Rhine, arriving there at 1200. The other units were to move
into the zone within twenty-four hours. In the interest of
secrecy, the time for preparing the troop movements was to be
brief; state, municipal, and party officials who were to assist in

---

[32] Meissner, *Staatssekretär unter Ebert-Hindenburg-Hitler,* p. 409. Neurath
said Hitler was serious about friendship with France. *I.M.T.,* Part 17, p. 118.

[33] It appeared in the *Midi* (Paris), the two newspapers having the same
publisher. *Völkischer Beobachter,* March 1.

[34] The Germans made an effort to get the interview withdrawn, since it had
not been published before the Chamber voted, but the *Midi* (Paris) was already
on the streets. Otto Abetz, *Das offene Problem,* p. 78.

[35] Meissner, *Staatssekretär unter Ebert-Hindenburg-Hitler,* p. 409; *cf.* François-
Poncet, *Fateful Years,* pp. 191-193.

the billeting of the men were not to be informed until 0800 on
Z-day; and persons on leave were not to be recalled. To preserve the peaceful character of the operation, Blomberg ordered
that military security and precautionary measures were not to
be taken without his express consent. Should the other Locarno
powers adopt countermeasures, the War Minister reserved the
right to take appropriate action.[36]

When the German Government announced, on March 5,
that the Reichstag would assemble the following week in order
to receive a foreign policy statement from the Chancellor, foreign emissaries and correspondents in Berlin surmised that the
Locarno Pact would be declared invalid because of the ratification of the Franco-Russian Treaty. Related to this opinion
was the report that Hitler would immediately demand the
abolition of restrictions on the Rhineland. A New York *Times*
correspondent wrote that immediate military reoccupation of
the zone was not believed included in the Government's plan.[37]
But a reporter for the *Manchester Guardian* had a better source
of information. He wrote that the German high command had
opposed a decision for military reoccupation of the Rhineland
because it was too great a risk for the German army. Hitler
was said to have imposed his decision.[38]

This announcement was scarcely off the wire when, on
March 6, the Reichstag meeting was moved up one week. This
abrupt change was connected with the decision of the League
to give Italy and Ethiopia one week to accept arbitration before imposing the oil embargo. With Italy threatening to leave
the League and to cancel her obligation under Locarno, Foreign Minister Flandin was again pressing London for a supplementary British guarantee to compensate for the loss of Italy.[39]

---

[36] Nuremberg doc. C-159, *Nazi Conspiracy and Aggression*, VI, 974-976.
[37] Guido Enderis, March 6.
[38] March 7.
[39] Pierre Étienne Flandin, *Politique française, 1919-1940* (Paris, 1947), pp.
194-195, 197; Churchill, *Gathering Storm*, p. 191; *Völkischer Beobachter*, March
4, 6, 7; *Times* (London) March 6.

The estrangement of Italy and Britain's reluctance to assume additional obligations must have convinced Hitler that the time was at hand to move into the Rhineland.[40]   William L. Shirer, an American correspondent, noted in his diary that Hitler would probably put an end to the demilitarized zone, but the sending of troops was judged too risky.[41]   The announcement that the representatives of the Locarno powers were being called to the Foreign Office prior to the assembling of the Reichstag added support to the opinion that the Rhine Pact would get an official burial.

If the Chancellor had decided before March 6 that Z-day would be on the following day, the secret was well kept. Available evidence points to the conclusion that the final decision was made on March 6.   Supporting this theory is General Manstein's remark that he had only one afternoon in which to prepare the time-schedule for the march.[42]   Moreover, the secret order to the navy did not go out until March 6.[43]   The choice of Saturday was important, since the British ministers and Parliament would be scattered for the week end and the French would have two days to "sweat it out" before the British cabinet could meet.   Hitler must have believed that countermeasures against the *fait accompli* would be taken immediately or not at all.   Consequently, any obstacles that could be raised against such measures would improve his chance for success.

At noon, on March 7, when Adolf Hitler entered the Kroll Opera to make his foreign policy statement to the German Reichstag, in the presence of the emissaries of foreign powers,

[40] Atherton (London) to State Dept., March 8. *U.S. For. Rel.*, I, 213; G. M. Young, *Stanley Baldwin* (London, 1952), p. 222; Dodd to State Dept., March 8. *U.S. For. Rel.*, I, 215.

[41] Shirer, *Berlin Diary: The Journal of a Foreign Correspondent* (New York, 1941), p. 49.

[42] International Military Tribunal, *Trial of Major War Criminals*, XX, 603.

[43] Nuremberg doc. C-194, *Nazi Conspiracy and Aggression*, I, 442, and VI, 1020-1021.   Activity of the navy was confined to reconnaissance duty in the North and Baltic Seas.   Navy men abroad were instructed to forego celebrating in order not to give a false picture of the *Führer's* intentions.

the press, and galleries packed with spectators, operation *"Schu-lung"* was four hours old. Advance units of the army were entering the Rhine cities and fighter planes of the Luftwaffe were over Cologne. The Chancellor talked for ninety minutes to the cheering delegates, most of whom were in uniform. Beginning with the "gray November day of 1918" and the sad consequences of the Great War, he moved on to enumerate various unsolved political and economic questions of the day, among which was the need for space for the sixty-seven million Germans. Next he attacked the claim of the Bolshevists to mastery of the world, recounted his attempts for a reconciliation with France, and reviewed the position Germany had previously taken with respect to the Franco-Soviet Treaty. This pact, he said, was directed solely against Germany, and, since it had invalidated the Locarno Treaty, the latter no longer applied to the Rhineland. The Chancellor listed seven proposals for guaranteeing European peace, proposals which had been delivered earlier to the representatives of the Locarno powers. The climax came when the *Führer* announced that German troops were then moving into "their future garrison posts in the western provinces of the Reich. . . ." Finally, he appealed to the German people to strengthen his hand by endorsing the National Socialist party in a new Reichstag election, and, bidding for a favorable reception abroad, he announced that Germany had no territorial demands to make in Europe.[44]

Those who witnessed the performance and who commented afterward generally held that the speech was one of Hitler's best. The delegates cheered until they were hoarse, especially when the Chancellor attacked Russia.[45] The *Times* (London) correspondent believed the friendly allusions to Britain were

[44] Special edition *Völkischer Beobachter*, March 8; *Verhandlungen des Reichstags*, IX Wahlperiode 1933, Vol. 458, 63-76. For excerpts in English, see Baynes, *Hitler's Speeches*, II, 1271-1293. The new election was scheduled for March 29.

[45] *Times* (New York), March 8; Meissner, *Staatssekretär unter Ebert-Hinden-burg-Hitler*, p. 410.

designed to throw upon the French Government the responsibility for the course which Germany was now adopting and, at the same time, to placate England.[46] Shirer, who was sharply critical of the affair, noted in his diary that a few diplomats thought the Rhineland action meant war; most thought Hitler would get away with it. Shirer observed, too, that Blomberg was extremely nervous during the Chancellor's speech.[47] Dodd said the speech was impressive,[48] while Messersmith, the American ambassador in Vienna, commented on the occasional belligerent tone in the oration. It was a peace speech, Messersmith reported, held in a warlike tone. Unless France and Britain showed some determination in the matter, he predicted that the Nazi element in Austria would grow stronger and would thus improve their chance for a successful revolt.[49]

The people of Berlin were less enthusiastic over the remilitarization than were the members of the Nazi-packed Reichstag, and, in government circles—particularly in the Wilhelmstrasse and in the War Ministry—there was serious concern over how France and England would react to the move.[50] The enthusiasm of the Rhinelanders, on the other hand, was genuine. As soon as the news of the re-entry of German soldiers was announced—in some cases by the use of Nazi sound-wagons—the townspeople quickly hoisted flags, jubilant crowds filled the streets, church bells were rung, and young girls showered flowers on the marching soldiers. In the evening torchlight parades were staged in the Rhineland cities, in Berlin, and in other cities of the Reich. The one in Berlin, reviewed by Hitler and his ministers from the balcony of the chancellery, was said to have included 15,000 storm troopers.[51] French consuls in the Rhineland cities reported to their embassy in Berlin that the soldiers were received with great enthusiasm, but

[46] March 9.   [47] *Berlin Diary*, pp. 49-51.
[48] To State Department, March 8; *U.S. For. Rel.*, I, 215.
[49] Memorandum, March 9; *U.S. For. Rel.*, I, 224-225.
[50] Meissner, *Staatssekretär unter Ebert-Hindenburg-Hitler*, p. 410.
[51] Tolischus, *Times* (New York), March 8; Shirer, *Berlin Diary*, pp. 54-55.

the "symbolic" units referred to by Hitler consisted of nineteen infantry battalions and thirteen artillery sections.[52] Although this pattern of flags, flowers, and fanfare in the Rhine cities was spontaneous, it was encouraged by government and Nazi officials. The military order of March 2, one will recall, directed the commander-in-chief of the army to inform state, municipal, and party officials in the Rhineland of the proposed re-entry of troops after 0800 on Z-day. Consequently, loudspeakers were installed in prominent places in the cities and towns for the purpose of transmitting Hitler's speech to the public; flags went up on public buildings as if by some prearranged signal; and party and government officials turned out to give "official" welcomes to the commanding officers of the military units. By order of Heinrich Himmler, Reich Minister of the Interior, and Doctor Goebbels, Reich Minister for Public Enlightenment and Propaganda, flags were to be flown on two days, on March 7 to celebrate the day on which Germany regained her full sovereignty, and on March 8 to commemorate Heroes' Day.[53] To insure that the remilitarization was "properly" reported, the Propaganda Ministry had German correspondents appear at the Templehof Air Field at 0800, without informing them of their destination. They were then let in on the secret and flown to Cologne, Frankfurt, and other cities.[54]

With their eyes on the March 29 election, the Nazi leaders used every possible propaganda device to win credit for the events of March 7. Utilizing radios, telegrams, and newspapers, local leaders conveyed their thanks to their *Führer* for his act of liberation. The *Völkischer Beobachter*, organ of the Nazi party, published many of these messages.[55] In a radio address Gauleiter Terboven of Cologne, "speaking for all the men and

[52] François-Poncet, *Fateful Years*, p. 192; Dodd to State Dept., March 7; *U.S. For. Rel.*, I, 208.

[53] Special edition, *Völkischer Beobachter*, March 8; *Völkischer Beobachter*, March 9.

[54] Gunter d'Alquen, *Völkischer Beobachter*, special edition, March 8.

[55] From Cologne, Coblenz, Trier, Karlsruhe, Frankfurt, Bonn, etc.

women in the zone," thanked the Chancellor for the new freedom. In acknowledging this message, Doctor Goebbels assured
the Rhinelanders that the soldiers who entered the area were
not representatives of an outmoded *revanche* policy but were
"representatives of peace."[56] This statement was meant for foreign consumption.

The first two days of the reoccupation were uneasy ones for
the German Government. The number of troops involved was
not large[57] and only three battalions had crossed the Rhine, but
Hitler knew he had gambled heavily. He had, therefore, given
a secret order to the army to avoid a conflict and to withdraw
the three exposed battalions—at Aachen, Trier, Saarbrücken—
across the Rhine if France took counteraction.[58] On informing
his ministers of the accomplished fact on the morning of March
7, the Chancellor urged them to keep strong nerves and to
remain calm if alarming reports came in from foreign countries.
Obviously he was relying heavily on the seven peace proposals
to create a favorable impression abroad, particularly in England.[59]

Some observers were willing to concede victory to Hitler
on the morning of the second day (March 8), when the French
—instead of marching—called a meeting of the Locarno powers
and appealed to the Council of the League of Nations.[60] Shirer
wrote that the faces of Hitler, Göring, Blomberg, and Fritsch
were all smiles as they sat in the royal box at the State Opera

[56] *Völkischer Beobachter*, March 8.
[57] Meissner says the total strength was about 30,000. With storm troopers
and police units the number would have been much higher. *Staatssekretär
unter Ebert-Hindenburg-Hitler*, p. 410.
[58] Bernhard von Lossberg, *Im Wehrmachtführungstab: Bericht eines Gen-
eralstaboffiziers* (Hamburg, 1950), p. 11; Kordt, *Nicht aus den Akten*, p. 134.
Apparently this was discussed before the march. W. Foerster, *Generaloberst
Ludwig Beck sein Kampf gegen den Krieg* (Munich, 1953), p. 57.
[59] Meissner, *Staatssekretär unter Ebert-Hindenburg-Hitler*, p. 411.
[60] Belgium supported this move. The appeal was received in Geneva on
March 8. Germany was charged with violating Article I of the Locarno Treaty
and Articles 42 and 43 of the Treaty of Versailles. League of Nations, *The
League from Year to Year, 1936* (Geneva, 1937), pp. 69-70.

for the Heroes' Memorial Day service.[61]   Later, on the same
day, when disturbing reports came from Paris about the unusually strong indignation in the French press, the meetings
of the French General Staff, military activity in the Maginot
Line, and a sharply worded radio address by Premier Sarraut,
the possibility of a French counteraction unnerved the *Führer*.
For a while he believed the game was lost.[62]   Blomberg suggested the withdrawal of the three battalions to the east side
of the Rhine, but the Chancellor refused.[63]   After the crisis
had passed, he told Hossbach, his adjutant, that he did not
want to take on another such burden for ten years.[64]

Had the Chancellor known the real situation in France he
would not have worried.   The French General Staff had no
plan for a limited military action which could have forced a
German withdrawal from the Rhineland.[65]   Foreign Minister
Flandin learned of this inadequate planning a few weeks before
the German reoccupation.[66]   So, when the French cabinet met
on March 7 to consider the German challenge, General Gamelin recommended the calling up of reserves.   But this was
deemed inadvisable, partly because of the general election
scheduled for the first week in May.   Meetings continued into

[61] Shirer, *Berlin Diary*, pp. 55-56.   In the main address, Blomberg stated that
Germany wished no offensive war but would not fear a defensive war.

[62] Meissner, *Staatssekretär unter Ebert-Hindenburg-Hitler*, p. 411; Kordt,
Nicht aus den Akten, p. 134.   Those who witnessed his near-collapse were
told to keep quiet.   For the warning telegram from the three attachés in
London, see Hossbach, *Zwischen Wehrmacht und Hitler*, p. 98.

[63] International Military Tribunal, *Trial of the Major War Criminals*
(Nuremberg, 1948), XX, 603-604; Kordt, *Nicht aus den Akten*, p. 134.

[64] *Zwischen Wehrmacht und Hitler*, p. 23.

[65] Maurice Gamelin, *Servir* (Paris, 1946-1947), II, 199; André Géraud, *The
Gravediggers of France, Gamelin, Daladier, Reynaud, Pétain, and Laval* (New
York, 1944), p. 2.   The French army was too rigid to set any of its parts in
motion independently of the others.

[66] Flandin, *Politique française*, pp. 195-196.   He put the question directly
to the French Military Council and was told that the army was concerned
only with a defensive mission.   Some officials in France had expected this
German action.   Straus to State Dept., March 7, *U.S. For. Rel.*, I, 206-207;
François-Poncet, *Fateful Years*, p. 194.

the second day of the crisis with the same result.[67]   Although
Paul-Boncour thought the Foreign Minister did not insist on
his point of view, if he honestly desired military action against
Germany,[68] a majority of the ministers, including the three
heads of the fighting services, preferred to await domestic and
foreign reaction before making a decision.   Premier Sarraut,
Flandin, Mandel, and Paul-Boncour, however, advocated the
strong line.[69]   The shifting of defense forces into their positions in the Maginot Line was the only action taken.   If the
French ministers considered the support which might have
been expected from the allies in eastern Europe, they fail to
mention the fact in their writings.

The reaction of the French people and of foreign governments contributed in no way to a solution favorable to France.
Actually the indecision in the cabinet was a reflection of the indecision in the country.   Neither the so-called rightist journals
nor the leftist organs advocated military measures.[70]   Knowing
this, Premier Sarraut and Flandin made an effort to arouse
public opinion in favor of a miltary action.   Utilizing the radio,
Sarraut delivered an address to the French people on the evening of March 8.   The strongest statement in the speech was
the announcement that the French Government "was not prepared to leave Strasbourg under the fire of German cannon."[71]
The Premier also denounced Hitler's use of the *fait accompli*,

[67] Gamelin wanted adequate forces for any eventuality, even war. *Servir*, II,
201; Flandin, *Politique française*, pp. 198-199; Paul Reynaud, *In the Thick
of the Fight, 1930-1945* (London, 1955), p. 127.

[68] Paul-Boncour, *Entre deux guerres: Souvenirs sur la IIIe République* (New
York, 1947), III, 32.   Géraud blames Flandin for not insisting on military
action.   *Gravediggers of France*, pp. 390-392.   L. B. Namier draws the same
conclusion.   *Europe in Decay: A Study in Disintegration, 1936-1940* (London,
1950), pp. 22-23.

[69] Paul-Boncour, *Entre deux guerres*, III, 33-35; Gamelin, *Servir*, II, 201;
Géraud, *Gravediggers of France*, p. 276.   Leger, Secretary General of the Ministry of Foreign Affairs, also favored strong action.

[70] Flandin, *Politique française*, pp. 199-201.   Many conservatives were critical
of the Government for contracting the alliance with Russia, while among the
so-called leftists pacificism ran strong.

[71] *Figaro* (March 9) called the message energetic.

particularly while France was preparing for a general election. Finally, he rejected outright the seven proposals which the Chancellor had made to the Locarno powers as the basis for European peace.[72]

If the French were guilty of hesitancy in a matter affecting their security, the British contributed to this indecision. Having turned a cold shoulder to Flandin's request for a supplementary guarantee of her Locarno pledge before March 7, in the event that Italy should repudiate her obligation, Prime Minister Baldwin's Government had no intention of giving the pledge afterward. On the contrary, London exerted a restraining influence on Paris, exhorting the French to take no action until their Governments could act jointly and after full consideration.[73] When it became clear on the second day that the British would not support aggressive action, Flandin asked for the moral support of the United States. Specifically, he suggested that President Roosevelt make some public statement condemning on moral grounds the unilateral repudiation of treaties. In Flandin's opinion, the President's words would receive wide attention, particularly in England. To strengthen his request, the French minister told Straus, the American ambassador, that Hitler would now be able to hold the Rhineland with a minimum force while he turned his attention south and east toward Austria, Czechoslovakia, Poland, and Russia.[74] When informed that President Roosevelt could not make the speech requested, Flandin expressed the hope that the American press might give some support to the French view.[75] Grasping at another straw, he encouraged Prime Minister Van Zeeland of Belgium to take the lead in demanding sanctions,

[72] Ibid., March 9; Manchester Guardian, March 9; Abetz, Das offene Problem, p. 79.

[73] "A velvet carpet for retreat," writes Churchill. Gathering Storm, p. 194; Atherton (London) to State Dept., March 8, U.S. For. Rel., I, 214.

[74] Straus, to State Dept., March 8; U.S. For. Rel., I, 216-217.

[75] Hull to Straus, March 10, and Straus to State Dept., March 11; ibid., I, 228, 234.

since Belgium was the innocent party in the case. This tactic was also intended to influence the British to stand with France.[76] But the British were unmoved.

This divergence in policy was also manifested in the attitude Paris and London took toward Hitler's peace proposals. Whereas the French rejected them outright, the British accepted them as a basis for negotiation. On this olive branch the *Führer* held out the prospect of a new demilitarized zone on both sides of the frontier; a twenty-five year nonaggression pact with Germany, France, and Belgium; renewed guarantees by Britain and Italy of the pact; inclusion of the Netherlands in the treaty; an air pact; nonaggression pacts with Germany's neighbors in the east similar to the German-Polish Treaty; and the return of Germany to the League of Nations.[77] One will have to admit that the proposals were artfully contrived and comprehensive, but they were intended to serve only as a screen.

Despite Flandin's plea for support and a parallel request for the British Government to influence their press for a common action against Germany, Baldwin and Eden made no public statement until Monday, March 9.[78] Opinion was strongly for peace, and the Foreign Secretary's calm speech in the House of Commons on that day was endorsed wholeheartedly by the British press.[79] A *Times* editorial called the speech "admirable," and promised to support the Government's intention to "rebuild for the future."[80] Excerpts taken by the *Times* editors from the *Daily Telegraph, Daily Mail, Morning Post, News Chronicle, Daily Express, Daily Herald,* and *Star*

[76] Straus to State Dept., March 11; *ibid.,* I, 234-235.

[77] *Völkischer Beobachter,* March 8; *Nazi Conspiracy and Aggression,* VIII, 397-398; Dodd to State Dept., March 7, *U.S. For. Rel.,* I, 208-209.

[78] Atherton to State Dept., March 8; *U.S. For. Rel.,* I, 213-214, and 241-242.

[79] Great Britain, *Parliamentary Debates, HC* (hereinafter cited as *Parl. Debs.*), 5th ser., cccix, 1812-1817. Though critical of Germany for the unilateral repudiation of the Locarno Pact, Eden promised to support France if she were attacked during the period of negotiation on the peace proposals.

[80] *Times* (London), March 10.

indicated a strong desire to accommodate Germany.[81] Von
Ribbentrop later called this understanding of Germany's point
of view a decisive factor in the crisis. Many Englishmen, he
said, agreed that no nation, great or small, could be denied the
right to defend itself.[82]

The Rhineland crisis was all but over for the Germans on
Monday, March 9, but the French wanted Germany's action
condemned by the Council of the League of Nations and
fresh guarantees to replace the old Locarno. Both aims smacked
of face-saving. Having invited the representatives of the other
Locarno powers to Paris on March 10, Flandin proposed that
the signatories of the Treaty inform Germany that she must
withdraw her troops from the Rhineland before negotiations
could proceed toward a settlement. If Germany did not yield
to this demand, then the Locarno powers should petition the
League to levy sanctions against her. Eden, however, rejected
this procedure,[83] insisting that the matter should first be taken
before the Council of the League. Furthermore, in the interest
of calm deliberation, he got the delegates to agree to move the
discussions to London and to request the Council of the League
to hear the Franco-Belgian petition there.[84] The delegates
were therefore able to attend both meetings.

Since Eden had elected to play the role of arbiter, immediately upon his return to London he sounded the German Government on the possibility of a token withdrawal of the forces
sent into the Rhineland. At the same time, he asked Germany
to pledge not to send in more troops and not to erect fortifications in the Rhineland, at least during the period of the negotiations. The effort failed when Hitler refused to give the
pledges. Nothing, he said, could induce Germany to renounce

[81] *Ibid.*, March 10.
[82] Joachim von Ribbentrop, *The Ribbentrop Memoirs* (London, 1953), p. 57.
[83] Straus to State Dept., March 10; *U.S. For. Rel.*, I, 228-229; *Parl. Debs.*,
HC, 5th ser., cccx 1444.
[84] Alan Campbell-Johnson, *Eden: The Making of a Statesman* (New York,
1955), p. 128.

sovereignty over the Rhineland zone. Besides, if M. Sarraut thought that France could not leave Strasbourg under the fire of German cannon, it was equally intolerable for Germany to see open towns like Frankfurt, Freiburg, and Karlsruhe menaced by the guns on the French fortifications.[85]

When the representatives of the Locarno powers met in London, Flandin tried for two days to get some form of sanctions against Germany.[86] Should Germany go unpunished, he predicted that the whole group of middle European statesmen who favored co-operation with the western powers would—in the next two years—disappear, and the youth of certain of those countries whose inclinations were pro-German would control with Germany the destinies of central Europe.[87] Eden stubbornly resisted all arguments for sanctions, believing the matter could be solved by a new arrangement based on Hitler's proposals. The Belgian point of view was by this time closer to Britain's,[88] so Flandin yielded. The change of venue for the meeting of the Council of the League was, likewise, intended to facilitate discussions with Germany. As a signatory to the Locarno Treaty, she was invited to send a representative. Before accepting, however, Hitler asked for assurances that Germany would be treated as an equal and that his peace proposals would be considered. The Council complied with his request, and the Chancellor selected Ribbentrop to head the German delegation.[89]

In placing his case before the Council of the League, Foreign Minister Flandin offered to submit the question of the compatibility of the Franco-Russian Treaty and the Locarno Pact to the World Court. Then he asked the Council to de-

---

[85] Interview with G. Ward Price, *Daily Mail*, March 11; Stephen Heald and John W. Wheeler-Bennett, eds., *Documents on International Affairs, 1936* (London, 1937), p. 60.

[86] Sussdorff's (Brussels) memorandum, March 23; *U.S. For. Rel.*, I, 264.

[87] Atherton to State Dept., March 13, *ibid.*, I, 241-242.

[88] Sussdorff's memorandum, March 23, *ibid.*, I, 265.

[89] League of Nations, *The League from Year to Year*, pp. 70-71. For the story of Hitler's conditions, see Kordt, *Nicht aus den Akten*, pp. 136-138.

clare that Germany had violated Article I of the Locarno Pact
and Articles 42 and 43 of the Treaty of Versailles, so that Britain and Italy—the guarantors—could discharge their obligations and the Council could address recommendations to the
members of the League.[90] Van Zeeland supported this move,
after which France and Belgium introduced a resolution condemning Germany for her action. Litvinov, the Soviet delegate, made a strong plea for the resolution, but Eden thought
the Council's duty was to examine the situation in all of its
aspects. Hitler's strategy of tying peace proposals to the reoccupation had paid dividends, and Britain was now repaying
France for dragging her feet on the Ethiopian question.

Before the Council voted on the Franco-Belgian resolution,
on March 19, Ribbentrop presented Germany's side of the case.
He repeated the line taken by Hitler in the Reichstag speech of
March 7, after which the Council voted unanimously—with one
delegate abstaining and one absent—for the resolution. Ribbentrop made a short protest, to which Flandin gave a brief answer,
and the session was closed.[91] When the members of the League
took no supporting action for the Council's decision and the
discussions among the Locarno powers on Hitler's peace proposals came to naught,[92] the German Chancellor had won another round.

During the crisis German officials were wont to speak of
the reoccupation as a "symbolic" action. The designation was
appropriate, for the total effect of the Rhineland coup was symbolic of the weakening of France and of the strengthening
of Germany. Lacking the will to act independently of Britain,[93] France surrendered the key to her whole system of alli-

[90] League of Nations, The League from Year to Year, pp. 72-73.
[91] Ibid., pp. 73-82. Hitler had approved the speech before Ribbentrop left
Berlin. Kordt, Nicht aus den Akten, p. 139.
[92] For reports on some of these discussions see U.S. For. Rel., I, 264, 269,
272.
[93] Leger, Secretary General of the Ministry of Foreign Affairs, believed that
if France had acted her allies would have joined her. Gamelin, Servir, II, 202.
Churchill agrees. Gathering Storm, p. 193.

ances, a structure erected on the premise that the French army could effectively threaten Germany. From 1919 to 1936 this premise was valid, while the Rhineland was occupied by foreign troops or was demilitarized. After March 7, 1936, the remilitarized Rhineland contributed greatly to Germany's strength. Hitler could not only wall out the French army while consolidating his position in central Europe but could also threaten France.

The significance of the events of March 7 was not lost on the eastern allies: Russia, Poland, and members of the Little Entente. If France did not have the will to force the withdrawal of the German soldiers from the Rhineland in the interest of her own security, she could hardly qualify as a reliable ally. Ratification of the Franco-Russian Treaty, Hitler's pretext for the action, was completed by the French Senate. But the pact was never implemented by military arrangements and was never invoked. Poland's behavior, first promising to honor her alliance with France if war resulted from Hitler's move and later hedging on that promise,[94] is hard to explain without thinking in terms of the shifting of power away from France and toward Germany. Czechoslovakia, Yugoslavia, and Romania were likewise forced to reconsider their arrangements with France.[95] In Prague, Benes and Masaryk thought that Hitler had gone too far, but they did not regard the German-Czechoslovak arbitration agreement as voided.[96]

The Nazi victory in the Reichstag elections of March 29 should not be interpreted as an endorsement of Hitler's Rhineland coup; controlled elections only measure the effectiveness of the controls. But it would not be too much to say that

[94] Poland had an alliance with France and a nonaggression pact with Germany. For the controversy over Foreign Minister Beck's promise, see Richard Breyer, *Das deutsche Reich und Polen* (Wurzburg, 1955), pp. 155-164; Léon Noël, *Une ambassade a Varsovie, 1935-1939; L'Aggression allemande contre la Pologne* (Paris, 1946), pp. 128-129; Jozef Beck, *Final Report* (New York, 1957), pp. 109-111.

[95] Glorney Bolton, *Czech Tragedy* (London, 1955), p. 123.

[96] Wright (Prague) to State Dept., March 14, *U.S. For. Rel.*, I, 246-247.

the German people endorsed the action. Of the few German newspapers claiming some degree of independent thought, the *Frankfurter Zeitung* stated on March 10 that Germany would resist to the end any effort on the part of the Locarno or League powers to apply sanctions. To the argument that the prestige of the League of Nations demanded at least the application of economic measures, the editorial answered that if the League had thought of its prestige at the right time it would have been compelled to remove the disparity of arrangements in the Rhineland long ago. In welcoming the removal of this last restriction on German sovereignty, the Germans could not have comprehended that they were also removing one of the most important brakes on Hitler's unbridled ambition. A few of the older Reichswehr generals may have understood this, but their views were discredited by the Chancellor's success. And when the man with the "intuition" proposed greater things, these few were silenced. The will of the *Führer* would dictate the fate of the Third Reich.

FRENCH REACTION TO
THE SPANISH CIVIL WAR,
JULY-SEPTEMBER, 1936

J. Bowyer Bell

On July 19, 1936, vague reports of a military rebellion in Spanish Morocco began appearing in the Paris newspapers; suddenly the insistent rumors of a new Spanish *pronunciamiento,* which had been circulating both in diplomatic circles and on the street corners of Europe, became reality. Within a few days it became obvious that a swift coup d'état had failed and Spain was involved in a civil war of uncertain length. Another of the endless changes in Spanish Governments would have had little significance in Europe or in France; but this time the rival factions attracted the interest and support of various non-Spanish individuals and parties. The Republican Government in Madrid portrayed itself as the defender of democracy, socialism, and the rights of man. The rebels, soon to be united under General Francisco Franco as the Nationalists, in their turn sought, often in language not unlike that of fascism, support from conservatives, Catholics, and all the forces of order. Few recent events in so short a period engendered so much passionate interest or resulted in such intimate involvement as did the Spanish crisis during the summer of 1936. All varieties of political faiths and creeds were quickly committed; for in Spain, for the first time, all the ideologies of the twentieth century—political, religious, social, and economic —seemed in clear view to clash in open battle. Thus, almost from the first week of the war, observers assumed that those European governments motivated by militant ideologies were going to be deeply involved, in theory if not in practice, in Spanish events. Automatically and with more than a little justification, Germany and Italy were assigned to the Nationalists, and Soviet Russia and possibly France were placed in the Republican camp. Neither the official newspapers, the partisan politicians, nor the official reactions seemed to deny this early division of Europe into two opposing camps.

In Paris for the first few days it was difficult to distinguish smoke from the fires inside Spain; but it was obvious, even then, that France might have to re-examine, for the first time in decades, her Spanish policy.[1] For the most part, in the years after World War I, Spain's position in French eyes had been that of a weak but satisfactory border state, whose internal difficulties and continuing governmental chaos had not affected Madrid's relation to French security. With the creation of the Spanish Republic in 1931 and the rapid rise to power and influence of ideological political parties, interest in Spain's internal conflicts had quickened but not to the extent of giving the Quai d'Orsay deep concern. The victory in the February, 1936, elections of the Spanish *Frente Popular*, an ill-matched assortment of moderate, radical, and revolutionary parties, had brought forth, momentarily at least, some concern from multifarious segments of French political opinion. Again, none of these reactions was particularly intense, since Spanish politics

[1] In France much of the unofficial response was immediate and extreme; it took the Quai d'Orsay and the cabinet somewhat longer to arrive at an official reaction. "When hostilities broke out on July 17th, everyone had already taken his definite stand. The Right, instantly, automatically, came out for Franco (twenty-four hours previously, practically no one had ever heard of him). The Left, naturally, came out for the legitimate Government." Pierre Lazareff, *Deadline* (New York, 1942), p. 132; cf. the early editorial position of *journaux d'opinion: L'Action Française* (royalist) or *L'Humanité* (Communist).

had for so long been of little but academic interest. Those parties attempting to form the new French *Front Populaire* were encouraged by their counterpart's victory, while their opponents regarded with ill-concealed horror the triumph of revolution across the border. In any case, the February elections and the ensuing civil disorder had seemed to foretell no particular reorientation of French policy. There seemed to be no reason to suppose that a moderate Republican Government, even when it was supported by the Communists and opposed by the Fascists, would disturb Spain's traditional neutrality. Thus the tribulations of the Spanish Republic during the first half of 1936 had been watched with only vague interest, while France turned its attention to more immediate and pressing problems.

During the first months of 1936, France had been torn by a bitter electoral campaign, which had finally culminated in April and May with a victory of the *Front Populaire,* composed of the Radical-Socialists, Socialists, and Communists. A new cabinet made up of Radical-Socialists and Socialists, pledged to a vast program of social reforms, was formed on June 4, 1936, by the Socialist Léon Blum. Within a few weeks, Blum's Government had succeeded in passing scores of bills enacting a multitude of long overdue measures. Each of these bills had been opposed by the Right with a ferocity born of desperation; nevertheless, the forty-hour week and vacations with pay were introduced, the Bank of France reformed, the armaments industry nationalized, a wheat board created, and labor received a host of benefits ranging from collective bargaining to an immediate increase in wages. For weeks France seemed to be in the midst of a new revolution, as one law after another transformed the nation despite the frantic opposition of the Right. By the end of June there had been 12,142 sit-down strikes as labor became progressively more aggressive; and in panic or retaliation capital began moving out of France. The franc fell on the international exchange. Fascist leagues were forcefully dissolved and immediately sprang up under other names to oppose

with violence and intimidation the program of the *Front
Populaire*. The French press, never known for moderation, divided into two warring camps, each accusing the other of
treason.[2] With the factories filled with strikers, the streets with
political demonstrations, and bitterness and suspicion rife, the
news of the Spanish crisis could not have come at a worse time
for disinterested reflection. The country was in no condition
to examine the situation across the border logically and ration-
ally in relation to France's best interests rather than to the particular interests of individual parties and prejudices.

Even during the relatively calm periods before the victory
of the *Front Populaire,* there had been no real unanimity on
the foreign policy of France. The alternatives suggested were
often conflicting and contradictory; the proper ambitions, the
future position of France in Europe, even the methods to
achieve the rarely agreed-upon common goals were all unsettled. Many of the proposed policies could be achieved only
by completely negating the dearest ambition of some other
group. There seemed no foundation of common interest on
which to build, no platform which could unite the nation, and
no possibility of compromising the impossible alternatives.[3]
The Left generally wanted closer ties with Soviet Russia and
also Great Britain, in order to form a united front of democratic
and socialist powers to balance the growth of Nazi Germany
and Fascist Italy. Many of the moderates agreed that ties with
Great Britain should be the foundation of any future position
of France, while an agreement with Russia might be necessary
but distasteful. Other nominal members of the moderates and
part of the Right gathered around Pierre-Étienne Flandin

[2] André Géraud, *The Gravediggers of France* (Garden City, 1944), pp. 367-
368; Shepard B. Clough, *France: A History of National Economics* (New York,
1939), pp. 302-303.

[3] Charles A. Micaud (*The French Right and Nazi Germany, 1933-1939* [Dur-
ham, 1943], pp. 20-21) suggests on the Left alone, excepting the Communists,
three main trends: the doctrinaire pacifism of the Socialists, the Jacobin patriotism within the Radical-Socialists, and a determination to enforce collective
security.

could accept no agreement with Communist Russia, and instead felt that the ideal position for France would be a return to the position of Stresa in April, 1935, when France, Italy, and Great Britain united momentarily in the face of German rearmament. Most of the Right considered the Franco-Soviet pact of May, 1935, to be an abomination, and insisted that a *rapprochement* was possible with Germany and essential with Italy. There were those, still further to the Right, who cried "Better Hitler than Stalin" or in some cases "than Blum," and whose voices, often supported by wealth and influence, were raised in a plea for reorientation of France in the face of German strength and conservatism and the Communist menace.[4] The splits were wide and deep, even excepting the avid partisans of Russia to be found in the Communist party, or the articulate reactionaries of the Right, monarchist, antidemocratic, pro-Fascist, who longed for a return of the ancien régime and an end to the decadent Republic. The large shifting center of French politics, seldom under strict party discipline, could not come to agreement on either common allies or common enemies. The center was cut through with deep currents of Anglophobia, pacificism, isolation, and opportunism. There was a general distaste for Soviet Russia, but it ranged from a bitter, unyielding hatred to a desire for a *mariage de convenance*. Even within the *Front Populaire,* there could be no immediate automatic response to the situation in Spain which would assure complete support of the three parties, much less the nation.

As the seriousness of the situation in Spain became clearer day by day, and as the politicians and newspapers quickly chose sides, it was apparent that France, with her geographical vulnerability and her interest in the western Mediterranean, would

[4] The far Right tended to be extraparliamentary and revolutionary, concerned with ideology more than economic conservatism as was the parliamentary Right. In the summer of 1936 perhaps the most influential groups were those gathered about Charles Maurras' royalist *L'Action Française;* although there were other groups either pro-Fascist, pro-Nazi, or *bonapartiste* who shared many of the same prejudices.

soon have to find a policy. The French Government, because of its own composition and because of French strategic requirements, could hardly remain uncommitted. European opinion fully expected that the new French Premier, supported by the same political and economic groups that supported the Spanish Republic, would do all in his power to aid the Madrid Government. Involvement, the sale of military supplies, even overt French military intervention were freely predicted. The *Front Populaire* made no secret of its partisanship and Yvon Delbos, the new Foreign Minister, on the floor of the Chamber of Deputies later made the Government's position even more explicit: "No one would contend the legitimacy of the Spanish Government (prolonged applause from the Left and extreme Left) . . . we have no reason to hide our sentiments . . . the friendship of Spain is necessary to our frontier and to France's position in North Africa and the Mediterranean."[5]

While the *Front Populaire* had a majority in the Chamber, it could not speak for France since the entire Right was violently and irrevocably opposed to sending any assistance to the Spanish Republic. The French conservatives believed that the Nationalists, even if tinged with fascism, were infinitely preferable to the Republic, tainted by communism and anarchism. The capitalists of France, many of whose interests were involved in Spain, were afraid of the results of a victory by the socialist Republic, which they saw only as a harbinger of disaster and revolution for France. The French Catholics, particularly the hierarchy of the Church, saw the Nationalists fighting a crusade in defense of order and civilization. Catholic Paul Claudel later wrote a eulogy of the Nationalists, and even Liberal Catholics hesitated to support the Republic, much less eulogize it. Only a small minority, such as intellectuals like Jacques Maritain, François Mauriac, and Georges Bernanos,

[5] *Annales de la Chambre des Députés*, Vol. 159, Part II, 1936, col. 2330. Excerpts from Delbos' speech of July 31, 1936.

publicly denied the legitimacy of the *parti de la Croisade*.[6] The extreme Right had found a common cause with most of France's conservatives and many of the moderates; and their newspapers and speeches pleaded the cause of Franco with a crescendo of logic, as well as venom and invective. With the Socialist Blum in control of the Government, the conservatives were now in dread not only of a French Socialist revolution, but also of a Socialist crusade into Spain. This, many were sure, would lead directly to a war with two great militant anti-Communist powers, Germany and Italy. Thus the arch-menace of Europe, Soviet Russia, could watch the bastions of order and decency destroy themselves. Then, too, the dread of a war fought with an expanding militaristic Germany was a deep and penetrating terror to much of France. A German war fought over the partisan issue of Spain could hope to unite the Right only in despair, desperation, and perhaps revolution. Most of the nationalist Right had become pacifist and seemed not to care whether the peace were maintained under German hegemony or not, just so long as war and particularly revolution were averted. Thus the civil war in Spain intensified the fears of the entire Right, and even many of the Radical-Socialists held back from the unqualified shipment of military supplies to Madrid. Only the Socialists and Communists could see no need for hesitation, and were instant and vociferous in their demands for immediate aid to the Spanish Republic.

Blum admitted that the national interests of France demanded a continuation of the Republic; but other things were not as clear to him as they were to members of his party, since the Premier felt he was responsible not only to the Communists and Socialists, but also to the entire country. Yet the Spanish conflict was of immense importance, for he realized that, to a large extent, his program of reform might depend

---

[6] Micaud, *The French Right*, p. 113; a liberal French Catholic's views may be found in Jacques Maritain's introduction to Alfred Mendizabal, *The Martyrdom of Spain* (New York, 1948), pp. 1-49.

upon a strong and successful foreign policy. Since one of the
axioms of French postwar diplomacy had long been the continuation of Franco-British co-operation, it was immediately
obvious that any overt intervention in Spain might strain relations with the British Conservative Government. Men of the
character of Stanley Baldwin, Anthony Eden, and Neville
Chamberlain were not going to be enthusiastic about a French
expedition to support a Spanish Socialist Government—however
much the *Front Populaire* pleaded and however much France's
historical precedents insisted. Blum suspected that he could
not count on strong support, or even perhaps acquiescence,
from France's strongest friend. With the rising criticism of
the Right dividing the nation, Blum was faced with the possibility of losing the friendship of Great Britain and at the same
time involving France in an Italo-German war with only the
doubtful support of a distant and uncertain Russian ally. Blum
was faced with impossible choices and no foreseeable compromise: "I am a socialist; if I do anything that risks bringing
France into war it will be said that I did it for no other reason
than to defend the Reds in Spain, and I fear that half France
would not follow me."[7] There seemed to be no way to answer
the siren song of Spain and yet miss the rocks of war unsup-
ported by a united French people or even strong allies. Yet
without a democratic Spain, France would be caught in a three-
way vise between Italy, Germany, and Spain, presented with the
all-too-clear threat of a second front. Well might Blum cry,
". . . mon âme est déchirée."[8]

The barrenness of Blum's alternatives was not as yet bleakly
apparent when early on the morning of July 21 the new Spanish
Premier, José Giral, telephoned a request to the French Government asking for permission to purchase arms and ammunition. At the same time two officers of the Spanish air force were

[7] Carlo Sforza, *Contemporary Italy* (New York, 1944), p. 355.

[8] Léon de Poncins, *Histoire secrète de la révolution* (Paris, 1938). This
ultrareactionary book contains (pp. 108-126) an apparently authentic letter from
Ferdinand de los Ríos to José Giral.

sent to Paris as purchasing agents. In addition to the normal rights of sovereign governments under international law to purchase arms, the Spanish Government, in December, 1935, had signed a commercial treaty with France containing a secret protocol agreeing to the sale of military supplies; so that Giral probably expected no more than technical and administrative difficulties in Paris. In fact, Blum immediately agreed to Giral's request and asked Pierre Cot, Minister for Air, and Édouard Daladier, Minister of National Defense, to work out the details.[9] Later on the same day a cabinet meeting was held in Paris, primarily to discuss the three-power conference to be held in London on July 23, to consider Germany's violations of the Locarno Pact. It was still too early, during this meeting on June 21, for the formation of an official policy regarding Spain, but Blum and most of the cabinet were already known to be sympathetic to the Republican cause. The newspapers of the Right certainly suspected this sympathy and feared a positive policy of intervention; instead they insisted that France observe a policy of strict neutrality. If there had ever been any doubt, the violent, uncompromising opposition of the Right to a Spanish adventure was quickly clear. Then, on July 22, Blum was warned, during a telephone conversation with the French ambassador in London, Charles Corbin, that both Eden and Baldwin were fearful of any French intervention in Spain. Corbin added, to Blum's surprise, that there was pro-Nationalist sentiment in the British cabinet. Certainly the early indications were that the French cabinet was going to have considerable difficulty in accepting the policy of strong support for the Spanish Republic which Blum and the Left favored.[10] On July 23 the French delegation of Blum, Delbos,

[9] Pierre Cot, *Le Procès de la République* (New York, 1944), II, 307.

[10] Straus to the Secretary of State, Paris, July 27, 1936 (tel.), *The Foreign-Relations of the United States* (hereinafter cited as *U.S. For. Rel.*), 1936, II, 447-449; Cordell Hull, *Memoirs of Cordell Hull* (New York, 1948), p. 476. Pierre Cot (*Le Procès de la République*, II, 308) mentions the pro-Franco sentiment in the British cabinet, but in a letter to the author, May 4, 1957, he states that he is unable to answer in regard to the presence of pro-Franco members of the

Alexis Leger, and René Massigli flew into London for the three-power conference with the British and Belgian delegations. Leger as Secretary-General of the French Foreign Office was the most important permanent official of the Quai d'Orsay, while Massigli was Assistant Director of Political and Commercial Affairs. During this period, and perhaps for the last time, the high officials of the Quai d'Orsay could greatly determine policy, mainly because of the respect which Blum and Delbos had for Leger. The latter's bête noire was a new Holy Alliance of Germany, Italy, Spain, and Great Britain; so that he was determined, within the limits of his authority, to hold the friendship of Great Britain at any cost. Blum and Delbos, particularly the latter, were willing to listen to his advice on continued co-operation with the British; and Leger, in turn, made every effort for the cordial acceptance of the leaders of the *Front Populaire* by the British Conservatives.[11] Between the meetings on July 23 the French delegation entertained the British at a luncheon at the French Embassy, where Blum and Delbos discussed the Spanish situation with Eden, who was determined to persuade the French of the inadvisability of either British or French intervention. Eden informed the French that the Conservative cabinet intended to pursue a policy of strict neutrality and nonentanglement. The talks were extremely cordial; but Blum, while sympathetic toward the British views on Spain, and enthusiastic over Eden's fondness for Proust, did not commit himself on France's future policy in

---

British Government during this period. It may well be that there was no official support of Franco within the British Government; although, there is no reason to assume that there was not considerable private anti-Republican sentiment, which Corbin might well have reported.

[11] An excellent study of Leger may be found in Gordon Craig and Felix Gilbert, *The Diplomats, 1919-1939* (Princeton, 1953), chap. xii (by Elizabeth R. Cameron), pp. 378-405. It was at this first meeting of Blum with the British in a corridor which led to the conference room at 10 Downing Street, that Leger held Blum in conversation beside a statue of Disraeli, also a Jew and clearly a statesman and gentleman. *Ibid.*, p. 391.

Spain.[12]   French pressure for neutrality began the next day when the delegation's airplane landed at Le Bourget; Camille Chautemps was waiting and began at once to speak of the dangers of intervening in Spain.[13]   Rumors of French aid to the Republic had already begun to circulate widely; so that on the same day Blum had been lunching with Eden the French Foreign Office had felt it advisable to deny officially that the French Government expected to export arms to Spain, or that export licenses had been granted to private companies to sell airplanes to the Spanish.   For the moment, this declaration was to be the official policy of France; but on July 24, Fernando de los Ríos, a leading Spanish intellectual and later ambassador in Washington, arrived from Geneva and London as a special delegate from Giral, to facilitate the shipment of the military supplies the Spanish had requested on July 21.   He arrived to find, not only the rather equivocal statement of July 23 by the Quai d'Orsay, but also that the campaign in the Parisian press against intervention was in full voice.[14]

At ten o'clock on the evening of July 24, de los Ríos met with Blum, Delbos, Cot, Daladier, and Vincent Auriol, Minister of Finance, at the home of the Premier.   For two hours the possibilities of supplying Spain with military equipment, as well as the strategic importance for France of the continuation of the Spanish Republic, were discussed.   There was no opposition to sending aid to Madrid, and only Delbos was reticent, insisting that French airplanes could not be flown into Spain with French pilots.   After de los Ríos left at midnight, discussion continued until a solution was found in the matter of French pilots.   Cot went directly from the meeting to see de los Ríos, waking him and discussing the details of the com-

[12] *Times* (London), July 22, 24, 1936; Alan Campbell-Johnson, *Eden* (New York, 1955), p. 138.

[13] Louis Lévy, *Vérités sur la France* (London, 1941), p. 114.

[14] *Temps*, July 24, 1936; Cot, *Le Procès de la République*, II, 307; Poncins, *Histoire secrète de la révolution*, p. 108 ff.

promise solution.[15]   Despite the opposition of the Right, the
reluctance of the moderates, and the disapproval of Great Britain, it appeared on the night of July 23 that French sale of
military supplies to Madrid was again only a question of technical details.

On the following morning, de los Ríos again saw Cot and
then visited the Potez airplane plant, but unknown to him, all
during the day, his difficulties increased. *L'Action Française*
and *L'Écho de Paris,* making use of the revelations of the recently resigned pro-Franco counsellor of the Spanish Embassy
in Paris, were almost hysterical in opposition to the planned
French intervention.   Blum met with Albert Lebrun, President
of the Republic, telling him of the cabinet's intentions in Spain.
Lebrun was horrified at the prospect of a revolution or a war,
which he felt might develop from any such intervention in
Spain, and he asked Blum to call a special cabinet meeting for
four o'clock that afternoon where the entire question could
be discussed.   During the day, aided by the Right newspapers,
rumors of the cabinet's intentions spread and the fear of a war
without British aid began to frighten many of the moderates,
including members of the *Front Populaire*.   The position of
the Conservative Government in London weighed heavily on
the minds of the Quai d'Orsay; and Delbos, never enthusiastic
about the Spanish venture, was more than willing to listen
to reason.   De los Ríos again met with Blum for over an hour
immediately before the cabinet meeting to urge him to hold
firm.   Although Blum knew of the pressures building up, both
within the Government and in the press, he remained convinced of the significance for Europe and for France of the
Spanish struggle: "I will remain in my position at all costs
and in spite of all risks."[16]

[15] Cot, *Le Procès de la République,* II, 308-309; Poncins, *Histoire secrète de
la révolution,* p. 108 ff.
[16] Poncins, *Histoire secrète de la révolution,* p. 108 ff.

Fifteen minutes later, when the cabinet meeting opened, Blum found that he was in no position to maintain his stand uncompromisingly, primarily because many of his ministers were at best reluctant to aid Madrid openly. While there was general agreement on the need for the continuation of the Spanish Republic in the interests of French security, there was wide divergence of views on the risks France would be taking in intervening. The dissenters, however, urged prudence rather than outright refusal of Giral's request; this was due to the caution and second thoughts of many of the moderates, both in the Chamber and in the *Front Populaire*. Both Lebrun and Édouard Herriot, President of the Chamber, were opposed to granting Giral's request, fearing German and Italian recognition of Franco and a consequent flood of arms to Nationalists. Champion of an official policy of nonintervention, Chautemps was wholeheartedly in favor of doing nothing provocative. He was supported by Delbos who feared the British reaction, as did the Quai d'Orsay. Jules Malvy, President of the Commission of Finances of the Chamber of Deputies and an extremely powerful figure, supported a policy of neutrality toward Franco, whom he presented as a general of the Left, a Freemason, and a secular adversary of the Spanish Church. His position was supported by Caillaux, President of the Commission on Finances of the Senate, Georges Bonnet, and a host of deputies who had little taste for a Socialist crusade to save Madrid. Only Auriol,[17] Cot, and Daladier backed Blum in favoring immediate full-scale aid to Madrid. Even the secret clause of the Franco-Spanish commercial treaty of December, 1935, calling for the sale to Spain of 20,000,000 francs worth of munitions could not sway the reluctant members of the Government. Although there was no suggestion of denouncing the treaty nor dispute on the strategic sig-

[17] Vincent Auriol, *Hier Demain* (Paris, 1945), I, 47-48. "J'avoue avoir aidé, dès le premier jour, d'une façon occulte, l'Espagne républicaine et amie de la France contre l'Allemagne et l'Italie installées sur notre frontière du Sud et aux portes de communications avec notre empire africain."

nificance of the Spanish Republic, many in the cabinet felt
the sale of arms would be viewed in Berlin and Rome as French
intervention.   Such an intervention would release a flood of
Italo-German aid, more deeply divide Europe into ideological
blocs, and vastly increase the risks of war.   Finally, after a
long discussion, a compromise was reached.   The cabinet voted
to collect and prepare a shipment of arms, which would take
eight or ten days; during this period Admiral Darlan would
be sent to London to explain the French strategic reasons for
aiding Madrid.   In the meantime, a debate would be held in
the Chamber of Deputies to test political opinion, after which
the cabinet would re-examine the Spanish question unless shipments from Germany or Italy should demand the speeding
up of French shipments to prevent a defeat of the Republic.
While the official communiqué issued after the meeting of
July 25 stated that "le Gouvernement français refusait d'ac-
corder à la demande de Madrid," Blum still had every hope for
persuading his cabinet to accept his views on aiding Madrid.[18]
As the next few days passed in an atmosphere of rising crisis,
voices on both sides were raised still higher demanding action
or neutrality.   The Right press suspected that under the official
refusal to aid the Spanish Republic there lurked an increasing
stream of "unofficial" aid tolerated by the Blum cabinet.[19]   Almost the entire Left, particularly the more vocal Communists,
insisted that Blum should immediately and in quantity aid his

[18] Cot, in his letter to the author, May 4, 1957, particularly stressed that during this period the influence of Caillaux and Malvy was extremely important as
was Delbos' fear of a break with Great Britain.   He also pointed out that one
of the most avid partisans of the Spanish Republic was Daladier: "Il était donc
résolu à faire son mieux pour aider les Républicains espagnols—toutefois, pas
plus que personne à ce moment là, il n'aurait été partisan d'envoyer l'armée
Française au secours du gouvernement espagnol."   Cf. Cot, Le procès de la
République, II, 310-311.

[19] Straus to the Secretary of State, Paris, July 27, 1936, U.S. For. Rel., 1936,
II, 447-449.   Much of the "information" used by the Right newspapers at this
time was supplied through pro-Franco leaks in the Spanish Embassy.   Straus
noted that the Spanish ambassador, who had just resigned, told him on July 27
of existing proofs of the Franco-Spanish negotiations.

fellow Socialists and democrats in Spain. On the international scene, there were ominous rumblings as world Communism organized to aid Madrid, and reports of Italo-German aid to the Nationalists increased in number if not in authenticity. More important rumors of British pressure on Blum and the *Front Populaire* cabinet began to appear in the press and then on the floor of the House of Commons during question time. On July 27 Eden made Britain's position clear, if any clarification had been necessary: "there was no question of intervention by his Majesty's Government."[20] Somewhat later, Sir George Clerk, British Ambassador to France, apparently intimated to Delbos that not only did the British have no intention of intervening in Spain, but that it was quite possible that Britain would be reluctant to aid France should it become involved in an international conflict brought about by the sale of war material to the Spanish Republic.[21] Although overt British pressure was negligible, British views on French intervention carried considerable weight. Leger, prime advocate of the most intimate ties with Great Britain as France's only chance for survival, now began urging an official policy of neutrality on Blum and Delbos, with the additional possibility of an international agreement on nonintervention to localize the Spanish struggle and prevent open action by Hitler or Mussolini.[22] Leger's proposal, however, arose from his own interpretation of French interests rather than from dictation from London, and most of

[20] *Parliamentary Debates, House of Commons,* 5th ser., CCCXV, col. 1071.

[21] Julio Alvarez del Vayo, *Freedom's Battle* (London, 1940), p. 68; Alexander Werth (*The Twilight of France, 1933-1940* [New York, 1942], p. 117) writes, "On September 16, 1936 this [Clerk's visit] was publicly stated by Zyromski, one of the [French] Socialists' leaders." The date of the declaration is uncertain. Cot, in a letter to the author, May 4, 1957, writes that he did not know of such a *démarche,* but only of Delbos' insistence on the British position and need for continuing close ties with Britain. It is quite possible that Clerk's presentation of the British views could have been construed as a threat, but unlikely that it was or else Cot would surely have heard of it during the series of cabinet meetings in July and August.

[22] Craig and Gilbert, *The Diplomats,* p. 392.

the French moderates had needed no suggestion from London to persuade them of the advisability of neutrality.

The real source of tension was not Franco-British relations or the activities of the Left and Right in Paris, but the rising fear of Italo-German intervention. On Wednesday, July 29, in Rome, the French ambassador, Count Louis Charles de Chambrun, called on the Foreign Minister, Count Galeazzo Ciano, to announce that "the French Government and French firms will not furnish war matériel" to the Spanish Republic. Ciano, far from expressing pleasure at French concern for Italian sensibilities in Spain, expressed considerable skepticism of French neutrality when under questioning Chambrun admitted that his declaration was not yet all inclusive. Ciano made it clear that he felt such a declaration would still allow "unofficial" aid to reach the Republic.[23] In France, despite the uncertainty of the cabinet, the opposition of the British, and the danger of Italo-German intervention, the Left called for the formation of volunteer brigades to fight the Nationalists, collected funds on behalf of the Madrid Government, and continued to demand that military supplies be sent to the Spanish Republic.

Then, on July 30, three Italian airplanes were forced to land in French Morocco. They were Italian army planes flown by Italian army pilots and obviously on their way to General Franco.[24] Rumor had become reality with a vengeance; now

[23] Conversation between Chambrun and Ciano, Rome, July 29, 1936. Count Galeazzo Ciano, L'Europa verso la catastrofe (Verona, 1948), pp. 44-45. This unofficial collection of conversations and documents is somewhat suspect, since there is more than a little reason to suppose that it has been subjectively edited at least once. The English translation, Ciano's Diplomatic Papers (London, 1948), is often untrustworthy.

[24] Cot (Le Procès de la République, II, 312-313) gives the results of the official investigation by General Denain, which noted that the Italian planes still had military log books. Mario Donosti (Mussolini e l'Europa: la politica estera fascista, [Rome, 1945], p. 54), who wrote from confidential information, recalls that the planes crashed because they were sent so hastily by Mussolini, who had been surprised by the rebellion and wanted to aid Franco before the latter won a quick victory.

that it was known that the Italian Government intended to intervene, the fears of the moderates that Spain would be the fuse for a general European conflict appeared to have been verified. Even the most pro-Republican members of the cabinet realized that the risks of war over Spain were growing. Blum, however, remained adamant in his hopes, but he could count on the support of only Auriol, Cot, and Daladier.[25] Rather than be put in a position by his reluctant cabinet of refusing Giral's request, Blum began to consider resigning, a policy favored by Auriol; but a representative of the Spanish Republic persuaded him that even if he had to accept nonintervention the Republic would prefer him to remain as Premier.[26] Thus on the evening of July 30, Blum took another, and this time, less tentative step than the cabinet's declaration of July 25, toward unilateral nonintervention when he and Delbos advocated a policy of nonintervention to the Foreign Affairs Committee of the Senate. On the following evening Delbos and Blum tentatively advocated nonintervention before the Cham-

[25] Cot, in a letter to the author, May 4, 1957, commented on the dangers of war during this period. "Je ne pense pas qu'il y ait eu en réel danger de guerre pendant cette période. Les Allemands n'étaient pas prêts. A ce moment là l'Armée française était, dans tous les domaines, très supérieure à l'Armée allemande et Hitler le savait. Mais Hitler et les Généraux allemands ont 'Bluffé' et ont magnifiquement utilisé la guerre civile espagnole comme banc d'essai pour leurs matériels de guerre et pour l'entraînment de leur personnel." If this was Cot's opinion in the summer of 1936, he was almost alone in his estimation of the risks of war. Cf. Blum (*L'histoire jugera* [Montreal, 1945], p. 174 [August 20, 1937]) who says: "Pour juger la politique qualifiée de non-intervention, et surtout pour la comprende, il faut se référer aux caractères généraux de la situation européenne tels que nous les avons definis: existence d'un danger de guerre générale . . . ," and again (p. 172 [August 19, 1937]): "La politique qualifiée de non-intervention . . . s'explique en fait par les deux constations que nous avons cherché à mettre en lumière: d'une parte, un État de l'Europe créant la danger de guerre générale . . . ."

[26] Lévy, *Vérités sur la France*, p. 115. Cot (*Le Procès de la République*, II, 334) mentions Blum's intention of resigning but places the decision after a cabinet meeting on August 8. It is almost impossible to date several of the significant events exactly because of the vagueness of the source. Darlan's report from London, Clerk's *démarche*, and the first suggestion of an international nonintervention agreement are all examples.

ber of Deputies, despite both their own and the Left's enthusiasm for the Spanish Republic.

On August 1 the French Government appealed to the British and Italian Governments to accept an arrangement for nonintervention in Spain; but at the same time Paris announced that it might consider changing the decision of July 25 not to supply the Republican Government in view of the large amount of supplies going to Franco. Thus Blum hoped to keep a wire open to Madrid; for if nonintervention proved impractical, which seemed possible, France's position would still be undefined. On the same day, General Denain's report on his investigation of the Italian planes, found in Morocco, arrived in Paris; it was now conclusive that they were military planes, withdrawn from formations of the Italian air force, and apparently the shipment had been decided upon as early as July 15. Instead of the situation having become clarified in the eight-to-ten-day breathing spell decided upon in the cabinet meeting on July 25, the Government's position had become even more complicated, the risks had increased, the bitterness of the opposition grown, and the disapproval of the British solidified. Except for a hard core on each side, the cabinet remained wavering and uncertain while simultaneously negotiations were carried on to effect a policy of nonintervention and to perfect the possibilities of aiding Madrid.[27]

On August 2 the cabinet met again to consider the implications of the events during the past few days. Lebrun had once again advised prudence in the face of the proved Italian and probable German intervention, but Blum still felt it was the Government's duty to aid the Republic. Delbos reiterated the British fears and stressed the Conservative cabinet's com-

[27] Cot, Le Procès de la République, II, 312. The conservative Times in London on August 2 complimented the declaration of August 1: "a fine tribute to its [the cabinet's] coolness and its clear vision." Despite the reservations in the announcement, the Times implied that France had accepted nonintervention, an interpretation which was accepted independently by many of the moderates, who began urging concrete steps on Blum in order to prevent a sudden reversal.

plete opposition to the French agreeing to Giral's appeal; furthermore, it was soon known in Paris that Admiral Darlan's mission of explanation had failed in the face of British distaste for and suspicion of the Government in Madrid. Delbos then advised sending out a proposal for the adoption of common rules of nonintervention to the interested European powers and at the same time France could declare conditional nonintervention contingent upon the attitude of the other Governments. In the face of the growing uneasiness of the Radical-Socialists and the dangers of war, and more particularly in respect of British views, Blum agreed at last.[28] It was clear that a policy of French neutrality would be received with delight by the Right and with relief by many members of the *Front Populaire,* who, like Joseph Paul-Boncour, found nonintervention a satisfactory solution to France's dilemma:

It was not a question of knowing whether we ought to support the legal Government against the insurgents or the insurgents against the legal Government—if we had accepted the legal right to intervene, then Italy and Germany might have installed their influence in Spain. . . . The initial position taken was certainly reasonable and conformed to the interest of peace and to the interest of Spain, whereas as long as the war was prolonged there would be foreign intervention and thus the war would continue.[29]

[28] Cot, *Le Procès de la République,* II, 341.

[29] Joseph Paul-Boncour, *Entre deux guerres: Souvenirs IIIᵉ République* (Paris, 1945-1946), III, 73-79. Despite the most willing tolerance it is almost impossible to follow the tortuous logic of most of the proponents of nonintervention, who sought rationalizations for a policy generally favored for reasons of fear or prejudice. Paul-Boncour is unusual in admitting that the French Government had the right to sell arms to Spain, and would have been pursuing a policy of commercial intercourse, not partisan military intervention. Usually the major and unquestionable premise of the defenders of nonintervention was the equating of the quite legal and quite usual sale of arms to another government with an unwarranted and dangerous interference in a foreign war. Werth (*The Twilight of France,* p. 117) in a brief sentence summarizes much of the topsy-turvy reasoning during this period. On July 30, Werth asked a member of the Chamber of Deputies "why the Spanish Government could not at least *buy* what it wanted in France. He raised his arms to heaven and whispered mysteriously: '*Vous comprenez, c'est très délicate,* DÉLICATE!'"

The final decision of the cabinet was to send the non-intervention appeal, coupled with an announcement that the French Government would not send any arms to Spain, even in fulfilment of contracts concluded before the outbreak of hostilities; but Blum had not given up every hope that some way might be found to aid Madrid, and again the announcement was not unequivocal in that the French cabinet, in view of the aid known to be reaching the rebels, reserved its final judgment for the enforcement of the nonintervention decrees. This decision was confirmed by a communiqué of the Quai d'Orsay on August 3; but in the meantime, taking advantage of the obvious legal loopholes, Daladier and Cot had been hurriedly sending supplies to the Republican Government, including about fifty airplanes.[30]   Many of the friends of the Spanish Republic, although not in as advantageous a position as Cot and Daladier, felt that the final step toward official nonintervention had not yet been taken.   Members of the Left, both in and out of the Chamber, urged Blum to stand firm.   Léon Jouhaux of the giant General Confederation of Labor denounced nonintervention and most of the Left press showed considerable reluctance to agree to the cabinet's policy.   On the other hand, the Right press campaign for neutrality continued and immediate steps were taken to have Delbos apply the policy of nonintervention by Henry Berenger, President of the Senate Foreign Affairs Commission, and Jean Mistler, President of the Chamber Foreign Affairs Commission.   Both Corbin and Clerk continued to express the anxiety of the British, so the pressure on Blum to accept outright unilateral nonintervention increased.[31]

[30] Throughout his tenure in office, although scrupulously observing the "formal" restrictions, Cot continued to supply the Spanish to the best of his ability. Delbos in jest, but with more than a grain of truth, once called Cot a smuggler, the Air Minister replied that instead he was a *"juriste."* Cot, *Le procès de la République,* II, 332-333.

[31] *Ibid.,* pp. 343-344; cf. the editorial opinion in *L'Écho de Paris, Le Temps, Le Populaire* (Socialist), and *L'Humanité,* August 2-8, 1936.

While the situation remained fluid in Paris, British and French telephone conversations began on August 3, as the diplomats began to work more closely to achieve what the British hoped would be the common goal of an international nonintervention agreement. The British obviously welcomed the French initiative and had previously suggested the possibility of including both Germany and the Soviet Union as well as Italy in any such agreement.[32] Now that France had formally proposed the international agreement, which the British had so far refrained from publicly championing, London could turn its full attention to securing acceptance of the French plan. The tentative approach made to Italy on August 1 by the French had received only a noncommital reply; and on August 3, when Chambrun approached Ciano, he found him still unwilling to comment on the prospects of Italy accepting nonintervention, despite the immediate announcement by Great Britain on the same day accepting it in principle.[33] In Berlin on the following day, André François-Poncet, the French ambassador, was more successful. The German Foreign Minister, Constantin von Neurath, insisted that there was no need for Germany to sign a nonintervention declaration since his Government had neither sent nor intended to send aid to the Nationalists; furthermore, Neurath was not hesitant about accusing the French of aiding the Republic while Germany remained neutral. He was, however, willing to participate in further discussions and suggested that Germany might be willing to sign such a declaration if the other European powers including the Soviet Union did likewise.[34]

---

[32] *Times* (New York), August 1, 1936, reported that on July 31 the British Government had not been favorable to a three-power meeting as not "competent" to deal with the question since both Germany and Russia could still aid either side.

[33] Conversation between Chambrun and Ciano, Rome, August 3, 1936, in Ciano, *L'Europa verso la castastrofe*, p. 50.

[34] Memorandum by Neurath, Berlin, August 4, 1936, *Documents on German Foreign Policy, 1918-1945* (hereinafter cited as *Ger. Docs*), ser. D, Vol. III, "Germany and the Spanish Civil War, 1936-1939," pp. 29-30.

Whatever Neurath might have denied to François-Poncet, the German military supplies going to the Nationalists became an open scandal. The continued revelations of the press concerning such intervention greatly contributed to the French moderates feeling an increasing need for an effective nonintervention policy during the hectic week after the August 2 cabinet meeting. The reverse was true of the Left, which urged French intervention before the Republic was crushed. Where once the Right had found itself in a position of desperation, it was now the Left that grew desperate as the British and French diplomats, oblivious of the fate of the Spanish Republic, continued to pursue their negotiations to secure nonintervention. By August 7, despite constant pressure, Germany and Italy had still given no indication that they intended to accept the Anglo-French policy.[35]

On August 8 the cabinet met to hear the pleas of the partisans for jettisoning the nebulous nonintervention proposals before it was too late. The cabinet was again divided into three groups: a small minority who strongly favored unilateral nonintervention, a somewhat larger minority who favored immediate aid to the Republic, and the majority who listened to the Radical-Socialists pleading the dangers of war, and Delbos pleading the British views. Although Chautemps attempted to urge nonintervention as a policy which would win friends for the cabinet in the Senate, Blum insisted that the policy must be accepted on its merits and in consideration of the arguments before the cabinet rather than considerations of internal policy. Although Blum still favored intervention, he was again willing to accept the view of the majority that France accept nonintervention with the privilege of reconsideration. With French

[35] Belgium had accepted nonintervention and the United States had announced, in essence, a similar policy, but neither the British nor French had been able to persuade Ciano or Neurath. Cf. conversation between Chambrun and Ciano, Rome, August 5, 1936, in Ciano, *L'Europa verso la catastrofe,* pp. 51-53; and *le Temps,* August 6, 1936, for Delbos' interview with the Italian ambassador Vittorio Cerruti.

and British diplomats busy urging nonintervention and France already committed in all but the formal announcement to the policy, efforts to persuade the cabinet were almost foredoomed to failure.[36]

Although the decision of the cabinet was technically a conditional one, in reality the first steps toward unilateral nonintervention had already been taken. French diplomats for over a week had been attempting to negotiate an international agreement. Despite the Anglo-French efforts, the Germans were reluctant to be committed and in turn proposed extending the agreement to include Switzerland and the United States, governments traditionally opposed to international agreements.[37] In London the German embassy did give definite assurances to the Foreign Office that "Germany was not assisting the rebel generals, that she had not sent them any war material, and that she did not intend to do so."[38] By August 12 the situation in Paris brightened even further when Ciano announced that Italy, with some reservations, accepted the principle of nonintervention. Moscow had replied favorably and the Portuguese Foreign Minister, Armaando Moneirro, declared that Portugal had maintained a strict nonintervention policy and would continue to do so.[39] Despite the lack of any firm commitments in Berlin and Rome, the British and French on August 15 exchanged a note proclaiming an embargo on all

[36] Cot, *Le Procès de la République*, II, 316-319. Despite Cot's contention that it was not until after the meeting on August 8 that the cabinet accepted nonintervention, all the other evidence seems to indicate that the meeting on August 8 simply made explicit the implied policy of neutrality first announced by the Quai d'Orsay's press communiqué on July 24, and publicly announced after the July 25 cabinet meeting. Even before the cabinet meeting on August 2, nonintervention was generally accepted as the cabinet's intention. The turning point in the maneuvers to accept one of the two simultaneous policies the cabinet was following was the period between the landing of the Italian airplanes on July 30 and the cabinet's approval on August 2 of the first steps toward an international agreement taken on the previous day.

[37] Memorandum by Neurath, Berlin, August 8, 1936, *Ger. Docs.*, ser. D, III, 34-35.

[38] Alvarez del Vayo, *Freedom's Battle*, p. 45.

[39] *Temps*, August 10-13, 1936.

exports of war materiel to either party, effective as soon as Germany, Italy, Portugal and the Soviet Union agreed.[40] This was simply a unilateral declaration of the status quo, which when answered by the other powers would automatically effect a nonintervention embargo.

After staking everything on a nonintervention agreement, the French cabinet's position grew more desperate each day the Germans and Italians delayed; furthermore, the procrastination in Berlin and Rome seemed to increase daily the risks of war, which the Anglo-French policy had been intended to avoid. That the moderates in the French cabinet, including Blum and Delbos, were having difficulties defending their policy was not lost on the German Foreign Ministry nor was the fact that it was becoming increasingly obvious on whose doorstep the blame would rest if nonintervention failed.[41] On August 21 Italy agreed to the Anglo-French proposal with only minor reservations and on August 24, partly to cover an extension of the army service with a cloud of good intentions, Germany too accepted nonintervention:

I [Neurath] have convinced the Fuehrer that we cannot wait any longer to join the neutrality declaration, if we do not wish to be suspected of sabotaging the whole matter. . . . I considered it necessary to inform the French Ambassador today, since tomorrow the Fuehrer will announce the introduction of the two year service. It seems to me that it would be well for us at least to make known our desire to cooperate on the neutrality question before this announcement, which naturally will again occasion unfriendly comments in France and probably in England.[42]

Although there was, indeed, some suspicion of Germany's immediate motives in the timing of the acceptance, the general

[40] These notes as well as many of the documents concerning the various nonintervention agreements may be found in the appendices of Norman J. Padelford, *International Law and the Spanish Civil War* (New York, 1939), pp. 205-661. It should be mentioned that a single nonintervention agreement never existed except as a collection of individual notes, declarations, and laws.

[41] Welczeck to the Foreign Ministry, Paris, August 21, 1936 (tel.), *Ger. Docs.*, ser. D, III, 49.

[42] Neurath to Dieckhoff, Berlin, August 24, 1936, *ibid.*, ser. D, III, 56-57.

feeling was one of relief and delight in what the London *Daily Herald* called "Mr. Blum's triumph."

The two weeks after August 8 had been a difficult time for Blum, since despite his commitment of France to nonintervention he could not achieve a European agreement. With each passing day the Communists and many of the Socialists grew more restive. Yet at the same time, an attempt to reverse France's policy of neutrality grew more dangerous. Once again Blum seemed to be fated to be ground between the millstones of impossible alternatives; but Italo-German acceptance had come in time to end the delicate situation. Yet on August 26 Blum had in hand only paper guarantees, individual decrees of nonintervention rather than an international treaty, and no foreseeable means of enforcement. Nonintervention both in Europe and France rested on an uneasy foundation, so that the French suggested an international committee to meet in London to supervise the nonintervention agreements. The proposal met with a surprisingly favorable reception and the era of delays seemed to be over as various governments began replying almost immediately. On August 28, Italy declared a willingness to join, to the surprise of the Germans, who were once again left as the last holdout:

The reply of the Italian Government to the last French *note verbale* . . . was made sooner than was to be expected. . . . I believe that even the French Embassy was surprised by the reply. . . . That the Italian Government has attempted, by the way its reply has been formulated, to reserve far-reaching freedom of action for all contingencies is just as obvious as that it does not intend to abide by the declaration anyway.[43]

The Germans did not, however, accept the invitation to join the committee until September 4, when the British Government guaranteed to their satisfaction that "the work of the

[43] Plessen to the Foreign Ministry, Rome, August 28, 1936, *Ger. Docs.*, ser. D, III, 60.

Committee would not expand in an undesirable manner."[44]
Only the Portuguese declined to participate, but it was agreed
that, temporarily at least, the Committee would meet in London without them. Even without Portugal, Blum's policy of
nonintervention had become a European one when twenty-five
members of the Non-Intervention Committee met at last on
September 9, 1936, in the Locarno Room of the British Foreign Office.

Despite his triumph in London, the French Left was bitterly
resentful of the cabinet's refusal to aid the Spanish Republic;
furthermore, rumors of Italo-German aid were increasing rather
than diminishing, which further compromised the unpalatable
policy in the eyes of the Left. Crowds at Blum's Luna Park
speech in September were openly hostile and softened only
when the Premier asked, "Do you not think that we have after
all saved Europe from a war at a particularly critical moment?"[45] It was soon clear that if France had saved Europe
from war it had done so at the expense of the Spanish Republic;
for the extended hypocrisy of the Non-Intervention Committee
began when the patent evidence of German and Italian intervention was ignored. There followed thirty months of evasions,
denials, sterile discussion and contrived solutions and the too-

[44] Memorandum by Gaus, Berlin, September 4, 1936, *ibid.*, ser. D, III, 72-73.
In an interview on May 6, 1957, Speaker's House, House of Commons, London,
with W. S. Morrison, the Committee's first chairman, this British "agreement"
was mentioned. Morrison did not recall that the British had promised anything;
more likely it was a case of the British believing that the Committee would not
expand in an undesirable manner because Germany would respect its previous
commitments, while the Germans chose to assume that the British meant that
the Committee would not expand in any event. The first report of the Committee meeting, sent by Prince von Bismarck, German chargé d'affaires, must
have heightened the German impression of British hypocrisy: "Today's meeting left the impression that with France and England . . . it is not so much a
question of taking actual steps immediately as of pacifying . . . the Leftist
parties in both countries. . . . during my conversation today with Vansittart
. . . I had the feeling that the British Government hoped to ease the domestic
political situation for the French Premier by the establishment of the Committee." Bismarck to the Foreign Ministry, London, Sept. 9, 1936, *ibid.*, ser. D,
III, 82-84.

[45] Werth, *The Twilight of France*, p. 119.

clear evidence of avarice, cupidity, and fear, as the activities of the Committee lost all relation to the situation in Europe and in Spain. Diplomacy seemed to be carried on in a vacuum, as foreign armies fought in Spain behind the uneasy façade of the Committee in London. There is now little doubt that the blockade of the Spanish Republic, which resulted from the supposedly impartial activities of the Non-Intervention Committee, prevented Madrid from purchasing the arms needed to survive, while allowing the Italians and Germans to send Franco whatever he needed to win his victory. The distant and uncertain assistance of Soviet Russia and Mexico could not contend with the aid supplied by the Axis, although it allowed the Republic to hold out until 1939.

Even if Blum had assumed that nonintervention was going to be effective and consequently a solution to his dilemma during the first week of August, by the first week of September it was becoming increasingly apparent that the Italians and Germans were accepting it only as a matter of form and with more than a little bad grace. Within another month there could not be the slightest doubt that Berlin and Rome were, with a maximum of effrontery, denying all in London, while the campaigns and equipment of the Nationalists made their hypocrisy public knowledge. Yet the French cabinet, still motivated by the same considerations and dominated by the increasing risks of a reversal of policy, made no serious effort to reconsider its decision. Blum had accepted nonintervention to quiet the fears of war and the dread of losing Britain as an ally; he had hoped to heal the deep conflicts within French society. In September and October, as in July, the fears had increased and the splits deepened. While during the early negotiations with the Spanish, Blum openly favored assisting the Republic, he was by September not only tamed by the moderates but soon became a defender of a policy he despaired of but pursued because he seemed to have no alternative. After August 8 Blum was committed to nonintervention against his inclinations and intentions. He knew, furthermore, that its success and the possible lessening of tensions between the two rapidly forming blocs in Europe was based on the assumption of good faith on the part of two governments in which he had no faith.[46]

If the policy of nonintervention was a grievous error, if it allowed Germany and Italy a free hand in assisting Franco to a victory over a Government friendly to France, if it weakened the position of France strategically, if it showed up fatal weaknesses to cynical eyes in Berlin and Rome, then not only Blum but the cabinet, the *Front Populaire,* and ultimately France must share in the responsibility. In restrospect, however necessary and proper the policy seemed in the summer of 1936, it is now clear that its results could hardly have been more damaging to French security and prestige. Occasionally a nation may accept a diplomatic defeat from necessity and out of desperation, but in July, 1936, with only a minimum of risk, the cabinet could have allowed the legal sale of arms to Madrid and insured a Republican victory. Nonintervention was, instead, accepted as a policy born of prejudice among the moderates, fear within all, and a misinterpretation of France's diplomatic and strategic assets. France was as necessary to British security as the French thought the British were to theirs. The danger of war, as Cot suggested and as we now know, was mostly bluff. Blum's hope of appeasing both the French Right and Germany and Italy proved pointless since the former was irrevocably alienated from the *Front Populaire* in any case and the latter Governments were insatiable. Thus despite considerable sympathy for Blum and admitting the severe, and at times desperate position of the *Front Populaire* cabinet, the

[46] Cot, in a letter to the author, May 4, 1957, suggests the following as one of the reasons for Blum's acceptance of nonintervention: ". . . désir de ne pas apparaître, aux yeux de l'Europe et du monde, comme des adversaires déterminés et résolus des gouvernements de Hitler et de Mussolini; le gouvernement français désirait pratiquer à l'égard de ces gouvernements une politique modérée et de conciliation."

French policy would appear to have been a grim and costly mistake—a mistake based on faulty interpretation, on narrow prejudices, on a failure of nerve.

Ultimately the forces, pressures, the intrigues and machinations were concentrated and weighted within Blum. During the weeks of crisis, it is true, much of his freedom of action was eroded; his refusal to present Lebrun with a *fait accompli*, his willingness to listen, to comment, to consider, all narrowed and hedged about his ability to act independently as Premier rather than as merely another member of the cabinet. Yet the decision not to help the Republic must remain Blum's—no majority vote of the cabinet, no reluctance within the *Front Populaire*, no inclination toward resignation nor consideration of the general will can take away the last and final responsibility from the decision of the Premier. Nonintervention became his policy; he defended it in the Chamber, before his party, and to France. Blum had become the nexus where met all the contradictory and conflicting forces of French politics, the creeds and faiths of a dozen segments of opinion, along with the immense pressures of money and power, the sweet reasonableness of French logic, and the whispers of history. The result was that Blum, in the eye of the hurricane found himself, his Government, and France unable to move in any direction without the risk of what seemed to him a catastrophe.

As indecision and uncertainty continued, eliminating the possibility of decisive action by the Premier or the cabinet, the policy of France became officially one of negation, of doing nothing and of advocating such a course to others. Yet Blum accepted this policy of nonintervention in the name of France when he felt in his heart that it was against France's best interest, against his Government's and his party's policies, and perhaps more than all else against his own convictions as a man of the Left. He had found himself unwilling to risk abstract historical France for the sake of what in the summer of 1936 he knew to be France's best interests. He was unable either to channel or ignore the mounting pressures on his Government; he was unwilling to force his convictions on a deeply divided nation, so that finally he did nothing. The forces and powers balanced out in Blum; and France, led by the men of the Left, wandered down the road to appeasement, following reluctant leaders who knew in their hearts their policy was dangerous, perhaps more so than the risks they had refused to take. The road to appeasement soon turned sharply downhill, the journey became swifter, the possibility of starting over harder, and the risks of doing so greater. With each day, delay and inaction became in themselves a policy, gaining momentum and driving the Government, almost unknowingly, further along what was to be a one-way road. In retrospect it is reasonably easy to see that Blum allowed the decision to be made for him, that he refused to take positive action, that he would not endanger his coalition nor take the ultimate risk—however much France's fate warranted such a risk. Whatever the scholars, politicians, and critics were to say in later years, Blum, at the very core of his nation, tugged and torn by the forces ripping France apart, truly felt himself unable to act. Perhaps a stronger man or a more reckless one would have taken the ultimate risk; but Blum's mind, honed on subtlety and distinction, long trained in the delicate art of compromise so necessary within the sectarian Socialist party, could not. All sides were clear to Blum, all the alternatives apparent, and from these there was no one policy to be found, no certain decision which would knit together the raveled ends of French policy. When Blum cried desperately "My soul is torn," he spoke not only for himself and his Government but for France.

GRAND ALLIANCE
OR DAISY CHAIN

British Opinion and Policy Toward Russia,
April—August, 1939

William R. Rock

Two weeks after Hitler's legions overran Bohemia and
Moravia and destroyed the last remnants of Czechoslovak independence (March 15, 1939), Prime Minister Neville Chamberlain announced in the House of Commons an unconditional
guarantee to support Poland against aggression. A fortnight
later, following the Italian invasion of Albania, the guarantee
was extended to include Romania and Greece. Those pledges
marked a veritable revolution in British foreign policy. As a
result, Britain found that, whereas a month before she had
stood pledged solely, in Europe, to the defense of France and
Belgium, her obligations now stretched to the Black Sea and
the Aegean.

The problem facing the British Government thereafter was
twofold: to preserve the peace by persuading Hitler that any
future use of force would be met by force; and, since Britain
and France did not possess sufficient force to act as a deterrent,
to create it by an association of powers strong enough and determined to resist. Support, both diplomatic and military, had
to come from the East, from the association of Soviet Russia

and Turkey with the peace bloc. An immediate exchange of proposals between Britain and Turkey led to the conclusion of a treaty of mutual assistance in mid-May. But the gaining of Russian support for the expanding peace front presented a more complicated problem.

Chamberlain professed to a "most profound distrust of Russia," both ideological and military. He suspected Russian motives, which seemed to "have little connection with our ideas of liberty and to be concerned only with getting every one else by the ears," and doubted her ability to maintain an effective military offensive. Moreover, she was hated and mistrusted by such states as Poland, Romania, and Finland.[1] Chamberlain's viewpoints were undoubtedly shared by a number of his Conservative colleagues.

British military opinion considered Poland to be a more valuable ally than Russia, so Soviet participation in a mutual aid pact seemed of doubtful military value. This estimate of Russia's military effectiveness stemmed from the belief that the purge of the Russian Army in 1937 had left it in a gravely weakened condition. Even as late as 1941, British Staff circles felt that the re-establishment of the Red Army as an effective fighting force would require years.[2]

Within the cabinet, however, Lord Halifax, the Foreign Secretary, was willing to go to some length to reach an agreement with the Soviet Union. He was supported by Sir Samuel Hoare, the Home Secretary, and Lord Chatfield, Minister for the Co-ordination of Defense, who suggested both the importance of Russia as a deterrent to Hitler, even though her military strength might be at a low ebb, and the danger of pushing the Soviet into the Axis if no approach were made to her.[3]

[1] Keith Feiling, *The Life of Neville Chamberlain* (London, 1947), p. 403.
[2] Lord Halifax, *Fullness of Days* (New York, 1957), p. 210; Viscount Templewood, *Nine Troubled Years* (London, 1954), pp. 342-345; Lord Strang, *Home and Abroad* (London, 1956), p. 167.
[3] Templewood, *Nine Troubled Years*, p. 352.

There was also a growing public demand in Britain for the inclusion of Russia in the peace bloc. In the debate on the British guarantee to Poland in the House of Commons, April 3, it was immediately evident that, while political leaders of all hues welcomed the new commitment, many regarded it as only a first step in organizing the forces of Europe against aggression.[4] The peril of Britain's new situation and the urgency of enlarging the Anglo-Polish combination to embrace Russia and other powers were emphasized by Arthur Greenwood, deputy leader of the Labor party, Sir Archibald Sinclair, leader of the Liberal party, Winston Churchill, David Lloyd George, Anthony Eden, M. P. Price, and Hugh Dalton.[5] Churchill's and Lloyd George's remarks were particularly impressive, Churchill declaring:

To stop here with a guarantee to Poland would be to halt in No-man's Land under fire of both trench lines and without the shelter of either. . . . Having begun to create a Grand Alliance against aggression, we cannot afford to fail. We shall be in mortal danger if we fail. . . . The policy now proclaimed must be carried to success—to lasting success— if war is to be averted, and if British safety is to be secured. . . . Russia is a ponderous counterpoise in the scale of world peace. We cannot measure the weight of support which may be forthcoming from Soviet Russia. . . . No one can say that there is not a solid identity of interest between the Western democracies and Russia, and we must do nothing to obstruct the

[4] Since early 1938 explicit discontent with Chamberlain's policy of appeasement and a demand for "collective security" had emanated from sections of Parliament and the press. Though at first that demand took the form of a vague Labor-Liberal call for a return to the policy of the League of Nations, it assumed more definite form on March 14, 1938, when, after the German occupation of Austria, Winston Churchill proposed to the House of Commons his "Grand Alliance." (See footnote 6.) Hitler's subjugation of Czechoslovakia raised to fever heat the agitation for a more vigorous British foreign policy to meet the Nazi menace. These statements are based on the author's doctoral thesis, "The British Policy of Appeasement and Its Critics, 1938-1939," Duke University, 1956.

[5] A Labor deputation had met with Chamberlain on the night of March 30 to emphasize the party's view of the tremendous importance of Russia and, if possible, to get "something about Russia" put in the declaration of the guarantee to Poland. Hugh Dalton, *The Fateful Years: Memoirs, 1931-1945* (London, 1957), p. 238. But nothing had come of this.

natural play of that identity of interest. . . . The worst folly . . .
would be to chill and drive away any natural cooperation which
Soviet Russia in her own deep interests feels it necessary to afford.[6]

Lloyd George pointed out the military implications of the
new situation:

You have the Polish Army. . . . Well led, they have always
fought valiantly. . . . But . . . no valour, no training can stand
against an overwhelming artillery supported by a tremendous air
bombardment. . . . If we are going in without the help of Russia
we are walking into a trap. It is the only country whose armies
can get there. . . . I ask the Government to take immediate steps
to secure the adhesion of Russia in a fraternity, an alliance, an
agreement, a pact, it does not matter what it is called so long as
it is an understanding to stand together against the aggressor. Apart
from that we have undertaken a frightful gamble. . . . If Russia
has not been brought into this matter because of certain feelings
the Poles have that they do not want the Russians there, it is for us
to declare the conditions, and unless the Poles are prepared to
accept the only conditions with which we can successfully help them,
the responsibility must be theirs.[7]

The demand for the inclusion of Russia in the peace bloc
was intensified in the Commons debate of April 13. Chamberlain, speaking with great forbearance toward Italy despite
her invasion of Albania, was interrupted by cries of "What
about Russia?" Momentarily deserting his prepared typescript,

---

[6] Great Britain, *Parliamentary Debates, House of Commons,* Fifth Ser. (hereinafter cited as *Parl. Debs., HC*), CCCXLV, 2500-2502. Churchill had explained
a year earlier what he meant by a "Grand Alliance" when he reasoned in the
House of Commons on March 14, 1938: "If a number of states were assembled
around Great Britain and France in a solemn treaty for mutual defense against
aggression; if they had their forces marshalled in what you may call a grand
alliance; if they had their staff arrangements concerted; if all this rested, as it
can honourably rest, upon the Covenant of the League of Nations, agreeable
with all the purposes and ideals of the League of Nations; if that were sustained,
as it would be, by the moral sense of the world; and if it were done in the
year 1938 . . . then I say that you might even now arrest this approaching
war. . . . Before we cast away this hope . . . let those who wish to reject it
ponder well and earnestly upon what will happen to us if, when all else
has been thrown to the wolves, we are left to face our fate alone." *Ibid.,*
CCCXXXIII, 100.

[7] *Ibid.,* CCCXLV, 2507-2510.

the Prime Minister assured the House that the absence of any reference to Russia in his speech did not mean that Britain was not "keeping in the closest touch with the representatives of that country." The Government's task was difficult. It had to consider not only what Britain wished, but what "other people are willing to do." "I ask the House to believe," he concluded, "that without any prejudice, without any preconceived ideological notions, we are endeavoring to the utmost of our ability so to marshal the forces that are still in favor of peace and which are willing to resist aggression that our efforts may be successful."

In the ensuing debate Sinclair, Wedgwood, and Dalton chided that Chamberlain would have neglected completely to mention the Soviet Union had the reference (in Dalton's words) not been "dragged out of him by interruptions from this side of the House, almost as a dentist would extract a tooth." Labor leader Clement Attlee pressed for an alliance with Russia as the indispensable basis for building up a new system of collective security. Churchill, Eden, Haden Guest, Vernon Bartlett, and B. Riley forcefully concurred. Sinclair made it clear that only Russian co-operation could translate into ships, airplanes, and troops the guarantees that Britain was "sprinkling around Europe," while Eden re-emphasized Churchill's point of April 3: "It would clearly be suicidal to stop half-way." Dalton acknowledged the problem created by Polish and Romanian fears of Russia and suggested solving it within the framework of an Anglo-Franco-Russian alliance. He asked Sir John Simon, Chancellor of the Exchequer, who was to conclude the debate, whether the Government had any objection in principle to a triple alliance, adding: "If not, why are they letting time slip by without making a proposal; or will they tell us that they have made the proposal and that it has been turned down by the Russians?" When Simon spoke, he neglected the question until Dalton interrupted him by asking it again, then replied: "Though I cannot say that that particular proposition has been made, the hon. Gentleman and the House may take it that the Government is raising no objection in principle to any such proposition."[8]

The same intense concern for an immediate extension of the peace front to all countries willing to co-operate, and to Russia in particular, found forceful expression in the British press. The Liberal *Manchester Guardian* (April 1) declared that the Government must lose no time in passing from its "interim policy" to the "final scheme," which meant that "Russia must be brought into the plan." Later that journal (April 15) asserted: "An arrangement with Russia, whatever its precise form, has become the keystone of the peace front." In complete agreement were the Labor *Daily Herald* (April 1) and the Liberal *News Chronicle* (April 1), two newspapers which, among others, conducted a veritable campaign toward that end. The *Daily Herald* (April 10) declared that without Russia no policy of mutual defense could be complete, while the *News Chronicle* (April 10) maintained that a "steel-strong" alliance with Russia was the only hope for peace. The independent *Glasgow Herald* (April 4), the Unionist Cardiff *Western Mail* (April 13), the Labor *Leeds Weekly Citizen* (April 7), and the Liberal *Liverpool Daily Post* (April 4) concurred, the latter journal expressing the view on April 12 that the smaller powers of Europe would not be likely to join the peace front until Russia was included. Both the independent *Financial News* (April 14) and the independent *Financial Times* (April 14) feared lest the Government was blind to the absolute necessity of Russian co-operation, without which, the pro-Labor *Reynolds News* (April 2) warned, the whole system of guarantees would be a "hopeless failure."

Similar views found expression in the periodical press. The exclusion of Russia was "so mad as to be almost incredible," asserted the independent *Time and Tide* (April 1), while the radical *New Statesman and Nation* (April 1) declared that

[8] *Ibid.*, CCCXLVI, 15-140.

without Russia "the Grand Alliance is indeed a desperately dangerous and improbable affair." For the independent *Economist* (April 8), Russia was the "cement" that would give the peace front strength; there was no more urgent and vital diplomatic task than reaching a firm understanding with the Soviet Union, it declared (April 15). "The key to the whole situation is Russia," stated the nonpartisan *Spectator* (April 14), and the independent *Statist* (April 15) agreed.

Many journals pressed for the widening of the peace front without specific, though sometimes with implied, reference to Russia. "The language of an armed anti-Nazi European alliance will alone win respect from the desperate disciples of brute force," the independent *Sunday Pictorial* (April 2) said. The agreement with Poland must be followed "with parallel agreements on a wider scale," declared the Conservative *Daily Telegraph* (April 10). Even the pro-Government *Times* (April 4) suggested that "no power is excluded" from the developing peace bloc, a sentiment apparently shared by the Liberal Bradford *Yorkshire Observer* (April 4), in whose view "there should be no mental reservations" in securing support for the anti-aggression front.

The Government could be under no misapprehension, the *Daily Telegraph* (April 10) and other newspapers pointed out, "as to the depth to which public opinion in this country has been stirred." This "stirring" was substantiated by a Gallup Poll in Britain during the month of April which resulted in 92 per cent of those canvassed declaring in favor of a British alliance with Russia.[9]

All of these factors, combined with the common-sense logic that without Russian co-operation there could be no effective implementation of the guarantees to Poland and Romania, pressed upon the Prime Minister in mid-April, when he and the cabinet decided to make an approach to Russia.

[9] *Herald Tribune* (New York), May 4, 1939.

The vacillating course and eventual result of the British negotiations with Russia in the summer of 1939 are generally known;[10] but the intense interest of the British public in the negotiations, the widespread demand for a swift and conclusive alliance with Russia, and the public impatience with the Government's delay in bringing the conversations to a successful conclusion have been neglected in the chronicling of these abortive events, overshadowed by the prejudices, miscalculations, and suspicions of the day-to-day diplomatic developments.

Britain made her first concrete approach to Russia on April 15,[11] when Sir William Seeds, the British ambassador in Moscow, proposed to the Soviet Foreign Minister, M. Litvinov, that if any neighbor of Russia should be attacked, "the assistance of the Soviet Government would be available, if desired, and would be afforded in such manner as would be found most

[10] A detailed account, chronicling events from the published *Documents on British Foreign Policy, 1919-1939* (3rd ser., V-VII) recently appeared in Arnold J. and Veronica Toynbee, eds., *The Eve of War,* 1939 ("Survey of International Affairs," 1939-1946, x; London, 1958). The published British documents bearing on the negotiations have been concisely summarized by A. J. P. Taylor in an essay, "The Alliance That Failed," in *Englishmen and Others* (London, 1956). The account given by Sir Lewis Namier in *Diplomatic Prelude, 1938-1939* (London, 1948) is precisely accurate, though based almost entirely on contemporary newspaper reports. Other accounts of varying degrees of detail and emphasis, generally accurate though written without benefit of the British documents, may be found in: W. P. and Zelda K. Coates, *A History of Anglo-Soviet Relations* (London, 1944); John W. Wheeler-Bennett, *Munich:Prologue to Tragedy* (London, 1948); David J. Dallin, *Soviet Russia's Foreign Policy, 1939-1942* (New Haven, 1942); and Max Beloff, *The Foreign Policy of Soviet Russia, 1929-1941* (London, 1949), Vol. II. The course of the negotiations has also received considerable attention in the following British memoirs: Templewood, *Nine Troubled Years;* Strang, *Home and Abroad;* and Winston S. Churchill, *The Gathering Storm* (Boston, 1948).

[11] A month earlier (March 17) Britain had sought an "expression of opinion" from Russia, and received a reply proposing a conference of the British, Soviet, French, Polish, Romanian, and Turkish Governments to discuss the possibilities of common action. This Britain declined as premature, and suggested a four-power declaration of consultation in the event of a threat to the independence of any European state. Though Russia, after some hesitation, agreed, Poland vetoed this proposal. There is where the matter rested until Britain resumed the initiative in mid-April. Cf. *Documents on British Foreign Policy, 1919-1939,* 3rd ser. (hereinafter cited as *B.D.*), IV, 360, 385, 392-393, 400-401, 453-454, 467.

convenient."[12] The Soviet reply of April 17 went far beyond the scope of the British request, demanding a full-scale alliance with Britain and France for mutual assistance against aggression, as well as coverage for all the border states between the Baltic and Black Seas and immediate military conversations.[13] Starkly realistic, the Russian reply placed Britain in a quandary as to whether, in her opposition to aggression, she was willing to become full partners in an alliance with Russia. The Government hesitated in consternation. Several weeks of discussion followed among the cabinet, the Foreign Office, and the various Governments concerned, as to the possibility of some compromise between the Russian and British proposals.[14]

The Government feared that a straight pact of mutual assistance would provoke Germany and divide opinion at home. It was not ready to undertake obligations to any of Russia's neighbors other than Poland, Romania, and Turkey; nor did it like the idea of Russian aid for Poland and Romania whether they wanted it or not.[15] Perhaps the sharpest thorn in Britain's side was the attitude of Poland, which found the Soviet proposals most objectionable. The Poles feared that their interests would be subordinated to those of Russia and that the Soviet Government would treat Poland as a mere pawn.[16] Romania shared this fear of Russia, and the Romanian Foreign Minister lent weight to the Polish argument during a visit to London in late April.[17] Thus time was consumed by the British Government in a desperate attempt to reconcile the following objectives: not to forego the chance of receiving help from Russia in case of war; not to jeopardize the common front by disregarding the susceptibilities of Poland and Romania; not to forfeit the sympathy of the world at large by

---

[12] Seeds to Halifax, Moscow, April 15, 1939, *B.D.*, V, 215.
[13] Seeds to Halifax, Moscow, April 18, 1939, *ibid.*, V, 228-229.
[14] Templewood, *Nine Troubled Years*, p. 354.
[15] Strang, *Home and Abroad*, p. 164.
[16] Kennard to Halifax, Warsaw, April 19, 1939, *B.D.*, V, 244.
[17] Visit of the Romanian Foreign Minister, April 23-26, 1939, *ibid.*, V, 312-313.

giving a handle to Germany's anti-Comintern propaganda; not
to jeopardize the cause of peace by provoking violent action
by Germany.[18]

While the Government tried to resolve this dilemma, the
press ventilated the issue. The independent *Financial News*
(April 29) felt it "incumbent upon the British Government
. . . to conclude a firm agreement with Russia." For the pro-
Labor *Reynolds News* (April 16), the new approach to Russia
must bring concrete results or the last four weeks of feverish
diplomatic activity would have yielded nothing. While
guarantees strewn all over Europe might make a "pleasant-
looking daisy chain," without Russian assistance they would
not form a barrier to Nazi aggression which any military expert
could trust. The independent *Sunday Pictorial* (April 16)
declared that Britain had not yet "grasped the shield of im-
pregnable defence"; the contacts with Russia were not sanctioned by the British people for "an idle tête-à-tête." In the
view of the *Manchester Guardian* (May 3), any coalition which
did not include Russia would not impress Germany, would not
satisfy British public opinion, and would give no reasonable
security for peace. The Government must make "every effort
to appreciate the Russian point of view" and to convince the
Russians of Britain's determination and sincerity. "A close understanding with Russia is imperative," said the Liberal *Liverpool Daily Post* (May 8), "and failure to reach one would have
a serious effect on public feeling in this country."

The negotiations were going at a "snail's pace" lamented
the *Daily Herald* (May 3). Of Russia's willingness to accept
full responsibilities in the peace front there could be absolutely
no doubt. Every section of public opinion desired a rapid conclusion of the negotiations, yet they dragged on. A direct meeting between Litvinov and Halifax was necessary. The *News
Chronicle* (May 1) fully agreed with the *Daily Herald* and
urged that both political and military staff talks be initiated

[18] Halifax to Kennard and Hoare, F.O., April 28, 1939, *ibid.*, V, 357.

with Russia at once. The independent *Glasgow Herald* (April 19) emphasized the necessity of a close understanding with the Soviet Union by warning that material aid could reach Poland and Romania only through Russia.

A few newspapers took a less vigorous point of view. The *Times* (May 4) was willing to agree to "reciprocal undertakings for common action" with Russia, but feared that "a hard and fast alliance might hamper other negotiations and approaches." The Unionist Cardiff *Western Mail* (May 2) assured its readers that the Government fully understood the importance of gaining Russian support; it must be given time to complete the negotiations.

During the first days of May, Chamberlain was questioned repeatedly in the House of Commons on the course of the negotiations with Russia. He usually gave vague, placid replies, as on May 2: "We are carrying on discussions of a perfectly friendly character. There must necessarily be a great many details which have to be considered, and there are other Governments to be considered. . . . There is no want of goodwill on the part of His Majesty's Government."[19] Such responses did nothing to alleviate the anxiety of those who questioned the sincerity of the Government in approaching Russia and who suspected it was only wasting precious time. Churchill in particular was concerned about the delay. He felt it must be "vividly impressed" upon the Polish Government that the accession of Russia to the peace bloc might be decisive in preventing war, and that the British people, who had recently sacrificed an honored, ingrained custom in accepting compulsory military service, had a right to call upon Poland not to place obstacles in the way of the common cause. The Baltic states should be brought into the peace front, and, above all, time should not be lost.[20]

[19] *Parl. Debs., HC,* CCCXLVI, 1698.
[20] Winston S. Churchill, *Step by Step, 1936-1939* (New York, 1939), pp. 318-319.

While Britain continued to ponder her reply to the Soviet, a major change occurred in the Russian Foreign Office. Molotov replaced Litvinov as Commissar for Foreign Affairs. The British press reacted to the change with surprising calm. The *Times* (May 4) felt it a "remarkable thing" that Litvinov had not gone sooner and considered it "imprudent to assume" that any change in Russian foreign policy would follow. The *Manchester Guardian* (May 4) commented that "one cannot altogether avoid the suspicion that if the British Government had been whole-hearted in its efforts we should by now have secured Russian aid against aggression and Mr. Litvinov would still be Commissar for Foreign Affairs." In an editorial entitled "Litvinov," the *News Chronicle* (May 4) suggested only that Britain's hesitation was in large part responsible for the delay in the negotiations. Lack of comment in the press makes it reasonable to suppose that there was little appreciation of the possibility that Molotov's appointment might herald a reorientation in Soviet foreign policy.[21]

The change in Moscow provoked a fresh crop of questions about Russia in the House of Commons on May 5. Chamberlain, apparently rattled, vented a peevish displeasure on the Opposition. To Attlee's charge that the delays were causing uncertainty, he retorted: "I do realize that uncertainty is being created by a number of people who are all the time suggesting that if there is any fault it must be the fault of the British Government." This "purely partisan attitude" is not "conducive to the interests of this country, but I cannot be held responsible for that." When W. Gallacher suggested that Chamberlain make "personal contact in order to get Stalin's own view," Chamberlain snapped back: "Perhaps the hon. Member would suggest with whom I should make personal contact, because personalities change rather rapidly."[22]

[21] Russia assured Britain that no change of policy was to be assumed from Litvinov's departure. Halifax to Seeds, F.O., May 6, 1939, *B.D.*, V, 453.
[22] *Parl. Debs., HC,* CCCXLVI, 2220-2222.

Chamberlain's Parliamentary behavior did not go unnoticed by the press. The Bradford *Yorkshire Observer* (May 9) in particular was annoyed, declaring that his curt dismissal of questions about the Russian negotiations "hardly does justice to the wide anxiety which exists in the nation over many branches of home and international policy." The Government could not be blamed for negotiating carefully with Russia, but "in this country of all others, public opinion has many free outlets, and the Prime Minister seems sometimes to be too abrupt in the Parliamentary expression of it."

The British Government eventually reached the conclusion that something on the lines of its original proposal to Russia was still the best solution. Despite French warning to the contrary,[23] the British reply handed to Russia on May 8 was merely a recast formula of the first proposal reiterating the British suggestion that, in view of the British guarantees to Poland and Romania, "the Soviet Government would undertake that in the event of Great Britain and France being involved in hostilities in fulfillment of these obligations the assistance of the Soviet Government would be immediately available, if desired, and would be afforded in such a manner and on such terms as might be agreed." Britain's major criticism of the Russian proposal was that, "though logically complete," it took too little account of practical difficulties and would require too long a time for its negotiation. Automatic Soviet assistance to Poland and Romania, as proposed by Russia, presented those Governments with "difficulties" and placed them in a position which they found "embarrassing." While

[23] The French, in effect, favored a pact of mutual assistance, and Bonnet had so informed the Russian ambassador in Paris. Phipps to Halifax, Paris, May 3, 1939. *B.D.*, V, 404-406. Convinced of the urgency of a triple alliance, the French generally took a middle ground between the British and Soviet positions, trying to reconcile the lack of precision in the English formulas with the manifest wish of Russia for minutely detailed provisions. Cf. Robert Coulondre, *De Staline à Hitler: souvenirs de deux ambassades, 1936-1939* (Paris, 1950), p. 265; Grigore Gafencu, *Last Days of Europe: A Diplomatic Journey in 1939* (New Haven, 1948), p. 148.

the hesitation of Poland and Romania to be closely associated
with Russia might be considered unjustified, it existed and
had to be taken into account. For that reason, the better plan
was to start from what was "immediately practicable" and to
build upon that basis.[24]

Before Russia replied, the British Government was able
to announce that it had successfully negotiated a pact of mutual
assistance with Turkey.[25] This announcement met with universal approval in the press, and some newspapers made it an
occasion for re-emphasizing the need for an agreement with
Russia. In an editorial entitled "The Whole Hog," the *Daily
Herald* (May 13) proclaimed: "Now Russia must be brought
in!" The independent *Glasgow Herald* (May 13) and the independent *Statist* (May 20) hoped that Turkey would prove to
be "a point of contact" for the Anglo-Russian negotiations.

Russia's reply to Britain on May 15 maintained the original
Soviet position and demanded "reciprocity": a pact of mutual
assistance, a guarantee of the "States of Central and Eastern
Europe threatened by aggression including Latvia, Estonia, and
Finland," and "the conclusion of a concrete agreement . . . as to
forms and extent of assistance."[26]

A complete impasse had therefore been reached, and the
British Government was faced with the choice of breaking off
the negotiations or extending its limited guarantees to a comprehensive alliance with Russia. Several factors, including
the constant pressure in Parliament and the press, influenced it
in the latter direction.[27]

The House of Commons, which had not debated foreign

[24] Halifax to Seeds, F.O., May 6, 1939; Seeds to Halifax, Moscow, May 9,
1939, *B.D.*, V, 448-450, 483-487.

[25] *Parl. Debs., HC,* CCXLVII, 593.

[26] Seeds to Halifax, Moscow, May 15, 1939, *B.D.*, V, 558-559.

[27] Other influential factors were the signing of the "Pact of Steel" in Berlin
on May 22 and the crisis which was developing around the German militariza-
tion of Danzig.

policy for a month while the Government pursued negotiations with Russia, aired the question of Anglo-Russian relations again on May 19. "We have procrastinated seriously and dangerously," declared Lloyd George on that occasion:

> I cannot imagine a government taking the risk which the present Government has taken . . . in failing to come to terms with Powers whose assistance to us will not only be useful but . . . essential. . . . Russia offered to come in months ago. For months we have been staring this powerful gift horse in the mouth. . . . What is the good of this political snobbery . . . ? The issues are too tremendous for that. . . . Why do we not make up our mind, and make it up without any loss of time, that we should come to the same terms with Russia as we do with France?[28]

Attlee felt that the line taken by the Soviet Government was the only "realist one." The vast majority of the British people, he believed, felt that the best hope of preventing further aggression was a firm union among Britain, France, and Russia. Yet week by week questions about those negotiations were answered by: "You must not interfere in these delicate negotiations while they are going on." What was the Government waiting for?

A completely different note was struck by Chamberlain. Lloyd George seemed to him "almost to go out of his way to find . . . evidence of the imminence of some frightful catastrophe." The pledges to Poland, Romania, and Greece were "first aid treatment." It still remained to get support for those assurances from any quarters able and willing to give it, but the Government was trying to avoid "what I call opposing blocs." It was endeavoring to build up a peace front against aggression, not an alliance between Britain and other countries, and "we should not be succeeding in that policy if, by ensuring the cooperation of one country, we rendered another country uneasy and unwilling to collaborate with us." Chamberlain felt "there is a sort of veil, a sort of wall, between the two

[28] *Parl. Debs., HC,* CCCXLVII, 1812-1815, 1820.

Governments [Britain and Russia] which it is extremely difficult
to penetrate."

When Sinclair, like Attlee, tried to elicit the Government's
objections to the Russian proposals, the Prime Minister reacted with obstinacy and embarrassment: "I am not going any
further than I have gone already. . . . I must walk warily. . . .
We are not concerned merely with the Russian Government.
We have other governments to consider. . . . I am not going
any further. . . . Refrain from pressing us unduly to disclose
the exact point where the difficulties arise."

Churchill cut through the Prime Minister's remarks with
a statement of hard facts: after many weeks of negotiation,
there was a complete deadlock. The differences had not been
stated, nor the objection to making an agreement "in the
broad and simple form proposed by the Russian Soviet Government." What was wrong with the Russian proposal of a
triple alliance? Churchill went on:

> I do not know whether I can commend it to my right hon.
> Friend by adopting a simile selected as a special compliment to
> him. It is like setting up an armoured umbrella, under which
> other countries would be invited to take shelter. . . . If you are
> ready to be an ally of Russia in time of war . . . why should you
> shrink from becoming the ally of Russia now, when you may by
> that very fact prevent the breaking out of war? I cannot under-
> stand all these refinements of diplomacy and delay. . . . You will
> not extend your responsibilities, or your burdens, by extending your
> guarantees to cover all those countries [Latvia, Estonia, and Fin-
> land]. . . . You are in it up to the neck already, and the question
> is how to make your system effective, and effective in time.[29]

It was Eden's firm conviction, too, that an understanding
with Russia would be "a definite gain to peace," and "the
sooner, the more complete, the more far-reaching that agreement, the better." If Britain were going to build a deterrent
to aggression, it would be folly not to build the most powerful
deterrent possible. How could a tripartite alliance based on

[29] *Ibid.*, CCCXLVII, 1843-1844.

complete reciprocity be thought to run counter to the peace front? "After all, France has already her own arrangements with Soviet Russia. No one thinks that they run counter to the peace front." There were difficulties in any course Britain might pursue. Having embarked on one, it was wise to pursue it with vigor and conviction.

When Sinclair eventually spoke, he tried to convey to the Government "the impression of blank astonishment and deep disappointment which is felt abroad by men of all parties, by all friends of peace and justice, at the attitude of His Majesty's Government towards Russia." The Government's pretexts for not accepting Russia's offer were "feeble and ridiculous." "What you require for keeping a door shut when somebody is trying to get through it," Sinclair continued, "is merely bulk and weight. That is why Russia would be so useful to the cause of peace at the present time." Without her, Britain could not preserve peace.[30]

In the press, agitation for the conclusion of a pact with Russia gained momentum. The *Daily Telegraph* (May 20), believing that "the Government would . . . be interpreting the general desire of the country . . . by coming to an arrangement with Russia with as little further delay as possible," asserted (May 22) that the future could not be risked for the sake of a formula. When Britain had already gone far beyond her traditional policy, "the nicely calculated less or more becomes otiose and irrelevant." To the Liberal *Liverpool Daily Post* (May 17), Russia's demand for reciprocity seemed a considerable commitment, but "small compared to the British guarantees to Poland and Rumania." Britain could not feel secure without a Russian agreement, it declared (May 25), and if that implied a defensive alliance, then a defensive alliance there must be. The *Daily Herald* (May 8) was very emphatic: "The country is determined to have a Russian alliance. The country must have its Russian alliance!" The Government, it

[30] *Ibid.*, CCXLVII, 1812-1886.

maintained (May 24), could continue "to refine formulas or elaborate compromises" only at the cost of betraying national interests. The independent *Glasgow Herald* (May 11) considered an alliance with Russia "the most obvious means of checkmating aggression" and doubted (May 20) whether the suspicions of Poland and Romania were so deep that they could not be convinced that to accept help from Russia was better than the prospect of having to withstand a German onslaught while Russia stood aloof. In the view of the Liberal Bradford *Yorkshire Observer* (May 20), "British diplomacy should be less belated and more decisive." A substantial system of security could not be built without Russia, it claimed (May 24), and "Conservative opinion has begun to accept that condition, despite Chamberlain's recent refusal to recognize how national opinion feels on the point."

The *Manchester Guardian* (May 20) felt it "absurd" to rebuff Russia because the Government did not want "an alliance." In the view of the independent *Observer* (May 21), the argument for an alliance with Russia led "irresistibly to a consummation which shall put the final seal on a convincing, businesslike, decisive 'encirclement for defence' against Germany." "What is Chamberlain up to now?" asked the independent *Sunday Pictorial* (May 14). Russia was ready to sign a three-power alliance, but Chamberlain feared such an alliance might "embarrass" him. "Is he still dreaming of turning our friends into enemies, and our enemies into friends? Let us have action this week!" The *News Chronicle* (May 24) affirmed that "public opinion has long been convinced that a firm military understanding with Russia is essential if the peace front is to be made really effective." Other newspapers, such as the Unionist Edinburgh *Weekly Scotsman* (May 20), simply found it "gratifying" that the negotiations were being pushed ahead.

Similar opinions found clear expression in the periodical press. The nonpartisan *Spectator* (May 19) and the *New States-*

man and Nation (May 20) considered an agreement with Russia "the prime condition of peace." If Chamberlain's hesitations were based on the idea that a Russian alliance would lend support to the Nazi legend of encirclement, the *Spectator* warned, "Britain might as well go into isolation, for a government that resolves to make no move that Dr. Goebbels is capable of distorting can manifestly make no move at all." To the independent *Economist* (May 20), it would be a "great pity" if insistence on a purely tactical point should cause Britain to lose her last chance of building a decisively strong Eastern front. The Government would have much more reason on its side "if it makes a minor concession to attain its major aim." The independent *Statist* (May 13) considered the failure of negotiations with Russia "unthinkable," and the independent *Time and Tide* (May 20) expressed a similar view in a caustic editorial aimed at Chamberlain and entitled, "He Cannot Say. . . ." As for the Prime Minister's apparent fear that an alliance with Russia would frighten off the smaller countries, *Time and Tide* declared, there is "a law in physics established by Newton which he appears to have overlooked: the greater body attracts the lesser."

A few journals were satisfied that the Government was acting wisely. The *Times* (May 9) reminded its readers that the negotiations were neither simple nor purely bilateral, so a speedy conclusion could not be expected. The Unionist Cardiff *Western Mail* (May 11) did likewise, although it later (May 25) expressed disappointment that no agreement had yet been reached. The Government's reluctance to form a hard-and-fast triple alliance pleased the Conservative *Daily Mail* (May 11): "it might involve us in areas far beyond Europe."

After Britain's receipt of the Russian reply of May 15, there followed more discussions with France, Romania, Poland, and now with the Baltic states as well. Halifax attended a meeting of the Council of the League of Nations in Geneva and returned to London convinced that any agreement that Britain

might make with Russia would have to be along Soviet lines.[31]
He secured support in the cabinet, and the Government decided "after many meetings and searchings of heart" (Sir Samuel Hoare records) to continue the negotiations on the Soviet
basis. To save face, however, the British decided to cloak the
whole project under the Covenant of the League of Nations.[32]

Accordingly, the new proposal dispatched on May 25 accepted the principle of mutual assistance and provided that the
contracting powers—acting in accordance with the principles
of the League—"would concert together as to the methods by
which such mutual support and assistance could, in the case of
need, be made most effective." But this support and assistance
was to be given "without prejudice to the rights and position of
other Powers."[33]

Molotov rejected this proposal. It was "cumbrous," "vague-
ly-worded," made effective co-operation dependent upon the
"interminable delays" of League procedure and was, therefore,
"no serious contribution." Typical of British reserve, it was
calculated to insure the "maximum of talk and the minimum
of results." Russia wanted effective guarantee of action, he
declared, not words and conversations.[34]

On June 2 Russia again proposed a pact of mutual assistance, insisting in effect on the deletion of all reference to the
League and the inclusion of direct guarantees to Belgium,
Greece, Turkey, Romania, Poland, Latvia, Estonia, and Finland. In addition, the Soviets now demanded that the political

[31] Alan Campbell Johnson records that Halifax received "abundant information that Germany was working with accustomed thoroughness for agreement
with Russia," and the Foreign Minister—if indeed he had condoned the cabinet's
refusal to consider the Soviet plea for a tripartite pact in the beginning—"certainly revised his opinions at Geneva." *Viscount Halifax: A Biography* (London, 1941), pp. 529-530. Halifax says nothing of this in his memoirs.

[32] Kennedy to the Secretary of State, London, May 24, 1939, *Foreign Relations
of the United States: Diplomatic Papers, 1939* (hereinafter cited as *U.S. For.
Rel.*), I, 259-260; Templewood, *Nine Troubled Years*, p. 354; Strang, *Home and
Abroad*, p. 167.

[33] Halifax to Seeds, F.O., May 25, 1939, *B.D.*, V, 679-680.

[34] Seeds to Halifax, Moscow, May 27, 28, 1939, *ibid.*, V, 701-702, 710-712.

pact become effective only after the conclusion of a military convention.[35]

The issue was clear. Russia would not join in the peace front unless Britain and France guaranteed the Baltic states, but the British Government was not inclined to force upon those states arrangements which they did not want.[36] British disappointment at Russia's reply was summarized in one terse statement in the *Times* (June 5): "The result is a completely new draft . . . or as it should be called, the Three-Power pact, eleventh edition, revised and enlarged, private circulation only."

Disheartened though the Government was,[37] it continued to seek a solution, impelled partly by the growing conviction of the Soviet's importance and partly by the persistent agitation in Parliament and the press. Chamberlain announced in the Commons on June 7 that a representative of the Foreign Office would go to Moscow to convey to Seeds full information as to the British attitude on all outstanding points.[38] The choice then fell upon William Strang, head of the Central European Division of the Foreign Office and a former Counsellor in the Moscow Embassy.

The British press generally approved the decision to send Strang to Moscow, although the prospects for his success engendered little enthusiasm. For example, the *Manchester Guardian* (June 8) and the *Daily Mail* (June 8) called it "a wise move"; the Liberal *Liverpool Daily Post* (June 13) passively hoped for his success; and the independent *Glasgow*

---

[35] Seeds to Halifax, Moscow, June 2, 1939, *ibid.*, V, 753-754.

[36] The Baltic states and Finland, apparently fearing Russian assistance as much as German aggression, had made it clear in London that they strongly opposed any proposal of automatic assistance. Cf. Foreign Office Memorandum, June 12, 1939, *ibid.*, VI, 35; Strang, *Home and Abroad*, p. 170.

[37] Chamberlain told Joseph Kennedy, the American ambassador in London, that he was "not at all sure he would not call the whole thing off." Kennedy to the Secretary of State, London, June 9, 1939, *U.S. For. Rel.*, I, 272.

[38] *Parl. Debs., HC*, CCCXLVIII, 400-401. The Government's first idea was to recall Seeds for consultation, but he was ill at the time and unable to travel.

Herald (June 8) declared that it would be a sign of Britain's "seriousness in this matter." The opinion was expressed in some quarters that a higher official should have been chosen to make the trip. The *New Statesman and Nation* (June 10) felt that Strang's appointment would strengthen the suspicion that more delays were intended; "it is so obvious . . . that one of the principal Cabinet Ministers ought to go." The independent *Economist* (June 10) opined: "That Lord Halifax himself or Sir Robert Vansittart has not been chosen to visit Moscow . . . may not be a pity according to whether the choice was directed by motives of prestige . . . or by a conviction that agreement is so close that Mr. Strang's help will be sufficient to obtain it." Even the *Daily Mail* (June 8) admitted, albeit derisively, that "to have sent a bigger man would no doubt have satisfied the dramatic instincts of the Russians." "Send Lord Halifax," demanded the *News Chronicle* (June 8).

Despite the generally calm reception of the Strang mission by the press, it had by no means lost interest in the Russian negotiations. The demand for their conclusion continued, although the comments of most newspapers came to be tempered more by calm anxiety than the earlier violent impatience. The Liberal Bradford *Yorkshire Observer* (June 1) and the independent *Glasgow Herald* (June 7) asserted that the Government must realize that what Russia asked was not unreasonable. The Labor *Leeds Weekly Citizen* (June 2) agreed: "Russia sees the European situation through clearer eyes than does our Prime Minister, and her remedy for the disease is sound and logical." If just a "fraction of the soothing qualities" which the Government had used on Germany were applied to Russia, the *Manchester Guardian* (June 10) maintained, "Britain would be much better off today." The conduct of the negotiations was "too reminiscent of the old diplomacy" for the independent *Financial News* (June 9). Seemingly representative of majority opinion was the considered view of the Liberal *Liverpool Daily Post* (June 1):

There has been far too much niggling on our part. We ought to have tried at the outset to understand the Russian standpoint and make prompter efforts to meet it. Instead we have hesitated so long that a situation has been created which may cause irritation in some quarters. It is deplorable that that should be the case, and it is to be hoped that steps will at once be taken to put an end to the difficulties over the pact with Russia, which is so necessary for resistance to aggression.

On June 15 Britain proposed a compromise, providing for immediate action by the contracting parties if one of them went to the assistance of another state which had consented to receive aid. There would be consultation only if one of them considered its security "menaced by a threat to the independence or neutrality of any other European power."[39] Russia immediately rejected this, replying that, since she had been asked to join in guaranteeing Poland, Romania, Greece, and Turkey, a British refusal to guarantee the Baltic states would put Russia in a "position of inequality, humiliating to the Soviet Union." Perhaps the only solution, therefore, was to return to a simple defensive pact covering only direct attack on one of the signatory powers.[40] This was unacceptable to the British, for it would be of no benefit in protecting Poland and the other states already guaranteed by Britain.[41]

The British tried again on June 22, suggesting that the alliance should operate in case of aggression "which, being directed against another European state, thereby constituted a menace to the security of one of these three countries" (the contracting parties). But when the Soviets asked who would decide whether the aggression constituted a menace to the security of one of the contracting parties, the British negotiators could only reply that "nothing was said in our draft on this point," and the proposal collapsed.[42]

[39] Foreign Office Memorandum, June 12, 1939, *B.D.*, VI, 39.
[40] Seeds to Halifax, Moscow, June 16, 1939, *ibid.*, VI, 85-86.
[41] Halifax to Seeds, F.O., June 19, 1939, *ibid.*, VI, 104-105.
[42] Seeds to Halifax, Moscow, June 22, 1939, *ibid.*, VI, 140-141.

Again the British were disheartened, and "several members
of the Government" doubted the wisdom of continuing the
negotiations.[43] But in the press and Parliament, agitation persisted. The *Manchester Guardian* (June 24) expressed the
almost universal feeling when it deplored the "interminable
delay" and chided both sides for acting like "two bankrupt
horse-brokers engaged in the sale of an unsound nag," instead
of two countries with common interests discussing the best way
to meet a common danger. Duff Cooper, a former cabinet
member, writing in the *Evening Standard,* was more pointed
in his reference to British hesitation:

When a man is attacked on a dark night by a couple of gang-
sters and there comes round the corner a powerful looking individual who seems inclined to render assistance, the man who is so
attacked will not pause to inquire whether his potential ally is a
Roman Catholic or a Plymouth Brother, nor even will he insist on
testing his muscles before accepting his help.[44]

In the Commons, Chamberlain was subjected to incisive
questioning almost daily,[45] frequently in none too genial terms.
"Does the Prime Minister not realize," Hugh Dalton asked on
June 12, "that these very long delays . . . are causing disquiet
in the country and . . . doubt as to whether His Majesty's Government really mean business in this matter at all? Are they
not spinning out time until they can wriggle back again to the
Munich policy?"[46] "In what year does the Prime Minister
expect Mr. Strang's visit to be concluded?" asked W. Leach on
June 21.[47] Other comments were as caustic. In addition, the
demand that a cabinet minister go to Moscow to negotiate

[43] Templewood, *Nine Troubled Years,* pp. 361-362.
[44] Quoted in Duff Cooper, *The Second World War* (New York, 1939), p. 294.
[45] Laborite Hugh Dalton took it upon himself to question Chamberlain
about the negotiations at least once, and sometimes twice, a week. This, Dalton
hoped, would help to quicken the British replies to Russia, since Chamberlain
would prefer to answer that "the ball was in the Russian's court and that he
was awaiting a reply from them." Dalton, *The Fateful Years,* p. 246.
[46] *Parl. Debs., HC,* CCCXLVIII, 881-882.
[47] *Ibid.,* CCXLVIII, 2204.

was expressed with increasing frequency. But Chamberlain refused to countenance such a mission, dismissing its suggestion with curt, piquant replies, even denying that the Russian Government had ever asked for the visit of a British minister, despite the fact that, on June 12, Maisky had invited Halifax to Moscow, though admittedly "when things were quieter."[48]

The "enormous interest" of the British public in the Moscow negotiations is attested by the German ambassador in London, Herbert von Dirksen. Optimistic announcements, he recorded, were greeted with loud cheers; Molotov's cold pronouncements with "disciplined disappointment." In his view, it was the "political public" which, by its "doggedness, fanaticism, almost hysteria," urged on the negotiations and "compelled the Government to make greater and greater concessions in order that the pact might be concluded as speedily as possible."[49]

Contemporary British writers agreed with Dirksen's view. "The friendship between His Majesty's Government and the Soviet Union has only ripened in the forcing house of a very warm public opinion," wrote Wedgwood Benn in the *Contemporary Review* (July, 1939),[50] while the divergence of opinion between the British people and the Government was suggested by M. Wolf in the *Nineteenth Century* (June, 1939):

> The British nation, with an almost unanimous voice, demands a Pact with Russia as an indispensable condition of the country's safety. . . . Public opinion . . . has swung decisively over to the view that only a marshalling of all the forces that are willing to oppose aggression in a solidly built peace front can save peace.

[48] Halifax to Seeds, F.O., June 12, 1939, *B.D.*, VI, 50-51. Halifax doubted whether his going to Moscow would serve any good purpose. He felt that since Molotov was obliged at every stage to consult his Government, the same would apply to any British representative. Johnson, *Halifax*, p. 531.

[49] Herbert von Dirksen, *Moscow, Tokyo, London: Twenty Years of German Foreign Policy* (Norman, Oklahoma, 1952), p. 221. Dirksen's Survey of His Ambassadorship to London, September, 1939. *Documents and Materials Relating to the Eve of the Second World War* (New York, 1948), II, 173-174.

[50] Wedgwood Benn, "The Prospect for European Peace," *Contemporary Review*, CLVI, 4.

In this the opinion of the public has far outdistanced that of the
Government.[51]

So it was that at the end of June, the British Government,
disposed to tell Russia "to go jump into the Baltic Sea or any
other sea they can find, except that they have been under constant pressure from all their friends who say that the failure of
a Russian pact would be psychologically bad for England" (so
Halifax told Joseph Kennedy)[52] continued the negotiations with
Russia.

Britain notified Russia on July 1 that she was willing to
agree that the alliance should operate in the event of aggression
against "another European state whose independence or neutrality the contracting country concerned felt obliged to defend
against such aggression." Molotov felt it necessary to give this
new British draft precision by adding a roll of the countries to
be defended. Britain agreed on the condition that Holland,
Luxembourg, and Switzerland be included, but Molotov refused, arguing that this introduced a "new element" which
Russia could not accept: these states did not recognize the
Soviet Union. Further, Molotov insisted that the agreement
provide for cases of "indirect aggression," which he defined as
"an internal *coup d'état* or the reversal of policy in the interests of the aggressor."[53] This was "completely unacceptable"
to the British, to whom aggression "is to be understood as covering action accepted by the State in question under threat of
force by another power and involving the abandonment by it
of its independence or neutrality."[54] Molotov rejected this
definition, offering a new one of his own: "Action accepted by
any of the above-mentioned States under threat of force by
another Power, or without any such threat, involving the use

[51] M. Wolf, "The European Situation," *Nineteenth Century*, CXXV, 646,
648.

[52] Kennedy to the Secretary of State, London, June 29, 1939, *U.S. For. Rel.*,
I, 276.

[53] Seeds to Halifax, Moscow, July 1, 4, 1939, *B.D.*, VI, 230-231, 249-250, 251.

[54] Halifax to Seeds, F.O., July 6, 1939, *ibid.*, VI, 277.

of territory and forces of the State in question for purposes of aggression . . . and consequently the loss of, by that State, its independence or violation of its neutrality." He further declared that the agreement would include Holland and Switzerland only "if, and when, Poland and Turkey conclude pacts of mutual assistance with the Soviet Union."[55]

Again the British objected, maintaining that such a formula would "undermine our whole moral position in Europe." On July 17, they resubmitted their formula of July 8; Molotov again rejected it. The British then proposed a new draft protocol omitting Holland and Switzerland and providing for consultation only "in the event of aggression by a European Power against a European State not named in the foregoing list." Without rejecting this proposal, Molotov raised a new point: his Government would also insist upon a military agreement, without which "the political part would have no existence."[56]

By this time the negotiations had begun to drag to such an extent that even some sections of the press began to lose heart. The *Manchester Guardian* declared on July 13: "It is coming to be realized here that Russian procrastination is methodical." The *Times* (July 19) observed that after twelve weeks the negotiations had become "a dispiriting theme, lacking now even the joy of the chase."

But the spirit of hope and urgency had by no means disappeared. The *Daily Herald* (July 6), the *Manchester Guardian* (July 6), and the Unionist Cardiff *Western Mail* (July 8) concurred in the view that Britain and Russia should sign the mutual assistance pact upon which they were in apparent agreement; then, with the development of greater trust and confidence, negotiations on "wider matters" could proceed from there. "No more delay!" demanded the independent *Sunday Pictorial* (July 9). "What about that pact?" asked the *News*

---

[55] Seeds to Halifax, Moscow, July 10, 1939, *ibid.*, VI, 310-311.

[56] Halifax to Seeds, F.O., July 12, 1939; Seeds to Halifax, Moscow, July 18, 1939, *ibid.*, VI, 333, 375-376.

Chronicle (July 29); it still must be pursued "boldly and reso-
lutely" until "signed, sealed, and delivered." "The sands are
running out," warned the Labor *Leeds Weekly Citizen* (July
28) in an editorial entitled "To Be, Or . . . ?" For the independent *Statist* (July 8), the adhesion of Russia was still the
primary need of the peace bloc; for the *National Review* (July),
Russia was as indispensable to Britain in 1939 as she had been
in 1914. A Russian alliance was essential to convince the
world that Britain was willing and able to resist further aggression, echoed the *New Statesman and Nation* (July 1) and the
independent *Economist* (July 8).

By mid-July a stir of considerable proportions had developed in Britain for the inclusion of Churchill in the cabinet.
Since he was among the foremost advocates of a binding alliance
with Russia, it is not unreasonable to suppose that this demand was in part an expression of the continuing desire for
the completion of the Russian negotiations. Many newspapers
reflected this surge of opinion. The *News Chronicle* (July 10)
said that the British public was "virtually unanimous" in desiring Churchill's presence in the cabinet, while the independent *Observer* (July 16) held that his exclusion was "repugnant
to the average man's notions of national common sense." The
Daily Telegraph (July 3), which had earlier found Churchill's
judgment on foreign policy wanting, now extolled his "un-
rivalled practical knowledge," his "vision, energy, and popular
appeal," and the *Manchester Guardian* (July 21) declared that
Chamberlain's acceptance of Churchill's services would be
"proof that he is determined to carry his policy to success."
Even the *Daily Mail* (July 5) felt that Churchill's "drive and
ability" would be "an asset to the country."[57] But Chamberlain
was utterly unwilling to entertain such a notion, and in his

---

[57] Besides the press campaign, posters were displayed in London demanding
"Churchill Must Come Back," and placards bearing similar slogans were carried
up and down before the House of Commons. Churchill declares that he was
surprised by this and had nothing to do with it, though he would have joined
the Government had he been invited. *The Gathering Storm*, p. 358.

stubborn refusal, Sir Samuel Hoare sees "a fault of his qualities." He resented outside pressure; therefore the more the
press clamored, the less likely Chamberlain was to listen. "Still
sure of himself and his program, he was opposed to changes that
might spoil his carefully laid plans."[58]

Throughout the month of July intensive questioning of the
Government on the Russian negotiations—including the advisability of sending a cabinet minister to Moscow—continued in
the House of Commons, the Prime Minister usually replying
with "I do not know"; "that does not depend on me"; or "I am
not in a position to say more." On July 12 Noel-Baker, in-
tensely annoyed by Chamberlain's evasive answers, asked
whether, in view of three and one-half months of fruitless
negotiation and Russia's early willingness to come to some
agreement, the Government would consider publishing all the
proposals which had been put forward on both sides "in order
that public opinion might assist towards a solution . . . upon
which the peace of the world probably depends." To this
earnest inquiry, the Prime Minister gave the irritatingly simple
reply: "No, Sir."[59]

The continued pressure on the Government to hasten the
conclusion of the Russian negotiations was acknowledged by
Strang in a July 20 letter to Sir Orme Sargent of the Foreign
Office. "We are being urged by our press and by our public
to conclude an agreement quickly," he wrote, "and the Russians
have good reason to assume that we shall not dare to face a
final breakdown of the negotiations." This made it certain
that if Britain wanted an agreement, "we shall have to pay
their price or something very near it." A treaty of mutual
assistance appeared to Strang as the best solution for "giving
satisfaction to our public" and for deterring a possible aggressor.
Looking backward, he suggested: "We should have perhaps
been wiser to pay the Soviet price . . . at an earlier stage, since

[58] Templewood, *Nine Troubled Years,* p. 387.
[59] *Parl. Debs., HC,* CCCXLVIII, 881-882.

we are not in a good position to bargain, and since, as the international situation deteriorates, the Soviet price is likely to
rise."[60]

Although the British preferred to settle the outstanding
political points before agreeing to military talks, Molotov rejected further political discussions without military conversations as "a needless waste of time." In a sudden reversal of
position, the Soviet Foreign Minister foresaw no "insuperable
difficulties," so the political questions could be settled during
the military conversations. Consequently, the British Government, which had already decided to agree to immediate military
talks if a breakdown in the political conversations seemed imminent, agreed on July 27 to undertake immediate military
conversations.[61]

After months of intense questioning in Parliament, Chamberlain was finally able to make a definite statement with regard
to the Russian negotiations on July 31, announcing that military talks would begin in Moscow "as soon as possible." In
the debate which followed, Sinclair urged that, as "urgent reassurance" about the negotiations, a man of "highest political
standing" should be sent to Moscow. Dalton condemned the
Government's "diplomatic dawdling" and "gross procrastination" and suggested that Halifax should go to Russia. In fact,
it would do no harm if Chamberlain himself were to exchange
views with Stalin.

Chamberlain maintained that the Government's willingness
to send a military mission to Russia before the conclusion of
the political conversations already constituted a move without
precedent in such negotiations. But this failed to satisfy Liberal P. L. Horabin, who observed in the Government "an in-
firmity of purpose," and asked it to ponder the words of Crom-
well used in that House: "I beseech you, by the bowels of
Christ, to believe that you may sometimes be a little wrong."

[60] Strang to Sargent, Moscow, July 20, 1939, *B.D.*, VI, 422-426.
[61] Seeds to Halifax, Moscow, July 24, 1939; Halifax to Seeds, F.O., July 21,
1939; Seeds to Halifax, Moscow, July 28, 1939, *ibid.*, VI, 456-460, 427-429, 521.

Eden regretted that the Government had not made up its mind two months earlier to send "the most authoritative mission to Moscow," including some official who could negotiate directly with Molotov. Why not send a political mission along with the military mission and attempt to finish the whole thing in one week? he asked. A direct approach was more likely to produce results than any other method, and since Germany appeared to be using the same technique in Danzig that she had employed in Czechoslovakia, the rapid conclusion of an agreement with Russia was all the more essential.

Haden Guest, Wedgwood, and W. Gallacher spoke to the same effect, the former urging "the addition to the military mission of a number of representatives of all parties in this House" with a view to gaining "a greater understanding of the peoples of the Soviet Union in order to bring the negotiations . . . to a successful conclusion." Wedgwood suggested sending part of the British Fleet to the Baltic as a sign of British determination and good will, while Gallacher flatly denied the genuineness of Chamberlain's desire for a pact with Russia since he had neither sent a cabinet minister to Moscow nor invited Molotov to London.[62]

While the press generally was pleased with Chamberlain's announcement of the military mission, the wearisome and abortive course of the political conversations had dulled some of the earlier enthusiasm. The *Manchester Guardian* (August 1) expressed what seemed to be the general feeling, hoping that the dispatch of the mission would soften whatever political difficulties remained. The British Government was not entirely to blame for the long delays, but any further delay on its part which could be avoided would be inexcusable.

There was surprisingly little comment in the press on the composition of the mission. Although it did not include any of the Chiefs of Staff,[63] no dissatisfaction was evident. The

[62] *Parl. Debs., HC,* CCCL, 1993-2100.
[63] It was deemed advisable for them to remain in Britain because of the

Liberal *Liverpool Daily Post* (August 1) did suggest, however, that a "prominent member of the Government" should accompany the mission "to make the occasion all the more impressive."

On August 2 the Russian negotiations were prominently mentioned in a heated debate in the House of Commons on the question of summer adjournment. "What guarantee have we," asked Greenwood, "that when our backs are turned the Government will not throw in their hands on this question of a triple alliance?" These negotiations are so important, Sinclair asserted, "that I do not think we ought to rise before they are completed." Tinker, Gallacher, and Sexton joined in expressing concern with the way the Government (as Sexton put it) "has dawdled and diddled along the road to a peace bloc with Russia." But the adjournment motion passed.[64]

The British and French military missions proceeded slowly to Moscow by sea,[65] arriving more than two weeks after the military conversations had been agreed upon. Their presence in Moscow implied no decisive concession, for the British mission was instructed: "Until such time as the political agreement is concluded, the Delegation should go very slowly with the conversations," and "until the political agreement is reached the Delegation must treat the Russians with reserve." Of the nineteen points of "general policy" included in the mission's instructions, eleven specified subjects which should not be discussed with the Russians or information which should not be given them.[66]

---

international situation. Templewood, *Nine Troubled Years*, p. 358. The mission was headed by Admiral Sir Reginald Plunkett Ernle-Erle-Drax, whose greatest distinction has been said to be that he had the longest name in the British Navy.

[64] *Parl. Debs., HC*, CCCL, 2427-2516.

[65] Many reasons have been put forward for going by sea, among them the idea that Russia was in no great hurry, the need of the two missions to compare notes before arriving in Moscow, and reluctance to fly officers on active duty across Germany by military airplanes in peacetime. Cf. Toynbee, *The Eve of War, 1939*, p. 480; Templewood, *Nine Troubled Years*, p. 358.

[66] Instructions to the British Military Mission to Moscow, August, 1939,

Once the talks began, however, the British delegation found it quite difficult to go slowly. It was immediately put in an awkward position when Admiral Drax, the leader, had to confess that he had no written credentials (he got them, eventually, on August 21) and was empowered only to negotiate, not to sign a military convention.[67] On August 14, the third day of the conversations, the Russians asked whether, in the event of German aggression, they could move Soviet troops across Poland and Romania. This was the decisive question. The British were unable to answer because according to their instructions the Soviet Government should pursue that matter directly with Warsaw and Bucharest. But Russia insisted upon a definite reply before proceeding further.[68] The talks were adjourned, never to be resumed except to reach agreement on indefinite adjournment.

Britain reluctantly, and France more eagerly, pressed in Warsaw for agreement to the passage of Soviet troops, but the Poles refused, suspicious of Russian intentions, fearful lest the Soviets were "attempting today to reach in a peaceful manner" what they had "attempted to obtain by force of arms in 1920."[69] No inquiry was made of Romania.

Meanwhile, no progress had been made in the political conversations. On August 17 Halifax submitted to Seeds four alternative proposals for dealing with indirect aggression.[70] But they were withheld pending the resumption of the military talks and consequently never reached Molotov.

Events had far outrun the course of the Anglo-Russian conversations. On August 23 the Russians signed a nonaggression

---

B.D., VI, 762-764. The American chargé in London reported that the British mission was told to make every effort to prolong its discussions until October 1. Johnson to the Secretary of State, London, Aug. 8, 1939, *U.S. For. Rel.*, I, 294.

[67] Minutes of the First Meeting of the Anglo-Franco-Soviet Military Delegations, Aug. 12, 1939, *B.D.*, VII, 563.

[68] Minutes of the Fourth Meeting of Anglo-Franco-Soviet Military Delegations, Aug. 14, 1939, *ibid.*, VII, 571-575.

[69] Kennard to Halifax, Warsaw, Aug. 20, 1939, *ibid.*, VII, 85-86.

[70] Halifax to Seeds, F.O., Aug. 17, 1939, *ibid.*, VII, 42-44.

pact with Germany, and although the British and French missions lingered in Moscow for several days, the die had most certainly been cast.

Whatever emotions the British experienced following the news of the Nazi-Soviet Pact, recrimination was not among them. Though staggered and perturbed by the contradictions of the past, only the needs of the future claimed attention. The Government issued a communiqué declaring that the Nazi-Soviet Pact would in no way effect its obligation to Poland,[71] and a determination to honor Britain's pledge found unanimous expression in the press and Parliament. As succinctly stated by the *Manchester Guardian* (August 23) and the *Daily Herald* (August 23), that pledge was not conditional upon Russian support; therefore it remained unaltered. In the House of Commons, reconvened in special session on August 24, the same feeling was at once evident. Although a few speakers seized the opportunity to blast Chamberlain's policy toward Russia, most agreed that this was no time for recrimination. Speaking for Labor, Greenwood expressed keen disappointment that the peace front had not been strengthened by the addition of the Soviet Union, but he did not propose "to rake over the embers of the days that are behind us."[72] Russia had made her choice, and that was that. It remained only for Britain to make clear her resolve to stand firm without Russian support.

In reviewing the British negotiations with Russia in the summer of 1939, there can be little doubt that Britain "quibbled" too much during the early stages of the talks,[73] just as there can be no doubt that Russia, enabled to do so by the strength of her position, bargained unscrupulously in an effort to sell her support—or at least her neutrality—to the highest bidder. Nothing could have been less engaging than the way in

[71] *Times* (London), Aug. 23, 1939.

[72] *Parl. Debs., HC,* CCCLI, 13, 14-60.

[73] Strang admits in his memoirs that the Government was "unreasonably slow" in accepting the principle of a three-power alliance. *Home and Abroad,* p. 166.

which the Russians conducted the negotiations, snubbing and disparaging British efforts to meet their declared wishes, refusing to compromise, and raising new points and difficulties. But it was also a mistake on the part of the British Government to treat the Soviet Union like a suppliant and to begin the conversations with suggestions which were both ludicrous and humiliating; it was a further mistake to go on haggling about every concession, thus rendering Britain unconvincing; it was a third mistake to send a junior official to Moscow to buoy the sagging negotiations.[74]

What the British Government did not seem to realize was that Soviet mistrust of British policy—based in part on the rude rejection of Russia's March 18 proposal for a conference on the possibility of common action and the exclusion of Russia from all exchanges by which Britain sought to build the peace front for four weeks thereafter—was at least as profound as their own mistrust of Russia, and might lead the Russians, as it eventually did, to conclude a mutually advantageous pact with Hitler. Rumors of a pending Nazi-Soviet deal were constantly dismissed as improbable, and as late as the end of July, Britain foresaw "no danger of an imminent breakdown" in the conversations.[75]

Nor did the British Government seem acutely aware of the diplomatic pit into which it had thrown itself or the risk of annihilation which it had deliberately incurred by the guarantees to Poland and Romania—action which (in the words of Arnold Toynbee) "invited disaster" if not followed at once by

[74] Strang claims that his mission was only a "routine assignment" for a junior Foreign Office official, and that the Russians never showed resentment that he, rather than a major official, had come to Moscow. *Ibid.*, pp. 158-159. But it certainly did nothing to inspire Russian confidence in British sincerity.

[75] Halifax to Seeds, F.O., July 28, 1939, *B.D.*, VI, 525. The British had some knowledge (though not full details) of the Nazi-Soviet conversations. Cf. Strang, *Home and Abroad*, pp. 194-196; William L. Langer and S. Everett Gleason, *The Challenge to Isolation, 1937-1940* (New York, 1952), pp. 124-125; Ernst von Weizsacker, *Memoirs of Ernst von Weizsacker* (Chicago, 1951), pp. 189-190.

total mobilization of Britain's resources, a zealous effort to
build up an effective coalition of powers for containing Germany, and generous measures for equipping both Britain and
any countries willing to join her with the armaments necessary
for withstanding a German attack.[76]

The guarantee to Poland, Strang records, "was designed, no
doubt, among other things, to meet what was recognized to be
an imperative demand by public opinion that Poland should
not be allowed to go the same way as Czechoslovakia." "An
improvisation" drafted on the afternoon of March 30 by Chamberlain, Halifax, and Cadogan, it "seems to have sprung fully
grown from the Ministerial mind," with no canvassing of political and military advisers.   In the scurry of giving the guarantee, "the military aspect of the problem went by default."[77]
The same might also be said for the guarantee to Romania.
In effect, then, the British Government was not thinking in
terms of military power in making these commitments; it was
thinking in terms of a principle.   But principle alone could
not defend Poland and Romania, and although this fact was
vividly put to the Government from time to time, especially
by Lloyd George, it made no significant impression.   The British Government, in fact, apparently conceived alliance with
Russia as a diplomatic maneuver, not as a prelude to action.
Rating Poland and Romania more valuable military allies than
Russia, there would be no point in getting Soviet assistance if
Poland and Romania then broke away.[78]   Moreover, Chamberlain and some of his colleagues feared that an alliance with
Russia might infuriate Hitler and make war inevitable, a war
which might yet be averted by other means.

The Soviet nightmare was a German invasion of Russia, a
war in which she might have to fight alone and receive the Ger-

[76] Toynbee, *The Eve of War, 1939*, p. 38.

[77] Strang, *Home and Abroad*, pp. 161, 193.   Cf. Dalton, *The Fateful Years*,
p. 237; Templewood, *Nine Troubled Years*, pp. 347-348.   Strang doubts whether
the taking of time would have made any difference in this action.

[78] Strang declares that "this error in appreciation had a powerful effect on
policy." *Home and Abroad*, p. 167.

man attack on Russian soil instead of going out to meet it in the Baltic states, Poland, and Romania. But Chamberlain's policy was based on the tacit assumption that Britain had nothing to fear for herself, and that she still had the power to assert herself as the arbiter of Europe whenever she chose to do so. Britain, therefore, neither shared nor understood this Russian fear. She never dreamed that within a year she would be threatened with invasion. Hence Russia's demand for a direct alliance seemed irrelevant, and the Russian fear of attack through the Baltic states only an excuse for aggression.[79] Were the Russian fears unreasonable? Only those can answer who know whether Britain would have stood by Russia to the death without the experience of Dunkirk and the blitz.

Throughout the negotiations, Britain was faced with an inherent contradiction in her policy which she was unable to resolve. Her aim was to find a means of protecting the small countries of Europe against the threat of German invasion, yet the price of enlisting Russia's aid in this undertaking seemed to involve exposing those countries to a threat from Russia which they regarded as at least equally serious. Having sacrificed Czechoslovakia to Germany, Chamberlain and his colleagues apparently were determined not to consent to the coercion of any other small country by a great power, whether that power were Germany again or Russia. But it never seems to have occurred to them that an unwillingness to sacrifice small countries to Russia was not the same thing as an unwillingness even to displease them by making a defensive alliance with Russia. The lengthy discussions on "indirect aggression" showed the difficulties which British "principles" raised, and it is not surprising that Russia—especially in view of Chamberlain's statement in the Commons on March 15 to the effect that Czechoslovakia had perished as a result of "internal disruption"—sought for ulterior motives instead of accepting British scruples at face value.

[79] See Taylor, *Englishmen and Others*, p. 164.

It may well be asked why Chamberlain, who had been so
oblivious to violations of international morality in dealing
with Hitler and Mussolini, was so insistent upon "principle" in
dealing with Russia.   Why was the British Government so
concerned about the "feelings" of Poland and Romania and
so blind to the "feelings" of the Soviet Union?   Evidently it
never occurred to Chamberlain and his colleagues that the dis-
like and suspicion between Poland and Romania on the one
hand, and Russia on the other, might be reciprocal, and that,
by insuring the co-operation of Poland, they had made the
Soviet Union uneasy and reluctant to collaborate in the peace
front.   The guarantees to Poland and Romania had made it
very difficult for Britain to take the one step needed to make
them effective by associating Russia with their implementation.
But the full seriousness of this was not seen at the time.   When
confronted with the Soviet Union, Chamberlain's mind was
completely closed to sympathetic understanding like that with
which he viewed Poland, and this attitude lent color to the
charge of prejudice leveled against his Government from time
to time.

But the explanation probably goes even deeper than that.
It is difficult to escape the conclusion that Chamberlain did not
fully appreciate the danger of the German threat to Europe.
He could not believe that the rantings of *Mein Kampf* were
a manual of daily conduct from which Hitler would not deviate,
nor did he ever seem quite able to convince himself that de-
tached reasonableness might not have any influence with Hitler.
Why, then, should Britain tie herself up in an unnecessary
alliance with the highly suspicious Soviet Union?   This point
can be made in another way by asking how, if this were not
true, the Government's dilatoriness in pushing defense preparations and rearmament can be satisfactorily explained.

To have overridden the fears of Poland and Romania,
Halifax contends, would have been offensive to the bulk of
British opinion and would have seemed justifiable only for the

sake of some "large and secure advantage." But on the British estimate of Russian strength, "the advantage was neither large nor secure."[80] This is a highly debatable judgment of British opinion and an acknowledged misjudgment of Russian strength.

In looking back, Strang admits in his memoirs: "Cold reason suggests that we should have gone straight to the Russians and left the Poles to their fate if they would not come with us." But Chamberlain's Government, he feels, just could not have done this, and whether a "more imaginative and far-sighted government" could or would have done so, and what, then, would have happened in Europe, "no man can say."[81]

The question of whether there were any conditions on which Russia was prepared to conclude an agreement with Britain cannot be answered until some future generation sees the archives of the Kremlin, and perhaps not even then. But the evidence available casts doubt upon Halifax's declaration: "I gravely doubt whether anything that we or the French could have said or done in 1939 would have had the smallest effect in leading Russia to accept a position calculated to invite sharp and early reaction from the German side."[82] The word "anything" covers a vast area. Had the Russians been concerned merely with alarming Hitler and dragging out the negotiations, they should have caused the delays. But the rhythm of the exchange of proposals, graphically indicated by A. J. P. Taylor,[83] found the Russians replying at first within three days, five days, six days; thereafter usually on the same day. The British at first took three weeks, twelve days, thirteen days, and thereafter a week or more on each occasion. From this, the Russians appear to have been anxious to conclude an agreement, while the British were slowing things down. Moreover, the British decided on July 23 to agree to military talks,

[80] Halifax, *Fullness of Days*, pp. 209-210.
[81] Strang, *Home and Abroad*, p. 194.
[82] Halifax, *Fullness of Days*, p. 211.
[83] *Englishmen and Others*, pp. 163-164.

yet the mission did not reach Moscow until August 11, only to reveal that it had no credentials. Here again, it appears that the British, not the Russians, negotiated reluctantly, perhaps with one eye on Hitler—and all the more so in the light of Sir Samuel Hoare's later admission that in the spring and summer of 1939, Russian participation in a mutual aid pact with her neighbors seemed, in the Government's eyes, "politically and geographically impossible."[84]

If Chamberlain, however, ever had a serious notion of breaking off the talks with Russia—and he apparently had on several occasions—he was never given the opportunity, for the pressure on him from Parliament and press was relentless.

It seems probable that both sides wanted an agreement, but not the same agreement. Britain wanted a promise of Russian aid "if desired"; Russia wanted a precise alliance for mutual assistance. Each move by one side increased the suspicion of the other. It is likely that at the outset of the negotiations, Russia was prepared to conclude an agreement provided that Britain could convince her that she was prepared to resist Hitler at all costs, which to Russia meant sacrificing such inessentials as moral scruples over the feelings of the small countries lying between Russia and Germany. But she was equally prepared to pocket the immediate gains which a Nazi-Soviet pact might bring her.[85]

In the final analysis, the British were more determined to keep Russia out of Poland and the Baltic states than to secure her aid against Germany. They did neither, salvaging from the wreck only their reputation, to which, A. J. P. Taylor attests,[86] Englishmen attach great importance.

[84] Templewood, *Nine Troubled Years,* p. 345.

[85] Strang lends support to the belief that Russian policy had not been pre-determined, declaring: "We make a mistake if we suppose that Soviet policy is always exactly calculated, clearly defined, and unhesitatingly pursued. . . . The Soviet Government have much the same difficulty in determining their foreign policy as other governments do." *Home and Abroad,* p. 197.

[86] *Englishmen and Others,* p. 167.

The policy necessary to avert disaster, at least as Toynbee saw it nineteen years later,[87] was not put into action until sometime after Hitler's defeat, and then not by Britain but by the United States. Whether it would have deterred Hitler in 1939 must remain one of the "ifs" of history, but there can be little doubt that its application would have materially shortened the war and saved Europe and the world untold suffering if war had come in spite of it.

[87] See above pp. 331-332.

TWO CONSTANTS
IN RUSSIAN FOREIGN POLICY

John Clinton Adams

I.

In an essay entitled "The Foreign Policy of Russian Czarism," published in 1890, Friedrich Engels summed up and brought to a climax the hostile views which he and Karl Marx had taken for many years of the nature, motives, objectives and techniques of Russian foreign policy. Then as now that policy seemed an enigma to many observers; Engels' solution of the riddle was terse:

The Russian diplomatic corps forms, so to speak, a modern Jesuit order, powerful enough in case of necessity to overcome even the whims of the Czar and to become master of the corruption within Russia, in order to disseminate it abroad the more plentifully; a Jesuit order recruited originally and preferably from foreigners. . . . It is this secret society, recruited originally and preferably from foreign adventurers, which has raised the Russian Empire to its present plenitude of power. With iron persistence, eyes set fixedly on the goal, not shrinking from any breach of faith, any treason, any assassination, any servility, distributing bribes lavishly . . . it is this gang which has made Russia great, powerful and feared, and has opened up for it the way to world domination.[1]

Sixty-three years later Professor Toynbee explained Russian international behavior as part of the "encounter between the

[1] K. Marx, and F. Engels, *The Russian Menace to Europe,* P. W. Blackstock and B. F. Hoselitz, eds. (Glencoe, 1952), p. 26.

world and the West"; Russia is a type of the "world," defending itself against the West by adopting western technology as a material weapon, a process beginning with Peter the Great, and a western ideology, Communism, as a spiritual weapon.[2]

Between the extremes represented by the nineteenth-century German zealot and the mid-twentieth-century English philosopher stretches a spectrum of judgments with respect to the nature and sources of Russian foreign policy. One of the most controversial questions involved in the general problem may be formulated in these terms: is the foreign policy of the Soviet Union a new policy, the diplomatic expression of Marxism-Leninism, which must by reason of its origin differ generically from the foreign policies of all non-Communist states, or is Soviet policy essentially only a continuation of the traditional policy of the Russian emperors? The argument in favor of the first alternative is that Imperial Russia pursued the same limited objectives and was actuated by the same motives as other great powers; like them it colonized peacefully; like them it was sometimes guilty of violent conquests and the economic exploitation of weaker peoples. But Russian emperors never suffered from "messianic" compulsions to conquer the world, nor did they invent and try to realize long-range plans of aggression. Russian policy was in no way the unique product of a psychological syndrome known as "Russian character"; it was the policy followed by all contemporary states. Soviet policy, on the other hand, is an all-embracing plan for the attainment of global supremacy, based upon a non-Russian ideology propagated by the present rulers of Russia; it is thus qualitatively and quantitatively different from the policy of the emperors and this difference of principle must never be obscured; in Professor Karpovich's happy aphorism: "Soviet diplomats behave as they do, not because they are Russians, but because they are Communists."[3]

[2] See A. J. Toynbee, *The World and the West* (New York, 1953).
[3] M. Karpovich, "Russian Imperialism or Communist Aggression," *New Leader*, June 4 and June 11, 1951.

The opposite view pretends to see through the hammer-and-sickle emblem and discover the old double-headed eagle behind it; it maintains that the foreign policy of a state such as Russia is determined by unchanging factors and thus tends to remain constant irrespective of the form of government adopted by that state; mere ideologies are quite insufficient causes to bring about fundamental changes. It is not Communism that menaces the world, but Russian power, as any powerful state menaces its neighbors; if Russian power were destroyed, Communism, as a threat to the free world, would disappear. Expansion is the normal process for all states, and the expansion of Russia caused grave concern in the West before the Communist Manifesto was written, more than a century before Lenin seized the state power in 1917. Russian policy today is not different from what it always was:

> In their main features the foreign policy methods of Soviet Russia have remained similar to those originated by Ivan I, domesticated by Ivan III, generalized by Peter I, and westernized by Catherine II. . . . To sow discord among actual or prospective enemies, to conquer them from within by Trojan horse techniques, by fostering groups disloyal to the political principles of their own countries and subservient to those of the Kremlin,—these are measures which have become commonplace appurtenances of Soviet policy.[4]

The importance of Communism to Russian policy, in this view, is not that it altered that policy in any way, but that the Communist leaders built a heavy industry which made Russia one of the two military powers in the world today; the ideology of Marxism-Leninism is simply one more weapon in Russia's arsenal. The policy of Russia under the Communists remains unchanged; but the power of Russia to achieve her objectives has been immensely increased.[5]

The first of these analyses denies any continuity between the foreign policy of Imperial Russia and that of the Soviet;

---

[4] Marx and Engels, *Russian Menace;* editors' introduction, pp. 13, 14.

[5] See H. R. Rudin, "The Continuity of Russian Imperialism," *Yale Review,* Spring, 1953.

the second not only affirms that continuity but denies that the Communists have altered anything; they have merely succeeded, by increasing Russian military power, in intensifying the traditional policy. Both explanations, in my judgment, fail to describe the phenomenon completely, and thus commit the common fallacy of neglected aspect. To deny the persistence of certain traditional Russian policies into the Communist era seems to me sheer sentimentality; to deny that international Communism intends the conquest of the world seems wilful blindness to reality. The truth appears to be that the objectives of traditional Russian foreign policy remain unchanged within the larger ambit of Soviet world-policy. As I have expressed it elsewhere:

> The Soviet Union does not behave like other states in its international relations because it is unlike any other contemporary state, except those created in its own image. In the first place, it is a sovereign great power, and as such its foreign policy is influenced by the same factors which condition or determine the foreign policies of other states: geography and economics. We should expect Russia, whether ruled by tsars or commissars, to pursue policies aiming at the subjection of the Baltic States, Poland and East Prussia, control of the Straits of the Black Sea, and a dominant position in the eastern Balkans, Iran, Manchuria and probably Korea. Two centuries and a half of Russian history confirm our expectations.
>
> But in addition to pursuing these goals, which are limited, though extensive, the Soviet Union is the headquarters of a conspiracy to overthrow by force all non-communist governments and establish a communist system throughout the world.[6]

In the absence of agreement as to the general nature of Russian policy it is not surprising that there should be no agreement concerning the factors, singly or in combination, which have produced that policy. Here we encounter monists, dualists and pluralists. An early twentieth-century view, redolent of the Social Darwinism popular at the time, was that Russia's evolution

[6] J. C. Adams, "The Teacher of Social Science and the World Crisis," the *Dartmouth Alumni Magazine,* Feb., 1954, p. 28.

is governed by nature's law of growth. . . . Given a people with a colonizing instinct and schooled by their environment to endure and conquer; given an absolute power with its roots set deeply in vital religion; and modern Russia is the inevitable result.[7]

This explanation simply begs the question, and is a warning against the dangers of dogmatism, but it is popular to the present day, owing unquestionably to the great authority of Klyuchevsky, who sponsored it. We are not directly concerned, however, with unsupervised migrations of people, or with the deportations carried out by Imperial and Soviet authorities, or with the unfettered initiative of ambitious frontier generals in Central Asia, but with the foreign policies of official Russia, Imperial and Soviet.

It is perhaps not as fashionable as it was to ascribe Russia's international behavior almost exclusively to economic causes, even in Soviet historiography, although the policies of the First Moscow and Petersburg Periods can be portrayed with some plausibility as the product, successively, of what the late Professor Pokrovsky used to call "boyar imperialism," then the desire to secure sea-transit for grain exports and to find markets in the Far East for Russian textiles and metal goods; Soviet domination of the "peoples' democracies" has recently been explained exclusively in economic terms as a consequence of the inefficient and wasteful Soviet system which has compelled the bureaucratic rulers of Russia to appropriate the resources of the enslaved states. But while it is possible to demonstrate the presence of economic motives in the determination of a particular policy, it is by no means self-evident or convincing beyond reasonable doubt that economic considerations did more than subserve the basic determinants of Russian policy, and it can be shown that in some very important cases the policy of the Imperial Government was carried out despite patent economic disadvantages; one striking example is the history of the strategic railroads constructed before World War I.

[7] F. H. Skrine, *The Expansion of Russia* (2nd ed., Cambridge, 1904), p. 1.

I have ventured to doubt the adequacy of some popular explanations of the course of Russian foreign policy over the last two centuries and a half, while conceding that each assigned cause may have operated in one or more areas, at one or more times, with varying degrees of effect. Other explanations when analyzed might prove to be insufficient causes of the phenomenon taken as a whole: the "urge to the sea," as Professor Kerner poetically termed the search for warm-water ports, can be and has been transformed into a monist explanation of Russian foreign relations. The Russian scholar Kornilov,[8] writing before 1917, presented a persuasive and cohesive theory of Russian history which explained both domestic and foreign policy until the middle of the nineteenth century as the result of an overriding necessity for military strength, and I believe that he came close to the truth. My own reflections have led to the belief that most of the theories previously mentioned may be likened to algebraic expressions which have been partially decomposed into prime factors: they are correct but they can be further simplified. It will be argued here that the prime factors determining Russian foreign policy from the reign of the first prince of Moscow to the present time are only two in number: geography and the Russian character. Geography supplied the prerequisite for what I shall call the "inertial momentum" of Russian policy; the Russian character, in my belief, manifests certain traits which do not change over the centuries. I shall try to show that these constants generate a foreign policy distinguished by extreme consistency, whether directed from Moscow or Petersburg, and by uniquely Russian qualities.

II.

The nature and sources of Russian foreign policy evoke manifold and contradictory explanations; the results of that policy are beyond dispute: territorial expansion on a scale unequaled in history, from Kievan Russia at its height in the

[8] A. Kornilov, *Modern Russian History* (2 vols.; New York, 1916).

eleventh century, which may have comprised an area of 400,000
square miles, to the present Russian empire of over 8,500,000
square miles. This expansion began in the First Moscow Period
of Russian history, and approached its maximum during the
Petersburg Period; at the beginning of the Second Moscow
Period the area under Moscow's control shrank until the situation superficially resembled the First Moscow Period at the
time of John IV, but Moscow soon recovered most of Petersburg Russia. Eventually, as a result of World War II, Moscow
not only completed the ancient task of "gathering in the
Russian lands," by annexing Bukovina and Carpatho-Ukraine
(Podkarpatska Rus) but extended Russian domination, through
so-called "peoples' democracies," beyond any previous limits.
This enormous achievement demands closer inspection.

Petersburg's conquests were spectacular and a cause of concern to all Europe; it is easy to ignore the geographically more
remote but indispensable acquisitions of pre-Petrine Muscovy,
especially those made by John III and John IV. Unable as yet
to break the power of Poland-Lithuania on the west or the
khanates of the disintegrating Golden Horde on east and south,
John III and his son made war on their own kind. The small
territorial rectangle around Moscow in 1300 had been increased
through servility and rapacity to a much larger, irregular poly-
gon by the time John III ascended the throne in 1462; his conquest of the once lordly and great Novgorod, with its vast holdings in North Russia, more than doubled the size of the Muscovite state; he and his son, Basil III, extended its frontiers to
the west and south past Tver, Pskov, and Smolensk. These
last gains chipped away bricks in the wall between Muscovy
and Europe; John IV turned east and smashed the wall separating Muscovy from Asia. He besieged the Khanate of
Kazan, which blocked the middle Volga, with an army estimated as high as 150,000 men, and a siege train of artillery
under German direction, and captured the city in 1552; four
years later he annexed the Khanate of Astrakhan, on the Caspi-

an Sea, the last remnant of the Golden Horde. Russia now controlled the whole Volga basin and was henceforth a new neighbor for Iran; the penetration of Siberia was begun, partly by private interests and in many cases by Cossacks and refugees from Muscovite absolutism and oppression. A century after the fall of Kazan Cossack explorers stood on the shores of the Sea of Okhotsk 7000 miles from Europe; in 1649 Khabarov occupied the Amur basin and hostilities with China began, ending in a Russian defeat that led to the Treaty of Nerchinsk, 1689, by which Russia demolished her forts along the Amur and the Russo-Chinese boundary was pushed to the Gorbitsa River and the mountain chain north of the Amur. Regular commercial relations between Russia and China were not established until after the death of Peter the Great, by the Treaty of Kiakhta, ratified in 1728, which permitted trade only at the town of Kiakhta, but allowed the Russians to maintain an ecclesiastical mission in Peking which assumed some diplomatic functions. No further changes in the official relations between Russia and China occurred until the middle of the next century. But Russian explorers and merchants continued moving east; they crossed into Alaska, made it a Russian province and, in 1812, built Fort Ross in Northern California, the frontier outpost of "Russian America."

The century following the death of John IV was as chaotic and bloody as any in Russian history; it began with the *Smutnoe Vremya,* or "Time of Troubles," ten years of confused civil wars and invasion that reached their climax when the Poles captured Moscow and ended with the establishment of the Romanov dynasty. During the middle of the century complicated wars took place between Muscovy and Poland, which were concluded by the treaty of Andrusovo, 1667; the Poles ceded to Moscow all Ukraine east of the Dnepr; the city of Kiev, on the right bank, was ceded theoretically for only two years, actually for all subsequent time. The century ended with the accession of Peter I, who was destined to initiate the

Petersburg Period in Russian history, to make Muscovy part of the European diplomatic system and, at least in dress and armament, a European country.

The Petersburg Period in Russian foreign policy was characterized by assaults on a series of geographic objectives, repeated at suitable intervals until the objectives were obtained; this fundamental process continued until Imperial Russia crashed and the Second Moscow Period began. Peter himself is chiefly remembered for his blow to the north which "smashed open a window on Europe." The Great Northern War, plotted by Peter and Augustus the Strong of Poland against the youthful Charles XII of Sweden, found both aggressors, and particularly Peter, unrealistically optimistic with respect to Russia's strength and that of Poland. Study of this prolonged and amorphous war reveals the following features, some or all of which have been characteristic of every modern war fought on Russian territory: at the outset Russia suffered immediate and serious reverses, owing to unpreparedness and inefficiency; the enemy found it possible to effect deep penetrations into the country; Ukrainian nationalism could be utilized as a weapon against Russia, but the weapon was unpredictable and unreliable; the occupation of Russian territory did not compel the Russian Government to make peace; diplomatic intrigues on the part of the Russians paralleled every stage of the military campaigns. The Treaty of Nystad, 1721, brought Russia part of Karelia, Ingria, Estonia, and Livonia, access to the Baltic Sea, and a water road to Europe nine months of the year. The foundation of St. Petersburg, May, 1703, symbolized the fact that geographically, economically, diplomatically, and militarily, Russia had drawn nearer to Europe. Having participated in a European coalition against a European state, Russia could now be reckoned a European power, although not yet a great power.

Throughout the eighteenth century Russian diplomacy assumed increasingly a European character and European scope;

it was influenced by family connections with the dynasties of Holstein and Mecklenburg and by the general European balance of power; Russian policy-makers devised far-reaching diplomatic "systems," grandiose in theory though never fully realized in practice. During most of the century Russia aligned herself with Austria against France, whose persistent hostility, despite the intervening distance, testified to the influence acquired by Russia in European affairs. The rise of Prussia presented Russia an opportunity to gain influence in the moribund Holy Roman Empire, since the growth of Hohenzollern power intensified the division of the Germanies, while the new rival of the Hapsburgs was still weak enough to require support from either France or Russia. Russia's involvement in European affairs, as contrasted with Muscovy's virtual isolation, was emphasized by her participation, not only in the War of the Polish Succession (1733-1738) but in the War of the Austrian Succession and the Seven Years' War, whose origins were to be found in central Europe, North America, and India. For the first time Russian troops took Berlin, in 1760.

Access to the Baltic having already been secured by Peter the Great, the main directions of expansion during the reign of Catherine the Great, 1762-1796, were to the west and south, at the expense of the decaying Polish Republic and the Khanate of the Crimea, against the latter of which, after initial success, Peter had been ludicrously ineffectual. Russia, Prussia, and Austria subjected Poland to the First Partition in 1772, by which Russia obtained the White-Russian districts of Polotsk, Mogilev, and Vitebsk plus a section of Livonia: an area of about 36,000 square miles with an estimated population of nearly two million, mostly Orthodox Russians. By the Second Partition, 1793, Russia seized the districts of Vilna and Minsk, Eastern Podolia, and Volynia: this time the plunder amounted to 89,000 square miles and three million people. The Third Partition, 1795-1797, brought Courland, Lithuania, Western Podolia, and Volynia under Russian rule. Poland disappeared from the map, not to reappear as an independent state until 1919; the transaction seems to have shocked even eighteenth-century consciences.

Catherine's intervention in Polish affairs eventually provoked the Ottoman Padishah into a war which included as a curious incident the only Russian naval victory ever to be attained in the Mediterranean (won with the help of English naval commanders), brought Suvorov into prominence as a soldier, and was concluded by a monument of diplomatic astuteness, the Treaty of Kücük Kaynarca, 1774. The Crimea, previously a Turkish vassal state, was proclaimed independent under the rule of its Khan, "of the line of Jengiz Khan," and "dependent on God alone" as the Treaty piously expressed it; Catherine annexed the peninsula in 1783. The Treaty established Russia on the coast of the Black Sea, where a battle fleet soon came into being, based on Sevastopol; it ceded to Russia the area between the Dnepr and the Bug rivers, and certain territories elsewhere, granted Russia the right of free navigation on the Black Sea and passage of the Straits for her merchant vessels, and established a vague precedent for future intervention in behalf of her coreligionists in the Ottoman Empire. A later war against Turkey ended in 1791 with the Treaty of Jassy, which extended the Russian frontier from the Bug to the Dnestr, the frontier of Bessarabia.

All in all Catherine had added 200,000 square miles to the Russian Empire, and millions of new, non-Russian subjects. Russia was not merely a European power, she was a great power as she moved into the era of the French Revolution and Napoleon. Russian foreign policy under Emperors Paul and Alexander I vacillated almost irrationally in reaction to causes which seem trivial today, but an autocrat's whim, be he emperor or party boss, can set big battalions marching. Russian troops fought the French at intervals in Italy, Switzerland, Austria, and East Prussia for nearly ten years before Alexander met Napoleon at Tilsit in 1807 to change sides and receive his share in a partition of the world. His first instalment was Finland, conquered forthwith from Sweden, and he sent Russian troops to Belgrade in support of the Serbian revolution which had been in progress since 1804. But in 1812, as the Grand Army concentrated on the Niemen, Alexander protected his southern flank by making peace with the Turks at Bucharest; he received Bessarabia and abandoned the Serbs to Turkish vengeance.

If Napoleon, when he invaded Russia on June 23, 1812, had aimed at Kiev it is conceivable that he might have roused Ukrainian nationalism, as Charles XII had planned to do during the Great Northern War a century before; he aimed instead at Moscow. Deep penetration of Russian territory did not destroy Russian capabilities; ultimately it brought the Russians to Paris and then to the Congress of Vienna, where Russia obtained most of Poland. Metternich might be the "coachman" of Europe, but for the next forty years the Russian emperor was its policeman, with a standing army of one million men, which Emperor Alexander I liked to call his *"prépondérance politique."* England was retreating toward isolation, France had made its supreme, and final, bid for continental domination, Austria faced the growing force of nationalism, Prussia was a Russian satellite, and Russia, which had entered the European diplomatic system a scant century before, dominated Europe.

Aside from the "Ruthenians" in Galicia and Bukovina, the process of "gathering in the Russian lands" was now complete, if the gathering-in be construed as the reunion of all branches of the Russian people in one sovereign state. Already the expansion of Russia had brought under her control many non-Russian peoples: Finns, Poles, Romanians and Crimean Tartars, as well as many tribes, mostly Turkish, inhabiting Siberia, indicating that the dynamic of Russian growth was something more than the desire to unify the Russian people. The objective pursued by Imperial Russia from 1815 until the revolution in 1917 with persistence and flexibility, an objective of such importance to Russian statesmen that it was called "the historic mission," had nothing to do with uniting the Russian people, although attainment would bring about a very significant expansion of the Russian Empire: it was to establish control over the Straits of the Bosporus and the Dardanelles, thereby converting the Black Sea into a Russian lake, or, if direct control should prove impossible, to reduce the Ottoman Empire to the status of a doorkeeper whose job was to keep the door locked to the fleet of any nonriparian power.

Russian diplomacy employed many tactics to realize the "historic mission," including armed assistance to subjects rebelling against their legitimate sovereign, the Ottoman Padishah. When the Greek revolution, after dragging on for years, seemed likely to be suppressed by the Padishah's nominal vassal, Mehmet Ali of Egypt, Russia fought Turkey and won Greek independence by the Treaty of Adrianople, 1829. Emperor Nicholas I, or his diplomatic advisors, had escaped between the horns of a dilemma: the duties of Russia to her oppressed co-religionists in Turkey and her duties as guarantor of legitimacy, the status quo, and the Concert of Europe, by asserting that her dealings with Turkey had nothing to do with the problem of Greece. If so, the liberation of Greece may be regarded as the by-product of a Russian victory which was followed by the annexation to Russia of the mouth of the Danube, and land in the Caucasus region, including the Black Sea coast from Anapa to Poti. The Turkish Danubian principalities, Moldavia and Wallachia, while remaining under Turkish suzerainty, were to receive an "independent national government" and were in fact placed under Russian protection. Most of the Romanian people were now subject to Russia.

Abruptly reversing her traditional policy of hostility toward Turkey, Russia next offered to protect Mahmud II from his rebellious Egyptian vassal, whose forces, superior in every way to those of the "Sublime Government," conquered Syria and menaced Constantinople. Russian warships entered the Bosporus early in 1833 and 10,000 men were landed on the Asiatic shore, in response to a Turkish request for help; as the Turks put it: "A drowning man clings to a serpent." The subsequent Treaty of Hunkâr Iskelesi provided for perpetual friendship and a defensive alliance between the two states; Russia unilaterally guaranteed the independence of Turkey; Turkish assistance to Russia was limited to closing the Dardanelles against any foreign warship. Well might Nesselrode write: "Our intervention in the affairs of Turkey has acquired a basis of legality." This favorable state of affairs was soon terminated after a second Turko-Egyptian crisis had involved England, Russia, and France, and even Austria and Prussia: Hunkâr Iskelesi was superseded by the Second Treaty of London, which substituted a collective guarantee of the closure of the Straits for the unilateral Russian guarantee.

The Russo-Turkish alliance of 1833 represented a maximum of Russian influence in Turkey which has not been achieved since, and which was soon to be diminished. Among its many other consequences, the Crimean War checked the extension of Russian power to the south by the simple expedient of neutralizing the Black Sea "in perpetuity," which severed the Russian naval spearhead pointing toward the Straits. The Treaty of Paris, 1856, also attempted to block the future advance southward of Russian land power by compelling Russia to cede a strip of southern Bessarabia bordering the Danube to Moldavia, abolishing the Russian protectorate over Moldavia and Wallachia, and substituting a collective guarantee; these arrangements created conditions which soon resulted in the union of the Principalities as the new state of Romania (1857-1861) subject to the suzerainty of the Ottoman Padishah.

Russian policy in the south lapsed perforce for nearly fifteen years while at home the Great Reforms took place as the direct consequence of a defeat which demonstrated that the Russian military colossus was no match for the technological superiority of western armies, however inefficient western leadership might

be. An opportunity to slip the fetters of the "Black Sea
Clauses" was presented by the Franco-Prussian war of 1870;
Russia had several times during the previous decade shown herself favorably disposed to Bismarck; in 1866 she frankly regarded Prussia as "the avenging instrument of Russian wrath"
upon an Austria whose policy in the Crimean War had indeed
astonished Europe by ingratitude for Russia's suppression of
the Hungarian revolution in 1849; in October, 1870, a month
after the French cuirassiers vainly charged the Prussian squares
at Sedan, a Russian circular to the Great Powers denounced the
"Black Sea Clauses." Prince Gorchakov explained that "it
would be difficult to maintain that the written law . . . retains
the moral validity which it may have possessed at other times."
The powers reaffirmed the sanctity of international law and
recognized its successful violation.

Seven years later Russian troops stood on the littoral of the
Sea of Marmora and in sight of the dome of St. Sophia. This
time Russia had exploited Balkan nationalism: uprisings of
Serbian *rayah* in Herzegovina, a prematurely exploded revolt in
Bulgaria followed by Turkish massacres; Serbia and Montenegrin military defeats in a war they had impulsively begun with
Turkey. The Treaty of San Stefano, imposed by Russia upon
the Turks in 1878, revealed a new design for indirect conquest:
the creation of a Bulgarian state stretching from the Danube
to the Aegean and from Albania to the Black Sea, clearly intended as a Russian satellite and the base for a final assault on
Constantinople. The Russian advance was halted, this time
short of war, by a European coalition dominated by Great Britain; the Congress of Berlin reduced the size of Bulgaria and
granted full independence to Serbia, Montenegro and Romania.
Russia received Batum, Kars, and Ardahan from the Turkish
enemy; her ally Romania was forced to retrocede southern
Bessarabia despite the Romanian blood that flowed before the
defenses of Plevna in Russia's behalf; the British delegate read
a menacing and vague statement which seemed to imply that

under certain circumstances England might not respect the principle that the Straits were closed to non-Turkish warships.

Russian military and diplomatic satraps, often working at cross purposes, dominated Bulgaria for the next five years. When Bulgarian politicians, or the newly chosen prince, Alexander of Battenberg, proved recalcitrant, Russian officers in the Bulgarian army might be abruptly recalled to Russia. In 1886 Russia instigated a conspiracy of Bulgarian army officers who kidnapped Prince Alexander and forced his abdication; when a counterrevolution succeeded, Battenberg was informed that a Russian envoy was on his way to take charge in Sofia; he appealed to the Russian Emperor, who bluntly disapproved his return to Bulgaria. Battenberg's successor, Prince Ferdinand, was viewed without enthusiasm in Petersburg and went unrecognized until 1896; meanwhile Russia financed and organized groups of dissident Bulgarian émigrés, with headquarters at Odessa, who fomented subversive activities in Bulgaria. By 1894 Russian policy in the Near East had changed to support of the status quo, except for occasional plots to seize the Straits by a sudden descent of the Black Sea Fleet, and the march of Russian Empire was directed elsewhere.

After the Crimean War halted Russia expansion toward Constantinople the Empire immediately began to expand in the Far and Middle East. Between 1857-1860 the left bank of the Amur River was annexed and the Ussuri region on the right bank, between the Ussuri River and the Gulf of Tartary; in 1860, near the Korean border, the Russians founded a city with the optimistic name of Vladivostok (Rule of the East). The northern half of the island of Sakhalin had been occupied in 1853; in 1875 the Japanese reluctantly ceded the southern half in return for the Kurile Islands. By that time the most distant province of the Russian Empire, Alaska, had been abandoned. In 1821, desirous of making the northern waters exclusively Russian, Emperor Nicholas I issued a decree that prohibited non-Russian vessels from engaging in "commerce, whaling, and fishing, and all other industry" north of the fifty-first parallel, and from approaching Russian-occupied islands and coasts in the Pacific closer than a distance of 100 (Italian) miles. This represented the extremity of Russian claims, which were reduced in 1824 to the line 54° 40', while freedom of navigation and fishing in the Pacific were conceded. Once the retreat began it continued until 1867, when the Russian flag ceased to fly over the American continent. Secretary of State Seward purchased Alaska for $7,200,000, although the Russians would have taken $5,000,000; there is reason to believe that unwillingness on the part of Washington politicians to ratify the purchase of "Seward's Ice-box" was softened by $200,000 worth of Russian bribes. It is alarming to imagine the military situation which would be faced by the United States if Alaska, instead of being a new member of the United States, were still Russian territory.

As the Russian tide flowed into the Far East it simultaneously inundated the Middle East and Central Asia. Here the work had been begun by Peter the Great; immediately after concluding peace with Sweden in the north, he started a war of conquest against Iran. Desultory hostilities occurred in the course of the eighteenth century and became outright war with Iran again in 1804, after Russia proclaimed the annexation of the Caucasus. The Treaty of Gulistan, 1813, secured for Russia the right to maintain a battle fleet in the Caspian, and sovereignty over a large tract of mountainous country between the Black and Caspian seas that happened to contain the bulk of the oil resources of the Caucasus. Another war with Iran, in 1827-1828, brought Russia further territorial gains at Iran's expense by the Treaty of Turkmanchai. The tempo of advance in these regions was rather slow, at first, and the pacification of the Caucasus required some thirty-four years, to 1864; but during the next sixteen years, from 1860-1876, far-reaching expansion occurred in Turkestan; Russian frontier generals conquered the fierce Moslem Khanates of

Kokand, Bokhara and Khiva, sometimes against orders from St. Petersburg; Kokand was annexed, the other two became protectorates. Based on Krasnovodsk, a recently founded port on the eastern Caspian, the Russians next conquered the Turkoman tribes, after capturing Gök-Tepe in 1881; they occupied Merv in 1884, arousing "mervousness" in London, and appeared to be threatening Herat, then considered to be the gateway to India.

Expansion through outright annexation virtually came to an end at this point; indirect expansion by domination and exploitation found a huge and rich objective in Manchuria, destined to be controlled, not by Russian bayonets, but through railroads and banks. By 1904 Japan had been ejected from the Asiatic mainland, the Chinese-Eastern railroad linked Siberia with Vladivostok across Manchuria, and the Southern-Manchurian Railroad stretched from its junction with the Chinese-Eastern at Harbin down to ice-free ports: Port Arthur and Dalienwan (Dalny, Dairen), which had passed into Russian possession in 1897-1898 by occupation and a twenty-five year lease extorted from China. The squadron based on Port Arthur represented potentially a still further extension of Russian power but its existence was short-lived; the Treaty of Portsmouth, New Hampshire, in 1905, after the Russo-Japanese War, substituted the influence of Japan for that of Russia in most of Manchuria, including Port Arthur and Dalienwan.

Russia arranged with Great Britain the partition of Iran, in 1907, even as she turned back to the Balkans and the "historic mission"; a few years later Austro-Russian rivalries in the Balkans helped detonate World War I. In March, 1915, attempting to keep an already war-weary Russia from a separate peace, or worse, Britain and France reversed their traditional policy and agreed that Russia might take possession of the Straits after an Allied victory; this change of policy was indeed, as the Foreign Office put it, "in total contradiction to the viewpoints and sentiments which have always predominated in

England and which have not at all disappeared today." With
the prize almost in reach, Imperial Russia came to an end in
1917, and the Second Moscow Period began.

Two years later the embattled Bolsheviks struggled to maintain themselves in a Russia shrunk to less than its dimensions
at the time of the accession of John IV, suffering invasion by
enemies old and new and torn by civil war; they succeeded, at
great expense, and reached a state of truce between the old
world and the new Soviet Russia by the middle 1920's. The
imperial boundaries had in general been regained, with certain
significant exceptions: Finland was now an independent state,
and the principle of self-determination of peoples had been
realized on the Baltic by the creation of three new sovereignties:
Estonia, Latvia, and Lithuania. To the west, the principle of
self-determination and desire on the part of France and England to erect a *cordon sanitaire* between Europe and the Bolshe-
vist infection had combined to revive Poland: as though rising
refreshed from a slumber of more than a century the Poles
almost mechanically attacked Russia; after being rescued from
defeat they managed to push the Polish-Russian frontier one
hundred fifty miles east of the ethnically correct Curzon Line
by the Treaty of Riga, 1921. Bessarabia swung pendulum-like
to Romania. Moscow failed in efforts to utilize the weapon of
proletarian revolution in the Baltic states, in Berlin, Munich,
and Budapest, in Bulgaria and northern Iran; exported Communism to China with considerable success, despite Chiang Kai-
shek's purge of the Kuomintang; and seemed to accept, as other
creeds had done, an indefinite delay in the coming of the last
judgment.

National-Socialist Germany's rise to European predominance in the 1930's posed a threat and an opportunity; when it
became probable that collective security against the German
menace could not be attained, owing to the equivocal policy
of England and France, Moscow abruptly abandoned the policy
of a "united front against Fascism," in favor of a second Treaty

of Tilsit. The Russo-German pact of August 23, 1939, envisaged a partition of the Baltic states: Finland, Estonia, and
Latvia would fall within the Soviet sphere, Lithuania would
go to Germany; Poland would be subjected to its Fourth Partition by Russia and Germany, this time along the Narew-Vistula-
San line; Bessarabia would swing back from Romania. After
the outbreak of World War II and the rapid collapse of Poland,
Moscow and Berlin revised their arrangements so that Poland
was partitioned along the Curzon Line, which in effect gave
ethnic Poland to Germany; Russia was compensated by Lithuania. Moscow demanded and acquired military bases in
Estonia, Latvia, and Lithuania; territorial concessions on the
part of Finland were enforced by a short war. In June and
July, 1940, as Germany conquered France and the end of World
War II seemed imminent, Russia annexed Estonia, Latvia,
Lithuania, and Bessarabia, together with the Bukovina. During the autumn of 1940 there was talk of a four-power pact
between Russia, Germany, Japan, and Italy by which the signatories would divide the world into spheres of influence;
Hitler explained that Russia's future lay in the direction of the
Persian Gulf and India. Moscow's conditions for joining
the proposed pact were more limited and explicit: undisputed
influence in Finland, Bulgaria, and northern Iran; a Russian
base at the Dardanelles. A month later Hitler signed Direc-
tive 21, Operation Barbarossa, the plan of attack on Russia.
The German invasion of Russia began June 22, 1941; it came
to a halt on December 5 with the Fourth Panzer Group twenty-
five miles from Moscow, in a temperature of forty below zero.
Large areas of Russian territory were occupied and admin-
istered by Nazi officials, the notorious *"Goldfasanen"*; the support of the Ukrainians and other nationalities was contemptu-
ously rejected and the entire Slavic population except the Cossacks was classified as subhuman; the Jews were exterminated.
The Germans found it impossible to compel the Russian Government to make peace, despite the occupation of more and

more land, and after the Russians encircled and annihilated the German Sixth Army before Stalingrad the death agony of the Third Reich began. At the end of the war the Russian flag flew over Berlin, and also, as the result of her brief intervention against Japan, over Manchuria and North Korea.

Russia retained the regions acquired during her alliance with Nazi Germany, annexed most of East Prussia, and in addition received Carpatho-Ukraine (Podkarpatska Rus) from Czechoslovakia, not an enemy state; her annexations amounted to 274,000 square miles with a non-Russian population of about twenty-four million. They gave her for the first time common frontiers with Norway, Czechoslovakia, and Hungary. In the Far East Russia recovered all of Sakhalin from Japan and also the Kurile Islands; forty years after the Treaty of Portsmouth she recovered Imperial Russia's position in Manchuria: a thirty-year lease of Port Arthur and joint operation with China for thirty years of the Chinese-Eastern and Southern-Manchurian Railroads, now known as the Changchun Railroad. Outer Mongolia, which had been drifting toward Russia since before the Revolution, was conceded by China to be independent. Moscow also demanded of the Turks a military base at the Dardanelles; they refused, strong in the support of the United States. A puppet Communist government was briefly established in Northern Iran just after the war, but American and British protests, and publicity in the United Nations, resulted in the withdrawal of Russian troops after which Teheran smashed the revolt.

The territorial acquisitions of Russia were small compared with the expansion of Russian influence in Europe and elsewhere after World War II, resulting from the establishment of Communist Governments in Eastern Europe, China, North Korea and Indo-China. During the first years of the Second Moscow Period the Communists had summoned the proletariat of a number of countries to class warfare without significant results. After 1945 they were more realistic. They exported the revolution and imposed Communist Governments on the countries they controlled unless the local Communists, as in Yugoslavia, were strong enough to crush capitalism without help from Moscow. One by one, the countries of Eastern and Southern Europe became "peoples' democracies": East Germany, Poland, Czechoslovakia, Hungary, Albania, Yugoslavia, Romania, and Bulgaria. Yugoslavia soon asserted and maintained independent membership in the Communist world; revolts flared in East Germany and Poland; revolution in Hungary was defeated by the Russian army. In general the "peoples' democracies" were only projections of Russian power and perhaps, eventually, future members of the Soviet Union.

In the Far East, the Chinese Communists were aided to some extent by Russia in overthrowing the Government of Chiang Kai-shek, but there can be little doubt that they accomplished this mainly by themselves, nor did they ever yield complete direction of their policy to Moscow. The North Koreans and Chinese failed in the Korean War, 1950-1953, to extend the soviet system to South Korea; in Viet Nam, the Communist forces of Ho Chi-minh defeated the French and became masters of the country down to the seventeenth parallel. By 1958 approximately one third of the planet stood under the flag of Communism, and the origin, center, and strength of this movement was Moscow.

III.

The survey of Russian expansion in the previous section reveals definite and persistent patterns of behavior in Russian external relations, lines of advance against objectives on every side of the Muscovite nucleus. The work of Peter the Great on the Baltic was undone by the Revolutions of 1917; it was done again in 1939-1940 by Joseph Stalin. Poland was partitioned three times by Catherine the Great, annexed almost completely by Alexander I, restored to the European family of nations in 1919, partitioned for the fourth time by Stalin in 1939. It was ruled for years after World War II by a Russian viceroy in the person of Soviet Marshal Rokossovsky, and at the present time it enjoys an autonomy within the Russian sphere as precarious as it is limited. Bessarabia is once again Russian territory; Bulgaria and Romania are so nearly a part of Russia that they possess little international personality. Until very recently Iran was to a certain extent under Russian protection, because a Soviet-Iranian Treaty, signed in 1921, permitted the Russian army to enter the country in defense of Iranian independence; something like the imperial sphere of influence obtains in Manchuria and northern Korea. Soviet authorities have continued the traditional attempts to realize the "historic mission." It is clear that these constant patterns are not connected with a specific form of government, for they remain the same whether Russia is ruled by tsars or commissars; they must be the product of constant factors.

One of these constant factors is surely the absence of any significant natural obstacles in the three great lowlands making up the Eurasian continent called Russia. The east-west highway through the forests north of the Pripyat Marshes brings European power to Moscow and beyond. Rivers, portages, and valleys and the railroads, canals, and roads that follow their course open the way to the Volga and Siberia; the north-south axis, from the Baltic Sea to the Black Sea and the Caspian, recalls the old trade route "from the Varyags to the Greeks"; the steppe road runs from the Carpathians to the Amur: it is history's longest highroad for invasion and counterinvasion.

In the mechanics of political expansion natural obstacles exert the effect of friction: they tend to prevent motion or to bring it to a halt if it has begun. In the absence of friction Newton's First Law permits an inertial momentum, once created, to continue indefinitely. Application of the analogy to Russian geographical conditions seems justified by the history of innumerable invasions of Russia from almost every direction over many centuries; the two invasions from the west in the nineteenth and twentieth centuries have been only the best-known and most spectacular. Invaders of Russia at all times have been able to penetrate the country deeply and to occupy large areas; it is then, at least in modern times, that the problem of forcing a military decision presents itself. Modern Russia accepts defeat in war only at a peripheral point: the Crimea, Manchuria; the invaders who aimed for the center eventually reached Poltava, the Beresina, and Stalingrad. Irresolute Russian leadership made World War I an exception to this rule of history. Space and climate have been formidable allies of the Russian army, while inertial momentum carries an invader deeper and deeper into a country which seems to have no throat to seize, no heart to pierce. Before the Napoleonic invasion Gneisenau predicted that after losing two battles Alexander I would cede Petersburg and Moscow and content himself with Kazan and Astrakhan, but Rostopchin was a better prophet, when he assured the emperor that "l'empereur de Russie restera toujours formidable à Moscou, terrible à Cazan et invincible à Tobolsk,"[9] although, as Mackinder pointed out long ago, "Napoleon at Moscow had very nearly marched right across the inhabited Russia of his time, and therefore across the territory which could afford supplies to the contending armies."[10] Engels summed up the geographical peculiarities of Russia in these words:

The country itself, turned toward Europe on one side only, was thus open to attack only at that point; it was without a vital center, the conquest of which could force a peace. Because of its lack of roads, its expanse, its poverty of resources, it was almost absolutely protected from conquest. Here was an unassailable power position made to order for those who understood how to take advantage of it. . . .[11]

In brief, then, the absence of natural obstacles encouraged invasion along well-defined routes, but the country offered an

[9] N. K. Shil'der, *Imperator Aleksandr Pervyi* (4 vols.; St. Petersburg, 1904-1905), III, 373-375.

[10] H. J. Mackinder, *Democratic Ideals and Reality* (New York, 1919), p. 149 and n.

[11] Marx and Engels, *Russian Menace*, p. 27.

invader almost no objectives for a mortal blow, while his
lengthening supply lines invited the knife of partisan warfare,
and the impassable mud of October held him fast until the
arrival of the Russian winter. The same geographical conditions likewise exerted their influence on the occasions when
Petersburg or Moscow took the offensive; once the Russian
armies moved, inertial momentum, which brought invaders to
Moscow, brought the Russians to Warsaw and Berlin.

During the last centuries the main axis of advance into
Russia has been from west to east but earlier, as we have seen,
the case was not so simple. Viewed as a whole, the history of
Russia is the history of a people unprotected by natural boundaries, defending itself on every side against predatory foes
whose invasions swept along on the wings of inertial momentum; the Russian counterattack began in the fifteenth century,
aided by the same momentum, and is still in progress. I have
no wish to depreciate Klyuchevsky's profound generalization
that the history of Russia is a history of colonizations[12] when
I suggest that it is also a military history from John III to the
present day, and that as a direct result of the geographical factor
military considerations have exercised a decisive influence on
the policy of all Russian governments from that time to this;
the familiar dictum that foreign policy is the outward push of
domestic forces does not apply in general to Russia. It seems
to me on the contrary that the inward push of external forces
molded the Russian state into a military monolith in which the
chain of command ran from palace to camp, to paraphrase de
Custine; that domestic policy was the servant of foreign policy;
and that the desire to maintain and increase military power
repeatedly brought transformations of internal political and
economic institutions: examples are the *oprichnina* of John
IV, the Petrine reforms, the emancipation of the serfs, and

[12] "Istoriya Rossii est' istoriya strany, kotoraya kolonizuetsya." V. Klyuchevsky, *Kurs russkoi istorii* (Moscow, 1937), I, 20.

the First Five Year Plan. Nothing could be clearer than the words of Stalin in 1931:

> The Mongol Khans beat [Old Russia]. The Turkish beys beat her. The Swedish feudal lords beat her. The Polish-Lithuanian "squires" beat her. The Anglo-French capitalists beat her. The Japanese barons beat her. They all beat her—for backwardness. . . . That is why we must no longer be backward. . . . We are 50 to 100 years behind the advanced countries. We must make good that distance in ten years. Either we do it, or they crush us.[13]

For centuries the rulers of Russia could claim that although their tactics might seem aggressive the underlying strategy was defensive; to push their frontiers far enough from the centers of government and power to insure national security. Where in Europe should such frontiers lie? Pondering this problem a century ago, Karl Marx concluded that:

> . . . the natural frontier of Russia runs from Danzig, or perhaps Stettin, to Trieste . . . the conquest of Turkey by Russia would be only the prelude for the annexation of Hungary, Prussia, Galicia, and for the ultimate realization of the Slavonic Empire which certain fanatical Panslavist philosophers have dreamed of.[14]

The Iron Curtain does indeed follow approximately that line, but there is no necessity to suppose that it represents Moscow's final solution of the problem of security for the present Russian empire. Security is not a line on a map, it is a state of mind, in this case, the state of the Russian mind.

In order to save space I shall take for granted the proposition that if a mean could be obtained of the mind-sets of a large sample of the Russian population it would differ significantly from means obtained by sampling the German population or the American population, or any population born to the heritage of western Christendom. One need not accept Mr. Gorer's tantalizing theses concerning the traumatic effects of swaddling clothes on the Russian psyche; is it not inevitable

---

[13] I. V. Stalin, *Sochineniya* (Moscow, 1951), XIII, 38, 39, *passim*.
[14] Marx and Engels, *Russian Menace*, p. 133.

that minds molded by a tradition deriving from Byzantium, from the Tartar yoke, from centuries of invasion and counter-invasion, a tradition, moreover, that knew no High Middle Ages, no Renaissance and Reformation, should differ from western minds? The gradual evolution of western culture contrasts with the discontinuities and leaps of Russian history, as de Custine perceived in 1839:

> Russia alone, belatedly civilized, has been deprived of a profound fermentation and of the benefit of a slow and natural cultural development, because of the impatience of her leaders. Russia has missed the ground work which forms great peoples. . . . Adolescence . . . has been lost to Russia. Her princes, and especially Peter the Great, counting time for nothing, made her pass violently from infancy to virility.[15]

Two characteristics of the Russian mind concern us here: extreme suspicion, and a sense of mission. Each of these traits has provoked descriptions and explanations over the centuries that affirm beyond reasonable doubt its existence and persistence; indeed, what could be better proof of the unchanging qualities of the Russian mind than the fact that comments written a century ago, or nearly four centuries ago, often read like the latest news from Moscow? Let me quote an English observer in the sixteenth century:

> This desperate state of things at home [in Muscovy] maketh the people for the most part to wishe for some forreine invasion, which they suppose to bee the onely means to rid them of the heavy yoke of this tyrannous government. . . . You shall seldom see a Russe a traveller, except he be with some ambassadour, or that he make a scape out of his countrie. Which hardly he can doo, by reason of the borders that are watched narrowly, and the punishment for any such attempt, which is death if he be taken. . . . Neither doo they suffer any stranger willingly to come into their realm. . . . As for the truth of his word, the Russe for the most part maketh small regard of it, so he may gaine by a lie and a

[15] *The Journals of the Marquis de Custine,* P. P. Kohler, ed. and trans. (New York, 1951), p. 323.

breache of his promise. And it may be said truely (as they know best that have traded most with them) that from the great to the small (except some fewe that will scarcely be found) the Russe neither beleeveth anything that an other man speaketh, nor speaketh any thing himselfe worthy to be beleved. These qualities make them very odious to all their neighbors. . . .[16]

Writing in 1839, the Marquis de Custine reported that "the diplomatic corps and Westerners in general have always been considered by this Government . . . and by Russia as a whole, as malevolent and jealous spies."[17] Stalin warned the Eighteenth Party Congress in 1939 that "foreign espionage services will smuggle spies, murderers and . . . wreckers into our country." A member of the Soviet Military Mission in Washington informed General Bedell Smith that Russians considered all foreign officials "potential spies."[18] In such anti-Western novels as N. Shpanov's *Podzhigateli* ("The Warmongers"), the United States is depicted as placing its main reliance on espionage and bribery. From chronic suspicion as well as past history is born the abnormal and extreme defensiveness of the Russian outlook; an excellent example of this is the Communist doctrine of "capitalist encirclement." Throughout the period between the two World Wars Soviet Russia was declared to be encircled by capitalist states planning to deliver a joint attack upon the first and only existing socialist state. After World War II had brought the Russian frontier west of Berlin and given Moscow predominance in Europe, the question arose whether capitalist encirclement had at last been broken. The answer from the Kremlin was that "capitalist encirclement is not a geographical concept." Less than a year after the end of World War II, it was announced in the Soviet press that "so long as the capitalist world exists, the possibilities of a new war and of bandit attacks

[16] Giles Fletcher, *Of the Russe Commonwealth* (London, 1591) (London, 1856, for the Hakluyt Society), pp. 45, 63, 152.
[17] *Journals of the Marquis de Custine*, p. 9.
[18] *Ibid.*, p. 9.

on the USSR are not excluded."[19]   Moscow cannot feel secure
so long as a capitalist state exists anywhere in the world.   Extreme defensiveness is dialectically transformed into unlimited
aggression in the name of security against a hostile world.

A second trait of the Russian mind is as perceptible over
the generations as chronic suspicion and defensiveness: its sense
of mission, the conviction that Russia is the bearer of a new
and higher truth to be served, protected and propagated, that
a new age is coming, or has come, and will have no end.   So
the monk Filofey assured Emperor John III (1462-1505): Rome
had fallen because it had betrayed true Christianity; Byzantium
had fallen because it had been willing to accept union with
Roman Catholicism: ". . . thou art the only Christian ruler.
Observe, then, and heed, pious ruler, that all Christian king-
doms are joined in thine alone, that two Romes have fallen,
but the third stands, and a fourth will not be; thy Christian
kingdom shall not be handed over to others."[20]   The mission
here was to maintain the purity of the only true and orthodox
faith, the faith of Holy Russia, against a gentile world; something of the same theme resounds in the concluding words of
Emperor Nicholas' manifesto to the revolutionaries of 1848,
before his armies moved: "God is with us!   Give ear, ye nations,
and submit, for God is with us!"

The superiority of Russia, and the Slavic peoples in general, was the theme of Slavophilism and Pan-Slavism in the nineteenth and early twentieth centuries.   The superiority of Russia
to the West is expounded calmly but with burning conviction
in the works of A. S. Khomyakov: the West has contaminated
the minds of Russians, and denationalized them; its influence
must be removed in order that Russians may find themselves.[21]
Pan-Slavism drew up an appropriate political program: unifica-

[19] *Krasny Flot,* July 18, 1946; V. Mikheev, "O kapitalisticheskom okruzhenii,"
Bol'shevik, Aug. 16, 1951, No. 16, pp. 58-62.
[20] N. Berdyaev, *Istoki i smysl russkogo kommunizma* (Paris, 1955), p. 9.
[21] See especially "Razgovor v Podmoskovnoi," in A. Khomyakov, *Izbrannye
Sochineniya,* N. S. Arsen 'ev, ed. (New York, 1955).

tion of all Slavs in an empire ruled by the Russian Emperor, acquisition of Constantinople, destruction of the German, Austro-Hungarian and Ottoman Empires. "And so," wrote Danilevsky in the Bible of Pan-Slavism, "for every Slav . . . after God and his Holy Church,—the idea of Slavdom must be the highest idea, above freedom, above science, above education, above every earthly treasure. . . ."[22] During the reign of Nicholas I, Pan-Slavism was suspected of concealing democratic or revolutionary tendencies, but as early as 1855 Karl Marx warned: "It is no longer Russia alone, but the Panslavist conspiracy which threatens to build its realm on the ruins of Europe";[23] in 1867 a Slavic Congress took place in Moscow that sealed an alliance between the younger Slavophiles and Russian nationalists and made Russia the center of the Pan-Slav movement. During World War II the authentic Pan-Slav note was struck in Russian propaganda, and a magazine entitled *The Slavs* appeared; Stalin's victory proclamation of May 9, 1945, might have been written by Fadeev: "The century-old struggle of the Slavic peoples for their existence and independence has ended with victory over the German occupiers and German tyranny."[24]

In the Second Moscow Period the mission has been to preserve the infallible doctrines of Communism from corruption and to disseminate them throughout the entire world. It is worth noting that the creeds which have been adopted and fostered by Russians are all of foreign origin. The theory of the "Third Rome" probably originated in Bulgaria; the whole doctrine of Slavophilism was presented to the Russians ready-made by German scholarship; "Scientific Socialism" is the work of Marx and Engels. It is also true that in every case the creed tended to assume a Russian character and to become identified with Russian nationality. In the days of Muscovy the names

[22] N. Ya. Danilevsky, *Rossiya i Evropa* (3rd ed.; St. Petersburg, 1888) chap. vi, p. 133.

[23] Marx and Engels, *Russian Menace*, p. 89.

[24] *Bol'shaya Sovetskaya Entsiklopediya*, "SSSR," p. 276.

"Orthodoxy" and "Russian" became synonomous: Orthodoxy was the "Russian faith" (*Russkaya vera*); Russians could be referred to as "the Orthodox" (*Pravoslavnye*). The tendency of Slavophilism and Pan-Slavism to assume increasingly Russian forms has been mentioned already; the views of the Slavophil Tyuchev seem indistinguishable from extreme Russian expansionism when he dreams of a Russian empire that shall include seven internal seas, an empire stretching "from Nile to Neva, from Elbe to China, from Volga to Euphrates, from Ganges to Danube!"[25] Little or no difference can be discerned here between Slavophilism and the purely Russian ambitions revealed by Catherine the Great's exclamation: "Could I live for two hundred years the whole of Europe would be brought under Russian rule";[26] or Koropatkin's notation in 1903 that Nicholas II "has grandiose plans in his head: to capture Manchuria for Russia and to annex Korea. He is dreaming also of bringing Tibet under his domination. He desires to take Persia, and to seize not only the Bosporus but also the Dardanelles."[27] It has been the same with the creed of Communism; its conquests have in every case been Russian conquests. Even before World War II Berdyaev wrote:

Instead of the Third Rome, [the Communists] succeeded in bringing into being the Third International, and many traits of the Third Rome were transferred to the Third International. The Third International is also a holy realm, and it is also founded upon an orthodox faith. In the West it is very poorly understood that the Third International is not international, but the Russian National Idea. It is a transformation of Russian messianism. [Western Communists] do not understand that in joining the Third International they are joining the Russian people and are [helping to] realize its messianic mission.[28]

In this connection, I suggest that this newest "Russian faith" will confront a most serious crisis if the growing power

[25] See Ivanov-Razumnik, *Ispytanie v groze i bure* (Berlin, 1920), p. 28.
[26] Quoted in M. T. Florinsky, *Russia* (2 vols.; New York, 1953), I, 604 n.
[27] *Krasny Arkniv*, II (1923), p. 31.
[28] Berdyaev, *Istoki i smysl russkogo kommunizma*, p. 118.

of Red China should embolden its leaders to dispute Moscow's primacy in the Communist world.

All of the creeds adopted by the Russians have been hostile to Western civilization, no matter how much they have contradicted each other. To Muscovy the West was the home of abominable heresy; the Slavophils of the nineteenth century saw the relationship as a conflict between light and darkness: Holy Russia—Slavic, idealistic, and religious—was at war with Europe's atheism, materialism, and, above all, revolutionary movement. Today Russia is more than ever at war with the non-Communist West, but by a gigantic paradox the treasures in whose defense the battle rages have been exchanged, and now Russia fights for atheism, materialism, and, above all, the revolutionary movement against Europe's religion, idealism, and "reaction." Only history is capable of such ironies. "Servility to the West" (*nizkopoklonstvo pered zapadom*) is an actual crime in Russia today, more that it ever was in the days of the Slavophils, who never denied that the West had much to commend it. But the unmeasured hostility of the Russian Communists is the latest and sharpest manifestation of an attitude that can be traced from Pushkin's *Klevetnikam Rossii* through the nineteenth and twentieth centuries to A. Blok's *Dvenadtsat'* and *Skify,* and to Mayakovsky and contemporary Russian literary propaganda: Russia is no part of the West; Russia is the custodian of higher truths that are destined to prevail; the West is stained with sin and doomed to destruction.

In this essay I have asserted that the continuity of Russian foreign policy is not seeming but actual, and that it is the product of two constants: geography and the Russian character. The principle of inertial momentum has a limited range; beyond the Eurasian lowlands it does not function. The other constant, combining chronic suspicion of the outside world, expressed as desire for maximum security, with a compulsion to

propagate an intolerant faith, whose triumph everywhere is regarded as the only way complete security can be attained, will
operate to expand the frontiers of Communism to the limits of
Russian power.

THE PRINTED WRITINGS
OF EBER MALCOLM CARROLL

A Preliminary Bibliography

Frederic B. M. Hollyday

1. *Books*

Origins of the Whig Party. Durham, North Carolina: Duke University Press, 1925. Pp. viii, 260.

French Public Opinion and Foreign Affairs, 1870-1914. New York and London: The Century Company, 1931. Pp. viii, 348.

Germany and the Great Powers, 1866-1914: A Study in Public Opinion and Foreign Policy. New York: Prentice-Hall, 1938. Pp. xv, 852.

With Dr. Fritz Theodor Epstein. *Das nationalsozialistische Deutschland und die Sowjetunion, 1939-1941: Akten aus dem Archiv des Deutschen Auswärtigen Amts.* Washington: Department of State, 1948. Pp. xliv, 416. German edition of *Nazi-Soviet Relations, 1939-1941: Documents from the Archives of the German Foreign Office,* ed. R. J. Sontag and J. S. Beddie (Washington: Department of State, 1948).

Co-editor. *Documents on German Foreign Policy, 1918-1945. From the Archives of the German Foreign Ministry.* Series C (1933-1937). Washington: U.S. Government Printing Office; London, H.M. Stationery Office, 1957 ff. One volume to

date. Series D (1937-1945). Washington: U.S. Government
Printing Office; H.M. Stationery Office, 1949 ff. Ten volumes
to date. German edition, *Akten zur Deutschen Auswärtigen
Politik, 1918-1945.* Series D (1937-1945). Baden-Baden: Imprimerie Nationale, 1950 ff. Six volumes to date.

II. *Articles and Essays*

"The Michigan Ambulance Section in France," *Michigan
Alumnus,* XXV (June, 1919), 586-590.

"Politics during the Administration of John Quincy
Adams," *South Atlantic Quarterly,* XXIII (April, 1924), 141-
154.

"French Public Opinion on War with Prussia in 1870,"
American Historical Review, XXXI (July, 1926), 679-700.

"A Project for a Guide to the European Press," *Bulletin of
the International Committee of Historical Sciences,* II (January, 1930), 427-431. Compare pp. 431-438, for the comments
of Wilhelm Mommsen, Charles Seignobos, and Kingsley Mar-
tin.

"Recent German Publications and German Foreign Policy,"
American Political Science Review, XL (June, 1952), 525-541.

"Franklin D. Roosevelt and the World Crisis, 1937-1940,"
South Atlantlic Quarterly, CII (January, 1953), 111-128.

"Ways to Best Communism," *Saturday Review of Literature,* XXXVIII (May 21, 1955), 40.

III. *Book Reviews*

Arnold J. Toynbee, *The Western Question in Greece and
Turkey: A Study in the Contact of Civilization* (2d ed.;
Boston and New York: Houghton Mifflin Company, 1923),
South Atlantic Quarterly, XXIII (January, 1924), 85-86.

Archibald Henderson, *Washington's Southern Tour, 1791* (Boston and New York: Houghton Mifflin Company, 1923), *North Carolina Historical Review*, I (April, 1924), 176-179.

Edward M. East, *Mankind at the Crossroads* (New York: Charles Scribner's Sons, 1923), *South Atlantic Quarterly*, XXIII (April, 1924), 191-193.

W. K. Wallace, *The Passing of Politics* (New York: The Macmillan Company, 1924), *South Atlantic Quarterly*, XXV (July, 1926), 100-101.

C. E. Playne, *The Neuroses of Nations* (New York: Thomas Seltzer, 1925), *South Atlantic Quarterly*, XXV (July, 1926), 333-335.

M. S. Stanoyevich, *Slavonic Nations of Yesterday and To-day* (New York: H. W. Wilson Company, 1925), *South Atlantic Quarterly*, XXV (July, 1926), 340.

Poultney Bigelow, *Seventy Summers* (2 vols.; New York: Longmans, Green and Company, 1925), *South Atlantic Quarterly*, XXVI (January, 1927), 97-99.

M. E. Vermeil, *L'Empire allemand, 1871-1900* (Paris: E. de Boccard, 1926), *American Historical Review*, XXXII (April, 1927), 654-655.

Sidney Bradshaw Fay, *The Origins of the World War* (2 vols.; New York: The Macmillan Company, 1928), *South Atlantic Quarterly*, XXVIII (April, 1928), 209-210.

G. P. Gooch and Harold Temperley (eds.), *British Documents on the Origins of the War, 1898-1914.* Vol. I, *The End of British Isolation;* Vol. II, *The Japanese Alliance and the French Entente;* Vol. III, *The Testing of the Entente;* Vol. XI, *The Outbreak of War: Foreign Office Documents, June 28-August 4, 1914,* collected and arranged by J. W. Headlam-Morley (London: H.M. Stationery Office, 1926-1928), *South Atlantic Quarterly*, XXVIII (January, 1929), 97-100.

Hermann Oncken, *Napoleon III and the Rhine: The Origins of the War of 1870-71* (New York: Alfred A. Knopf, 1928), *Journal of Modern History*, I (June, 1929), 313-315.

Winston S. Churchill, *The Aftermath* (New York: Charles Scribner's Sons, 1929), *South Atlantic Quarterly*, XXVIII (July, 1929), 319-320.

Georges Clemenceau, *In the Evening of My Thought* (Boston and New York: Houghton Mifflin Company, 1929), *South Atlantic Quarterly*, XXIX (January, 1930), 98-99.

Heinrich Eduard Brockhaus [Hermann Michel, editor], *Stunden mit Bismarck, 1871-1878* (Leipzig: F. A. Brockhaus, 1929), *American Historical Review*, XXXVI (October, 1930), 147-148.

Ministère des Affaires Étrangères, Commission de Publication des Documents relatifs aux Origines de la Guerre de 1914, *Documents diplomatiques français, 1871-1914*. Première Série (1871-1900), tome I, 10 mai, 1871—30 juin, 1875; tome II, 1 juillet, 1875—31 décembre, 1879 (Paris: Imprimerie Nationale, 1929, 1930), *American Historical Review*, XXXVI (January, 1931), 393-394.

J. W. Headlam-Morley, *Studies in Diplomatic History* (New York: Alfred H. King, 1930), *South Atlantic Quarterly*, XXX (January, 1931), 93-95.

Walter Consuelo Langsam, *The Napoleonic Wars and German Nationalism in Austria* (New York: Columbia University Press, 1930), *South Atlantic Quarterly*, XXX (January, 1931), 95.

G. P. Gooch and Harold Temperley (eds.), *British Documents on the Origins of the War, 1898-1914*. Vol. IV, *The Anglo-Russian Rapprochement, 1903-1907;* Vol. V, *The Near East, 1903-1909;* Vol. VI, *The Anglo-German Tension, 1907-1912* (London: H.M. Stationery Office, 1928-1930), *South Atlantic Quarterly*, XXX (January, 1931), 96-97.

Bernadotte E. Schmitt, *The Coming of the War: 1914* (2 vols.; New York: Charles Scribner's Sons, 1930), *South Atlantic Quarterly*, XXX (April, 1931), 206-208.

Donaldson Jordan and Edwin J. Pratt, *Europe and the American Civil War* (Boston and New York: Houghton Mifflin

Company, 1934), *Political Science Quarterly*, XLVII (March, 1932), 138-140.

Ministère des Affaires Étrangères, Commission de Publication des Documents relatifs aux Origines de la Guerre de 1914, *Documents diplomatiques français, 1871-1914*. Première Série (1871-1900), tome III, janvier, 1880—mai, 1881 (Paris: Imprimerie Nationale, 1931), *American Historical Review*, XXXVIII (October, 1932), 116-117.

Ministère des Affaires Étrangères, Commission de Publication des Documents relatifs aux Origines de la Guerre de 1914, *Documents diplomatiques français, 1871-1914*. Première Série (1871-1900), tome IV, 13 mai, 1881—20 février, 1883 (Paris: Imprimerie Nationale, 1932), *American Historical Review*, XXXVIII (July, 1933), 759-760.

Ministère des Affaires Étrangères, Commission de Publication des Documents relatifs aux Origines de la Guerre de 1914, *Documents diplomatiques français, 1871-1914*. Première Série (1871-1900), tome V, 23 février, 1883—9 avril, 1885 (Paris: Imprimerie Nationale, 1933), *American Historical Review*, XXXIX (January, 1934), 329-330.

W. L. Middleton, *The French Political System* (New York: E. P. Dutton and Company, 1933), *Political Science Quarterly*, XLIX (March, 1934), 149.

Kent Roberts Greenfield, *Economics and Liberalism in the Risorgimento: A Study of Nationalism in Lombardy, 1814-1848* (Baltimore: The Johns Hopkins Press, 1934), *South Atlantic Quarterly*, XXXIV (January, 1935), 114-116.

Chester Wells Clark, *Franz Josef and Bismarck: The Diplomacy of Austria before the War of 1866* (Cambridge, Massachusetts: Harvard University Press, 1934) *American Historical Review*, XL (July, 1935), 737-738.

Ebba Dahlin, *French and German Public Opinion on Declared War Aims* (Stanford: Stanford University Press, 1933), *American Journal of International Law*, XXIX (October, 1935), 730.

George Barnard Noble, *Opinions and Policies at Paris, 1919. Wilsonian Diplomacy, the Versailles Peace, and French Public Opinion* (New York: Macmillan Company, 1935), *American Journal of International Law,* XXIX (October, 1935), p. 730.

Pearl Boring Mitchell, *The Bismarckian Policy of Conciliation with France, 1875-1885* (Philadelphia: University of Pennsylvania Press, 1935), *American Historical Review,* XLI (January, 1936), 383-384.

Alexander C. Flick, *Modern World History since 1775,* revised by Witt Bowden (New York: F. S. Crofts and Co., 1935), *Annals of the American Academy of Political and Social Science,* CLXXXIII (January, 1936), 291-292.

William L. Langer, *The Diplomacy of Imperialism, 1890-1902,* (2 vols.; New York: Alfred A. Knopf, 1935), *Annals of the American Academy of Political and Social Science,* CLXXXIV (March, 1936), 231-232.

Ministère des Affaires Étrangères, Commission de Publication des Documents relatifs aux Origines de la Guerre de 1914, *Documents diplomatiques français, 1871-1914.* Première Série (1871-1900), tome VI¹, 8 avril, 1885–30 décembre, 1887 (Paris: Imprimerie Nationale, 1934), *American Historical Review,* XLI (April, 1936), 542-544.

J. Wallas-Rudiger, *La Belgique et l'équilibre européen: documents inédits* (Paris: Berger-Lavrault, 1935), *Journal of Modern History,* VIII (September, 1936), 378-380.

Ch. de Chavanne, *Avec Brazza: Souvenirs de la Mission de l'Ouest Africain, mars, 1883–janvier, 1886* (Paris: Librairie Plon, 1935), *American Historical Review,* XLII (January, 1937), 391.

Louis L. Snyder, *From Bismarck to Hitler: The Background of Modern German Nationalism* (Williamsport: the Bayard Press, 1935), *American Historical Review,* XLII (April, 1937), 595.

H. A. L. Fisher, *A History of Europe* (3 vols.; Boston and

New York: Houghton Mifflin Company, 1935-1936), *South Atlantic Quarterly*, XXXVI (April, 1937), 229-232.

Ministère des Affaires Étrangères, Commission de Publication des Documents relatifs aux Origines de la Guerre de 1914, *Documents diplomatiques français, 1871-1914*. Première Série (1871-1900), tome VII, 1 janvier, 1888—19 mars, 1890 (Paris: Imprimerie Nationale, 1937), *American Historical Review*, XLIII (July, 1938), 861-862.

Ministère des Affaires Étrangères, Commission de Publication des Documents relatifs aux Origines de la Guerre de 1914, *Documents diplomatiques français, 1871-1914*. Première Série (1871-1900), tome VI^2, 4 mars, 1885—29 décembre, 1887 (Paris: Imprimerie Nationale, 1938), *American Historical Review*, XLIV (July, 1939), 982.

Ministère des Affaires Étrangères, Commission de Publication des Documents relatifs aux Origines de la Guerre de 1914, *Documents diplomatiques français, 1871-1914*. Première Série (1871-1900), tome VIII, 20 mars, 1890—28 août, 1891 (Paris: Imprimerie Nationale, 1938), *American Historical Review*, XLV (October, 1939), 220.

Franz Borkenau, *The New German Empire* (New York: Viking Press, 1939), *Annals of the American Academy of Political and Social Science*, CCVIII (March, 1940), 195-196.

James R. Mock and Cedrick Larson, *Words that Won the War: The Story of the Committee on Public Information, 1917-1919* (Princeton: the Princeton University Press, 1939), *South Atlantic Quarterly*, XXXIX (April, 1940), 234-235.

Ministère des Affaires Étrangères, Commission de Publication des Documents relatifs aux Origines de la Guerre de 1914, *Documents diplomatiques français, 1871-1914*. Première Série (1871-1900), tome IX, 23 août, 1891—19 août, 1892 (Paris: Imprimerie Nationale, 1939), *American Historical Review*, XLV (July, 1940), 961.

Otto Strasser, *Hitler and I* (Boston: Houghton Mifflin Company, 1940), *Social Studies for Teachers and Administrators,* XXXI (December, 1940), 373-374.

Irma Christina Barlow, *The Agadir Crisis* (Chapel Hill, North Carolina: The University of North Carolina Press, 1940), *American Historical Review,* XLVI (January, 1941), 406-407.

Oron James Hale, *Publicity and Diplomacy, with Special Reference to England and Germany, 1890-1914* (New York: D. Appleton-Century Company, 1940), *Journal of Modern History,* XIII (June, 1941), 258-259.

Jane Scrivener, *Inside Rome with the Germans* (New York: The Macmillan Company, 1945), *South Atlantic Quarterly,* XLV (April, 1946), 258-259.

Carlton J. H. Hayes, *Wartime Mission to Spain, 1942-1945* (New York: The Macmillan Company, 1945), *South Atlantic Quarterly,* XLV (July, 1946), 386-389.

Oscar I. Janowski, *Nationalities and National Minorities* (New York: The Macmillan Company, 1945), *South Atlantic Quarterly,* XLV (October, 1946), 512-514.

The Ciano Diaries. The Complete Unabridged Diaries of Count Galeazzo Ciano, Italian Minister of Foreign Affairs, 1939-1943 (New York [Garden City]: Doubleday and Company, 1946), *South Atlantic Quarterly,* XLVI (January, 1947), 129-132.

Franz Schoenberner, *Confessions of a European Intellectual* (New York: The Macmillan Company, 1946), *South Atlantic Quarterly,* XLVI (January, 1947), 133-135.

Corey Ford and Alastair MacBain, *Cloak and Dagger: The Secret Story of OSS* (New York: Random House, 1946), *South Atlantic Quarterly,* XLVI (April, 1947), 284-285.

Ministère des Affaires Étrangères, Commission de Publication des Documents relatifs aux Origines de la Guerre de 1914, *Documents diplomatiques français, 1871-1914.* Première Série (1871-1900), tome X, 21 août, 1892—décembre, 1893 (Paris: Imprimerie Nationale, 1945), *Journal of Modern History,* XXII (June, 1950), 170-172.

Germany, 1947-1949: The Story in Documents (Washington: U.S. Government Printing Office, 1950), *South Atlantic Quarterly*, XLIX (October, 1950), 534-535.

Louis Fischer, *The Soviets in World Affairs: A History of the Relations of the Soviet Union and the Rest of the World*, (2d ed., 2 vols.; Princeton: The Princeton University Press, 1951), *South Atlantic Quarterly*, LI (January, 1952), 194-195.

Joseph Berry Kennan and Brendan Brown, *Crimes against International Law* (Washington: The Public Affairs Press, 1950), *Far Eastern Quarterly* (now Journal of Asian Studies), XI (August, 1952), 470-471.

James K. Pollock and Homer Thomas, *Germany in Power and Eclipse: The Background of German Development* (New York: D. Nostrand, 1952), *Journal of Central European Affairs*, XIII (April, 1953), 84-85.

Harold F. Gosnell, *Champion Campaigner: Franklin D. Roosevelt* (New York: The Macmillan Company, 1952), *American Historical Review*, LVIII (April, 1953), 664-665.

Walter H. Kaufman, *Monarchism in the Weimar Republic* (New York: Bookman Associates, 1953), *Journal of Central European Affairs*, XIII (July, 1953), 191-192.

Crane Brinton, *The Anatomy of Revolution* (2d ed.; New York: Prentice-Hall, 1952), *Journal of Political Economy*, LXI (August, 1953), 364.

Herbert Feis, *The China Tangle: The American Effort in China from Pearl Harbor to the Marshall Mission* (Princeton: The Princeton University Press, 1953), *South Atlantic Quarterly*, LIII (April, 1954), 275-276.

William L. Langer and S. Everett Gleason, *The Undeclared War, 1940-1941* (New York: Harper and Brothers, 1953), *South Atlantic Quarterly*, LIII (April, 1954), 280-282.

Gustav Hilgar and Alfred G. Meyer, *The Incompatible Allies: A Memoir-History of German-Soviet Relations, 1918-*

1941 (New York: The Macmillan Company, 1953), *South Atlantic Quarterly*, LIII (April, 1954), 301-303.

Henry L. Bretton, *Stresemann and the Revision of Versailles* (Stanford: The Stanford University Press, 1953), *Journal of Central European Affairs*, XIV (July, 1954), 192-193.

Wilma Höcker, *Der gesandte Bunsen als Vermittler zwischen Deutschland und England* (Göttingen: Musterschmidt Wissenschaftlicher Verlag, 1951), *Journal of Central European Affairs*, XIV (July, 1954), 205-206.

Hans Kohn, *German History: Some New German Views* (Boston: The Beacon Press, 1954), *American Historical Review*, LX (October, 1954), pp. 100-101. See the exchange of correspondence between Gerhard Ritter and Eber Malcolm Carroll on this review, in the *American Historical Review*, LX (April, 1955), 774-775.

Boyd C. Shafer, *Nationalism: Myth and Reality* (New York: Harcourt Brace and Company, 1955), *Journal of Southern History*, XXI (August, 1955), 387-388.

Heinz Pohle, *Der Rundfunk als Instrument der Politik: Zur Geschichte der Deutschen Rundfunks von 1923/38* (Hamburg: Verlag Hans Bredow Institut, 1955), *American Historical Review*, LXII (October, 1956), 134-135.

Ernst Hanfstängl, *Unheard Witness* (Philadelphia: J. P. Lippincott Company, 1957), *South Atlantic Quarterly*, LVI (Spring, 1957), 281-282.

Hans Bausch, *Der Rundfunk im politischen Kräftespiel der Weimarer Republik* (Tübingen: Mohr, 1956), *Journal of Modern History*, XXIX (June, 1957), 186-187.

W. N. Medlicott, *Bismarck, Gladstone, and the Concert of Europe* (London: University of London, the Athlone Press, 1956), *American Historical Review*, LXII (July, 1957), 890-891.

A. J. P. Taylor, *Englishmen and Others* (London: Hamish

Hamilton, 1956), *American Historical Review*, LXIII (April, 1958), 722.

Joseph J. Mathews, *Reporting the Wars* (Minneapolis: University of Minnesota Press, 1957), *American Historical Review*, LXIV (October, 1958), 72-73.

Index